Racial Migrations

NEW YORK CITY AND THE REVOLUTIONARY POLITICS OF THE SPANISH CARIBBEAN, 1850–1902

Jesse E. Hoffnung-Garskof

PRINCETON UNIVERSITY PRESS

Princeton & Oxford

Published by Princeton University Press
41 William Street, Princeton, New Jersey 08540
6 Oxford Street, Woodstock, Oxfordshire OX20 1TR

press.princeton.edu

Library of Congress Control Number: 2018965752

First paperback printing, 2021
Paperback ISBN 978-0-691-21837-3
Cloth ISBN 978-0-691-18353-4

British Library Cataloging-in-Publication Data is available

Editorial: Eric Crahan and Pamela Weidman
Production Editorial: Leslie Grundfest
Text and Jacket/Cover Design: Pamela Schnitter
Cover images: (Top): From Rafael Serra's *Ensayos políticos,
sociales y económicos*, 1889; (Bottom): Bird's-eye view of New York
with Battery Park in the foreground and the Brooklyn Bridge
on the right. Lithograph, 1873. Restored by Adam Cuerden.
Production: Erin Suydam
Publicity: Alyssa Sanford
Copyeditor: Cindy Milstein

This book has been composed in Bell MT Std

Racial Migrations

Para Paulina, compañera, colega, amor

CONTENTS

CAST OF CHARACTERS

Roughly in Order of Appearance

THE PRINCIPALS

Rafael Serra. Politician, civil rights activist, journalist, educator, and cigar maker. Founder of La Liga. Born in Havana, Cuba, 1858.

José Martí. Poet, politician, journalist, and diplomat. Founder and leader of the Cuban Revolutionary Party (1892–95). Born in Havana, Cuba, 1853.

Sotero Figueroa. Journalist, publisher, and typesetter. Born in San Juan, Puerto Rico, 1853.

Gertrudis Heredia de Serra. Midwife and community leader. Married to Rafael Serra. Born in Matanzas, Cuba, 1856.

Manuela Aguayo de Figueroa. Seamstress. Married to Sotero Figueroa. Born in Toa Baja, Puerto Rico, 1855.

Juan Gualberto Gómez. Politician, civil rights leader, and journalist. Born in Sabanilla del Encomendador, Matanzas, Cuba, 1854.

Juan Bonilla. Journalist, lodge leader, civil rights activist, and cigar maker. Born in Key West, Florida, 1869.

Gerónimo Bonilla. Cigar maker, Odd Fellow, and revolutionary. Born in Havana, 1857.

Francisco Gonzalo "Pachín" Marín. Poet, journalist, and typographer. Cofounder, with Sotero Figueroa, of the Club Borinquen. War correspondent for *Doctrina de Martí*. Born in Arecibo, Puerto Rico, 1863.

THEIR FAMILIES

Cayetano Heredia and María del Socorro del Monte. Parents of Gertrudis. Residents of Matanzas. A man of the Carabalí nation and the oldest daughter of Rita del Monte.

Rita del Monte and Sebastián Campos. Leaders of the Lucumí cabildo, Fernando VII. Godparents to more than twenty persons in Matanzas. Owners of at least one slave.

Marcelina Montalvo and Rafael Serra (Sr.). Parents of Rafael. Residents of Havana. Born in Cuba.

Chuchú Serra. Seamstress and teacher. Rafael Serra's aunt.

María Rosendo Fernández and José Mercedes Figueroa. The parents of Sotero Figueroa.

Dolores and Francisco Bonilla. Homemaker and shoemaker, respectively. Parents of Juan, Gerónimo, and Francisco Bonilla.

Francisco Bonilla. Cigar maker, Freemason, and impresario. Brother of Juan and Gerónimo Bonilla.

Ramón Marín. Liberal publisher and educator. Owner of the Establecimiento Tipográfico El Vapor in Ponce. Uncle of Pachín Marín.

KEY FIGURES

In Puerto Rico

Rafael Cordero. Teacher and cigar maker.

Alejandro Tapia y Rivera. Liberal author and historian.

José Julián Acosta. Liberal publisher, author, and politician.

Román Baldorioty de Castro. Liberal teacher, author, and politician. Founder of the Puerto Rican Autonomista Party.

Pascacio Sancerrit. Liberal author. Head of production at Acosta's printing house. Mentor to Sotero Figueroa.

Juan Morel Campos. Musician and composer associated with the musical style known as *danza*. Author, with Sotero Figueroa, of *Don Mamerto*.

In Matanzas

Gabriel de la Concepción Valdés (Plácido). Artisan and poet. Accused of conspiracy and executed by the Military Commission in 1844.

Pilar Poveda. Midwife and community leader. Sentenced to a year of labor by the Military Commission in 1844. Mother-in-law of Plácido.

Miguel Failde. Tailor, composer, and musician associated with the musical style known as *danzón*.

Martín Morúa Delgado. Artisan, journalist, and politician. Ally and mentor of Rafael Serra, who later became a bitter rival.

In Havana

Saturnino Martínez. Spanish-born labor leader, journalist, and cigar maker. Editor of *La Aurora*. Employed in the same workshop as Rafael Serra.

Nicolás Azcárate. Liberal lawyer, journalist, and politician. Ally of Saturnino Martínez and supporter of Juan Gualberto Gómez.

Count of Pozos Dulces (Francisco de Frías). Cuban aristocrat, agronomist, intellectual, and journalist. Editor of *El Siglo.*

Gonzalo Castañón. Conservative journalist and colonel of the pro-Spanish militia, the Voluntarios. Killed in Key West in 1871.

Fermín Valdés-Domínguez. Medical doctor, socialist, and close boyhood friend of José Martí. Chief of staff for General Máximo Gómez during the final war of independence.

Antonio Bachiller y Morales. Professor at the University of Havana and secretary of the Economic Society of Cuba. Later a member of the Cuban Junta in New York.

Benjamín Céspedes. Physician. Author of *Prostitution in the City of Havana.*

In Key West

Salomé Rencurrel. Lodge leader and cigar maker. Neighbor of the Bonillas and a member of the Sandoval household in New York. A supporter of *Doctrina de Martí.*

Juan María Reyes. Factory reader, journalist, and politician. Writer for *La Aurora* and *El Siglo* in Havana. Editor of *El Republicano* in Key West.

José Margarito Gutiérrez. Cigar maker, labor leader, and journalist. Principal author of the "Protest" of the Cubans of color in Key West, in 1881. Correspondent for *La Fraternidad.*

THE COMMUNITY

Lorenza Geli and Magín Coroneau. Cubans who arrived in New York as domestic servants in wealthy households. Later members of La Liga, and witnesses to the marriage of Gerónimo Bonilla and Isabel Acosta.

Lafayette Marcus. Seaman, waiter, and caterer. One of the first Cubans of African descent to settle independently in New York. Founder of the Sol de Cuba Masonic lodge.

Magdalena Sandoval. Cuban migrant. Member of the St. Philip's Episcopal Church. Matriarch and domestic manager of the household at 89 Thompson Street.

Germán Sandoval. Cuban cigar maker and community leader. Founder of the Logia San Manuel. Resident of 89 Thompson Street and later 231 East Seventy-Fifth Street. Married to Magdalena Sandoval.

Philip White and Elizabeth Guignon. Prominent members of the St. Philip's Episcopal Church. Hosts of society functions and literary soirees. Philip was a pharmacist and a member of the Brooklyn Board of Education.

Carlos and Sarah Crespo. A clerk in a cigar store and a seamstress, both Cubans, who lived in the home of Philip White and Elizabeth Guignon. Members of the St. Philip's Episcopal Church.

Charles A. Reason. Engraver, officer in the Sons of New York, and nephew of Charles L. Reason.

Harriet Reason. Landlady at several properties on West Third Street. After the death of her husband, Charles A. Reason, she married the Cuban violinist Alfredo Vialet.

Charles L. Reason. Mathematician, educator, and civil rights leader. Principal of the "colored" grammar school on Manhattan's West Side.

Bibián Peñalver and Carolina Roger. Confectioner and seamstress, respectively. Parents of Pastor Peñalver, whom they sent to New York to study at the school of Charles L. Reason in 1876.

Pastor Peñalver. Violinist and band leader who played functions in both African American and Cuban clubs and societies. A founding member of La Liga.

Pantaleón Pons. Cigar maker who lived and worked with Germán Sandoval and Salomé Rencurrel. A founding member of the Logia Sol de Cuba.

Agustín Yorca. Cigar maker. Served as a witness for more than two hundred Cubans who naturalized in New York between 1870 and 1900.

THE EXPEDITION

Flor Crombet. Oriente-born general in the Cuban insurgency. The son of a French planter and a woman of partial African descent.

Máximo Gómez. Dominican-born general in the Cuban insurgency. Commander in chief of the Army of Liberation in the final war of independence.

Antonio Maceo. Oriente-born general in the Cuban insurgency. Hailed by some as the "bronze titan," he suffered continual racist suspicion and accusation from white separatists as well as Spanish propagandists.

Agustín Cebreco. Oriente-born general in the Cuban insurgency. Politician allied with Rafael Serra in the early years of the Republic of Cuba.

Pedro Prestán. Lawyer and property holder in Colón, Panama. Participant in the Liberal uprising in Caribbean Colombia in 1885. Executed for alleged arson and racial rebellion.

BACK IN NEW YORK

La Liga and The Clubs

Manuel de Jesús González. Author and cigar maker from Santiago de Cuba. Treasurer of La Liga, and close comrade of Serra and the Bonillas.

Rosendo Rodríguez. Puerto Rican cigar maker and revolutionary. Officer in La Liga. President of the Club Las Dos Antillas. Member of the New York Advisory Council.

Augusto Benech. Cuban cigar maker and revolutionary. Member of La Liga. Founder of the Club Las Dos Antillas and the Club Guerrilla de Maceo.

Modesto Tirado. Puerto Rican typographer, publisher, and politician. Member of La Liga. Officer in the Club Borinquen. Politician in Eastern Cuba after the war.

Pilar Cazuela de Pivaló. Puerto Rican revolutionary and community leader. Member of La Liga and officer of the Club José Maceo. Married to Silvestre Pivaló.

Silvestre Pivaló. Cuban cigar maker and revolutionary. A member of La Liga and officer in the Club Las Dos Antilllas.

Pedro Calderín. Cuban restaurant owner and community leader. President of La Liga, agent for La Igualdad, treasurer of Club Guerrilla de Maceo, and leader of several other clubs and associations.

Arturo Schomburg. Puerto Rican revolutionary, Freemason, and historian. Secretary of the Club Las Dos Antillas. Founder, with John Bruce, of the Negro Society for Historical Research.

Josefa Blanco de Apodaca. Cuban midwife and revolutionary. Leader, with Gertudis Heredia, of the women's groups associated with La Liga. Mother-in-law of Juan Bonilla.

Isidoro Apodaca. Cigar maker and revolutionary. Leader of the clubs Las Dos Antillas and Manuel Bergues Pruna. Husband of Josefa Blanco.

Dionisia Apodaca de Bonilla. Cuban American revolutionary. Daughter of Isidoro Apodaca. Stepdaughter of Josefa Blanco. Member of La Liga. Married to Juan Bonilla.

Dominga Curet de Muriel. Puerto Rican revolutionary and community leader. Officer of the Club José Maceo.

Manuel Bergues Pruna. Journalist, politician, and insurgent officer. Leader of the abstention effort in 1893. First man of color to serve as a public prosecutor in Santiago. Member of the Club Las Dos Antillas.

Antonio Vélez Alvarado. Puerto Rican advertising agent and publisher. Cofounder of the Club Borinquen.

Other New Yorkers

T. McCants Stewart. Minister and lawyer who argued important civil rights cases. Member of the Brooklyn Board of Education. Proponent of African American political independence.

T. Thomas Fortune. Journalist, publisher, and civil rights activist. Editor of the *New York Globe, New York Freeman*, and *New York Age*. Founder of the Afro-American League.

William Derrick. Minister and politician, originally from the West Indies. Pastor at the Bethel AME Church on Sullivan Street. Republican Party operative.

Henry George. Journalist, economist, and author of the widely read book *Progress and Poverty* (1879). Candidate for Mayor of the New York Labor Party in 1886.

Rev. Ernest Lyons. Pastor of St. Marks Methodist Episcopal Church on Manhattan's West Side. Civil rights advocate and Republican Party leader.

The Study Group

Enrique Trujillo. Cuban publisher, journalist, and publicist. Editor of *El Avisador Cubano* and *El Porvenir*. An outspoken opponent of José Martí.

Fidel Pierra. Lawyer and businessman. Autonomista who joined the Cuban Revolutionary Party after Martí's death. Promoter of the Cuban cause to the North American public.

Gonzalo de Quesada. Lawyer and politician raised in a wealthy exile family. Teacher at La Liga. Personal secretary to José Martí. Later head of the Cuban diplomatic mission in Washington, DC.

Enrique José Varona. Cuban philosopher. Editor of *Patria*. Fierce opponent of Sotero Figueroa and Rafael Serra. Leader of the Study Group.

Emilio Agramonte. Cuban lawyer, musician, and socialite.

Tomás Estrada Palma. Cuban lawyer, teacher, and politician. Delegate of the Cuban Revolutionary Party and plenipotentiary minister of the Provisional Government of Cuba in the United States. President of Cuba from 1902–6.

Manuel Sanguily. Cuban journalist, politician, and member of the Study Group.

Eduardo Yero. Cuban journalist and politician. Ally of Manuel Bergues Pruna, Rafael Serra, and Sotero Figueroa. Personal Secretary of Tomás Estrada Palma and editor of *Patria*.

ENDINGS

Evaristo Estenoz. Cuban civil engineer, military officer, and politician. Founder of the Independent Party of Color and leader of a rebellion in Eastern Cuba in 1912. Corresponding member of the Negro Society for Historical Research.

John Edward Bruce. African American journalist and intellectual. Founder, with Arturo Schomburg, of the Negro Society for Historical Research.

Figure 1. *From top left, clockwise* Rafael Serra, Sotero Figueroa, Juan Gualberto Gómez (The New York Public Library Digital Collections), and José Martí (University of Miami Library, Cuban Heritage Collection, Cuban Photograph Collection).

Figure 2. *From top left, clockwise* Juan Bonilla, Germán Sandoval, Agustín Cebreco, and Antonio Maceo (The New York Public Library Digital Collections).

Figure 3. La Liga: 1. Santos Sánchez, 2. Justo Castillo, 3. Olayo Miranda, 4. Aquiles Brane, 5. Isidoro Apodaca, 6. Luis Vialet, 7. Enrique Sandoval, 8. Modesto Tirado, 9. Juan Román, and 10. Gerónimo Bonilla (Serra, *Ensayos políticos, sociales y económicos*).

Figure 4. La Liga: 11. Ana M. de Benavides, 12. Dionisa Apodaca de Bonilla,
13. Josefa Blanco de Apodaca, 14. Lorenza Geli de Coroneau, 15. Carmen
Miyares de Mantilla, 16. Isabel V. de Bonilla, 17. Mariana Rivero de Hernández,
18. Candelaria de Graupera, 19. Josefa N. de Cárdenas, and 20. Pilar Cazuela de
Pivaló (Serra, *Ensayos políticos, sociales y económicos*).

Figure 5. La Liga: 21. Sixto Pozo, 22. Eligio Medina, 23. Pastor Peñalver, and 24. Rosendo Rodríguez (Serra, *Ensayos políticos, sociales y económicos*).

Figure 6. Officers of the Club Guerilla de Maceo: 1. Benito Magdariaga, 2. Olayo Miranda, 3. Antonio Gomero, 4. José Fernández Mesa, 5. Dámaso Callard, 6. Joaquín Gorosabe, and 7. Pedro Calderín (Serra, *Ensayos políticos, sociales y económicos*).

Figure 7. Consuelo Serra, above and Arturo A. Schomburg (The New York Public Library Digital Collections).

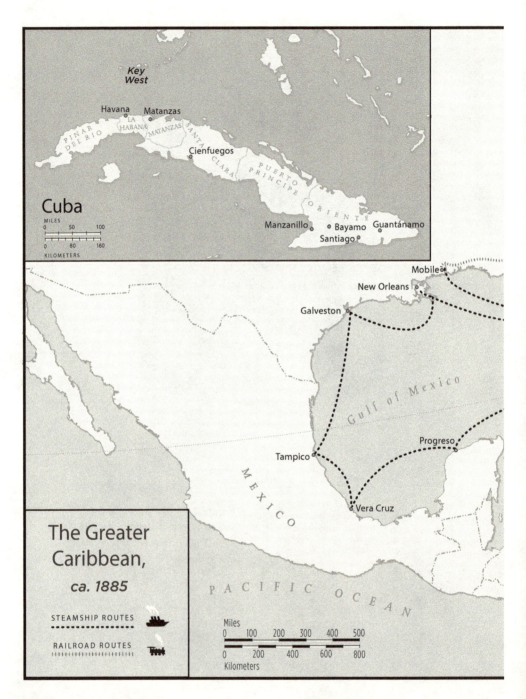

Cuba

MILES
0   50   100
0   80   160
KILOMETERS

Key West

Havana   Matanzas
LA
HABANA   MATANZAS
PINAR
DEL RIO
SANTA
CLARA   Cienfuegos
PUERTO
PRINCIPE
ORIENTE
Manzanillo   Bayamo   Guantánamo
Santiago

Mobile
New Orleans
Galveston
Gulf of Mexico
Progreso
Tampico
MEXICO
Vera Cruz
PACIFIC OCEAN

The Greater
Caribbean,
ca. 1885

STEAMSHIP ROUTES

RAILROAD ROUTES

Miles
0   100   200   300   400   500
0   200   400   600   800
Kilometers

Map 1

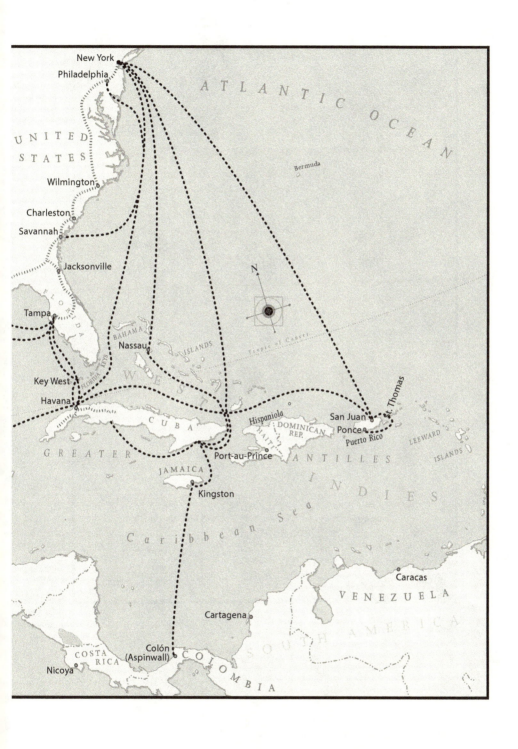

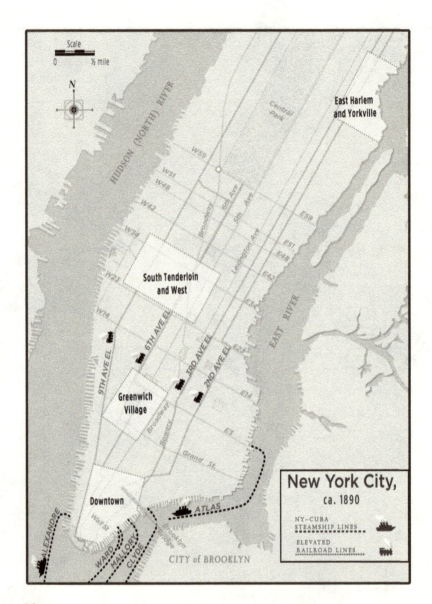

Scale

0 ½ mile

N

HUDSON (NORTH) RIVER

Central Park

East Harlem and Yorkville

W59

W57

W48

W42

Broadway

6th Ave

5th Ave

Lexington Ave

E59

E57

E48

E42

W34

W23

South Tenderloin and West

W14

EAST RIVER

9TH AVE EL

6TH AVE EL

3RD AVE EL

2ND AVE EL

E23

E14

Greenwich Village

Broadway

Bowery

E3

Grand St.

Downtown

West St.

ATLAS

Brooklyn Bridge

ALEXANDRE

WARD

MALLORY

CLYDE

CITY of BROOKLYN

New York City,
ca. 1890

NY–CUBA
STEAMSHIP LINES

ELEVATED
RAILROAD LINES

Map 2

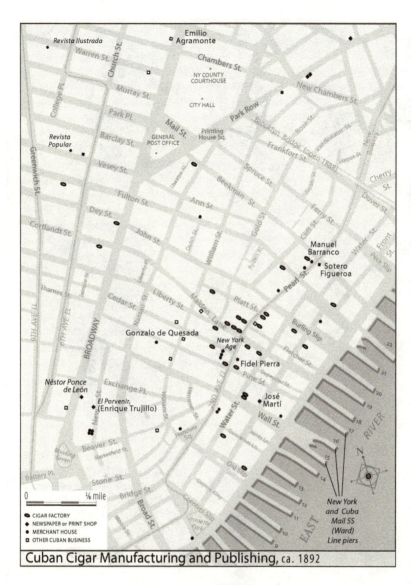

Cuban Cigar Manufacturing and Publishing, ca. 1892

Map 3

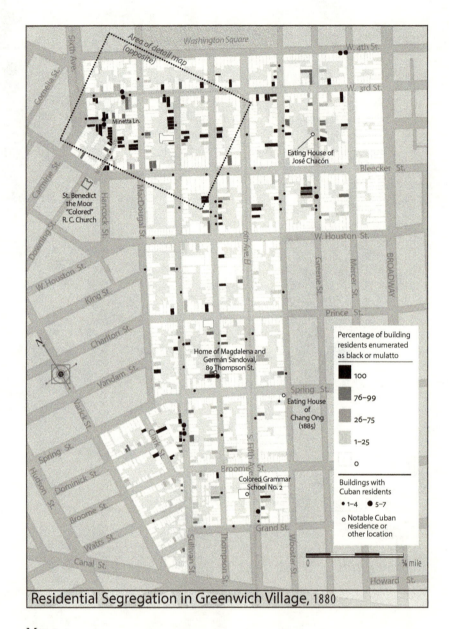

Residential Segregation in Greenwich Village, 1880

Map labels:

Washington Square
W. 4th St.
W. 3rd St.
Sixth Ave.
Cornelia St.
Minetta Ln.
Area of detail map (opposite)
Eating House of José Chacón
Bleecker St.
Camine St.
St. Benedict the Moor "Colored" R. C. Church
Hancock St.
MacDougal St.
W. Houston St.
Downing St.
6th Ave. El
Greene St.
Mercer St.
BROADWAY
W. Houston St.
King St.
Prince St.
Charlton St.
N
Home of Magdalena and Germán Sandoval, 89 Thompson St.
Vandam St.
Spring St.
Varick St.
Eating House of Chang Ong (1885)
Spring St.
Clark
Broome St.
So. Fifth Ave.
Hudson St.
Dominick St.
Colored Grammar School No. 2
Broome St.
Watts St.
Sullivan St.
Thompson St.
Grand St.
Wooster St.
Canal St.
Howard St.

Legend:

Percentage of building residents enumerated as black or mulatto

- 100
- 76–99
- 26–75
- 1–25
- 0

Buildings with Cuban residents

- 1–4
- 5–7
- Notable Cuban residence or other location

0   ⅛ mile

Map 4

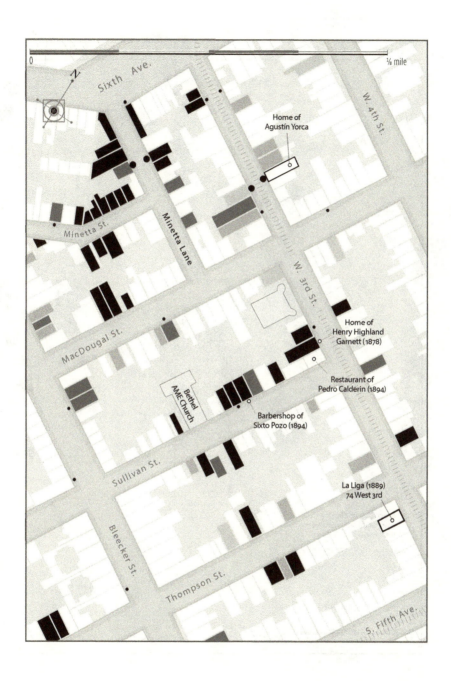

0

⅛ mile

Sixth Ave.

W. 4th St.

Minetta St.

Minetta Lane

W. 3rd St.

MacDougal St.

Home of
Agustín Yorca

Home of
Henry Highland
Garnett (1878)

Restaurant of
Pedro Calderin (1894)

Bethel
AME Church

Barbershop of
Sixto Pozo (1894)

Sullivan St.

La Liga (1889)
74 West 3rd

Bleecker St.

Thompson St.

S. Fifth Ave.

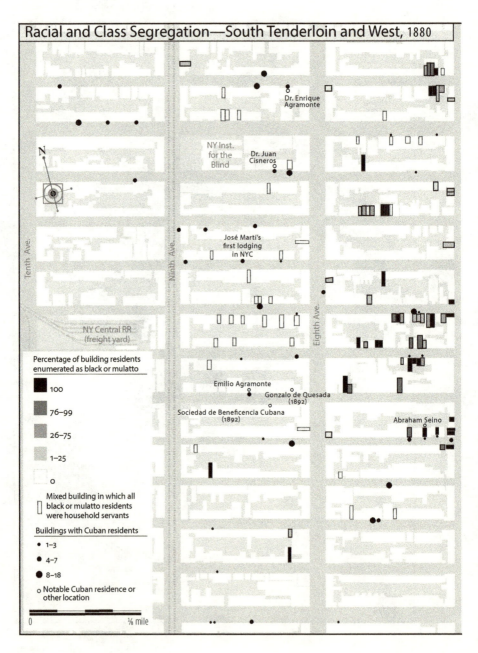

Racial and Class Segregation—South Tenderloin and West, 1880

Dr. Enrique Agramonte

NY Inst. for the Blind

Dr. Juan Cisneros

Tenth Ave.

Ninth Ave.

Eighth Ave.

N

NY Central RR (freight yard)

José Martí's first lodging in NYC

Percentage of building residents enumerated as black or mulatto

- 100
- 76–99
- 26–75
- 1–25
- o

Mixed building in which all black or mulatto residents were household servants

Buildings with Cuban residents

- 1–3
- 4–7
- 8–18
- o Notable Cuban residence or other location

0   ⅛ mile

Emilio Agramonte

Gonzalo de Quesada (1892)

Sociedad de Beneficencia Cubana (1892)

Abraham Seino

Map 5

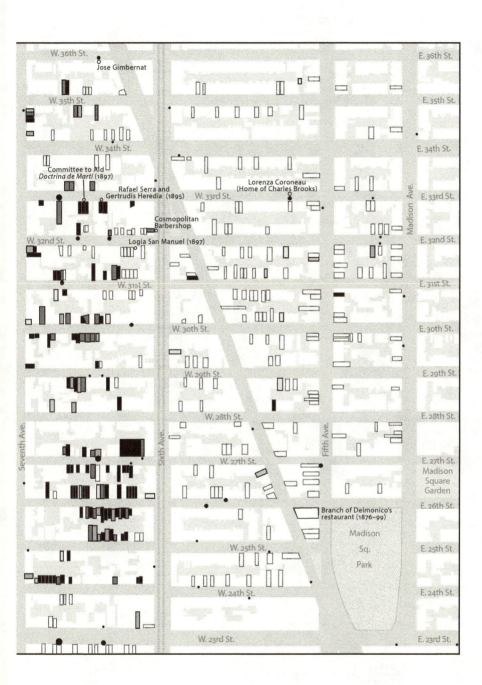

W. 36th St.

Jose Gimbernat

W. 35th St.

E. 36th St.

E. 35th St.

W. 34th St.

E. 34th St.

Committee to Aid
Doctrina de Martí (1897)

Rafael Serra and
Gertrudis Heredia (1895)

Lorenza Coroneau
(Home of Charles Brooks)

W. 33rd St.

E. 33rd St.

Cosmopolitan
Barbershop

Logia San Manuel (1897)

W. 32nd St.

E. 32nd St.

W. 31st St.

E. 31st St.

W. 30th St.

E. 30th St.

W. 29th St.

E. 29th St.

W. 28th St.

E. 28th St.

W. 27th St.

E. 27th St.
Madison
Square
Garden

Branch of Delmonico's
restaurant (1876–99)

E. 26th St.

Madison

W. 25th St.

Sq.

E. 25th St.

Park

W. 24th St.

E. 24th St.

W. 23rd St.

E. 23rd St.

Seventh Ave.

Sixth Ave.

Fifth Ave.

Madison Ave.

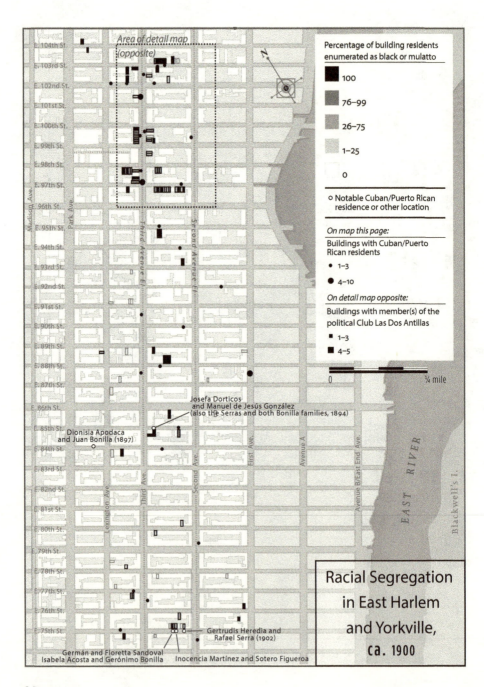

Area of detail map
(opposite)

Percentage of building residents enumerated as black or mulatto

■	100
▨	76–99
▨	26–75
▨	1–25
□	0

○ Notable Cuban/Puerto Rican residence or other location

On map this page:
Buildings with Cuban/Puerto Rican residents
• 1–3
● 4–10

On detail map opposite:
Buildings with member(s) of the political Club Las Dos Antillas
■ 1–3
■ 4–5

0   ¼ mile

E. 104th St.
E. 103rd St.
E. 102nd St.
E. 101st St.
E. 100th St.
E. 99th St.
E. 98th St.
E. 97th St.
96th St.
E. 95th St.
E. 94th St.
E. 93rd St.
E. 92nd St.
E. 91st St.
E. 90th St.
E. 89th St.
E. 88th St.
E. 87th St.
E. 86th St.
E. 85th St.
E. 84th St.
E. 83rd St.
E. 82nd St.
E. 81st St.
E. 80th St.
E. 79th St.
E. 78th St.
E. 77th St.
E. 76th St.
E. 75th St.

Madison Ave.
Park Ave.
Third Avenue El.
Second Avenue El.
Lexington Ave.
Third Ave.
Second Ave.
First Ave.
Avenue A
Avenue B/East End Ave.

EAST RIVER

Blackwell's I.

Josefa Dorticos
and Manuel de Jesús González
(also the Serras and both Bonilla families, 1894)

Dionisia Apodaca
and Juan Bonilla (1897)

Gertrudis Heredia and
Rafael Serra (1902)

Germán and Floretta Sandoval
Isabela Acosta and Gerónimo Bonilla   Inocencia Martínez and Sotero Figueroa

**Racial Segregation
in East Harlem
and Yorkville,
ca. 1900**

Map 6

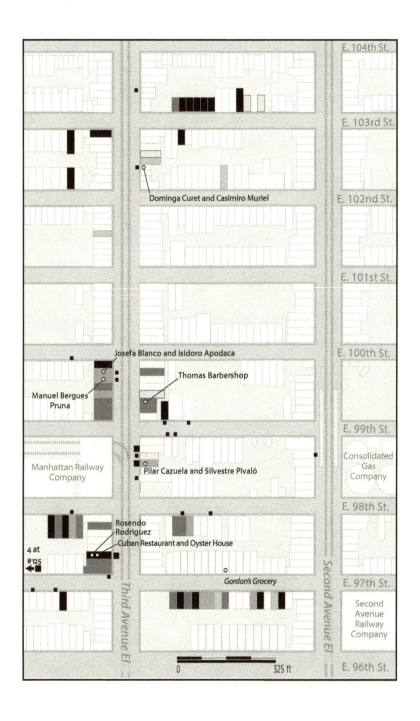

E. 104th St.

E. 103rd St.

Dominga Curet and Casimiro Muriel

E. 102nd St.

E. 101st St.

Josefa Blanco and Isidoro Apodaca

E. 100th St.

Thomas Barbershop

Manuel Bergues
Pruna

E. 99th St.

Manhattan Railway
Company

Pilar Cazuela and Silvestre Pivaló

Consolidated
Gas
Company

E. 98th St.

Rosendo
Rodriguez

Cuban Restaurant and Oyster House

4 at
#125

E. 97th St.

Gordon's Grocery

Second
Avenue
Railway
Company

Third Avenue El

Second Avenue El

0   325 ft

E. 96th St.

Racial Migrations

PROLOGUE

Radial Lines

On a bitter cold January evening in 1890, on the first floor of a row house on West Third Street in Greenwich Village, a group of Cuban and Puerto Rican immigrants gathered in two wallpapered rooms. Most of the men in attendance had already spent the day rolling tobacco in New York City's cigar factories, or waiting on tables and cooking in the nearby restaurants that catered to cigar workers. The women had spent the long day sewing, washing, keeping house, and tending the children who now sat on their laps. In their spare time, at gatherings like this one, these men and women had also found ways to become readers, musicians, teachers, poets, journalists, and revolutionaries. Illuminated by gaslight and heated by a small coal stove, the apartment held a piano, a table and chairs, and a bookshelf with the works of Plutarch, Herbert Spencer, and Joseph Ernest Renan as well as books of poetry in Spanish. The double doors between the two rooms stood open, and the crowd sat in rows of chairs stretching from one room to the other. As on so many nights, the group directed its attention toward a speaker, a handsome man with dark-brown skin and elegantly shaped sideburns. A framed portrait of this same man hung by the door of the flat. His name was Rafael Serra. He had led the effort to create, in this warm apartment, an organization called La Liga, an educational and recreational society dedicated to the welfare and uplift of Puerto Ricans and Cubans of "the class of color"—the class to which he and almost all those in the audience proudly belonged.[1]

No one yet used the term "Afro-Latino."[2] In Cuba, where slavery had been abolished only four years earlier, as in Puerto Rico, where slavery ended only thirteen years before that, officials referred to the people in this community as *negros*, *morenos*, *pardos*, and *mulatos*—words that expressed varying degrees of blackness. English-speaking New Yorkers typically called them "Cuban Negroes," if they noticed them at all. In the great swirl of humanity that descended on New York in the late nineteenth century, they were a tiny current, numbering in the hundreds in a city that was home to hundreds of thousands of newly arrived immigrants. Understandably, their experiences hardly register in classic accounts of immigration, race, and urban politics in this period. Yet the stories of these revolutionaries provide a window on the world through which they moved. As migrants, they boarded steamships to cross the narrow expanses of water that separated the islands from one another and from the rising imperial power to the north, experiencing firsthand the varied systems of racial domination created in each society in the wake of slavery. As settlers, they negotiated New York City's evolving color line, and the porous boundary between Latin American migrant communities and African American communities. As exiles, they used the resources, networks, and insights that they had built as migrants and settlers to intervene in nationalist politics, especially the struggles to overthrow Spanish colonialism in Cuba and Puerto Rico. This book tells their remarkable stories.

These stories are not exactly forgotten. The presence of a second speaker at the inauguration ceremony that frigid night in January ensured that Serra and a handful of others who helped to organize La Liga would be remembered, at least by historians of Cuba. This second speaker was the poet, journalist, and diplomat José Martí, a white man. His portrait hung opposite Serra's near the door of the flat. Martí would later create the Cuban Revolutionary Party and lead the effort to organize a rebellion against Spain. He would die in the early days of the war that he helped to launch and would then become the most celebrated figure in Cuban history: the Father of the Fatherland, the Apostle of Liberty, the Martyr of Dos Ríos.[3] In the chill of January 1890, however, the prospects for independence from Spain were hardly auspicious, and Martí was still a long way from becoming a nationalist hero. A previous attempt at revolution, the "Ten Years' War" from 1868 to 1878, had failed to win independence from Spain or secure the abolition of slavery on the island. A second "Little War," from 1879 to 1880, also failed to separate the island from Spain, but did spur the gradual abolition of slavery by 1886. The divisions that had emerged during these wars still ran deep among Cuban exiles in New York—disagreements between artisans and manufacturers, between veterans of the military campaigns and civilians, and between black settlers and white. Despite his credentials as an intellectual, Martí was not particularly beloved by any of these groups. The community that gathered at La Liga was the exception. Martí had helped to gather the resources to create La Liga. He volunteered to teach classes in the apartment on West Third Street, and he brought a handful of other white professionals and businessmen with him to teach as well. Serra and his allies, along with these teachers, became Martí's inner circle as he began to build a broader following among working-class exiles and, with that support, to rebuild the separatist movement.[4]

Thus the central characters in this book helped to organize and shape one of the great freedom struggles of the nineteenth century. Sotero Figueroa, a Puerto Rican typesetter, did the work to transform Martí's manuscripts into lines of print. He was the publisher of Martí's newspaper, *Patria*, and part of the team that edited it. Francisco Gonzalo "Pachín" Marín, another Puerto Rican, gave thunderous speeches at nationalist gatherings before eventually volunteering to fight and die in the Cuban insurgency. Juan Bonilla, a cigar maker born in the Cuban enclave in Key West, was a Freemason and a spiritist. He wrote for *Patria*, for the leading black newspapers in Havana, and for the African American press in New York. Serra, the founder of La Liga, was a cigar maker and politician from Havana. After Martí died, Serra published his own newspaper in New York. When the war of independence was won, Cuban voters twice elected him to the Cuban House of Representatives. Gertrudis Heredia, a midwife, led various women's groups at La Liga. One of the first black women to study obstetrics at the University of Havana, she delivered babies in the migrant community in New York. She was also Serra's wife. Though they earned their livings as artisans, these revolutionaries had access to printing presses and made extensive use of them, leaving a detailed record of their own thought. They were articulate observers of their own lives and of the immigrant worlds that they helped to construct.[5]

The lives and writings of these early Afro-Latino and Afro-Latina New Yorkers thus provide an opportunity to reconsider the history of race and revolution in the Spanish-speaking Caribbean. It was in conversations with this group of men and women that Martí—drawing on the popular ideologies of the earlier independence struggles—disavowed the reigning international scientific consensus about black inferiority. Together with him, the founders of La Liga proclaimed racial division and inequality to be a product of social prejudice, not nature. The revolution, they argued, would avoid class and racial conflict by assuring the inclusion of all Cubans in a just social order. The struggle against Spain was an effort to secure a republic "with all and for the good of all," as Martí famously phrased it. Serra and his allies also worked with Martí to reassure wealthier white Cubans—many of whom worried that a revolution might unleash a black rebellion on the island—that black Cubans were ready to forgive the sins of slavery and "forget their color." In a free Cuba, Martí proclaimed, there would be "no whites nor blacks, only Cubans."[6]

This idea of a nation that would transcend race left an ambivalent legacy. As an ideal, the republic "with all and for the good of all" stood in clear contrast to the politics of segregation and white supremacy that were gaining ascendance in the United States at the time. Even more than a hundred years later, the idea of a nation with no racial divisions continues to be emblematic of an alternative, or even of resistance, to the ideas about race that came to dominate in the United States. Recalling the principle of a nation for all, for instance, Cubans successfully instituted universal manhood suffrage after the defeat of Spanish forces, even against the wishes of the leadership of the occupying force from the United States. This alternative has been particularly important for the many people from the Caribbean who came to live within the orbit of the United States, both as colonial subjects in the territory of Puerto Rico and as migrants and racialized minorities on the mainland.

Yet the ideas of racial transcendence that emerged within the Cuban and Puerto Rican independence struggles, like variants of this notion that persist in many parts of the Americas, were a double-edged sword. As a shared revolutionary project, the call for a nation without racial divisions could provide leverage in struggles to combat entrenched racial inequality. But the call to forget race could also be used to subsume "particular" concerns (such as the welfare of persons of color) into the ostensibly "collective" interests of the fatherland. Worse still, many Cubans and Puerto Ricans would later choose to interpret the legacies of the independence struggle, and particularly their contrasts with the violence of segregation and disenfranchisement in the United States, to suggest that the Caribbean nations had *already* transcended any history of racial oppression at the moment of their founding, making further discussion of racial inequality unnecessary or even racist. For decades, scholars in Latin American studies engaged in heated debates over Cuban and other Latin American "myths" of racial harmony. Should the promise of a society that would transcend race be celebrated as an effective strategy for pursuing social justice? Or should it be debunked as a cynical tool for stifling independent antiracist activism? Increasingly, scholars have moved away from such a stark set of choices. The ideal of a nation without races was hardly a literal description of Cuban or Puerto Rican social reality, but it was more than simply a mechanism for imposing the interests of a dominant class. The ideology espoused by Martí became the terrain on which various actors, including people of African descent, positioned themselves in struggles over the shape of their movement and the society that it would produce.[7]

The point of returning to the stories of the people who gathered around Martí at La Liga, then, is not to resolve the long-standing debate over whether Martí's promises of racial inclusion lent themselves more to the pursuit of racial equality and social justice or to efforts to preserve an unequal and unjust status quo. The point is rather to ask what led Serra, Figueroa, and the other exiles of color in New York to invest so thoroughly in their relationship with Martí. Why did they accept the call to demonstrate patience and forgiveness in the name of national unity? Why did they choose to promote the idea of a nation for all and with all as if it were Martí's idea instead of their own? How did they manage to assert themselves in the nationalist struggle without giving up their right to form independent associations or to demand equal treatment as people of color? But perhaps most especially—given the ways that comparisons with the racial politics of the United States inform most writing about race in Puerto Rico and Cuba—what role did their experiences in the United States play in shaping the coalition politics that they helped to create around Martí? These are the questions that new attention to the lives, travels, and writings of Serra, Marín, Heredia, the Bonillas, and Figueroa—and to the larger community within which they organized—can help to answer.

Many years after the first gatherings at La Liga, one of Serra's supporters described the two-room apartment on West Third Street as "something like the central point of a vast sphere where all of the radial lines of a resurgent patriotism converged."[8] This probably overstates the case, as many key participants in the revolutionary struggle never came to New York or passed through the doors of La Liga, and because La

Liga was only one of several important institutions built by this community of exiles. But the idea of a central sphere through which many radial lines—or life trajectories—converged provides a useful way to imagine the interconnected stories of migration, writing, and politics that I try to capture in this book. By tracing a handful of migrant revolutionaries along circuitous routes from the places of their birth through their convergence at La Liga, and then past the encounter with Martí into the period after his death, I have tried to construct a migrants'-eye view of the world that they inhabited, and to use that view to offer insight into the origins and evolution of their revolutionary thought. This is a variant of a technique that professional historians call "microhistory": a focus on the details of individual lives that are not necessarily typical or representative in any statistical sense. Such sustained attention to the personal experiences and thoughts of just a few individuals can reveal the contours of a time and place that are otherwise difficult for historians to capture or relate. Microhistory can be especially helpful in illuminating the spoken and silent constraints, terror, and spaces for negotiation that individuals marked by racial difference experienced within societies organized around racial domination.[9]

This book presents several microhistories that begin separately and, over time, intertwine. The idea of a "class of color," invoked in the founding documents of La Liga, intentionally expressed an ideal of unity within a group that was in fact quite diverse in its origins. Cubans and Puerto Ricans sometimes used the terms "class of color" or "race of color" to express (or dismiss) the fear that all people of African descent, free pardos and morenos as well as enslaved people, would unite in rebellion. Other times, the term "class of color" served as a euphemism for the most dignified and honorable subset of the free African-descended population. The founders of La Liga, along with other civil rights activists in Cuba, appropriated both meanings. They argued against the traditional divisions between brown and black people, and for unity, under the leadership of the dignified and honorable class of color, in the struggle against racism. Nevertheless, the people who joined in this call had experienced race in different contexts and different ways. Figueroa was born to parents described as pardo (light brown) in San Juan, the small administrative capital of Puerto Rico. Serra was the legitimate child of moreno (dark brown) parents in the opulent sugar metropolis of Havana. Bonilla was born and raised in a family that had come from Havana but lived in Key West. He grew up in neighborhoods shared with white Cubans and African Americans. Heredia was the granddaughter of the leaders of an Afro-Cuban *cabildo* (ethnic association) in the booming sugar port of Matanzas. Marín was the son of a mulato small businessman, and the acknowledged descendant of a prominent white family in the small conservative enclave of Arecibo, Puerto Rico. Following the model of radial lines converging on a central point, *Racial Migrations* opens by situating the main characters within the contexts where they were born, where they first entered public life, and where they first began to articulate ideas about race.

The story of the people who crossed paths in the gatherings at West Third Street is thus, in the first place, an effort of careful comparison. It provides an opportunity to illustrate two fundamental arguments about race that are easy for professional historians to assert, but can be difficult to bring to life for nonacademics. The first is that race is a social rather than a natural phenomenon. The institution of racial slavery existed in many parts of the Americas, producing strikingly similar consequences in each of the many societies that sought to integrate former slaves as free workers and citizens after emancipation. Nevertheless, the contours of how race actually worked—including how people were classified, and what legal and social consequences those classifications carried—could be markedly different in local contexts. The second is that the systems for organizing societies around race intersected, in each of these contexts, with other social hierarchies, including class, gender, and sexuality. Understanding the particular racial politics that this group of migrants articulated, including the decision sometimes to organize themselves as a class of color, and at other times to demand the right to be Cubans and Puerto Ricans without qualifiers, and eventually to position themselves as supporters of Martí, requires situating these decisions within the kinds of racial, class, and gender strictures they encountered in their places of origin.[10]

But if this story begins with comparisons, it quickly moves on to something else entirely. The men and women who listened to the speeches on that frigid January evening may have started their lives with different kinds of social identities, formed in diverse local contexts, yet they did not remain isolated from one another or confined within neatly demarcated racial systems. They moved through multiple spaces of conflict and negotiation over the aftermath of slavery: different parts of Cuba and Puerto

Rico, the British colony of Jamaica, the independent Republic of Haiti, and the French Canal Zone in Panama. They gathered observations about the workings of racial domination in each of these contexts, and adjusted their own perceptions of race and citizenship in response. They reflected on their home societies from the vantage point that they gained as travelers. Most of all, by the time they helped Martí to construct the idea of a nation that would transcend racial difference, they did so as settlers living in the segregated city of New York during the Gilded Age—at precisely the moment when white politicians in the United States made a hasty retreat from the promise of interracial democracy.[11]

"You do not know, nor can you suppose, how hard it is for the man of color to live in this northern land," Serra, the founder and leader of La Liga, wrote to a fellow exile named Tomás Estrada Palma.[12] Estrada Palma eventually replaced Martí as the head of the Cuban Revolutionary Party and later became the first elected president of Cuba. Because he had not experienced life in the United States as a man of color, Serra noted, Estrada Palma did not know what he and the organizers of La Liga knew about the workings of the color line in New York. Estrada Palma was also, as yet, unaware of the extent to which Serra and others at La Liga socialized and exchanged political ideas with African American activists and journalists in their adopted city. Nor have historians given much attention to the experience of "migrating while black" in late nineteenth-century New York. Yet the racial politics that unfolded within the Cuban and Puerto Rican independence struggle, so often contrasted to the racial politics of the United States in the era of Jim Crow, actually emerged, in part, as a result of the experiences of people of color living in the northern land, and participating actively in the racial politics and segregated social life of their adopted home. Together with the African Americans among whom they lived, and with whom they danced, married, formed fraternal lodges, and discussed current events, the members of the community that gathered at La Liga began to develop the sensibilities, politics, and even institutions of an African diaspora. They started to imagine and build ties among African-descended people across linguistic and national lines. These ties helped to strengthen rather than detract from their efforts to gain full citizenship within each national community. Indeed, these ties provide a necessary frame for understanding the remarkable nationalist resurgence that took place in the flat on West Third Street. And they are equally important for understanding the period after Martí's death, when Serra, Figueroa, and Bonilla worked to preserve their influence as the Cuban Revolutionary Party reconfigured around Estrada Palma, and as the revolutionary struggle was cut short by the US invasion of Cuba and Puerto Rico. Finally, the episodes of intimate encounter among intellectuals and activists of color across national and linguistic divides highlight the considerable uncertainty about how racial politics should and could evolve in both the United States and the Spanish Caribbean at the end of the nineteenth century.[13]

This is a work of narrative history. Historians often organize books around a set of arguments, usually taking issue with the claims of other historians and marshaling their evidence to support these claims. When we write for one another, we frequently pause to discuss our methods, especially when we have found a new source or a new way to answer a difficult question from a familiar source. I have chosen instead to build an interpretation through the telling of these intertwined stories without putting debates, theories, or methods in the foreground. The result is, I hope, something that reads more like a novel than like a textbook. I am, of course, deeply informed by and indebted to the work of many other scholars, brimming with excitement about the archives that I consulted and thrilled by the minutia of detective work required to piece these stories together. I am eager for readers to be alert to the extensive and challenging research that went into this book, and to the novelty of my approach. Yet I think there is something to be gained in focusing on the story, not least the possibility of engaging the interest and imaginations of readers beyond those already invested in the field. Those who are interested in the more arcane details of the historian's craft will find a full accounting in the endnotes, in a brief note on sources, and in a separate article, published specifically for historians, on digital research methods. A nineteenth-century novelist—like the ones whose books Serra and his companions read aloud to one another as they worked rolling cigars— might interrupt here to beg your patience, gentle reader, as the pieces of the puzzle are presented one by one and begin to fit together gradually over the course of the book. I ask for this same patience as the story moves among various locations and takes the perspective of different characters. I will do my best to provide reminders of what has come before and hints of what is yet to come. Only occasionally will I step back and reflect on how a particular episode fits with or reshapes what previous historians have written or supposed.[14]

Finally, I hope for your patience in dealing with the greatest challenge that I faced in writing this book. The rich body of texts that Serra, Figueroa, and others left behind, while offering remarkable insight into their social and intellectual worlds, also produce a great unevenness in this story. The individuals who left this extensive record of their own thoughts were almost always men. To a degree, this is an insoluble problem. Projects designed by Cuban and Puerto Rican men of color to insert themselves into a public sphere dominated by white men almost always depended on asserting their masculinity—their right to be treated as men. This often meant imposing new forms of exclusion on black women or accommodating existing forms of exclusion. In writing this book, I have faced difficult choices, like many other historians, about how to tell the story of those audacious projects without reproducing the erasure of women of color from the public record. I have no particularly good answer to this dilemma except to highlight the role of women when possible as well as the significance of sex and gender in stories about both women and men. Where the record falters, I have also sometimes opted to employ a degree of speculation. I have chosen to signal these moments with question marks, or with the words "maybe," "perhaps," or when there is good circumstantial evidence, "probably" or "almost certainly." These questions are not haphazard or fanciful but rather deeply informed by research. They allow me to bring in information that is crucial to the story without introducing new, unconnected characters. The idea is not to put words into the mouths or thoughts into the heads of people whose lives were so radically different from my own, or to abandon the historian's responsibility to documentation and evidence. It is instead to invite readers to participate in informed acts of historical imagination. Indeed, this is the underlying method of history-as-storytelling employed in the book as a whole. Let us start by imagining the places where the stories begin.[15]

▪ 1 ▪

Beginnings

Scattered, here one day, there the next, everywhere, jumbled like lost gems on a beach, unknown and sometimes despised in the indifferent multitude, the true heroes and the liberators of the future await the moment when they will put their ideas into play, when they will secure their triumphs.

—Rafael Serra, "Nadie lo sabe," 1894

How many setbacks would he not overcome and how much fortitude would he not develop before opening the way for himself, and rising, rising high to make himself admired by a society that was refractory toward all those of his race!

—Sotero Figueroa, *Ensayo biográfico*, 1888

Years later, the writer Lorenzo Despradel described La Liga, the "famous" educational and recreational society located at 74 West Third Street, as the meeting place where all the important elements of the nationalist movement crossed paths in the early 1890s.[1] We begin the tale of this convergence with a seemingly simple question: Where did these "radial lines" originate? Many generations of biographers, with a wide range of political agendas, have provided a fairly rich account of the childhood and early career of José Martí. But for the others who gathered to hear him speak at the apartment on West Third Street, the question of origins is difficult to answer. Nationalist writers—especially writers of color—frequently wrote and published sketches highlighting the literary and political accomplishments of men of "humble" origins, including some of those who passed through La Liga. But they faced a tension between the desire to emphasize how far their subjects had come—their extraordinary triumphs of self-making—and the likelihood that full disclosure about their origins would dishonor and tarnish their public reputations. Thus in his collection of biographical sketches of men of color who had lived in the United States, the black Cuban journalist Teófilo Domínguez noted only that the founder of La Liga, Serra, was born in 1858 in Havana, received a primary education, entered the cigar workshops of Havana, and "began to earn his own sustenance when he was scarcely thirteen years old!" Domínguez then shifted to the most important narrative action: "By his own efforts he continued to acquire varied knowledge."[2]

This emphasis on self-making—a quick pivot from obscure origins to an accounting of literary and political accomplishments—helped express the principle that a man's achievements mattered more than the circumstances of his birth. Rather than detail such circumstances, authors typically employed a range of polite phrases, including "from nothing," "from a humble cradle," "a child of the people," "obscure," and "among the disinherited of the earth."[3] They wrote hardly at all about women. Their vision of racial unity was heavily invested in a shared experience of manhood. Yet in the few exceptions to this rule, nationalist writers used similarly vague allusions. Martí himself reported on a gathering of a group of women of color organized by Gertrudis Heredia, describing "the heartfelt and modest speeches, spoken with the trepidation of a new bride, by women who, in that other life from which they come, the life of darkness and impiety, never learned the arts of association."[4] This way of discussing origins required few potentially embarrassing specifics of the particular obstacles that Serra, Heredia, and others faced on their way to becoming "something." But these details are exactly what would be most helpful, looking back from a distance of more than a century, to fully understand the beginning points of the lives that converged at La Liga, and the varied contexts of racial domination that gave rise to the visions of racial and class justice that these men and women espoused.

Still, it is possible to dig deeper into the circumstances of their "humble" points of origin. To make the task manageable, I focus here on the early lives of just three of the key personalities in the book. The first of these is Serra, cigar maker, poet, and politician. The second is Heredia, a midwife who became one of the few black women to complete a certification program in obstetrics at the University of Havana before joining her husband, Serra, in New York. There, the couple raised a daughter. Heredia, along with another midwife, led the various women's organizations affiliated with La Liga. The third is Figueroa, a Puerto Rican typesetter and journalist. Figueroa set the type, proofed copy, and oversaw the printing of Martí's newspaper, *Patria*. He was an official in the Cuban Revolutionary Party, and gave speeches alongside Martí and Serra at countless party events. Like Serra, he served as a bridge to working-class and black and brown constituents in New York. But he also helped to bring the relatively smaller community of Puerto Rican exiles under the umbrella of the Cuban Revolutionary Party. After Martí's death, Figueroa and Serra led the charge in defending a radical vision of "the Apostle's" legacy.[5] The experiences of three other figures help to fill in some crucial gaps around the stories of the first three. One is Manuela Aguayo, who married Figueroa in the late 1870s, but who died of tuberculosis several years before he moved to New York. The second is Juan Gualberto Gómez, the most important journalist of African descent and civil rights leader in Cuba from the 1870s through the end of the century, and a close ally to Martí, Serra, and Figueroa. The last is Martí himself, who was born in Havana only a few years before Serra, but grew up in wholly different circumstances.

These individuals—four men and two women; four Cubans and two Puerto Ricans; two people with dark-brown complexions, three with lighter-brown skin, and one regarded as white; a midwife, a seamstress, a typographer, two journalists, and a cigar maker—do not represent the full spectrum of diversity within the group that would later converge at La Liga. But their stories are sufficiently distinct from one another to provide a starting place, a sketch of the varied racial landscapes out of which they came. In fact, the differences among their stories are what prove to be most important. Like almost everyone associated with La Liga, all these characters except Martí were identified as members of the "artisan" class (urban, skilled workers) and as people "of color." Yet naming their class and racial status in this way provides little more information than the euphemistic allusion to their "humility." Indeed, precisely because of the seeming familiarity of the concept "of color," simply calling them intellectuals and leaders "of color" risks papering over the diversity of their experiences of race. To be an artisan "of color" in San Juan, the small administrative capital of Puerto Rico (where Figueroa was born and raised), was to fall within a range of experiences that was similar but not identical to the range of experiences perceived by people described as "of color" in Havana (where Serra was born), the opulent capital of Cuba's booming slave economy. To be the granddaughter of the leaders of an African ethnic society in Matanzas, Cuba's wealthy second city (as Heredia was), was not the same as to be the illegitimate daughter of a white politician in the small town of Toa Baja, Puerto Rico (as Aguayo was). To be a man was to experience color and class in ways that were dramatically different from the experiences of women. These tales of self-making share some important features but also differ in crucial ways.

A HUMBLE CRADLE

In 1856, a couple named Cayetano Heredia and María del Socorro del Monte brought their infant daughter to the cathedral in the city of Matanzas to be baptized. For a fee, the parish priest conducted the required ritual, applying holy oil to the child's head, washing clean the original sin with which she had been born, and advising two godparents of their spiritual obligations to the child. He gave the baby the name chosen by her parents, María Gertrudis. Then, at some point later that day or that week, he turned to the sacramental books that were in his charge in order to record the details of the ceremony. Cuba, one of the two remaining Spanish colonies in the New World, was a society without any civil registry and characterized by low levels of literacy. Sacramental registers were the closest thing to an official record of the identities and lineages of the people who lived on the island. Parish priests produced formulaic accounts of baptisms in a deliberate hand, inserting relevant details such as date, the name and sex of the child, and the names of parents, grandparents, and godparents. They also made important determinations of social status, indicating whether children were free or enslaved, and whether they were white. In the case of María Gertrudis, the priest copied the details of the event in a racially segregated baptismal register for pardos and morenos. He recorded that she was the daughter of Cayetano Heredia, "native of Africa," and María del Socorro del Monte, a woman born in Matanzas.[6] He then indexed the record by writing surnames and other details in the margins, and tucked the book away in the sacred repository. A second priest made the same determination in 1858 when Rafael Serra and Marcelina Montalvo, "free morenos from Havana," went to a local parish in Havana to baptize their son. This priest too inscribed José Rafael Simón Agapito Serra in the book set aside for baptisms of pardos and morenos.[7]

In Cuba at the midpoint of the nineteenth century, to be recorded in one of these separate baptismal books was to be assigned to an explicitly inferior social status. Ideas about racial difference provided the ideological backbone for the central feature of Cuban economic, political, and social life: the systematic enslavement and brutalization of Africans and their descendants. Even for those who were legally free, to be marked as pardo or moreno was a significant barrier to social standing. For instance, though there was technically no law against interracial marriage in the Spanish Empire, local officials in Cuba interpreted laws designed to prevent minor children and persons of noble blood from contracting "unequal marriages" without the consent of their families as an impediment to any marriage across color lines. This obstacle could only be overcome by obtaining permission from a representative of the Crown.[8] These practices derived from Spanish legal restrictions on the Christian descendants of Jews and Muslims based on a concept of inherited difference known as "impurity of blood." In the slave societies of the Caribbean the same restrictions were applied to people with the somewhat different inherited "stain" of blackness. And they persisted well after the concept of blood purity fell out of use in Spain itself. Beyond the question of marriage, to be accepted unconditionally as a person of rank, to be eligible for certain offices, to enter certain professions, and to be treated with honor and dignity by other persons of standing, required a public reputation as a white person.[9]

These two baptismal records offer a sure sign that Gertrudis and Rafael, who many years later would become migrants and community leaders in New York, were not born into such a reputation. Nor does it seem likely that the priests in question would have experienced much doubt in making their determinations about where the two children stood in the local racial hierarchy. Similarly, the priest in another Havana parish who baptized José Martí in 1853 would not have had much doubt about placing his record in the baptismal book for white persons. José, known to his family as Pepe, was the child of two Spanish immigrants to Cuba. His parents had neither significant property nor claim to aristocratic distinction, and they would later fall on hard times. But José's father was a professional military man—a position reserved for men who could prove their purity of blood. The idea of blood purity had its origins in attempts to manage the ethnic diversity within Spain, but in the colonies, the Martí family and other new arrivals from the peninsula were automatically granted the benefits of whiteness.[10]

Color was also a key element of social hierarchy in the other remaining Spanish American colony, the smaller Caribbean island of Puerto Rico. But the system for assigning color status did not work in precisely the same way. This is evident in the record produced in 1853, when José Mercedes Figueroa and María Rosenda Fernández brought their son Sotero to be baptized in the cathedral in San Juan. The priest fulfilled all the same rites: the anointment with oil, the admonition to the godparents, the collection of an emolument from the parents, and the recording of the act in a sacramental book. Yet this book was segregated on different principles. In fact, less than a year before Figueroa was born, the bishop of Puerto Rico had reviewed the sacramental books at the San Juan Cathedral and ordered priests to end the segregation of baptismal records by race. The bishop did not suggest that he favored the end of all racial distinctions or believed that all races were one. Nor did he offer any reason for the new policy. He merely specified that all free white, black, and brown people should appear in the same book, and only slaves should appear in a separate, second book. Under the bishop's orders, the priests at the cathedral crossed out the words "white persons" on the title page of the book previously reserved for whites, inserting the words "of all classes." Puerto Rican record keepers shifted the line of separation from race to legal status (free or enslaved), and began to leave race unspoken or to treat it obliquely, in contrast with record keepers in Cuba.[11] So although he had recorded the baptisms of Sotero's older siblings in the register for pardos and morenos, the priest recorded his birth in 1853 in the newly desegregated book, with no mention of his race or that of his parents.[12]

In all three cases, the priests recorded the status of these families with some variation of the phrase "native of Havana," "residents of this parish," and "of this city." These phrases were probably small details for those involved, but they are highly significant for historians seeking to understand exactly where these families stood within these two societies. In the 1850s, most people of African descent on both islands lived in rural settings, as either peasants or slaves. But both Cuba and Puerto Rico had long-established urban communities of African-descended artisans, peddlers, entrepreneurs, washerwomen, and seamstresses. Free colored tradespeople and their families were able to achieve, through economic success, a degree of honorable personhood. Service in local militias also granted some free men of color privileges, including pensions and immunity from civilian courts and jails. Authorities also permitted and even encouraged the expansion of associations for free people of color, including lay Catholic brotherhoods. It is not clear if any of the parents who appeared in these baptismal registers had attained this honorable status, but it is certain that they were "of the city," which in and of itself could be a mark of a certain distinction.[13]

Yet there were clear differences in the circumstances of free people on the two islands. The port of Havana, Cuba, was a required stopping point for the great fleet of the Spanish Empire in its heyday, home to a sizable administrative and military presence. Puerto Rico lay outside the main imperial trade routes. As in other remote parts of the empire, the small scale of economic production created relatively more space for people of African ancestry or mixed ancestry to live outside the bonds of slavery while reducing the number of people who could be considered white. Thus by the last third of the eighteenth century, free people of color constituted only one-fifth of the population of Cuba, but about half of the population of Puerto Rico.[14] These differences then grew even more dramatic when, over the subsequent half century, the economies of Cuba and Puerto Rico shifted toward the production of tobacco, coffee, and especially sugar for export. In both Cuba and Puerto Rico, this dynamism relied heavily on a new influx of enslaved people from Africa.[15] But the two islands differed dramatically in the scale of this shift toward slave production. During the period when Figueroa was a child, the enslaved population in Puerto Rico totaled only 41,738 as compared with 241,037 free people of color. In Cuba, when Heredia, Serra, and Martí were children, 370,553 people lived in slavery along with 232,493 free people of color. The contrast is even more marked if we break down the two islands by region. San Juan, where Figueroa was born and raised, remained a modest administrative and military capital, while most of the island's sugar production and most slaves were concentrated in the southern and western ports of Ponce, Guayama, and Mayagüez. Havana and Matanzas, in contrast, were not only grand modern cities and the principal ports in Western Cuba but the nearby countryside was also the most productive sugar region in Cuba (and the world).[16]

The massive growth of sugar production, and the corresponding growth of Havana and Matanzas, provided economic opportunities for some free people of color. But the burgeoning export economy also led to a growing and increasingly powerful Cuban planter class, and to widespread concerns among white Cuban intellectuals about the "Africanization" of the island. Cuban thinkers were acutely aware of the fate of the plantation society that the French had constructed in nearby Saint-Domingue, where African slaves had far outnumbered white colonists. Indeed, the Cubans had eagerly taken advantage of slave rebellions in Saint-Domingue in the 1790s to build their own sugar industry. Then they had watched as armies composed of former slaves waged a successful anticolonial revolution and established an independent black republic, Haiti. In this context, white intellectuals expressed ambivalence, if not outright hostility, toward pardo and moreno artisans and militiamen. They worried that the presence of so many black and brown people in the urban trades discouraged the immigration of white workers, and the "improvement" of the artisan class. They expressed concerns that free people harbored aspirations that would unsettle clear lines of social hierarchy and threaten the very stability of the slave system. And they regarded free pardos and morenos as the potential allies of slaves, part of a unified "African race" or "race of color."[17]

This shifting politics of race came to a head after 1844 when Cuban authorities discovered several planned slave uprisings in the countryside around Matanzas. A Military Commission conducted a widespread investigation, employing torture to uncover, or perhaps invent, a conspiracy for a coordinated attack on slavery, led by free people. The commission executed a dozen accused leaders, including Matanzas poet, silversmith, printer, and carpenter Gabriel de la Concepción Valdés (Plácido). The authorities also banished more than four hundred free men of color, and imprisoned more than a thousand. The Military Commission further confiscated the property of the accused in order to cover the cost of investigation, trial, and detention. This episode of state violence proved devastating to the economic fortunes of the most well-established African-descended families in the cities of Western Cuba. Though it is not clear whether any close relative of Gertrudis and Rafael came under suspicion, children baptized to free families in Havana and Matanzas in the 1850s grew up in the shadow of this violence. Indeed, Plácido's mother-in-law, the midwife Pilar Poveda, continued to act as a community leader in Matanzas well into the period of Gertrudis's childhood. Plácido's widow remarried a local violinist who had been imprisoned but not killed during the investigations. Their son Enrique later became a close friend and ally of Rafael and Gertrudis.[18]

So the two Cuban couples, Rafael Serra (Sr.) and Marcelina Montalvo, and Cayetano Heredia and Socorro del Monte, brought their children to be baptized in a period when white society in Havana and Matanzas worked to reinforce the boundaries between whites and nonwhites, eliminating the free colored militias and segregating public facilities. Cuban elites also organized to encourage the immigration of white people to the island in the hopes of insulating themselves against black rebellion and preparing for the transition from slavery. In 1854, rumors spread that the Catholic hierarchy and a liberal governor had plans to relax the restrictions on interracial marriage (as part of a project to promote sacramental marriage and crack down on consensual unions). This led to a backlash and a decree reinstating the broadest possible interpretation of Spanish laws governing unequal marriages. The principle at stake, however, was no longer the defense of the "purity" of individual white families, but rather a broader question of security. Intermarriage, opponents argued, would incite the aspirations of the race of color. By the 1860s, the authorities had stopped granting any licenses for "unequal" marriages. Priests likely held a range of views, but they dutifully continued segregating sacramental registries, maintaining racial divisions in the spiritual world and in the island's only system of public records.[19]

By contrast, the San Juan of Sotero Figueroa's childhood was comparatively insulated both from the influx of Africans and the wave of repression that swept Western Cuba. To be sure, Puerto Rico was a society profoundly marked by slavery. Nearly half a century had passed since a visitor had remarked "there is nothing more ignominious on this Island than to be black, or to be descended from them: a white man insults any of them, with impunity, and in the most contemptible language."[20] But such prejudices persisted. White families, government officials, and representatives of the church still shared a widespread consensus that "unequal" marriages ought to be discouraged. But concerns about such marriages continued to be a private matter related to the integrity of family honor, against a backdrop of pervasive racial mixture, rather than a political concern that interracial marriage would lead to rebellion and insecurity.[21] Worries about slave rebellions, especially after slave uprisings in Saint Croix and Guadalupe in 1848, led to a new set of legal punishments for free people of color who "rose up" against whites in Puerto Rico (the fa-mous Decree against the African Race). Clearly, the idea of a threat from a unified African race was not absent altogether. Those measures seem never to have been enforced and were quickly reversed.[22] Compared to their Cuban counterparts, wealthy Puerto Ricans seem to have been little concerned with segregating public space or sociability, or systematically undermining the status of free people, or at least they lacked the power to put such concerns into effect.[23] They were also much less successful than their Cuban neighbors at attracting Spanish immigrants, meaning that whiteness itself was often a fairly ambiguous status. As we will see, this does not mean that whiteness ceased to be an important component of social hierarchy in Puerto Rico. Yet it does help to explain why the seg-regation of sacramental documents no longer seemed necessary in Puerto Rico at midcentury, while the practice continued in Cuba.

In addition to segregating baptisms into distinct sacramental books, priests in Cuba and Puerto Rico (before 1852) often assigned additional distinctions according to degree of blackness, using the terms "pardo" (light brown), "moreno" (a more respectful way to describe someone per-ceived to be dark brown), and "negro" (a less respectful way to describe someone perceived to be dark brown). Public officials and notaries applied these categories too. Rafael's parents were morenos. Sotero's parents ap-peared with no racial descriptor on his baptism, but the priests described them as "free pardos of this city [San Juan]" on the baptismal records of two older children, created before the church desegregated sacramental records. It seems fairly sure that they and their children continued to be treated as pardo in their everyday lives, even after the change in church policy.[24] These were not trivial distinctions. The Spanish government, for instance, divided militias on both islands into three battalions: one for whites, one for free morenos, and one for free pardos. In Cuba especially, religious brotherhoods also frequently segregated pardos from morenos. These color categories were not defined simply or even principally by physical appearance. Color terms reflected perceptions of public behav-ior, relative economic status, and how other members of a person's family and social networks were positioned in the racial hierarchy too. They de-pended as well on how far removed a person was seen to be from captivity in Africa. "Negro," for example, was a word reserved, for the most part, for persons held in slavery or only recently manumitted. Colloquially, there were still more terms for particular combinations of complexion, hair texture, and facial features. Yet especially for free people of African descent, these various elements did not necessarily fit together in predictable or consistent ways. The ascription of a particular color status by a priest at the moment of baptism or by a notary at a later date was significant but not indelible. In fact, the color ascriptions assigned to a particular family on official documents could change over generations or over the course of the life of a single individual. In a few cases, individuals were able to mobilize official pressure to convince priests to amend the baptismal records.[25]

Despite these basic similarities between the use of color terms in Cuba and Puerto Rico, these gradations worked differently in different parts of the Spanish Caribbean. Census officials on both islands cared deeply about the question of race in their statistical estimates of population for the same reason: they believed that the numerical superiority of white residents was an important, and perhaps the most important, factor in the success of their aspirations for social stability, economic growth, and political freedom. But they diverged, along with the societies in which they were embedded, in the ways that they understood and represented racial categories. For one thing, official statistics, collected by mayors, parish priests, and neighborhood constables, consistently indicated that people of intermediate status were a much-larger proportion of the population in Puerto Rico. Cuban censuses in this period estimated that free pardos narrowly outnumbered free morenos. They also concluded, though, that there were more than twice as many enslaved "negros" as there were free people of color altogether. By contrast, Puerto Rican census takers considered that the free pardo population outnumbered free morenos by a factor of more than seven to one, and also far outnumbered people held in slavery on the island.[26]

The difference between an island where most persons of African descent were mixed and only distantly descended from slaves and another island where most persons of African descent were black and closely connected to slavery might be expected, given the difference in the scale of the recent sugar boom on each island. But island censuses were more than just a neutral accounting of racial groups; they required crucial decisions about how to count and sort diverse and variegated populations into racial categories. In Puerto Rico, officials generally counted in a way that expanded the middle of the spectrum, describing what they saw as a small and shrinking population of morenos. By midcentury, Cuban census commissions typically chose not to report the numbers of pardos and morenos separately, instead lumping these groups together as free people "of color."[27] This was consistent with the idea of a "class of color" that, authorities sometimes argued, was poised to "rise up against the whites." By the 1860s, even African-descended intellectuals and activists sometimes used the terms "race of color," or even "negro," to refer to all African-descended people, though specific individuals were still frequently identified as pardo, mulato, africano, or moreno.[28] The concept of a "class of color" or a "race of color" appeared in Puerto Rican public life as well, but its use was less frequent. Perhaps more important, while many Puerto Ricans understood African ancestry as an indelible stain on family lineage that could not be mitigated, in a society with little immigration from Europe, the borderline between pardo and white was typically a matter of reputation, and therefore open to considerable flexibility.

These differences in the mode of recording and counting race between Cuba and Puerto Rico, together with the differential status afforded to persons of mixed race in both societies, help to make sense of the "humble" origins of the three children at the heart of this story. Figueroa was the son of free urban "pardos" whose race went unspoken on the key official document that marks his early life, at a time when priests stopped referring openly to race. He would come of age in a period in which officials collecting racial data, including the local constable in his neighborhood, tended to see most Puerto Ricans of African descent as mixed rather than black. Meanwhile, Heredia was the daughter of an African-born man, and Serra was the son of free "morenos" in Western Cuba, where public officials sought to collapse the varied color statuses into the category "of color" or simply "negro," and to rigorously separate whites from nonwhites. Intermediate categories continued to exist in Cuba. But large numbers of African-descended people, including both Gertrudis and Rafael, lived at one end of the racial spectrum, and a large group of recent immigrants, including the family of Martí, lived at the other extreme. In fact, Martí's father was one of the officials responsible for counting and ascribing racial categories to the residents of Havana. After an undistinguished career in the military, Martí's father found a job as a *celador de barrio*, or neighborhood constable, responsible for keeping tabs on the local population.[29] In cities at the center of the plantation complex, Gertrudis and Rafael's blackness seems not to have been an open question, not something to be negotiated over the course of their lives. Figueroa, on the other hand, was already something other than black at the moment of his birth, and as we will see, his racial status continued to evolve over the course of his life.

Yet there are more wrinkles to the story. The priest who performed Gertrudis's baptism described her father, Cayetano, as a "native of Africa." On the baptismal record of her younger sister, their father appears as "of the Carabalí nation." Many, but not all, persons who were eventually identified as Carabalí in Cuba came on slaving ships originating in the port of Calabar, and received their ethnic descriptors in bills of lading and acts of sale. Cayetano's ethnic identification thus opens the possibility that he was born in one of the small, interconnected communities of the Cross-River Delta, near the border between present-day Nigeria and Cameroon, in which many of the people shipped through Calabar were taken captive. One way or the other, he almost certainly arrived in Cuba as a captive, destined for slavery.[30] We can only imagine the details of his transformation from a free person into a captive, and the luck and strength that allowed him to survive capture, movement within coastal Africa, separation from kin and from the resting place of his ancestors, the trauma of the sea voyage across the Atlantic, and the dangerous first years of enslavement in Cuba, known as "seasoning." Cayetano probably forged bonds with other people transported on the same slave ship. He likely received his Christian names and surnames from the persons who first purchased him in the Matanzas slave market.[31] He may also have participated in the Abakuá Society, an all-male secret fraternity in Havana and Matanzas that was closely associated with the initiation-based societies that helped to govern the Cross-River Region.[32] The baptismal records do not speak to this, nor do they give details about how, between his arrival in Cuba and the birth of his daughter, he managed a most extraordinary feat of self-making. How, in the middle of the immense and brutal profit-making machine of plantation society, did he make himself free?

Indeed, this is a question that must be asked about some member of the family tree of each of the free people of African descent in this story. For some, the last enslaved member of the family was many generations removed. Free people of African descent had lived on both islands since the first shipments of African captives arrived in the sixteenth century. But for Rafael Serra, like Gertrudis Heredia, the border between slavery and freedom may not have been far in the past. In a poem published in 1880, Serra declared that he had been born into slavery. "This is the shocking slavery," he wrote, "into which this writer was born."[33] This may well have been a rhetorical device rather than an autobiographical detail, as it contradicts the information on his baptismal record. Perhaps he meant figuratively that he was born in the time of slavery. Or maybe the person speaking in the first person in the poem was not intended to represent Serra literally. Later in life, however, Serra described himself as the "son of enslaved parents."[34] Here again it is possible that he was speaking metaphorically. Men in the independence movement often used the term "slavery" when referring to colonial oppression. Or perhaps his parents were free at the time of his birth, but like Cayetano, had previously been enslaved. The only other clue to his family's legal and economic position is a brief mention of an aunt, Chuchú Serra, whom Serra described as a seamstress and schoolteacher of "extremely humble" birth.[35] The emphasis, *extremely*, added to this common euphemism could suggest that she too was a slave who became free over the course of her life.

How, then, was such a thing possible? Perhaps, as sometimes happened, the persons who held Cayetano and Chuchú in captivity conceded the gift of freedom in return for loyalty or extraordinary service. It was more common, however, for enslaved people in Cuba to purchase their own freedom. Urban and domestic slaves in Cuba were frequently in a position to engage in some sort of independent economic activity. This allowed some to save for or to purchase their freedom in installments—a process called *coartación*.[36] To help understand this process, we can turn to an example about which historians know more (and introduce a historical figure who will come to play a major role in this story). Juan Gualberto Gómez was the most famous writer and politician of color in Cuba between the 1870s and the 1920s, a close ally of Martí, Figueroa, and Serra, and after independence a member of the Cuban Senate. Gómez was born on a plantation in rural Matanzas in 1854. His parents, Fermín Gómez and Serafina Ferrer, were enslaved domestic servants, Cuban born, of mixed racial ancestry, and apparently favorites of their masters. The family that held them in slavery allowed the couple to marry. They also permitted Serafina to take in sewing and Fermín to plant a vegetable garden, selling his produce in the market. Through these efforts, the two managed to save enough money to purchase Juan Gualberto's freedom prior to his birth, for a sum of twenty-five pesos. The priest inscribed this arrangement on his baptismal record. By the time Juan Gualberto was ten, Fermín and Serafina had purchased their own freedom as well and moved to Havana, where his mother operated a laundry, and his father sold fruits and vegetables.[37]

Perhaps Cayetano Heredia did something similar, earning the money to purchase his freedom while still legally enslaved. Maybe Chuchú Serra did the same thing. As a seamstress, she would have had precisely the skills necessary to undertake this sort of project. Alternately, either may have been a "rented out" slave, living independently from their masters, turning in a portion of their wages and keeping the rest for the purposes of self-purchase. Or perhaps they secured loans from relatives or members of a mutual aid association, possibly someone with a shared African ethnic identity, paying the money back once they were free and able to control their own wages. Maybe they depended on relatives (either blood relatives, shipmates, or kin created through godparentage) who were already free to help bear these costs. Maybe, once they were free, they did the same for other relatives.[38]

Generally speaking, people who had been born free enjoyed a higher social status than those who had become free during their lives, and people separated from slavery by several generations enjoyed higher status than those for whom the connection was easily remembered. So even in a context where the broad category "people of color" was increasingly salient, Gertrudis would likely be understood to have the lowest status of these three children, because of her close connection to Africa and slavery. Rafael might have had slightly higher status because his parents were creole, Cuban born, and possibly freeborn. Sotero might have higher status still, as a member of a family identified as pardo and with no close ties to slavery. What is more, his father, José Mercedes, had been born in Venezuela. The fact that he was an immigrant created a geographic as well as a generational distance from enslavement, effectively preventing Puerto Rican neighbors from obtaining specific information about just how his family came to be racially mixed, or how long ago.[39]

But things were never quite that simple. The priest who conducted a baptism for Gertrudis in Matanzas in 1856 was likely familiar with her family, especially her maternal grandparents, Rita del Monte and Sebastián Campos. Both del Monte and Campos were identified by various priests as of the "Lucumí nation." This, and the timing of Rita's baptism, suggests that Gertrudis's grandparents may have been born in the Bight of Benin, in the vicinity of the Oyo Empire, and may have been captured and sold into slavery during the civil wars that shook that region in the 1820s.[40] The baptismal record of Rita's oldest daughter (Gertrudis's mother) in 1831 identifies Rita as a Lucumí woman and the "slave of Captain José del Monte." Yet by the time of the baptism of her second daughter in 1843, she appeared as a "morena libre." At about the same time, she and her husband, Sebastián, first appeared in the church to serve as godparents to the child of another woman. By the time that Gertrudis was born thirteen years later, at least twenty more people had prevailed on Rita and Sebastián to serve as godparents. Some of their godchildren were infants, some were adults, some were enslaved, and some were free. Most remarkable of all, when Rita brought an enslaved woman of the Mandiga nation to be baptized, the priest reported not only that Rita was the woman's godmother but that she was also the woman's owner.[41]

By the year that Getrudis was born, colonial officials also recognized her grandfather as the leader of the cabildo Fernando VII. *Cabildos de nación* were societies made up of people who, having been wrenched from communities of origin, found others whose language and customs were intelligible, and reconstructed communal ties and spiritual practices under the umbrella of African "nations." In his role as leader of the cabildo, Sebastián managed funds and property, and organized dances and ritual gatherings. He was responsible for maintaining relationships with local priests, who had oversight of funerals as well public celebrations on feast days. For instance, when Gertrudis was eight months old, her grandfather received permission from the local authorities to lead his cabildo in the parade for the Feast of the Rosary, marching behind the banner of their patron, Santa Bárbara. Because the members of the cabildo Fernando VII were Lucumí, they knew this saint as the alter ego of the *oricha* named Changó, the deity of fire, lightning, drumming, and dance associated with the powerful city-state of Oyo. The year that she turned eight, her grandfather applied for and received permission to hold no fewer than forty-five dances at the cabildo headquarters on Calle Daoíz. Gertrudis, like other Cuban-born descendants of cabildo members, was technically not allowed to attend such gatherings.[42]

Sebastián and Rita's leadership may have reflected a high social status that they had previously enjoyed in Africa, or unusual spiritual power.

Or perhaps it stemmed from their ingenuity within the local economy in Matanzas or simply to good fortune (relative to others brought to Cuba in captivity). As head of the cabildo, Sebastián would also have had to negotiate with secular authorities, especially the local constable. Here again, the contrast between the ways that the characters in this story were inserted within the same set of social relations is stark. José Martí's father, Mariano Martí, served as constable in several neighborhoods of Havana. Mariano was, Martí's boyhood friend recalled, "one of those agents of authority who, when passing through the streets with his two bodyguards behind him, frightened away all evildoers, except for those who were his collaborators."[43] Mariano's official tasks included witnessing and certifying the election of cabildo leaders, and then interacting with those leaders to approve petitions to hold dances, collect taxes, impose fines, and sometimes mediate conflicts within the cabildos. It is not clear whether Gertrudis's grandmother, Rita, occupied an official position in the cabildo Fernando VII. But women played prominent roles in practical governance and the spiritual life of the Lucumí cabildos of Matanzas. Indeed, within the ritual and philosophical practices that Rita would have known as Regla de Ocha (and later generations called Santería), lineages of initiation and spiritual knowledge often passed through female lines.[44]

All this is highly significant for thinking about where Gertrudis and her family fit in the local social context. To Cuban society at large, being the daughter and granddaughter of formerly enslaved Africans might be seen as a severe defect. In the immediate world in which Gertrudis grew up, however, to be the oldest daughter of the oldest daughter of Rita and Sebastián was probably a sign of considerable prestige. To Martí, whose father had been part of the state apparatus that oversaw Afro-Cuban ethnic organizations, the fact that Gertrudis came from "that other life," the world of "darkness and impiety," made her a most unlikely participant in associational life. But to the African-born people of Matanzas, especially the people who were the godchildren or slaves of her grandparents, or members of the cabildo Fernando VII, Gertrudis may well have been born into a presumption of leadership.

A last crucial piece of information on these sacramental records complicates the question of status still further. Priests recognized both Rafael and Gertrudis (even Juan Gualberto Gómez, the child of people held as slaves) as legitimate children. Sotero, on the other hand, was illegitimate, a natural child. To be a natural child in San Juan, Matanzas, or Havana was wholly unremarkable. Marriage was both difficult and expensive, out of reach for a large majority of the population, in both Puerto Rico and Cuba.[45] Illegitimacy was thus a common element of poverty, and legitimate marriage was one of the ways that a small, self-conscious elite in the Spanish Caribbean imagined the distance between itself and everyone else to be the result of an inherent moral superiority rather than because of brutal systems of exploitation. In this sense, to be a natural child was similar in Puerto Rico and Cuba to having "impure" blood. Persons of high social rank, or "quality," regarded natural children as persons without honor, making them ineligible to use the titles "don" or "doña," rendering them unacceptable marriage partners for persons of high status, and excluding them from the priesthood, secondary education, and public offices.[46]

Yet illegitimacy was not simply a social defect parallel to nonwhiteness. The two defects actually overlapped to a great degree, both in terms of the people whom they excluded and the ways that elites thought about them. To understand this point it can help to consider the moment in 1855 when "Don Manuel Aguayo," a planter and the mayor of the Puerto Rican town of Toa Baja, brought his daughter Manuela to be baptized. Manuel was not married to the child's mother, a woman named Ezequiela Pulido.[47] This made Manuela a natural child. Her maternal lineage was also suspect. According to baptismal records in a distant parish in San Juan, her mother, Ezequiela, was the natural daughter of a woman reputed to be a parda and a man reputed to be white.[48] But it is unlikely that anyone checked those records, and the fact that Manuel appeared at the child's baptism left the racial status of the mother and daughter somewhat ambiguous. When men of high status confirmed their relationships to the mothers of their children through marriage, they could rescue those women from dishonor and their children from illegitimacy. Indeed, baptismal books in Puerto Rico were full of marginal notations indicating that subsequent marriages had converted natural children into legitimate children. Thus, when Manuel appeared along with her to recognize his daughter, Ezequiela's attachment with the mayor of the town seems to have influenced the priest, who recorded her as "Doña Ezequiela Pulido," affording her an honorific that suggested she was a woman of honor, legitimate and white.

Had Manuel gone on to marry Ezequiela that status would likely have been secure. But less than a year later Don Manuel married another woman, from an established local family, with whom he subsequently fathered several legitimate children.[49] This announced to the world that Ezequiela was an acceptable sexual partner but not a potential marriage partner. In the entangled logic of race and sex in the Spanish Caribbean, such treatment signaled to the world that Ezequiela was not of pure blood. Because members of the dominant classes typically considered women of African descent to be without sexual honor, their relationships with men outside marriage, even with more powerful white men, were thought to be the result of their intrinsically dishonest natures. When white women faltered, the logic went, they had likely been led astray. The honorable response was for the father to legitimate the child and restore the mother's honor by marrying her. When nonwhite women faltered, even when they were forced, there was no honor to be restored. Thus, in a society where public reputation about who was white was more important than official record keeping, marriages (or their absence) became "racializing mechanisms," fixing the status of women and children according to the treatment afforded them by powerful men. Manuel's decision not to marry Ezequiela, then, stamped Manuela with the defect of illegitimacy and a strong implication of impure blood. This implication would have been further strengthened when Ezequiela, still unmarried, brought a second child to be baptized. This time neither Manuel nor any other man stepped forward to acknowledge the child. Years later, when Manuela and her own husband, Sotero, brought their legitimate children to be baptized, the priests acknowledged her as the daughter of Don Manuel, but afforded neither Manuela nor her mother the honorific.[50]

The implications of illegitimacy for racial status were somewhat different in the case of unmarried couples of relatively equal status, like Sotero's parents, who seem to have lived as common-law husband and wife. But race and sex were still tied together. Church and government officials imagined the problem of illegitimacy (which they saw as a mark of the uncivilized culture of the Cuban and Puerto Rican poor) to stem primarily from the sexual improprieties that they attributed to women of African descent. So the priest who recorded Sotero's birth, while not marking his status as pardo or keeping a segregated sacramental book, recorded his identity in a way that strongly implied his racial status by denying his parents the honorifics "don" and "doña," and by marking him as a natural child. When he and Manuela went to have their children baptized, the priest recorded

Sotero without the honorific don as "the natural child of José Mercedes and María Rosenda," neither of whom were afforded honorifics.

But if prejudice against illegitimacy continued to be a tool for reinforcing racial inequality, efforts to secure legitimacy through church-sanctioned marriage could be a means for reducing the stain of racial difference or for claiming respectability despite indelible racial difference. Some free people of color in Cuba and Puerto Rico, especially those who served in militia battalions and worked in skilled manual trades, therefore took great pains to create and maintain legitimate lineages and "dense" networks of legitimate kin through marriage and godparentage. Even if these networks were exclusively composed of nonwhite people, if all were married and legitimate, this had the potential to attenuate their exclusion from public life in their cities.[51] It is in this sense notable that the Serras and the Heredias managed not only to free themselves but also to marry. Perhaps they took advantage of one of the periodic campaigns undertaken by church authorities in the 1850s to reduce sacramental fees and legitimate consensual unions. For some reason, however, Sotero's parents either did not seek this status or never managed it, though they apparently lived as husband and wife, and baptized four children together (three of whom later joined the respectable, married, artisan class). As a result, Sotero began his life not only as a pardo but also as illegitimate, though the ascription of this status too would evolve over the course of his life.

SCHOOL

Clearly, none of these children came "from nothing." Their projects of self-making began with grandparents who founded and ran community institutions and created broad networks of dependents (and purchased other human beings); parents who emigrated, who survived the Middle Passage, who purchased their own freedom, who baptized their children, and who married or who lived as if they were married. Yet in each case, the most important first step toward making their offspring into writers, public figures, or professionals was an education—something that could be obtained only against a backdrop of extremely adverse circumstances. Spanish law technically mandated that every municipality in Cuba and Puerto Rico create free public schools beginning in 1844.[52] But the number of people who actually attended primary school in the colonies was miniscule, especially in Puerto Rico. Wealthy Puerto Ricans resisted the taxes that would have been necessary to support public education, especially in rural districts where landed elites also had a vested interest in pressuring the children of poor families into field labor.[53] Officials settled on creating an insufficient number of schools and paying low salaries to teachers. Teachers, in turn, often absented themselves from schools altogether, paying a fraction of their stipends to substitutes to whom they left all the work of instruction. Public school teachers also generally charged tuition to those who could pay, treating nonpaying students as "spectators" rather than as pupils.[54] The consequences of these policies were dramatic. When Figueroa reached school age in the early 1860s, official statistics showed that only 8.3 percent of the population of Puerto Rico could read or write. The figures were significantly worse among the segment of the population identified as nonwhite, at 2.3 percent, and significantly better for those recorded as white, at 14.9 percent.[55] Education was the privilege of those who could pay for it, and secondary and higher education were, for the most part, the special privilege of people reputed to be white.

Because he lived in San Juan and because his parents did not require him to begin earning money at a young age, Figueroa was able to enroll in a school that was run as a charity by a cigar maker named Rafael Cordero. Cordero, identified as moreno by contemporaries, was not the only teacher of African ancestry in Puerto Rico. Nor was he the only teacher to accept children who were, as Figueroa would later put it, "disinherited by fortune." Especially after midcentury, teaching was an occupation of intermediate status, within reach for men from plebeian families (or men with unacknowledged ties to patrician families) seeking to enter the professions.[56] Yet when Cordero created his school in 1810, it was one of the only primary schools of any kind in the city. For fifty-eight years, he taught generation after generation of boys while still earning his living rolling cigars. Indeed, his workshop and his classroom were one and the same. By the time of his death in 1868, he was largely responsible for, as one writer put it somewhat condescendingly, "the little learning that a tenacious observer can discover in the class of color."[57] Nevertheless, his school was also one of the better options for white students in the city, even for some boys from well-situated families. As Figueroa himself put it, Cordero taught "a large number of the persons who today give brilliance to this society."[58]

This presented a significant opportunity for Figueroa. By the time that Figueroa started school at the beginning of the 1860s, Cordero was already a much-beloved elderly man, well known to colonial authorities, to local priests, and to neighbors of all social classes. Indeed, three men who had been Cordero's students in the 1830s, Alejandro Tapia y Rivera, José Julián Acosta, and Román Baldorioty de Castro, were, by the time Figueroa was a student, leaders of the emerging liberal reformist and abolitionist movement, and outspoken advocates for popular education. Tapia and Acosta enjoyed the privileges of uncontested whiteness. Baldorioty, as we will see, was illegitimate and therefore contended with some suspicion about his racial purity. These three men were at the heart of San Juan's small community of writers, teachers, and intellectuals—a new kind of urban elite without ties to landholding or inherited title. They had studied or traveled in Europe, and they developed what one writer has called a "militant desire for modernity," which they exercised through participation in government boards and commissions, and in one of the few institutions of civil society permitted by the Spanish monarchy, the Economic Society.[59] They looked around at their small capital, a grid of six streets by eight streets, with no public water supply, inadequately paved streets, no streetcars, and no opera house, and responded with disgust. They hatched projects to remake the center of the city, to regulate public behavior, and to develop public institutions, even as a growing population put pressure on the housing market, pushing poorer residents into a handful of new neighborhoods outside the city walls.[60]

More than anything, the liberal intellectuals in the Economic Society sought to improve education on the island, publishing textbooks, supporting the creation of secondary and technical schools, and fostering literary contests and prizes. These efforts mainly benefited the children of wealthier Puerto Ricans. But in theory, the reformists also favored education to uplift and civilize the poor.[61] This was advocacy of a particular sort. In their calls to educate poor Puerto Ricans, reformists described the varied popular cultures in Puerto Rico, especially those derived from African antecedents, as a wasteland of ignorance, barbarism, and superstition. They portrayed their own European training as universal civilization.[62] By the time that Figueroa entered school, these reformists had begun to cast Cordero—who had been their teacher—as a hero of liberal reformism, a man whose rudimentary training and Christian morality had kept a spark of enlightenment alive in Puerto Rico despite the dereliction of the colonial authorities. In 1858, "a group of good patricians" proposed that Cordero receive recognition in the form of membership in the Economic Society, though they never followed up on the idea.[63] While eager to recognize the "generous efforts" of Cordero and to congratulate themselves on their liberal racial attitudes, these reformists worked toward a society in which men like themselves would exert more control over the educational system, bringing the next stage of enlightenment to the Puerto Rican population. Their affection for their old teacher, however, seems to have been genuine, as was their support for his more brilliant students. So if their plans for reform had little impact on the lives of the great majority of Puerto Rican children of Figueroa's generation, for Figueroa himself, the close relationship between his teacher and the leaders of Puerto Rico's liberal reform movement would prove important.

The educational system was significantly more developed in Cuba than in Puerto Rico, especially in Havana, where official literacy rates reached 57 percent by the early 1860s.[64] In the first decades of the century, most teachers in Cuba were, like Cordero in Puerto Rico, free people of color without formal education or training.[65] Serra's aunt Chuchú was a teacher in this tradition. Similar to Puerto Rico, by midcentury a group of creole intellectuals supported education and scientific research, and advocated public schooling through the institution of the local Economic Society. Because of the enormous wealth produced by the sugar and tobacco industries, these reformists benefited from considerably greater resources than their Puerto Rican counterparts. They created a public library, supported literary societies, funded schools, and sat on boards to oversee curriculum and select teachers. These efforts were strongly inflected by their location at the center of the burgeoning slave society of Western Cuba. At the same time that the members of the Economic Society in Puerto Rico began to venerate El Maestro Rafael, members of the Economic Society in Cuba sought to remove teachers like Chuchú Serra from their posts. Such teachers, in the words of Antonio Bachiller y Morales, the secretary of the Economic Society, were "not only ignorant to the point of stupidity, but also unclean in their behavior and of the wrong race." They also sought to eliminate the "mixture of all classes and castes in a single classroom." In practice, this meant excluding students of color from public schools. The Spanish government instructed Cuban municipalities to provide segregated schools for children of color. Yet local authorities and the Economic Society ignored these directives, explained Bachiller, because of the "irresistible conviction" that it was too dangerous to educate children of color in the context of a slave society.[66] Bachiller would later flee to New York, where he would become an important figure in the Cuban Junta in the 1870s.

Both Martí and Heredia reached school age in the early 1860s, at a moment when the Economic Society had largely succeeded in imposing these reforms. Martí's father had lost his job as a petty official, and the family depended almost entirely on the income that his mother and sisters earned as seamstresses. But a family friend took on the expense of sending him to the premier secondary school in Havana, where he became a star student and the protégé of one of the great literary figures in Cuba, Rafael Mendive, a poet and abolitionist who served as principal of the school.[67] Things were different for Gertrudis. There were no longer any teachers of color in Matanzas. The census reported 1,178 free girls of color residing in the jurisdiction of Matanzas, about half of whom were school aged. But only 40 of them attended school.[68] There is no evidence as to whether Gertrudis was among this lucky few. It is clear that what minimal educational opportunity existed meant something different for girls of color than it did for boys. The most honorable occupation for women in Matanzas was to be married and employed in domestic chores, or in the supervision of a household staff, in one's own home. This kind of status required the presence of a male breadwinner and was strongly correlated with race. Girls like Gertrudis might aspire to this status, but because white men were prohibited from marrying them and nonwhite men faced severe economic constraints, they were almost certain to be engaged in paid work for most of their lives.[69] When looking for work, furthermore, the options were few. Washerwomen had more independence than women who performed domestic labor inside the homes of other families. Yet their independent movement through public spaces in the city subjected them to dishonor. White women therefore eschewed this trade. Seamstresses, on the other hand, could take in piecework, earning their living safely within the confines of private homes. As such, this occupation attracted many white women, including Martí's mother and sisters, who supported the family through his father's chronic unemployment. It was also one of the few occupations preferred by white women that was also open to women of color. Training in manual skills such as sewing, then, was one of the key advantages of schooling for girls who faced exclusion based on impurity of blood. Manuela Aguayo, who had been recognized but not legitimated by her father, the mayor, had the good fortune to learn this trade. Townspeople in Toa Baja (and her own family members) may have viewed her as other than white, but at least this reputation was not compounded by the need to work or conduct business in public.

The few opportunities that girls like Gertrudis had to attend school, including classrooms run by older seamstresses like Chuchú, therefore focused on teaching basic literacy and manual skills. These were more useful than academic subjects in expanding the limited life chances offered by the colonial and patriarchal economic system. There is no record of whether Gertrudis ever attended primary school or if she ever worked in any of these occupations. But she did learn to read and write. As we will see, Gertrudis eventually made her way through a more difficult path to become a licensed midwife, with a title from the University of Havana, and community leader.

Serra took the first steps toward becoming a teacher, journalist, and politician in nearby Havana.[70] By the time that Serra was old enough to begin school, none of Havana's more than sixty public schools (including the one attended by his future friend and ally Martí) reported any children of color in attendance. Serra probably attended one of eleven private primary schools for children of color in the city, or one of the three private primary schools that accepted both white and black students.[71] Again, it is interesting to draw on the better-known story of Juan Gualberto Gómez. Having secured the freedom of all its members, the Gómez family moved to Havana by the time Juan Gualberto was ten. He attended a private school run by Antonio Medina y Céspedes, a man usually identified as pardo.[72] Medina was part of the generation of intellectuals of color that had survived the repression unleashed in the wake of a suspected conspiracy including free and enslaved people in 1844. He was a tailor who worked creating sets and costumes in the elegant Teatro Tacón in the 1830s. Medina became a published playwright and journalist in the period before the repression, moving in the same circles as the poet Plácido. In the 1850s, as educational reformers worked to impose new standards, in large part to get rid of teachers that they considered to be of the "wrong race," he studied to obtain his certification as a teacher. In 1861, he opened a private school, El Colegio Nuestra Señora de los Desamparados.[73] Medina thus threaded the needle of the period of reform that followed the repression, and Gómez received his education in a space frequented by other survivors of the earlier era of pardo literary expression.

Serra likely attended one of the lesser-known and lower-status "incomplete" primary schools in the city. But his teacher was, quite likely, also a survivor of the period of repression and the efforts by reformers to "elevate" the teaching profession. The fact that his aunt Chuchú, a seamstress of "extremely humble" origins, operated this kind of rudimentary private school suggests that some of the adults in his family were literate, and committed to the project of self-making through education and teaching. This is crucial, as Serra's formal education (like Figueroa's and Heredia's) could only have come about as a result of a conscious investment of family resources in order to pay school fees and to clothe him appropriately. Public subsidies for education in Cuba went almost exclusively to white children.[74] Sending children to school also meant forgoing the income that their early entry into the workforce would have provided. It is unlikely that a seven-year-old child, no matter how remarkably gifted, could have conceived of this project independently, or carried it off without the support of parents or other adults.

FINDING WORK

With a few extraordinary exceptions, the professions remained closed to boys of color and to girls, independent of racial status, in San Juan, Matanzas, Toa Baja, and Havana at the end of the 1860s. This included even those who, like Heredia, Figueroa, and Serra, could read and write, and Aguayo, who had several well-connected male relatives. The trades remained the surest path toward economic stability and modest social standing, and almost all the people of African descent who later became community leaders, writers, and intellectuals on the two islands, and in exile, first became artisans. Figueroa became a typographer, Serra a cigar roller, and Aguayo a seamstress. Heredia, the granddaughter of Rita del Monte of the Lucumí nation, became a midwife. Let us begin with her story, as it is probably the most remarkable of the four. Like washerwomen, midwives moved independently around the cities of the Spanish Caribbean. Because such movement implied dishonor and racial impurity, for most of the colonial period the profession was almost entirely left to women of African descent, for whom it was a significant opportunity for economic gain and status. As late as the early 1860s, in the years that Gertrudis reached school age, the great majority of licensed midwives in Matanzas were women of color. The most famous midwife in Matanzas, Pilar Poveda, was the mother-in-law of the famed artisan and poet Plácido. When Plácido was executed as a supposed leader of the free people of color accused of provoking a slave rebellion in 1844, Poveda was sentenced to a year of forced labor for allegedly assisting him. She then moved back to Matanzas to resume her practice. She was a contemporary of Gertrudis's grandparents.[75]

Gertrudis came of age precisely as Poveda and other midwives of her generation faced not just political repression but also new pressures from medical and political authorities. In the same way that educational reformers recoiled in horror at the prospect of black teachers presiding over the classrooms of white children, doctors and government officials lamented the tradition of black women attending to white women in childbirth. Indeed, it is no coincidence that Economic Society secretary Bachiller y Morales described the teachers he deemed unfit for service as "intruding midwives." In the wake of the repression in 1844, medical reformers began a project to "elevate" the profession of midwifery, to bring it under the authority of doctors, and to attract white women. They instituted a training program for midwives at the Clínica de Partos of the Havana Hospital. They implemented new licensing rules that required midwives to be married and literate—a combination that proved nearly impossible for free women of color to accomplish. An additional requirement that midwives be of "good moral character" meant that women of color not only had to learn to read (in the near-total absence of schools) and marry in a church (though it was expensive, though they outnumbered black men in the city, and though they were legally prevented from marrying white men). They also had to overcome widespread stereotypes about their sexual dishonor, including depictions of them on the stage, in literature, and on thousands of cigarette packages that aimed to capitalize on the erotic fantasies of white men. Finally, authorities imposed steep new training and licensing fees as a barrier to entry for poor women. As a result, by 1869, there were no licensed midwives of color in Havana or Matanzas, although many probably continued to practice without a license.[76]

Remarkably, then, Gertrudis managed to become a midwife in the period after reformers had succeeded in their effort to make it a more respectable profession, precisely to exclude women like her. Most likely she began her training as an apprentice to an unlicensed midwife in Matanzas. Such training would have been shaped by the world into which she was born. Women in this world likely relied on midwives with practical skill, but also influence over the spiritual world (both Christian saints and Lucumí orichas), to face the most physically trying and dangerous moments of their lives. But in the mid-1880s, she enrolled in the clinical certification program at the University of Havana, at which point she had to pay seven and a half pesos and convince a physician with a professorship at the university to take her on for a three-year period of supervision. At the end of this period, she had to pay a fee of a hundred pesos, along with additional taxes. Finally, a committee of doctors administered an examination covering "anatomical and physiological knowledge of the pelvis and the reproductive organs" as well as diagnosis of presentations, and the care of mothers in labor and newborn infants. She also passed a practical examination, supervising the delivery of a baby under the watchful eye of her examiners. They judged her on the basis of a rigorous regime of hand washing and disinfection, on the proper attire (a clean apron and sleeves rolled up to the elbows), instruments (including a stethoscope), ointments (white Vaseline and under no circumstances almond oil), and the proper mixing and application of antiseptic washes. The tribunal approved her with a mark of "outstanding," granting the title of midwife to the woman they identified as "the morena, Gertrudis Heredia."[77]

The archives in Havana preserve almost no details as to how she managed any of this. It is clear, however, that she submitted her baptismal record to the university in application for her license. The unusual step that her parents had taken in getting married, decades before, made it possible for her to pass the scrutiny of university officials and enter the certification course. It is also clear that she submitted a copy of the sacramental record showing that she had married Serra in 1878. This provided her with further proof of her dignity and moral worth, without which she could not have attempted the examination. It established a distinction between her and other women in her community, including her sister-in-law María de Jesús Serra, who brought her daughter to be baptized a few years after Rafael and Getrudis married. The two women experienced the strangeness and joy of their first pregnancies and deliveries at about the same time, but the priest recorded the child born to María de Jesús as a "parda," child of a "free morena" and an unknown father. He was probably not literally unknown, of course, but rather could not be compelled to marry María de Jesús or recognize their child because she was black.[78] From a distance of more than a hundred years, the record demonstrates the deep injustices embedded in the concepts of legitimacy and sexual honor. At the time, it simply confirmed widespread beliefs about the indecency of black women, especially in their relationships with white men. Gertrudis was spared the worst consequences of this system because of her relationship with Rafael. Fortunately, her husband was also a proponent of women's education and, having already left Cuba by this point, had access to well-paying work in cigar factories in New York. He may well have contributed to the substantial resources that Heredia had to gather to pay for training and licensing fees.

It is impossible to know, but not to imagine, that when Gertrudis first appeared at the university, when she presented herself for annual reviews, when she interacted with her clinical supervisor, and when she returned to take her examination, she must have dedicated painstaking attention to her self-presentation. Her dress, movements, speech, and professional skills were likely judged differently because of white doctors' and patients' prejudices about black women. Indeed, only two years before Heredia took her examination, a white physician named Benjamín de Céspedes caused an upheaval in Cuban public life by publishing a collection of clinical case studies of advanced venereal disease. He based these on gynecological examinations of prostitutes. Céspedes called his book *Prostitution in the City of Havana*, framing the case studies with a historical and sociological account of the causes of prostitution that relied, mainly, on rabid denunciations of Cubans of color. He concluded that "in Cuban society's lymphatic organism, the purulent abscess of prostitution is rooted in the behavior of the colored race." Black and mixed-race women, he thought, were a dangerous source of contagion: "their intimate contact infects everything they touch."[79] Céspedes also offered a nearly pornographic account of the immoral and sensuous dancing of black and brown women. This was no surprise to the reading public in Cuba, which was already inundated with cigarette packages adorned with color images depicting mixed-race women as harlots. The book quickly became a best seller, receiving resounding praise from white journalists and reviewers, and righteous rebuttals from journalists of African descent.[80] As one of the first black women to receive advanced training in obstetrics at the University of Havana, Gertrudis had not only to contend with the stereotypes built by generations of reformers who had tried to remove black midwives based on the notion that they were illiterate, dirty, and "intrusive"; now, in the middle of her training, Céspedes ignited debate in the Cuban medical community with his account of the damage black and brown women had done with their "infernal machine of fornication."[81] What mechanisms of self-possession would be necessary for this young woman to overcome the burden of such stereotypes, to answer clearly and professionally the questions put to her by her examiners (all white men) on pelvic anatomy and the function of the reproductive organs?

On the other hand, the memory of a time when midwives of color attended all births in Western Cuba was not so far in the past. White women may have been more willing to contract Heredia's services because of this tradition, and their patronage may have bolstered her reputation as decent and moral. In this role, clients would have trusted her with their most intimate secrets: hidden pregnancies, attempts to avoid or end pregnancies, clandestine adoptions, and baptismal records written to conceal paternity or even maternity. Discretion was likely as important a quality as Christian morality for such a sensitive occupation.

At the same time, attending women of African descent, in moments of profound pain and joyful emotion, seems to have helped to make her into a trusted community leader, an heir to her grandmother. Maybe her professional training allowed her the satisfaction of providing scientific information about reproduction and sexual health to women who lived in "humble conditions," including labor and delivery, care of infants, and strategies to avoid or terminate pregnancy. Perhaps she infused the gift of this information with advice, and advice with judgment or condescension. Maybe she carried into her interactions with clients the message, prevalent among doctors in Havana and Matanzas, that maternal hygiene and Victorian morality were one and the same, and that black women, as a rule, were seriously deficient in both. Maybe her patients saw her careful attempts to present herself as "of good moral character," for the benefit of her professional reputation, as attempts to place herself above them. Maybe they saw the rituals of hand scrubbing, antiseptic washes, and stethoscopes as strange impositions on their expected routines of childbirth, which turned on intercession with saints or spirits, not on the invisible power of microbes.

Unfortunately, available documents offer almost no insight into these questions, so we are forced to use our imaginations about what might have been. We can discern a clue, however, in a report of Gertrudis's professional activities in the newspaper for the class of color, *La Fraternidad*. The mention of Heredia in *La Fraternidad* is brief, but the outlines of the case seem to be the following. Mrs. Concepción Morales, a woman of color honorably married to the newspaper's editor, Miguel Gualba, had a difficult labor requiring the intervention of a medical doctor, Mr. Cándido Hoyos, and two midwives. One was Gertrudis. The second midwife, Estefanía Barrera de Meireles, was a woman whom the medical examiners at the university recognized as white. How exactly this trio came to work together on the case is not clear.[52] Maybe Hoyos was a clinical supervisor from the university. Perhaps Heredia was attending to Morales on her own when the labor turned problematic, at which point she called the doctor. This would make sense given the social and political ties she had to the woman in labor. But where did the second midwife come from? Was she working alongside Heredia from the beginning? Did Doctor Hoyos bring her along when he received the call? Was this an implicit comment on his trust in Gertrudis or his attitude toward black midwives? We cannot be sure. It is notable, though, that the writer in *La Fraternidad* referred to the two as "the intelligent midwife Estefanía Barrera de Meireles," and as "the no less studious Sra. Gertrudis Heredia de Serra." For writers in *La Fraternidad*, her studiousness, her status as a married woman (indicated in the title Sra. de Serra), and her ability to traverse the narrowing path of opportunity to become a trained professional were clearly matters of pride. Is it too much of a stretch to imagine a tone of slightly wounded pride in this impeccably polite presentation of the "intelligent" midwife (whom doctors treated as "Doña Estefanía Barrera de Meireles") and the "no less studious" midwife whom they treated as "the morena María Gertrudis Heredia"?[53]

Figueroa's first step to becoming a professional writer in San Juan, when he finished at the school run by the cigar maker and teacher Rafael Cordero at the age of twelve or thirteen, was to obtain a position as an apprentice. He found one in the printing house owned by the most celebrated of Cordero's former students: teacher, abolitionist, and liberal politician José Julián Acosta. An apprentice *cajista*, or typesetter, would first be given the task of distribution: taking apart compositions at the end of a print run, sorting types, cleaning them, and putting them in the correct positions in the boxes for the next project. This meant learning to identify and put in its place every possible character, including italics, bold, and upper- and lowercase. It meant special attention to avoiding the most common mix-ups, confusing *6* and *9*, *p* and *q* (as in the expression "mind your *p*'s and *q*'s"), or *n* and *u* as well as learning technical and mathematical symbols, and understanding and sorting the many different sizes and shapes of blank types necessary to produce white space in a text. All this was complicated by the fact that types were made in the inverted image of the text they produced. A box of types badly sorted, or types that were mishandled, dropped, or badly cleaned, would undoubtedly subject an apprentice to the ire of the older, more experienced cajistas, who memorized the location of all the types to speed their work. When the typesetters reached into their "lower case" for an impeccable italicized *p*, that is exactly what they wanted to find.

Little by little, Figueroa would have been allowed to begin composing, transforming handwritten manuscript into lines of type. He would have started by composing three lines at a time, reaching for type with his right hand and aligning it in a small tray held in his left. Each line would be set, double-checked, and justified through the insertion of spacers to make the lines the same length. The trick was balancing the empty spaces between words and characters so that none were too close and none were too far apart. The lines were then carefully transferred to a wooden frame large enough to hold an entire page. Once a page was complete, the typesetter would print a proof and submit the results to the copy editor. With corrections in hand, Figueroa (once he had learned to read the specialized notations used for editing) could return to the page of type and carefully execute the corrections. This meant pulling free any misplaced types and replacing them, then checking justification and adjusting both vertical and horizontal alignments. After multiple rounds of proofs and corrections, on all the pages of a book, he might help with the *armado*. The typesetters made sure that all pages were the same size and similarly aligned, added page numbers, chapter titles, and notes, and then checked their work and made corrections before handing it off to the pressmen.[84] It was only once he finished his apprenticeship and moved into the work of setting that he would start to collect a salary. Wages earned through labor were a mark of passage to manhood in these workshops. The typographer and writer Juan Coronel (who later moved to Puerto Rico) remembered the first payment that he received as a young printer in Cartagena: "More inflated than a peacock, I arrived at my house to hand over all that I had earned in the first week. In the street, I wanted to stop passersby and show them the money, telling them: I obtained this with the efforts of my own hands."[85]

An ambitious young typesetter, eager someday to be a *regente*, or head of production, Figueroa would have studied each aspect of the printing process. He would have asked older workers to explain complex layouts such as statistical tables and figures, advertisements, mathematical or musical notation, and foreign-language composition. He would have taken pride in his own editorial skills, eager at first to make the job of the copy editor lighter and eventually to be able to perform as a copy editor (which he later did for the newspaper *Patria*). He would have learned the job of the pressmen, keeping up with advances in press technology (most San Juan shops worked with steam-powered cylindrical presses) in order to someday supervise all elements of production. He would have become a perfectionist, hoping to provide authors and publishers a beautiful product, visually elegant, technically sophisticated, and free of errata: errors noticed once it was too late to correct them and listed at the end of a volume—the shame of a typographer.[86]

He would also begin to absorb the particular ideological commitments shared by printers. Anyone who has spent an hour formatting a research paper, a poster, or a school newsletter knows the feeling of converting a fleeting bit of text into something durable and public. In the nineteenth century, however, the transformation from manuscript to newspaper, handbill, or book was the exclusive purview of printers. They tended to see this process as transcendent and themselves as the "operatives who worked at the loom of ideas, which take on eternal life as they are printed."[87] Given the high level of literacy and editorial skill required of them, their constant contact with writers, and the reverence with which they regarded the printed word, it is small wonder that print workers often tried their hand at writing. Indeed, print shops became one of the most common spaces for working-class self-education in San Juan, as in other parts of the Caribbean, Europe, and North America. Acosta himself later noted that when Figueroa became a writer, he merely followed "the beautiful example provided by his comrades in the art, the Franklins and Greelys in the American Union, the Michelets in France, and George Smith in England."[88]

Figueroa's own later writings also help to explain this trajectory within the particular context and small world of San Juan publishing. Of the handful of booksellers and authors in the city, several of those who had risen through the ranks of the print shops seem to have served both as models to emulate and as supporters encouraging him to take up writing. In his essay on "those who have most contributed to the progress of Puerto Rico," Figueroa highlighted Nicolás Aguayo, a man from a prominent white family. Orphaned as a child and left without economic support, he became an apprentice in a print workshop, where he studied independently, eventually becoming a secondary school teacher, an author, a member of the Economic Society, and an abolitionist. José González Chaves, another orphan, set up the first bookbinding workshop in San Juan. He eventually operated a leading bookshop. By the 1870s, his son, José González Font, became a publisher with a shop not far from where Figueroa worked. The publisher Pascacio Sancerrit was, Figueroa wrote, born "among the disinherited of the earth." Here the suspicions aroused by the familiar euphemism are confirmed by Sancerrit's baptismal record. He was the natural son of a free parda woman and a white man, and his baptism was recorded in the book reserved for pardos and morenos. Sancerrit began working as a guard in a merchant house at fourteen. He taught himself humanities, mathematics, and languages as well as typography. He eventually became a teacher, a journalist, and a prominent liberal publisher. These biographies offer clues both to the models that Figueroa adopted when forming his own intellectual ambitions, and to the network of mentors and patrons that he relied on.[89]

Without a doubt, the most important figure in this regard was Sancerrit, the head of production at Acosta's printing house when Figueroa became an apprentice there. Figueroa remembered that Sancerrit "encouraged in us our literary interests, when we took our first hesitant steps along the path that we still traverse without security; he indicated which authors we should consult in order to develop good taste; and lastly, with docile good humor, he looked over more than one of our meager productions, without a doubt to encourage us, signaling and applauding that which he judged to have some merit."[90] Yet Sancerrit was part of a broader group of intellectuals, including the owner of the print shop, Acosta, who also took an interest in Figueroa's progress as a writer. Acosta was a former student of Cordero and a central figure in educational reform efforts. He was also an abolitionist and a proponent of worker education. Through the efforts of men like Acosta and González Font, and through the diligent labor of their employees, print culture expanded rapidly in the second half of the nineteenth century, providing space for the emergence of many workers with intellectual aspirations.[91] Typographers' status, on the upper edge of the artisan world, was akin to (and interconnected with) that of school-teachers, who occupied the lower edge of the professional world. In late nineteenth-century Puerto Rico, teaching and printing were professions that required neither formal certification nor proof of purity of blood. In fact, almost all the men of color who became authors in Puerto Rico during this period were schoolteachers, typographers, or both.[92] Once he had established himself as a typographer, Figueroa married Manuela Aguayo, the natural daughter of a minor colonial official.

Following in the footsteps of Benjamin Franklin, Horace Greely, or Nicolás Aguayo was not a path open to Rafael Serra in Cuba. In the decades after the repression of 1844, the first workers' associations created by Cuban typographers, many of whom were Spanish immigrants, helped to close off opportunities in the print shops in Western Cuba to all but white men. When he finished schooling at the age of thirteen, Serra went to work in a cigar factory. The cigar trade was booming at the time. Havana had upward of five hundred cigar workshops employing more than fifteen thousand workers. These workshops ranged from small operations called *chinchales*, run independently by one or two artisans, to large factories employing hundreds of workers.[93] Apprentices in cigar factories were typically signed over to factory owners by their parents in an exchange of labor for training. They were often overworked and abused, frequently working alongside slaves, and sometimes punished by whipping. Serra would likely have begun with lower status tasks (often reserved for children and slaves), such as stripping stems or packing boxes with finished product. At the end of his apprenticeship, however, Serra was a trained *torcedor*, a roller. Though initially a difficult skill to master, rolling soon became a repetitive enterprise for experienced workers. Serra and his comrades sat for hours at benches, lined up at rows of desks on the workshop floors, using only a *chaveta*, curved blade, and careful movements of the hand to shape piles of cured tobacco leaves into stacks of Havana cigars. By the time Serra entered the trade, each year Havana workers provided hundreds of millions of these increasingly prized luxury items to the world market.[94]

Like print shops, the cigar factories of the Spanish Caribbean developed a worker culture of self-instruction as well as literary and political aspiration. Black teachers who were so common in the early part of the century, and who had become targets of reformers like Bachiller y Morales, were commonly cigar makers by trade. When Serra entered the factories, though, a new worker education movement had recently emerged, led by an Asturian cigar worker named Saturnino Martínez. Martínez attended lectures and recitals at the Liceo de Guanabacoa, an elite literary society, and became an assiduous patron of the public reading room of the Economic Society. In 1865, Martínez helped to create the first labor newspaper in Cuba, *La Aurora*. In it, he advocated self-education and the creation of mutual aid societies for cigar workers, deploying a stern moralizing tone. He also called on manufacturers to allow workers to read edifying texts aloud during working hours. In 1865 and 1866, workers in dozens of factories began contributing a fraction of their daily wages to make up for the pay lost by workmates who took turns reading to the group. Employers did not have to contribute anything except their permission, although they were encouraged to build platforms called "pulpits" on the shop floors. Employers also had veto power over exactly what texts could be read.[95]

Conservatives and the colonial government expressed concerns that reading in the factories would become a source of disorder or rebellion, banning the practice in 1866 and again in 1868. Others poked fun at what they considered ridiculous pretension.[96] Yet the nascent liberal reformist movement in Cuba, led by a lawyer named Nicolás Azcárate and an agronomist named Francisco de Frías (generally known by his title, Count of Pozos Dulces), celebrated artisan education as a way to instill an ideal of self-making among workers instead of socialism or rebellion. The reformist newspaper, *El Siglo*, to which both men contributed, joined *La Aurora* in its support for reading in factories, recommending that workers read "biographies of useful and good men, above all of honorable artisans, who offer the example of a Franklyn, printer, a Palissy, potter, of a Jacquard, weaver, of a Lincoln, lumberjack, of a Hartzenbusch, cabinetmaker, of a Watt, mechanic, of a Moratin, silversmith, and of a Johnson, tailor." In step with Puerto Rican counterparts like Acosta (whom they knew from student days in Madrid), the Cuban reformists saw education as a vehicle for instilling their own values among workingmen. They believed that reading in factories, paid for by workers themselves, would help foster thrift and self-discipline, at no cost to employers. This practice, it turned out, was also a potential training ground for collective action, though this was not necessarily something that reformists hoped for. Taking up a collection to support a reader was not so different from taking up a collection to help a sick comrade, a worker organization, or even comrades out on strike.[97] Serra was only seven years old when reading was first instituteed in Havana factories. At the time, many shops still employed enslaved people alongside indentured apprentices, Chinese contract laborers, and free workers, black, brown, and white. Free people of African descent constituted about half the cigar workforce. So the voices of factory readers reached a diverse audience. By the time that Serra was thirteen and began to work full time in the factories, the first Cuban war of independence was underway and reading was officially banned in the factories.[98]

LIBERALISM

Rafael Serra, in the cigar workshops of Havana, Sotero Figueroa, in the print shops of San Juan, and José Martí, then just starting high school, were thus situated at distant coordinates within the same broad intellectual world. Even as the leading liberal thinkers on each island began reaching out to artisans, they joined forces with one another to push for reforms within the Spanish Empire. In 1866, the Spanish Overseas Ministry invited patrician voters on both islands—a group of landowners, manufacturers, merchants, and professionals selected on the basis of their level of tax contribution to state coffers—to elect representatives for a commission in Madrid to discuss the possibility of colonial reforms. Several hundred voters from the two islands elected representatives, among whom were none other than Azcárate and Pozos Dulces (close on the heels of their campaign of advocacy for reading in the factories) as well as Acosta, the printer and supporter of worker education who (a few years later) would be Figueroa's employer. These men knew one another from their days as students, and were all allied with the same set of peninsular thinkers and politicians. The liberal reformists from the two islands joined forces against conservative representatives, who argued for the status quo. The liberal position was twofold: all Spaniards should enjoy more civil freedoms and tax reform, and Spaniards born in the colonies should have the same status as that enjoyed by Spaniards born on the peninsula, including representation in the Spanish Cortes. Conservatives argued that slave societies and societies with large free populations of African descent were too volatile to be invested with political freedoms. "Special laws" distinguishing the colonies from the peninsula, appointed governors, and a strong military presence were necessary to keep order in this context.[99]

Yet the liberals in the Cuban and Puerto Rican delegations differed on the key questions of race and slavery in ways that reflected the different circumstances in the two colonies. Acosta and the other Puerto Rican liberals proposed the immediate end of slavery, laying the substantive groundwork for what would become the abolitionist movement in Spain over subsequent decades. They further argued for opening higher education and the professions to people of color, and even extending rights of suffrage to all adult men who paid a minimum tax of twenty-five pesos, independent of color. This proposal even included persons previously enslaved so long as they could prove that they had been free for at least five years. The Puerto Ricans congratulated themselves that contrary to the warnings of conservatives, there was little danger of upheaval on their island. Back in Puerto Rico, the liberal schoolteacher and notary José Pablo Morales contended, "It is our good fortune that we have always treated the blacks better here." As a result, he wrote, in Puerto Rico there was "less hatred to be extinguished."[100] The Cubans, led by Azcárate and Pozos Dulces, agreed that slavery was detestable. They wished that the slave traders had never populated the island with Africans or tied the colony's economic fortunes to slavery. The Puerto Ricans, they added, were to be congratulated on their proposal. But it would never work in Cuba. Cuba's survival, they maintained, required that slavery be eliminated gradually, which is to say, no time soon.[101]

None of this should be taken to mean that Puerto Rican liberals favored a radically egalitarian society. They imagined a transition to free labor in which white patricians, guided by enlightened professionals and administrators, would remain firmly in control, in which most Puerto Ricans would provide docile labor for export production, and in which the majority of workers would not be black. Their belief that this transition could

be managed effectively rested on their view of Puerto Rican demograph-
ics, especially their optimism about free people of color. They argued that
the island was blessed with a large free peasantry, many of whom they
considered to be white or at least not dangerously black. These peasants
could be incorporated as productive free laborers in a revitalized plantation regime. Puerto Rico's large population of free people of color, "one
of the elements that contributes most to the future of that society," they
asserted, would serve as a crucial ally in the orderly transition to free
labor. Free people of color would act as a buffer, helping to integrate former slaves into a harmonious and stable social order. No legal restrictions
should therefore be placed on free people of color, Puerto Rican liberals
contended, lest they be pushed into resentment. The Cubans were much
less sanguine about the free population of color on their island, which they
described as "not without danger." They argued that *only* the whitening of
the Cuban population through immigration would bring stability, progress, culture, and morality to the island. White workers, they concluded,
were an "element of order and stability." Only white immigrants could be
expected "to propagate and perpetuate the culture of the spirit and the
greatness of the moral world." Immigration, they maintained, was thus
essential to the evolution of Cuba into a liberal society, and to the project
of gradual abolition.[102]

The divergent views expressed in the 1866 meetings in Madrid help to
situate Serra's experience as a young cigar roller in Havana and Figueroa's
as a young typographer in San Juan. The liberals who most actively sought
alliances with artisans in the late 1860s in San Juan and Havana, and who
gathered to discuss colonial reforms in 1866, differed in their regard for
free workers of African descent. The reformists who supported efforts at
worker education in Cuba were the same men who favored the civilization of the workforce through white immigration. Supported by reformists, Spanish-born workers made up a growing proportion of employees in
cigar factories, dominated the highest-skilled and highest-paying positions,
and occupied leadership roles in the first mutual aid societies and craft
unions, which did not include workers of color.[103] While Figueroa relied on
a network of mentors and allies among San Juan's reformists, Serra relied
on "his own efforts" to advance his education. These efforts were surely influenced by the culture of reading and self-education in the factories where
he worked, just as they were probably connected in some way with the

older traditions of black and brown teachers, like his aunt Chuchú, operating small schools for poor children of all colors. But there seems to have been no leading liberal thinker who took on the role of mentor for Serra in Havana in quite the way that Azcárate did for the Spanish-born Saturnino Martínez, and Sancerrit or Acosta did for Figueroa in San Juan.

The year after the meetings in Madrid, Puerto Rican writer Alejandro Tapia (who would also become a supporter of Figueroa's intellectual efforts) published the play *The Quadroon*, which used a story of romantic love between a white creole doctor and abolitionist and a woman of partial African ancestry, to offer a sharp critique of racial prejudice.[104] The play was pointedly set in contemporary Cuba, not Puerto Rico. This was a bit of a sleight of hand. There was surely plenty of racism to expose in Puerto Rico. Yet for all its flaws, during the 1860s the Puerto Rican liberal movement had begun to articulate opposition to both slavery and legal restrictions based on color. The Cubans had not.

This panorama would change radically, however, as a series of rebellions unfolded in the Spanish Empire in 1868. In particular, a decade of warfare in Eastern Cuba, the creation of a large Cuban émigré community in Key West, and a surprising, if short-lived, moment of democratic opening in Puerto Rico would create a new, quite-radical version of liberal ideology and new opportunities for artisans of African descent to assert themselves within the liberal movements. In Cuba this took shape, by the end of the first armed insurgency, as a movement to create educational and recreational societies for the uplift and integration of the class of color as well as newspapers, and the beginnings of a movement for full civil and political rights. It was in the context of these transformations that Figueroa, Serra, Gómez and other men in their generation—but almost never women—started to make the leap from worker to author.[105]

· 2 ·

The Public Square

If I consider it to be a great honor to be part of the working class and if my greatest satisfaction lies in earning my own bread at the cost of sweat and fatigue, I am also seduced by—and drawn by irresistible currents of feverish enthusiasm towards—the fierce battles of the press and the imposing demonstrations of the public square.

—Juan Coronel, *Un viaje por cuenta del estado*, 1891

On a Thursday night in New York in 1891, a year after the founding of La Liga, a group of Cuban and Puerto Rican immigrants arranged their chairs in a semicircle on the carpet in the main room of the social club. As they gathered, they sat talking, reading, and listening to music played on the piano, enjoying the company of friends while they waited for their teacher to arrive. La Liga was an instructional society, founded with a mission to provide educational opportunity for the men of the "class of color from Cuba and Puerto Rico." Rafael Serra, who had founded the club, described its goal as "raising, with spotless hands, the class that is now prostrate out of its inertia."[1] His formulation echoed the condescending logic of a broader movement, currently underway, to create charitable instructional societies for black and brown artisans in Cuba. The idea was to "advance the intellect and elevate the character" of a group systematically denied the benefits of public education, and therefore imagined to be woefully lacking in these qualities. But in practice, La Liga was actually something quite different. Rather than providing basic literacy, it was meant to supply training and advancement for men who "may have completed their primary education and show ostensible aptitude for careers or offices rarely held by members of the class of color."[2] Instead of a charitable institution for a prostrate class, this was a space of mutual aid created by ambitious artisans who were eager to make the leap to something else: to become professionals, writers, or politicians. They gathered in the "house of love and affection" several nights a week for classes in Spanish grammar, English, French, and history.[3] On these evenings, they worked to reshape their patterns of speech, of orthography, of vocabulary, and of syntax, and to fill gaps in their knowledge of history, science, and literature that might "give ammunition to those of little generosity who have had the means or opportunities to study more, and who sneer at those who have studied less."[4]

Of all the nights of the week, Thursday nights were the most important. Thursdays the men gathered for their seminar with José Martí, the man whose portrait hung on the front wall next to Serra's, and the man they referred to simply as "El Maestro," the teacher. While they sat reading and listening to music, and waiting for Martí, they each wrote out short essays and questions, leaving these *papelitos* unsigned on the table. At about nine o'clock, Martí would arrive, stirring up a flurry of warm greetings. To each man he offered a "frank handshake and an affectionate word." He asked them why they never came to visit him. "What, are we not friends already?" He observed the books that they sat reading, offering words of approval and recommendations for further reading. He told them that these Thursdays were also the most important night in his week. "You all know that when the world crushes my heart I come to be with you so that with your affection you can cure me."[5] When there were children present, he handed out candy. Martí then read aloud from the slips of paper that the men left for him on the table, responding to each one. He began with questions of style. They should strive to avoid "ugly words," he admonished, and should always choose simplicity and directness over literary flourish. (Martí's own prose, however, was frequently dense and intricately woven.) He also responded to their questions and propositions. These could be as simple as, "What is a peninsula?" But more often they touched on complex questions of philosophy, political theory, or classical history, such as, "What is the importance of the Senate in a republic?" Any of these would be enough to launch Martí into an impromptu disquisition on physics, psychology, natural history, politics, art, or political economy.[6]

Over time, the nights at La Liga became a key symbol of Martí's bid for leadership in the nationalist movement. Supporters arranged for journalists to come to witness the Thursday night gatherings, and the students of La Liga played the part of dutiful and diligent disciples for the purpose of propaganda. In print, Martí frequently celebrated his students, describing their "manly complaints."[7] La Liga, he later wrote, was "the home of ideas paid for over several years, with the sacrifice of their difficult wages, by a few Cuban workers, workers of color, those workers of ours, who, though it seems a joke to some of the more useless among us, have *Essays on Education*, by Spencer, *Bonaparte* by Iung or *Parallel Lives* by Plutarch open on their work benches, where fiercely and independently they earn their bread."[8] They, in turn, became his evangelists. They were to be defenders, after his death, of a radical interpretation of his legacy, arguing that a true reading of his doctrine required fulfilling the promise of inclusion and social justice, a nation "with all and for all." Former students at La Liga invested in upholding a mythical Martí, whose unstained memory aligned perfectly with the ideals to which the tragically imperfect politicians who followed him ought to have aspired. The remembrances of Thursday nights with Martí, in particular, became a lesson to the "timid *pueblo* that still does not say what it thinks," and to the "swollen and arrogant who want to be loved and still have not been able to understand why the *pueblo* felt so much love for El Maestro."[9] Figueroa wrote of a Martí who "came down from the pedestal" of native genius, and "sat at our table and shared our misery, our anguish, and our hope."[10]

Whether or not the evenings with Martí were really as transcendent as such accounts suggest, these recollections point to a crucial detail. Martí's former students frequently built explanations of their participation in his movement and of his unique qualities as a leader around descriptions of Thursdays at La Liga—evenings whose principal purpose was to support them in their efforts to remake themselves from dignified workers into writers and intellectuals. This was the context in which, together with Martí, they imagined a republic "without a single Cuban who did not feel himself to be a man."[11] The politics of race and Cuban nationalism could involve discussions about many things—slavery, labor, land, sex, or military service—but for the participants in the seminars at La Liga, it was centrally about their own right to be thinkers. When the radial lines of the resurgent nationalist movement crossed paths at La Liga, the politics of race and nationalism converged with a specific project of literary self-making and intellectual assertion.

These efforts at social mobility, from artisan to intellectual, did not originate in New York City. Nor were the evenings with Martí the first time that such efforts had intersected with the politics of reform and revolution. Indeed, long before the artisans who created La Liga met Martí, their political and literary activities were already shaped by the spaces that had been opened to them by the liberal political movements that emerged in the Spanish Caribbean in previous decades. To understand the Thursday nights at La Liga requires tracing the stories of Serra, a young cigar worker from Havana, and Figueroa, a young typesetter from San Juan, forward into the decade of the 1870s, when they first worked to transform themselves from honorable artisans of "humble beginnings" into men of public reputation. But here two new characters join our story as well: the brothers named Juan and Gerónimo Bonilla. The two eventually became close allies of Serra in all his activities in New York and prime movers in the project to build an instructional society. Indeed, it was the brothers Bonilla, both cigar rollers, who hosted the first meetings of what would become La Liga in their home—the flat that they shared on the first floor of the row house at 74 West Third Street in Greenwich Village. The younger of the two, Juan, then became Martí's most celebrated student at La Liga: the exemplary young worker who had managed to become a thinker, despite the prejudices of the world around him. *Patria* frequently published essays by Juan, introducing him to readers thus: "He reads and writes English the same as he reads and writes Spanish. He works as a cigar roller, and he knows the classics by heart, and contemporary literature too. He reads everything, but he thinks for himself. He is the secretary of societies, a correspondent for newspapers, a vehement reader, who always has his pockets filled with books. His greatest pleasure is a shelf of brainy and useful books."[12]

Along with Serra and Figueroa, no one served as clearer proof within the Cuban revolutionary movement of the capacity of black men for dignified citizenship, or their willingness to forgive the sins of their white countrymen, than Juan and Gerónimo. And their evolution into thinkers, writers, and citizens, like that of their comrades, began long before they arrived in New York. In fact, for the Bonilla brothers, it started when they were children and young men in the large Cuban exile settlement in Key West, Florida. These four writers and intellectuals—Figueroa, Serra, and the two Bonillas—shared an ambition that a contemporary described as an "irresistible current" that drew them out of the artisan workshops and into "fierce battles of the press and the imposing demonstrations of the public square." But which particular battles, which newspapers, and which imposing demonstrations afforded men of visible African ancestry an opportunity to enter the public square, and on what terms?

This question is more than strictly biographical. The differences among the kinds of opportunities for becoming a writer that Figueroa experienced in Puerto Rico, the Bonillas experienced in Key West, and Serra experienced in Western Cuba add another dimension to our understanding of the varied contours of race and racism in the world within which they moved, and help to explain the divergent strategies that they adopted in their struggles against racism. Missing from this comparison is the last of our principal characters, the aspiring midwife Gertrudis Heredia. It was no coincidence that both Martí and his students at La Liga saw their shared ideal of equality expressed as the principle that all "the sons of a nation" should "feel that they are men." No variant of liberal or nationalist politics in this period offered a visible role as active citizens—soldiers, voters, or writers—to women, although women were actually present in many forms of political mobilization. Heredia did not become an author in this period. As the men in this story began writing and publishing narratives of their own lives, and developing a politics of racial equality, they often made urgent arguments about the proper behavior, respectability, and dignity of black women in general. But the particular experiences or opinions of Heredia and the other women with whom they shared their lives were, for the most part, missing.[13]

RACE AND REVOLUTION

The question of which battles, which newspapers, and which demonstrations opened space for men of color to assert themselves as intellectuals and "sons of a nation" leads first to the tumultuous rebellions that unfolded in Spain and the Spanish Caribbean in 1868, each of which marked a turning point for these men and for many of their future allies in Puerto Rico, Cuba, Florida, and New York. The possibility that anticolonial rebellions would encourage broader challenges to social hierarchies was exactly the threat that, for nearly a century, had played into the considerations of wealthy Cubans and Puerto Ricans about the risks of separating from Spain. Yet following the 1866 meetings in Madrid to discuss colonial reforms, some urban liberals and some creole landowners made the choice to enter into new kinds of coalition with workers, rural smallholders, wageworkers, and even enslaved people. Several things contributed to this decision. First, the Spanish government rejected the recommendations of liberal representatives. Instead, officials waged a campaign of repression against liberals in Cuba and Puerto Rico (including removing them from their posts as teachers), and against the emerging tobacco worker movement in Havana (where reading in factories was banned by government order). Then by the end of 1868, the Spanish government engaged in an escalating trade war with the United States, cutting off access to North American markets. On the brink of ruin, some planters and some disaffected proponents of colonial reform began to think differently about the prospect of rebellion.

The rebellions began in September 1868 with an uprising in the Puerto Rican town of Lares, where coffee growers found themselves perilously indebted to Spanish merchants who controlled the coffee trade. They took the risk of rallying the landless peasants and enslaved workers who worked on their properties in a rebellion against the merchants. The rebels proclaimed the abolition of slavery and independence from Spain, but only a few prominent liberals, most notably the physician Ramón Emeterio Betances, took part in planning the uprising. Nonetheless, when authorities discovered the plan and easily put down the revolt, they depicted it as a sinister plot by the abolitionists and liberals. The Spanish administration unleashed yet another round of repression against the liberal movement in Puerto Rico, which would remain extremely cautious about any expressions of separatism over the next decades.[14]

The outcome was far different when, a month after the uprising in Lares, a group of cattle barons and sugar planters from the southeastern Cuban districts of Manzanillo and Bayamo declared independence from Spain. The men who led the rebellion were landowners from the parts of Cuba where plantation slavery existed on the smallest scale, where liberalism had the strongest foothold, and where people who counted as white were in the majority. As in Puerto Rico, wealthy creoles in this part of Eastern Cuba (and allies from the ranch lands of Central Cuba who soon joined the struggle) were less fearful of racial rebellion than their counterparts in Western Cuba or around Santiago. And like the indebted coffee planters in

Lares, the leaders of the rebellion had little to lose. High taxes and the loss of access to markets in the United States had brought them to the edge of insolvency. The insurgents adopted as their platform a now-familiar reformist project that would increase civil and political liberties, institute free trade, reform taxation, and protect property. But they were hardly radicals. Seeking to attract support from western planters and wanting to preserve the possibility of eventual annexation to the United States, they worked to avoid attacks on property. Like the Cuban representatives in Madrid two years before, they were reticent on the question of slavery. They manumitted their own workers on the condition that they join the rebellion in subordinate roles and promised to end slavery after the fighting was over. But they were intentionally vague about the terms.[15]

Nevertheless, the uprising launched a long insurgency known as the Ten Years' War (1868–78), radically transforming the possibilities for people of African descent to participate in anticolonial politics. This shift began as the fighting spread eastward into the jurisdictions of Santiago de Cuba and Guantánamo, where tensions over land and slavery had already been percolating for nearly a decade. In many ways, the social structure of this area was more similar to Puerto Rico than it was to Western Cuba. Santiago had a large free population of color in both the cities and the countryside. Many free people owned urban and rural property, and others rented land. This allowed for the spread both of subsistence farming and of small-scale food and tobacco production for market. A few families became so wealthy that over generations, they moved from the status of moreno to that of pardo to that of white. Many more people reached an ambiguous status that would have been familiar to residents of San Juan: their color status went unreported on some official documents, although they were not afforded the honorifics don and doña. Beginning in the 1850s, however, sugar plantations took root and grew in this region, absorbing land and displacing smallholders. This threatened the livelihoods and the social status of free people of color and of white peasants, forcing many into labor alongside enslaved workers.[16]

The independence struggle, launched by planters and ranchers in Manzanillo and Bayamo, spread eastward into Santiago and Guantánamo as men of modest social status, including many who were artisans or smallholders, and who were not white, joined the struggle and mobilized the disaffected rural population. For instance, José and Antonio Maceo, sons of a former militia officer and small rural property owner, recruited a broad network of kin and dependents into the struggle, and quickly rose in the ranks to become generals in the insurgent army. The Maceos and their allies led their forces in direct attacks on plantations, recruiting slaves into the rank and file of the rebellion. Their wing of the movement created its own political program including immediate abolition, the destruction of the plantation regime and distribution of land, and equal citizenship without privileges of race. Some of the white military commanders, notably the Dominican-born Máximo Gómez, also adopted this program.[17]

Although part of the same revolution, the military leaders who had mobilized the popular uprising in Santiago and Guantánamo disagreed bitterly on key issues with the civilian government of Cuba Libre, dominated by men from Manzanillo, Bayamo, and Puerto Príncipe. The civilian government did adopt the principle of antislavery in 1871, after considerable debate and pressure from the military faction. But the two wings of the movement continued to differ fiercely on a proposed invasion of Western Cuba. General Gómez proposed to send troops westward under the command of General Antonio Maceo to halt sugar production and destroy slavery, striking colonial rule at its heart—the export economy. Civilian leaders opposed this invasion both because of fears about nonwhite military leadership and because they did not want to destroy the economic system of Western Cuba. To the contrary, they wanted to attract support from western planters and politicians in the United States, and neither group was likely to favor an attack on plantation agriculture, carried out by black, brown, and white troops serving under black, brown, and white commanders. Differences on matters of strategy and personal loyalty further pitted individual civilian leaders against one another, and caused tensions among the various military chiefs as well. Meanwhile, the Spanish government and loyalists worked to stoke fears about the rebellion, circulating rumors that black officers kept harems of white women, and would eventually seek to take control of Cuba altogether, dominating and seeking vengeance against whites. By the mid-1870s, these divisions had largely stalled the insurgency, with the more cautious and conservative faction growing increasingly wary of the rising power of Maceo, and gradually abandoning the struggle.[18]

SAN JUAN AND PONCE: SOTERO FIGUEROA

The rebellion in Cuba combined with a quickly evolving political transition in Madrid to create new spaces for Figueroa to participate in liberal reformist politics. In 1868, only a few weeks before the beginning of the insurgency in Cuba, a group of military officers in Madrid deposed the queen of Spain. This inaugurated a process of political reform in the peninsula, including a more liberal constitution, a new king, and eventually a short-lived republic (1873–74). The liberal turn in Spain produced a contradictory political scene in Puerto Rico. In response to the uprisings in Lares and Oriente, the colonial government encouraged well-to-do Conservatives and others born on the peninsula to arm themselves as a militia corps, known as the Voluntarios. These militiamen took on the task of defending public order, accusing liberals of separatist leanings and sympathy with the Cuban insurgency. At the same time, the rising fortunes of moderates and liberals in Madrid, and a desire to outflank the Cuban insurgency, reopened the door to negotiations over reform in Puerto Rico. In the early 1870s, Puerto Ricans enjoyed new freedoms of the press and association, and even the right to elect local town councils and representatives to the Cortes (Parliament) in Madrid.[19]

For Figueroa, a man in his early twenties, this period coincided with his coming of age as a writer and journalist. Press freedom meant that for the first time, the workshop where he toiled, transforming manuscripts into printed pages, produced a liberal newspaper, *El Progreso*, published by his mentor, Pascacio Sancerrit. A boom in liberal publications allowed Figueroa to learn the mechanics of newspaper layout, the rhythms of deadline production, and the conventions of journalistic prose—skills that he would put to use founding his own newspaper and that would later make him an indispensable ally of Martí in New York. The expansion of the liberal press also created new opportunities for Puerto Rican writers of color to publish their work. The most prolific such writer was a man named Eleuterio Derkes, a schoolteacher in Guayama. Derkes began publishing his own newspaper during the liberal interlude. He also sent poetry and articles to *El Progreso* in San Juan and *La Razón* in Mayaguez, and published several pamphlets, plays, and books.[20]

The new electoral contests in Puerto Rico also further strengthened the nascent political alliance between liberal politicians, now the Partido Liberal Reformista, and urban artisans. In the first Puerto Rican elections held in 1869, only about two hundred men in San Juan contributed the minimum level of taxes to be eligible to vote. Another four hundred qualified because of their "capacities." Of these, about half were military personnel. The rest were public officials, a handful of pharmacists, lawyers, and doctors. In addition, about seventy men had the right to vote as *capacidades* (in the awkward usage of the day) because they were members of the Economic Society.[21] These were all categories in which people of acknowledged African descent were almost, if not quite entirely, absent. Yet the elections sent Román Baldorioty de Castro, a man of plebeian birth, to serve as a representative in the Cortes in Madrid. Baldorioty was a former student of Rafael Cordero who, after receiving a scholarship to study in Spain, became a schoolteacher and founded the Economic Society. Puerto Rican Conservatives unsuccessfully challenged his election to the Cortes on the grounds that he was illegitimate. Then opponents in the Cortes alluded disparagingly to his status as a mulatto. Baldorioty responded, "Because the pigment of the cutis does not signal differences in nobility and morality among men; my complexion is dark and I assure you . . . that there is a brilliance that will emerge with my words to enlighten these blackened consciences."[22] This statement likely appealed to artisans in San Juan, who also surely celebrated in 1870 when the Liberal administration in Madrid ended the practice of investigating the "purity of blood" of persons nominated for public office in Puerto Rico.[23]

Artisans got a chance to demonstrate their support for such policies in 1871, when a new electoral law allowed all free men over the age of twenty-five to present themselves to the authorities, demonstrate their ability to read and write, and request to be added to the voter lists under the concept of capacidad.[24] Puerto Rican liberals quickly reached out to artisans in their efforts to build an electoral coalition. Sancerrit—a member of the Economic Society whose mother was identified, on his baptismal record, as a free parda—led this effort. He was the perfect intermediary. "We saw him," Figueroa later remembered, "not only advise the slow and lazy that they should hurry to demand their voting rights, but also in some cases complete the necessary documents for those who were not accustomed to the practices of the representative system."[25] From the perspective of the Conservative press, this encouragement of new voters was an attempt to whip up anti-Spanish resentments among the rabble. Conservatives harassed newly enfranchised men when they registered their names on voter lists, and Conservative newspapers referred to new voters as "nauseating *capacidades* who have learned to sign their names expressly in order to get the vote."[26]

Nevertheless, with the support of these new voters, the Liberals won the 1871 contests handily. Nearly a decade later, in a play poking fun at Conservative politicians, Figueroa imagined the experience of a Liberal electoral victory from the perspective of a losing candidate:

> But the worst part was when we left the polling station: there were factions, there were insults, there were threats, and some even came to blows. I, who wanted to protest the elections, the same as my *compañeros*, said that there had been cheating in the canvassing of votes, and immediately I felt—(putting his hand to his hip) . . . an expressive caress that sent me home in more than a hurry.[27]

This may hint at Figueroa's own experience of the elections of 1871. Perhaps he and the other artisans at Acosta's workshop were part of the crowd that, emboldened by the Liberal ascendency, "caressed" the backsides of public officials on Election Day in 1871. Maybe he was part of the Liberal public that hooted at and jeered Voluntarios who dared appear on San Juan streets in uniform.[28]

Whether or not he participated in this levity, he could not have avoided the fallout when, within a few weeks after the elections, violent conflicts broke out between free residents of color in San Juan and the military. Accounts of how this violence began differ. Conservative journalists accused the "radical faction," recently victorious in elections, of riling up black and brown allies. The Liberals' idea, wrote the Conservative publisher José Pérez Moris (whose print shop was only a few buildings away from Acosta's), was to get their plebeian allies to provoke an incident that would force the governor-general to suppress the Voluntarios.[29] According to a report in the *New York Times*, tensions had been boiling over in San Juan for some weeks and "hot-headed" radicals in the Liberal contingent were encouraging "negroes" to begin a revolution. Then, on July 25, someone began throwing stones at Spanish soldiers during a concert in the Plaza de Armas. A soldier attacked a man described in the *New York Times* as a "dandified negro," thinking him the perpetrator. This set off a general riot, with fighting "wherever a Negro met a soldier or a soldier met a Negro." By the end of the evening, three soldiers and five "Negroes" were dead.[30] It is impossible to know if this characterization as "dandified" describes someone dressed in intentionally flashy clothing, with an emphasis on showing off. Perhaps this was a man who simply hoped to appear civilized, upright, and urbane—an honorable urban citizen—but whose dark skin made this self-presentation seem pretentious and dandified to the reporter. Figueroa, a young typographer and aspiring author with brown skin, who likely dressed in the best clothes that he could afford, and who had not previously experienced episodes of generalized racial violence in his city, had a different view of the events. He later recalled that "the persecution of the race of color reached a new extreme, with the army and the Voluntarios making attacks because they knew how to invent and maintain the pretext that the blacks were throwing stones at the armed forces."[31]

Figueroa was not eligible to vote in the 1871 elections because he had not yet reached voting age. Still, these were formative moments for his evolution as a Liberal Reformista author and orator. Liberals in Puerto Rico may have occasionally hoped to rouse free people of color to action by stirring up resentment toward Voluntarios or hinting at sympathy for the Cuban cause. But they were not generally eager to inspire rebellion. They advocated for equal status for the overseas provinces within a democratic Spanish nation as well as equal civil rights and freedoms for all Spaniards, whether born in Spain or the colonies, independent of race. In place of class struggle or racial strife, they proposed to build a harmonious relationship between intellectuals and enlightened workers based on universal education and the freedom of association. Men like Figueroa's employer, Acosta, therefore assisted in creating artisan associations in San Juan in 1872, and in Ponce and Mayaguez in 1873. These groups modeled their literary activities, libraries, theatrical performances, and dances on the institutions that Acosta and his peers had created for themselves, groups like the Literary and Artistic Circle (founded in San Juan in 1869).[32] People of African descent not only joined the new artisan institutions; they were prominent in the leadership.[33] Indeed, when a Spanish writer visited one of these clubs in the 1880s, the presence of black and brown men was so extensive that he identified them as "Negro societies."[34] Overall the artisan social world was racially integrated to a remarkable degree, and largely nonwhite, although it was certainly not free of racism. Acosta and his allies also invited a few exemplary artisans into their own societies, and helped them to publish in the expanding liberal press. Figueroa, for instance, joined San Juan's Literary and Artistic Circle, and was elected its secretary.[35]

The Liberals scored another victory when the Cortes in Madrid abolished slavery in Puerto Rico in 1873; slavery would continue in Cuba until 1886. This provided abolitionists in San Juan with yet another moment to take to the streets for a public act: a jubilee to celebrate the act of abolition. In a grand procession, carefully constructed to reinforce a message of social peace, a group of newly free persons marched silently behind the victorious abolitionists, led by Acosta. Another prominent liberal publisher circulated through the crowd hugging black people and kissing their children, shouting, "And to whomever would deny this great truth, saying that these slaves have not entered into their liberty without hatred, I will say that he lies!!" In the evening festivities, Figueroa, now twenty years old, the protégé of several prominent abolitionists, and "a young man with a bold semblance and an indomitable gaze," led the Literary and Artistic Circle in its formal presentation of thanks to the new, Liberal governor of Puerto Rico, Rafael Primo de Rivera. This seems to have been one of Figueroa's first forays as a speaker in the public square.[36]

The Liberal interlude in Puerto Rico came to an abrupt end in 1874, with the restoration of the monarchy in Madrid and a return to Conservative politics at the Overseas Ministry. This was a major formative event for Figueroa, who wrote of this period, "Despotic reaction enthroned itself on the Island." The new governor-general, Laureano Sanz, deposed the popularly elected Liberal town councils and mayors, replacing them with loyal Conservatives. He closed Liberal newspapers and suppressed Masonic lodges. Sanz removed Liberals from civil boards and teaching posts. At the same time, "the electoral lists were corrected and a great number of voters were removed." The Conservatives raised the minimum contribution that Puerto Ricans had to make in order to qualify as electors and reduced the category of "capacidad" from all men who could read and write to include only Spanish soldiers, government administrators, professionals, and teachers. These measures reduced the electorate in Puerto Rico from about twenty thousand in 1873 to about three thousand by 1878. The new suffrage laws had a disproportionate effect on literate urban men of low rank, including many who were not white and who had recently been enfranchised—the same men, Figueroa noted, who "at an earlier moment some intransigent Conservatives had called, uncivilly, nauseating *capacidades*."[37] This group included Figueroa, who reached voting age in this period. The widespread purge of Liberals from teaching posts was an indignity for wealthier men, but a serious hardship for those of lower status, who depended entirely on their income from teaching to support their families.[38]

Things were not quite so dire for men, like Figueroa, who earned their living as tradesmen. Despite increasing censorship, publishing continued to expand on the island, providing new opportunities for social mobility, if not free expression. In 1880, Figueroa moved to the southern city of Ponce, with permission from officials in San Juan to start his own newspaper there, *El Eco de Ponce*. The letter from San Juan advising local authorities in Ponce that Figueroa was to be permitted to publish a newspaper refers to him as "D[on] Sotero Figueroa, a resident of this Capital."[39] The official who drafted this letter would have been within his rights had he chosen not to refer to Figueroa as don because Figueroa was pardo, illegitimate, and a tradesman. But Puerto Rican elites, even colonial officials, continued to be relatively lax about such formalities.[40] Figueroa moved to the city having previously been an officer in San Juan's Literary and Artistic Circle, and having gathered sufficient resources to found his own print shop and to start publishing his own newspaper. This meant that he had access to a press and a workshop. He had the use of a set of types, and money to buy paper and ink. Figueroa also had ties of kinship with the secretary of the city government in Bayamón, his wife's father, and friendships with many leading Liberals.[41]

Ponce was the largest commercial hub in Puerto Rico at the time, the center of Puerto Rico's sugar industry as well as its booming coffee trade. Although sugar production was in a period of decline, cane fields still surrounded the small city, less than fifteen minutes' walk from the cathedral and buildings of the municipal government. But the small city had a burgeoning civil society dominated by planters and merchants who aspired to a model of wealth and modernity based on other leading cities of the Atlantic. The wealthiest men in Ponce, most of whom were members of the Conservative Party, gathered each afternoon at a sidewalk café on the corner of Calle Luna and Calle Marina to discuss business.[42] After the purges in the electoral rolls, local political power lay in the hands of about six hundred men still eligible to vote, either as property holders or as public employees.[43] These men held firm control over local government. Yet Ponce was also a center of liberal reformism. With even more success than their counterparts in San Juan, wealthy residents of Ponce teamed up with local intellectuals to construct a self-consciously patrician city center with paved public ways, lighted plazas, elegant architecture, and the ornate Teatro La Perla. They founded schools, newspapers, asylums, a library and reading room, and a credit union, and held an industrial and agricultural exposition. In the wake of abolition, Ponce's men of letters (including many who had opposed the end of slavery) quickly consolidated a message that slavery had ended because of their own foresight and enlightened generosity.[44] Ponce was populated by thousands of workers recently freed from slavery too. Despite their comparative lack of interest in imposing formal segregation, city leaders remained intensely concerned with race. They expressed a belief in the superiority of whiteness, and its fundamental link to values of progress and civilization. They also sought to control the terms of the transition to free labor in cane production, to crack down on crime and vagrancy, and to police working-class sexuality. All these activities carried racial (among other) meanings.[45]

In his first forays into journalism, against this backdrop, Figueroa did not propose to represent the views of a generalized black race or a respectable class of color, as his Cuban contemporaries did at almost exactly the same moment. Nor did he attempt to speak for the broader working class, as Puerto Rican typographers Ramón Morel Campos and Ramón Romero Rosas would do a decade later.[46] Figueroa instead adopted a voice as a commercial publicist, working for the progress of the Playa neighborhood. He presented himself as an author, unmarked by color, rank, or class. *El Eco de Ponce*, he promised, would fulfill a necessary function for the progress of the city and of humanity. Perhaps more important for the propertied class that might purchase or read advertisements, *El Eco de Ponce* would serve as a "tireless defender" of the interests of "agriculture, industry, and commerce."[47] In *El Eco de Ponce*, Figueroa adopted positions that focused mostly on what he called modern civilization: a constellation of economic dynamism, effective statesmanship, and technological advancement. He sought to extend this definition of modern civilization—an ideal that he shared with many patrician readers (including the government inspectors who carefully read each issue)—to include specific elements of political liberalism, a set of values about which many of those same potential readers were lukewarm or indifferent. For example, he celebrated the opening of a new library as a victory for those opposed to "obscurantism." He also argued for freedom of the press, on the model of the United States. He promised "to speak the truth, as much of the truth as is permitted by the law or decree that currently governs journalism, without fear of ridiculous threats or base impositions."[48] As a result, he suffered imprisonment and fines in multiple instances for his criticisms of the colonial order. This was a fairly typical occurrence for a liberal newspaperman in late nineteenth-century Puerto Rico: local officials offended by an article simply instructed the Civil Guard to halt publication, to impound all issues in circulation, and to arrest the publisher.[49] Finally, Figueroa represented himself as an arbiter of good taste, beauty, and intelligence—someone who spoke for "those who know how to feel the beauty in art," and those who "admire the great concepts of intelligence and appreciate that which is truly great and good."[50]

The opportunity to project oneself in this kind of voice may have been part of the transcendent quality that typographers attributed to the act of setting type. So long as printed pages were crafted by an expert in grammar, orthography, and composition, a printing press made it possible to create a public identity that was not immediately or visibly tied to social class, legitimacy, color, grooming, dress, or manners of speech. There were not many journalists in Ponce, however, and a good portion of the reading public would likely recognize him as the same man who traveled through the narrow streets of the city. Whether readers knew him to be an artisan turned publisher, thought of him as a man of color aspiring to be an author, or saw the categories of artisan and urban man of color as overlapping, his unflinching assertion of the authority to judge probably made those who observed him take notice. This self-assurance is especially notable in contrast to some of his Cuban contemporaries, who prefaced interventions in the public sphere with protestations of their limited education and unworthy opinions.

Figueroa's claim to be a spokesman for civilization and beauty was an implicit argument about racial and class equality. Yet he also applied the broad concept of modern progress to the elimination of racial privileges.

When a charitable institution made available two seats in the school for indigent girls from Ponce on the condition that they be white and the product of legitimate marriages, Figueroa (who was neither) responded in *El Eco de Ponce* that true charity "accepts no hierarchies and distinctions other than those of talent, and would cease to fulfill its august mission on earth if it were to sustain privileges that are created by prejudice and that civilization will cause to disappear."[51] In other situations, one suspects that Figueroa took pains not to address instances of racism directly. He reported, for example, on a performance by a company of *bufos cubanos*, a style of popular theater from Cuba that depended heavily on ethnic and racial stereotypes, many played by white actors in blackface. This type of performance typically depicted a *mulata* (an alluring mixed-race woman hopelessly in love with a white man), a *negro bozal* (an uncultured black man speaking Africanized Spanish), and a *negrito* (a happy black man or woman singing and dancing *guarachas*, in stylized imitation of black musical practice). As Figueroa wrote, "And although it is true—as other colleagues have noted—that art does not emerge unscathed from its caricatures, even the most phlegmatic viewer will split his sides with laughter and pass the time in diversion."[52] Of all these caricatures, the one that seems likely to have been the most troubling to a typographer of African descent seeking recognition as a writer and arbiter of good taste is the *negro catedrático* (a "black professor" who put on airs of erudition, comically misusing academic terms). More troubling still would have been the play *Los negros periodistas* (performed in Puerto Rico in 1880), in which the comical "professor" is a former slave who wins the lottery and uses the proceeds to found a newspaper, to great hilarity.[53]

The report on the bufos cubanos highlights the delicate tightrope that Figueroa walked as an aspiring journalist from the artisan class. It also points toward his growing involvement in Ponce's theatrical scene. A year after this review appeared, a leading acting company (known for its performances of Cuban bufos) performed Figueroa's own debut work as a playwright, a one-act *zarzuela* (musical comedy) called *Don Mamerto*. His need to work with these performers may have been a factor in Figueroa's muted criticism of the blackface genre. The performance of *Don Mamerto* took place at Ponce's Teatro La Perla, the center of the city's patrician cultural scene. The play was an irreverent comedy about a young liberal lawyer in love with the daughter of the title character, a corrupt Puerto

Rican official. Although Don Mamerto publicly fulminates against "heretics, Masons, and liberals," he is not an ideological Conservative but rather a pragmatic and craven one. He explains, "If I were to permit myself to have my own ideas, and these, by misfortune, were contrary to the ones espoused by those in power, I would be deprived of my future and my salary." On the same principle, Mamerto opposes the match between his daughter and a young liberal because "knowledge is a food that offers very little nutrition for the stomach, and I think that Luis, with all his science, has quite enough of it already to die of hunger."[54] The play ends happily with a Liberal Party victory in Madrid. News arrives that the young lawyer will receive an official position, Don Mamerto removes his objection to the match, and the marriage can go forward.

The play makes clear allusion to a tradition of liberal dramas in which an elite family objects to a marriage to a person of partial African ancestry or unknown lineage. Those who knew the playwright surely also recognized the resonance between the story line and his own marriage to the daughter of a Conservative functionary. Figueroa, however, chose not to make color prejudice, social rank, or legitimacy an explicit part of his story. In *Don Mamerto*, the drama stems from the discrimination that talented liberals experienced because of their ideas. This was a politics of social equality that consciously constructed color prejudice not as a distinct social problem (shared by aspiring intellectuals and former field slaves) but instead as one aspect of a broader assault on dignified manhood, part and parcel of a constellation of colonial ills (shared by a range of intelligent men in the liberal coalition). To present a drama about the ways that a corrupt and idiotic colonial society unfairly prevented talented liberals from earning a living and consummating their role as patriarchs through legitimate marriage was not simply to cover or displace a complaint about racial prejudice. Rather, it made merit and manhood into the central unifying problems of colonialism, and the triumph of men of merit over aristocratic privilege and corrupt patronage a single solution to a range of social ills, including "preoccupations" of color. This vision evolved over time, but remained relatively intact into the period that Figueroa allied himself with Martí, who promoted Figueroa into positions of prestige and responsibility based on his merits while almost never mentioning his racial status.

Figueroa partnered with a local musical celebrity, Juan Morel Campos, to create the music for *Don Mamerto*. Morel Campos was also a man of partial African descent, known for his role in popularizing the dance form most associated with Ponce's artisan class, the syncopated rhythm called *danza*.[55] The danza, and by extension the recognition of Morel Campos as a great composer and musician, was fast becoming a symbol of a form of Puerto Rican nationalism that incorporated the cultural expressions of the mixed-race working class as artifacts of authentic creole identity. Alejandro Tapia, who relocated to Ponce in these years too, thought that danza was "characteristic of our climate and our sensibilities." Liberals like Tapia, however, also expressed concerns that the danza, which included an extended figure in which couples held one another in close embrace, swaying their lower bodies to the steady looping rhythm, might be *too* black. It should be purged, he wrote, of "the influence of voodoo and Africa," and should be "stripped of all that it has of voluptuousness."[56] Another liberal writer argued against teaching Puerto Rican children the "feminine" and sensual danza, and recommended instilling instead the "the sacred round of Work and Progress, to the cadence of the solemn harmonies of Science, Justice, and universal Fraternity."[57] What considerations must have figured into Figueroa's decisions to dance or not when his collaborator Morel Campos played at local functions? Was he conscious that certain movements of the hip or pelvis would be seen as signs of blackness, and would therefore disqualify him as an intellectual? Was he conscious that some might see in him a natural tendency to perform the danza authentically because of his brown skin and curly hair, or that others might perceive his skin and hair differently if they saw him perform the danza authentically? Were Figueroa and Morel Campos conscious of the nascent connection between artisan popular culture and an emerging nationalist sentiment among elite liberals when they inserted a danza with nationalist lyrics, *La Borinqueña*, at the end of their play?

The fact that the play was an unflinching parody of Puerto Rican officialdom, an insult to the same politicians who repeatedly fined and jailed Figueroa for expressing his ideas over the next several years, provided an additional message about the capacity for wit and daring of an aspiring author who, after all, was still an artisan and a pardo. Shortly before the play opened, Figueroa's newspaper, *El Eco de Ponce*, folded. He then directed a second newspaper, *La Avispa* (The wasp), which also lasted only a few months.[58] And he returned to wage work as a typographer, principally in the workshop owned by liberal publisher Ramón Marín. Just at the moment of his greatest artistic triumph, his path from artisan to author took a step backward. In helping to physically produce the newspapers published in this shop and simultaneously contributing articles to them, he became part of the inner circle of Ponce liberals, created by Marín—the son of an enslaved woman—and by Román Baldorioty de Castro—the former student of Rafael Cordero who had risen from plebeian birth to be a representative in the Cortes and had now, because he was prevented by the authorities from working as a teacher, fallen on hard times. Baldorioty began publishing a newspaper out of Marín's shop in these years.[59]

More than a decade later, a Spanish writer sneered that Martí had surrounded himself with "mulattoes" who went to New York in order to "pass themselves off as persons" even though in Puerto Rico "they never amounted to anything more than bad typesetters."[60] Yet officials and conservative writers in Puerto Rico rarely, if ever, put this sort of derision in print, although they may well have taken the opportunity to diminish men like Figueroa in the public spaces of the city, withholding respectful treatment as "don" or insisting that he give way on the narrow sidewalks. There were surely numerous ways that the wealthy men who controlled the government and institutions of Ponce communicated their sense of superiority. Liberal allies, however, impressed by Figueroa's bravado and his skill as a writer, seem to have continued to make space for him in their social world—their newspapers, their literary societies, their café conversations, and even their families. They took the opportunity to confirm his status as "Don Sotero Figueroa," supporting his efforts at self-making, relying on him as an intermediary with the broader world of artisan associations, while securing their own bona fides as men with progressive ideas about rank and merit. By the time that Figueroa met Martí, he was well acquainted with the promises and pitfalls of friendships with this kind of liberal.

KEY WEST: GERÓNIMO AND JUAN BONILLA

The two men who would host the first meetings of La Liga in their living room in New York City had experienced the political transformations touched off by the revolution in central and Eastern Cuba in quite a different context: as boys growing up in the newly emerging Cuban settlement in Key West, Florida. At the same time that cattle ranchers and planters in Eastern Cuba began a rebellion to protest the trade war that Spain had undertaken with the United States, a group of Cuban tobacco entrepreneurs developed a different strategy to avoid the most severe consequences of the new tariff walls. By importing raw tobacco and thousands of skilled workers from Cuba, and manufacturing "Havana" cigars inside the United States, they took advantage of a growing market while avoiding the high duties on the importation of finished cigars.[61] Key West was an ideal spot for these enterprises, only six hours from Havana on the steamships that arrived weekly, and also connected by steam and sail to markets in New York City and New Orleans.[62] Over the decade of the Ten Years' War, a large portion of the Cuban cigar industry moved to Key West, tripling the island's population and making it one of the principal ports on the gulf coast of the United States. In Key West, nationalists and labor leaders were beyond the reach of Spanish authorities, able to organize openly and publish with relatively little molestation, expressing ideas that were dangerous even to hint at in Havana.

Yet something else was going on in Key West: an experience of exile that transformed, rather than just allowing into the open, the relationship between liberal and labor politics and activism by people of color. Although Cuban nationalists liked to say that Key West was more Cuban than North American, it was also a city in the southern United States, in the midst of the tumultuous period of political renegotiation after the Civil War. As such, the southern city provided a workshop for Cuban workers and nationalists to develop new kinds of interracial politics—unlikely as that might seem—and it offers a fascinating parallel to the short period of expanded suffrage in Puerto Rico.

Gerónimo and Juan Bonilla were the children of a shoemaker named Francisco and a homemaker named Dolores, who moved their family from Havana to Key West shortly after the war began in Eastern Cuba in 1868. At the time of the 1870 census, Gerónimo was thirteen, and Juan (who had been born in Key West) was one. A third brother, Francisco, was three. Francisco also later moved to New York, where he worked in cigars and was at one point the manager of a Cuban dance orchestra.[63] But he was never active in Cuban politics to the same degree as his brothers. When they arrived in Florida, the Bonillas joined a small minority in the growing immigrant community. At the time of the 1870 census, census takers identified only seventy-four Cubans in Key West as black or mulatto, while recording more than nine hundred Cubans as white.[64] These seventy-four included seven of the eight members of the Bonilla household (Juan, the eighth member, was also listed as black, but was a native-born Floridian). Although their father was a shoemaker, the boys grew up to be cigar rollers and spent their childhoods in a community dominated, as no other in the hemisphere, by the cigar industry. Like other Cubans of color in the city, the Bonilla family lived in a small cluster of households composed of black and mulatto Cubans, in a neighborhood where the vast majority of residents were counted by census takers as white Cuban cigar makers.[65]

In Key West, workers preserved the institutions of shop floor reading and worker education, but linked both to the populist wing of the nationalist movement, as it had emerged in Oriente, and to a new project of interracial solidarity. Juan María Reyes (formerly a contributor to the Havana newspapers *El Siglo* and *La Aurora*, the papers that had campaigned in favor of factory reading in the early 1860s) led this effort. Reyes became a full-time *lector*, circulating among and reading aloud in multiple factories without actually working there. He used his position as a reader and his newspaper, *El Republicano*, to build support among workers for the independence movement. In 1871, organizers opened the San Carlos Society for Instruction and Recreation (Club San Carlos), which unlike similar institutions in Cuba, invited the participation of both white and black workers, and housed a school that enrolled both white and black children. At the same time, anarchist organizers within the factories began to promote the principle of worker solidarity across racial lines. Workers put this principle into practice during an unsuccessful strike in 1875, supported by Reyes and the populist nationalists.[66] Gerónimo and Juan grew up and became skilled craftsmen within the worker enclave in Key West. They listened to the nationalist lectores, and learned about the Paris Commune and the new ideas of socialism and anarchism from comrades in the shop.

Most remarkably, there is strong evidence that the Bonillas grew up among men who took part in a form of political engagement that was novel for Cuban workers of any color: men who voted in local, state, and federal elections. Reconstruction era politics were in full swing in Key West during summer 1870, and newly arrived Cuban workers were a key component. Reyes and other Cuban independence leaders helped hundreds of cigar makers to present themselves in front of Key West judges to declare their intent to become US citizens in time to vote in the elections that were scheduled for November of that year. Those Cuban voters helped the Republicans win control of Key West and Florida governments. Key West was the largest city in Florida at the time, and the Cubans became an important power block in state politics. In exchange, Reyes and other Cuban leaders received patronage positions from the Republican Party. Posts in the customhouse and good relationships with local magistrates facilitated the illegal smuggling of weapons and other supplies to the insurgency.[67]

The Bonillas became involved in these political efforts through a strange twist of historical fate. When they first arrived in Florida in 1868, the United States allowed only "free white persons" to become citizens through naturalization. But in early 1870, Republicans in Washington, DC, drafted a bill reforming the rules for naturalization. The main goal was to put stricter controls on the certification of new immigrants as voters by judges in Democratic precincts in northern cities. Near the end of debate, an aging abolitionist who still advocated full citizenship for African Americans proposed an amendment striking the word "white" from the naturalization statute. His proposal nearly killed the bill. Western lawmakers and some labor groups objected vehemently that this would open the door to the naturalization of Chinese immigrants. Republicans eventually found a compromise. In summer 1870, President Ulysses S. Grant signed a bill that left the phrase "free white persons" in the statute, but extended the right to naturalize to persons of "African nativity or African descent" as well. Since few people of African descent seemed likely to move to the United States, few in Washington objected to the new wording. It was understood to be a symbolic gesture to a key Republican constituency, African Americans, that would have little practical effect.[68]

Yet the change in the naturalization statute had a major unintended impact on Cuban politics in Florida. Only months after Grant signed the bill, Cuban nationalists would for the first time began to mobilize electoral coalitions across class lines. Because of the new naturalization law, black and brown Cubans could help swing elections and shift the flow of political appointments. Even before insurgent leaders in Oriente adopted the principles of abolition and citizenship without regard to race, and at almost the precise moment that electoral reforms allowed literate artisans to participate in elections in Puerto Rico, this act of Congress allowed the nationalists in Florida (or forced them) to appeal to black men as voters.

As a result, Francisco Bonilla, the black shoemaker whose sons would grow up to be close supporters of Martí, was among the first of the new Cuban voters to claim US citizenship, on October 1, 1870. One of the men who went with him to naturalize on that day was Salomé Rencurrel, a cigar maker who was the Bonillas' immediate neighbor. Years later, Rencurrel lived in the same apartment as the Bonillas in New York, where also he became an important community leader.[69] Francisco and Salomé thus became two of the first black Cubans to become full voting citizens of a republic—any republic. This meant not only the right to vote but also the right to participate in the give-and-take of patronage politics and public spectacle that this kind of citizenship entailed. There is no way to know whether any Cubans took part in the Election Day celebration of "negroes," who according to an unsympathetic observer, drove around the city "in a wagon with a brass band, shouting and jeering and generally making themselves offensive to the white citizens." Nor is it possible to determine whether any Cubans took part in the brawl that unfolded at a Republican meeting in 1872 after group of white men proposed to split off, creating their own "respectable white party."[70]

It is clear, though, that the integration of Cuban exiles into local social institutions and electoral politics did not always align white Cubans with the project of black citizenship. In 1872, nationalist exiles formed a Masonic lodge in Key West, but voted to exclude men of color from initiation and to prohibit "speaking about race" within the lodge. Cubans of color responded by creating their own lodge, named for Abraham Lincoln.[71] That same year, a segment of the Cuban movement defected to the Democratic Party, which promised support to the insurgency that had not been forthcoming from Republicans. With the Cuban vote divided, the Democrats temporarily took over the government in Key West and, more significantly, won control of the Florida state government in the elections of 1876. The federal government withdrew troops from the state later that year and Democrats quickly undertook a project of legal reform and terror designed to disenfranchise black voters in the state[72] When Francisco Vicente Aguilera, an insurgent leader from Eastern Cuba, visited Key West in these years, he discovered that the white Cubans in Key West were "very distant from the people of color." According to his account, someone in Key West was engaging in a campaign of propaganda, telling black and brown Cubans that "the current revolution has not been made to help them," and that they should form their own movement "to avenge all the offenses committed against them during the era of slavery," especially the tortures and wrongful convictions perpetrated in 1844.[73] The era of slavery, it is worth noting, would not come to an end in Cuba for another decade. It is difficult to know, in any event, whether this call to arms was actually circulating among Cubans of color in Key West, or if Aguilera was merely inferring the motive of racial vengeance from reports of the formation of independent black social or political institutions, within or outside the nationalist fold. But the willingness of some in the nationalist coalition to create segregated institutions and to join forces with the Democrats was likely part of the problem.

The leadership of the exile movement included many like Aguilera, men from the planter class who had adopted the principles of abolitionism and full manhood citizenship late in their lives, and unevenly. As historian Ada Ferrer notes, "On the one hand, [insurgent leaders] clearly asserted the equal right of all Cubans to make or serve the nation; on the other, they made it evident that each group had different degrees of right to the very title of 'Cuban.'"[74] Yet the war and exile had begun to change Cuban liberal politics in fundamental ways. When Aguilera discovered the breach between white and black Cubans in Key West, he called a meeting of the Cubans of color, including most likely Francisco Bonilla and Salomé Rencurrel. Aguilera listened to their complaints and (at least to his own satisfaction) answered their concerns. He mediated the mutual resentments expressed by white and black Cubans. The Cubans of color in the city then organized and hosted a dinner to celebrate the resolution of racial tensions in the city (suggesting that they continued, despite the emergence of unsegregated nationalist and labor organizations, to maintain their own social networks and leadership). Meanwhile, other nationalist leaders continued to appeal to men like Bonilla and Rencurrel for votes. Carlos Manuel de Céspedes, son of the planter who had led the first rebellion in Bayamo, ran successfully for mayor of Key West in 1875. Gerónimo naturalized several weeks before this election.[75] Céspedes and other nationalists also rallied workers to the Republican ticket in the 1876 presidential race.[76]

A decade later, the principal at the "colored" high school in Key West, Lemuel Livingston, reflected on the difference between white Cubans and other white people in Florida. The white Cubans surely had their prejudices, he reflected, but "don't consider it a religious duty, based on pure hatred and cussedness, to throw things in one's way and crush manhood and life out of him because he has pigment in his cuticle." Livingston, a graduate of Howard University, was also a journalist and a leader in the Republican Party. He was part of a successful effort to preserve black voting rights and Republican rule in Key West until the Democratic state legislature revoked the city charter in 1889. The unusual attitude among white Cuban Republicans, he thought, was crucial to making Key West "the freest" town in the South.[77]

The active presence of African Americans, like Livingston, within these emerging political coalitions was a key difference between the experience of the Bonillas in Key West and the experience of Figueroa in San Juan, where Liberals created similar electoral coalitions at precisely the same moment. In Key West, interaction with African Americans was a crucial feature of life outside politics as well. The Bonillas became conversant in multiple worlds, both Cuban and African American. Juan may have attended the school at the San Carlos, which famously taught both white and black children. But the San Carlos school faced frequent financial shortfalls, operating intermittently in these years. He and Francisco may also have attended one of the small private schools operated by Cuban exiles, a Catholic school that was organized specifically for children of color, or one of the colored public schools in the city, run by important African American Republicans like Livingston.[78] A traveler to Key West noted that "the children of the poorer classes of Cubans" played together with African American children in the neighborhoods that they shared "on a footing of social equality."[79] It is not clear whether this writer meant to say that both white and black Cuban children played with African Americans, or just with black Cubans. For that matter, it is not clear whether he regarded any of the poorer class of Cubans as properly white. Either way, contact with African American children in Key West was probably a factor in the role that the Bonillas took on later in life as pivotal figures in alliances between Cubans and African Americans.

This unusual context for the evolution of Cuban politics can be seen clearly in the 1880 census, at which time the Bonilla family lived on a block shared with several African American families (as well as both white and black Cubans). They lived next door to James English, a mulatto barber and Republican leader who served as a registrar of voters and on the County Commission. Gerónimo may have been old enough to discuss Republican politics over the porch railing with English and other neighbors. The man who knocked on the Bonillas' door as part of the canvasing effort for the 1880 census was an African American blacksmith named Robert Gabriel, a Republican member of the Key West City Council and the grand master of a local Odd Fellows lodge, a fraternal organization that claimed membership from the same black artisans, teachers, journalists, and preachers who took the lead in black Republican activism. Here was a second point of contact for the Bonillas. In 1876, Cubans of color formed the Logia San Rafael, an Odd Fellows lodge with a charter from Gabriel's fraternal organization. It is not clear whether Gerónimo joined this lodge while living in Key West.[80] But activity within this Odd Fellows and within Republican Party politics in New York were both essential staging grounds for Gerónimo's and Juan's leadership in the later efforts to create La Liga, and recruit black and brown Cubans into the Cuban Revolutionary Party.

HAVANA AND MATANZAS: RAFAEL SERRA (AND JUAN GUALBERTO GÓMEZ)

Accounts of the multiracial labor movement, of strikes, of political campaigns, and of interactions with African Americans in Key West would undoubtedly have reached Rafael Serra in Havana by the end of the Ten Years' War, especially as migrants from Key West began returning for visits to Cuba in the late 1870s.[81] Yet to speak of such things in Western Cuba was to take a risk. The pro-Spanish party in Havana asserted its power, organizing a militia force known (as in Puerto Rico) as the Voluntarios. This militia was under the command of peninsular merchants and manufacturers, who drafted peninsular workers to be foot soldiers. The Voluntarios forced Cuba's Liberal reformers into silence or exile, even during the brief period of Republican rule in Spain. The Spanish government did deploy the pardo and moreno battalions in the war, and even employed some enslaved people to the defense of empire in exchange, eventually, for their freedom. But during the war, there was no electoral mobilization or publishing in Havana comparable to the events that unfolded around Figueroa in San Juan, no Election Day antics, no celebrations of abolition (still more than a decade away), and certainly no recruitment of black workers into an expanded system of elections and patronage, as in Key West.

Yet Havana was not wholly quiescent nor wholly shut off from the political transformations taking place in Oriente, San Juan, and especially Key West. The episode that most clearly demonstrates this interconnectedness was a polemic between the exile journalist Juan María Reyes and Gonzalo Castañón, editor of a conservative Havana newspaper, a man who also served as a colonel in the Voluntarios. The two first squared off in their respective publications. Then Castañón, having traveled by steamer to Key West to challenge Reyes to a duel, lost his life in an exchange of fire with a Cuban baker. News of the episode electrified Key West, but reverberated throughout the Spanish Caribbean as well. Voluntarios took to the streets in Havana looking for opportunities to exact revenge. As in the rioting after the elections in San Juan that same year, they frequently attacked men of color. This would likely have been an important aspect of the unfolding of events around Castañón's death, as understood by a thirteen-year-old Serra.[82] But the episode also contributed to an altered political landscape as officials in Havana began to target well-to-do creoles. The authorities imprisoned a group of medical students in Havana, accusing them of defiling Castañón's tomb, and executed eight of the prisoners. The confrontation between a nationalist journalist in Key West and a conservative journalist and militia captain thus became a formative moment in the political evolution of a generation of Cuban professionals. This generation included the young Martí, whose closest boyhood friend, Fermín Valdés Domínguez, was one of the medical students arrested and sentenced to hard labor (though not one of those killed). Martí had also been sentenced to hard labor for the possession of letters that appeared to link him to separatism. After serving part of their sentences, Martí and Valdés Domínguez received clemency and fled to exile in Spain, where they then attended university and began their own careers as authors by publishing denunciations of the political repression in Cuba. They were in Spain during the brief Liberal ascendency of the early 1870s, which included parliamentary debates over the expansion of suffrage and abolition of slavery in Puerto Rico and the short-lived Spanish Republic.[83]

Another episode several years later hints at other networks of clandestine resistance linking Havana to San Juan, Key West, and Oriente in this period. In 1875, police in Havana arrested Bartolomé Duarte, whom they identified as a "moreno" coachman born in Puerto Rico. Investigators found that he was in possession of US currency, a revolver and cartridges, and letters indicating that he had a "commission to smuggle out the members of his race, and to get them aboard ships leaving for Key West," where allies helped them embark for Oriente to join the rebellion. They found evidence that Duarte had already helped at least two men escape from slavery in this fashion.[84] There is no indication as to how widespread this kind of activity, akin to the Underground Railroad in the United States, was among coachmen or other free artisans of color in Havana. Nor is it clear whether the fact that Duarte was originally from Puerto Rico points to any broader links among artisans and abolitionists on the two islands.

It is clear, however, that political alliances of the kind that had emerged in Key West and Puerto Rico in the early 1870s arose later in Western Cuba, and coalesced more slowly. Under the peace agreement signed by the more cautious faction of the insurgency in 1878, the Pact of Zanjón, Cubans gained many of the limited political reforms that Puerto Ricans had enjoyed for a decade: permission to form associations and to publish newspapers, so long as they did not advocate independence. They could also, for the first time, form political parties to compete in new elections, fielding candidates for municipal offices and for representatives to the Cortes. As in Puerto Rico, after the retrenchment of the mid-1870s, suffrage was limited to men who were wealthy enough to pay a minimum level of taxes, or who were considered capacidades as professionals, proprietors, military officers, prizewinning artists, or government administrators. As in Puerto Rico, this electoral law strongly favored the pro-Spanish contingent, including many peninsular merchants, manufacturers, and bureaucrats. Nevertheless, the new electoral system allowed for wealthy and middle-class creoles to organize themselves to pursue measured reform within the colonial system too.[85] This was an alternative that most Cuban intellectuals and property owners (including many former insurgents) increasingly preferred to the radicalizing separatist movement, which Spanish propagandists continued to depict as a black rebellion.

A newly formed Liberal Party argued for continuing to pursue the remaining goals of the insurgency through the newly created legal means of advocacy and party politics. But the party took a narrow view of what these goals were, reminiscent of the aims of the liberals in the Cuban delegation to Madrid in 1866: the extension of the Spanish Constitution to Cuba, the gradual abolition of slavery, white immigration, and tariff reform. The more radical faction of the insurgency, led by Maceo, had not been party to the peace agreement, did not accept its terms, and soon began organizing in exile for a return to armed conflict. Maceo and his allies argued that the Liberals had betrayed the cause of the revolution by accepting peace without securing the abolition of slavery or the independence of Cuba. One of the most bitter of these indignities was the fact that the leadership of the newly formed Liberal Party, while calling for loyalty from people of color, supported neither universal suffrage, equal civil rights, nor immediate abolition. The Liberals preferred gradual abolition, after an extended period of "apprenticeship" in which former slaves would be forced to keep working for the people who had enslaved them.[86]

These restrictions aside, the period after the Pact of Zanjón did produce new kinds of newspapers and political institutions, within which intellectuals of color, including Serra, could intervene. On the more progressive margins of the Liberal Party, labor leader Saturnino Martínez and lawyer Nicolás Azcárate, the pair who had helped to institute reading in cigar factories a decade earlier, sought to rebuild the alliance between liberal reformists and artisans that had been interrupted by the war. They promoted the creation of worker education centers and advocated immediate abolition and universal suffrage.[87] Martínez also worked to create the new Union of Workers in the Tobacco Industry, which attracted more than four thousand workers in Havana in the year after the end of the war. This union reflected the increasing circulation of anarchist ideas, including the principle of antiracism. Also, because it expressly included workers from the various occupational categories in cigar making, the union brought workers of different social status (rollers, selectors, and strippers) together into one organization, though it is not clear how quickly the organizations serving each trade group integrated.[88] Serra worked in the same factory as Martínez, and his first documented political activities comprised "assiduous labor" to help create this union.[89] Over time, the Liberal Party (later renamed the Autonomista Party) incorporated Azcárate's group, and began to reach out more broadly to artisans and men of color as potential allies.

Yet the emergence of multiracial labor alliances, and the desire of some politicians to mobilize support from black and white workers, did not signal the creation of a broader worker or political culture that had moved beyond traditions of racial segregation. This can be seen in the proliferation of separate worker institutions and newspapers created by and for artisans of color, often with their own ties to the leading political factions. Conservatives offered help for black and brown Cubans creating their own "colored" versions of the *casinos de españoles*, social clubs for Spanish loyalists. Liberals encouraged black and brown workers to create their own versions of the artisan educational clubs promoted by Azcárate and Martínez. These Societies for Instruction and Recreation were commonly known as *sociedades de color*. Within them, a new civil rights leadership emerged in Cuba, advocating for educational opportunity, desegregation of public facilities, and expanded political rights.[90] These clubs were Serra's second and much more extensive experience of political organizing. Indeed, they became the main platform for the evolution of a whole generation of Cubans of African descent who become writers and politicians in this period.

The most prominent of the new civil rights activists was Juan Gualberto Gómez, the son of a couple who though enslaved on a plantation in Matanzas, managed to save enough money to purchase his freedom and their own. His parents sent him to school and then, with the help of their former owners, to Paris for training as a carriage maker. In Paris, Gómez left his apprenticeship and began working as a journalist. He served as a translator for Francisco Vicente Aguilera, the Cuban insurgent leader and exile who had attempted to mediate conflicts between black and white Cubans in Key West in 1874. Gómez then moved to Mexico, home to a considerable colony of Cuban exiles by the last years of the war. There he worked as an agent for the Cuban musician, Claudio Brindis de Salas, known as the "black Paganini." In Mexico he met Azcárate, who encouraged him to return to Cuba. In Havana, Azcárate invited the young journalist to speak at elite literary functions, and encouraged his efforts at publishing, teaching, and advocacy. Azcárate also apparently introduced Gómez to Martí, also recently returned from exile and an avid participant in events at Azcárate's literary society, the Liceo de Guanabacoa. In April 1879, with support from Azcárate and other high-profile Liberals, Gómez opened a school for children of color in Havana and began publishing a newspaper called *La Fraternidad*, in which he advocated full civil rights, education, and uplift for people of color.[91]

Serra made his mark at almost exactly the same moment in the neighboring city of Matanzas (two hours away by train), where he moved shortly after marrying Heredia. In August 1879, four months after the appearance of the first issue of *La Fraternidad* in Havana, Serra helped to found the Society for Instruction and Recreation called La Armonía (Harmony). He raised funds for and operated a free primary school in the home that he shared with Heredia on Calle Daoíz, in close proximity to the Lucumí cabildo long run by her grandparents. He taught reading, writing, grammar, geography, linear drawing, and arithmetic to more than thirty-five students. He also briefly edited a newspaper called *La Armonía*.[92] This was a rapid transformation for a young man from a worker and labor activist to an educator, journalist, and black civil rights leader. He had attended primary school and had an aunt who was a teacher so it is perhaps not too surprising that he had managed to educate himself to the point where he could teach basic subjects to those with even less schooling than he had. But where did he acquire the experience needed to begin publishing a periodical? He was not a typesetter, like Figueroa. He did not have many years of experience working as a journalist abroad, like Gómez. One possibility is that he relied on white allies, including several founding members of the La Armonía Society who were educators or journalists, and part of the same literary circles as Azcárate and Martí. Such men may have offered assistance with the practical matters of producing the first issues of his newspaper, editing, proofreading, contacts with printers, or help with start-up costs, possibly in exchange for an expectation that Serra would support their political endeavors.[93]

The support that men like Gómez and Serra received from white literary types and advocates of popular education was, however, a double-edged sword. In 1880, the government decreed an end to slavery and the creation of a new system of "apprenticeship" that required former slaves to continue working for former masters for a period of eight years. The leaders of the Liberal Party in Cuba favored this move. Nevertheless, they remained deeply concerned with what they termed "the social question," by which they meant the presence of large numbers of people soon to be freed from slavery. The Liberal politician Rafael Montoro, for instance, considered that "nothing good can be expected of the new social class," and that "the most difficult and arduous problem" consisted in "making them worthy of freedom and civilization."[94] Even those on the democratic fringe of the Liberal Party, like Azcárate, remained concerned with what they saw as the deep moral and cultural failings of Cubans of color. In Azcárate's view, support for civil rights and mutual aid societies organized

by men such as Serra went hand in hand with efforts to suppress the cabildos de nación, with their immoral and "savage exhibitions. . . . [Since]
slavery has disappeared and blacks are now equal to whites before the
law," he wrote in 1881 (five years before the end of the apprenticeship
system, and at a moment when the law did not in fact treat blacks and
whites equally), "they have the most interest in seeing the cabildos disappear from the Island so that people of color will gather in charitable
and cooperative associations and establish casinos, liceos, and other circles
dedicated to cultivated diversions and useful instruction." The point of
the new sociedades de color was precisely to instruct and civilize black
Cubans, to prepare them for participation in Cuban society.[95]

It is not clear whether this kind of pressure influenced relations between the members of Serra's La Armonía and the members of the cabildo
Fernando VII, founded by Heredia's grandfather and still in operation
nearby on Calle Daoíz as late as 1878.[96] It is likely that Serra and Heredia
drew on the resources and relationships created by an older generation
of community leaders born in Africa. This would not have been unusual,
as many cabildo leaders applied to convert their organizations into sociedades de color in this period, along the lines advocated by Azcárate. For
instance, the members of several cabildos in the Havana neighborhood of
Jesús María formed the Unión Fraternal society, separating themselves
from "other elements of the same race, with less culture, who devoted the
cabildo to African religion."[97] Sometimes, these distinctions took the form
of disputes, such as those that unfolded in Key West between members of
a society who saw themselves as "on the true path to progress" and Africans who "still danced according to the custom of their country."[98] Perhaps
these kinds of conversations also took place between the participants in
La Armonía and the members of the cabildo Fernando VII. On the other
hand, some scholars have argued that the public rejection of African-
derived cultural practices was a necessary facade for the sociedades de
color, and that behind closed doors, many of the newly created associations
secretly carried on as before.[99] Perhaps, then, Serra and the other founders of the Sociedad La Armonía were privately respectful of the Lucumí
elders in Heredia's family, even as they participated in a project of uplift
and "civilization" imagined by some as an effort to supplant the cabildos.

Whatever his private views on Afro-Cuban spirituality and music, it
seems clear that Serra already sympathized with the project of Cuban

independence, though he could hardly say so in his newspaper. The peace settlement in 1878, which achieved neither independence nor abolition, left a substantial portion of the Cuban insurgent movement unsatisfied. After the negotiations over the treaty completely excluded the more radical military faction from Oriente, Maceo and other African-descended officers, along with many white comrades, denounced the settlement and went into exile. Then, in August 1879, just as Serra began publishing *La Armonía*, separatists began a new insurgency in Oriente, known as the Little War. Guillermo Moncada, a former carpenter from Santiago and a man of visible African descent, led the uprising, which key members of the Liberal Party disavowed. As before, the government attempted to construe the new rebellion as a race war, targeting repression in ways that supported this claim. This included blocking the entry of persons of color at Cuban ports, presumably to prevent the arrival of black revolutionaries from Key West, New Orleans, and Jamaica. The choice that Spanish officials made to racialize the rebellion thus had a disproportionate impact on black and brown émigrés in Key West who could not travel back and forth from Cuba as usual.[100]

Serra apparently joined a clandestine revolutionary club in Matanzas during this period, at the same time that Gómez and Martí organized similar clubs in Havana.[101] Yet in his efforts to become an author and teacher, Serra offered a carefully constructed alternative to the image, spread by the government, of the savage black bandit. The first issue of *La Armonía* announced, "Our flag is the flag of order."[102] Serra and his allies explained that far from sowing the seeds of disunion, the goal of the society was to "harmonize all the races and all of the social classes, beneath the sacred maxim of fraternity." This ideal (also expressed in the title of Gómez's newspaper, *La Fraternidad*) corresponded to the reigning ideology of class harmony within Spanish Republicanism as transposed onto Cuban race relations. The way to harmonize Cuban society, black writers argued, was to guarantee basic civil rights to the class of color.[103] *La Armonía* hoped to "bring about the disappearance of the prejudices of birth and these barriers that have dominated all humanity for so many centuries." Racial equality would not produce instability, according to this assertion, so long as public education and well-regulated associations were available to ensure "morality" and the "guarantee of public tranquility."[104] In fact, though Serra could not say so openly in Matanzas in 1879, this commitment to tranquility and social harmony was in no way a disavowal of the uprising in Oriente. In later writings, he made similar arguments that the separatist revolution itself was the enemy of disharmony and disorder.[105]

Serra's newspaper, *La Armonía*, did not last long. By the beginning of 1880, it ceased publication, likely because of limited funds. He soon started collaborating on the production of a weekly paper edited in Matanzas by Martín Morúa Delgado, a cooper of mixed African ancestry and an aspiring writer. Already in the late 1870s a rift had opened between Morúa and Gómez.[106] The two exchanged barbs in their newspapers, and would remain rivals throughout their careers, even after they both became senators in the days of the first Cuban republic. In later years, Serra would be a close ally and supporter of Gómez, but as he made his first forays into journalism, Morúa, although only slightly his senior, served as his mentor and guide. Serra later recalled working "under his direction and following his advice, which I accepted because I viewed him as more enlightened than me, which in reality he was."[107] Serra published poetry and political writings in Morúa's *El Pueblo*. In at least one instance, he took over as editor of the paper during Morúa's absence.[108]

The ability to appear in print made Serra a public figure in Matanzas, though in contrast to *El Eco de Ponce* (where Figueroa adopted a voice as raceless arbiter of good taste and defender of progress), Morúa and Serra made their first forays into publishing as representatives of the class of color.[109] They responded to the concerns of Liberal allies who debated the "social question," arguing that the sociedades could guide the "colored race" toward the new modes of public behavior, civility, and enlightenment that were necessary for citizenship.[110] Taking on this role, they negotiated an almost-impossible performance of public respectability. At that very moment, Cuba's leading form of popular entertainment consisted of bufos with white actors in blackface representing *negros catedráticos*, who used ridiculous, stylized speech, including mangled Latin and misused scientific terms. Onstage, negros catedráticos lectured benighted *bozales* (blackface characters who spoke Africanized Spanish) on the need to give up their savage ways. The joke was that people of such limited culture should lecture *anyone* on the proper ways to be civilized. Their attempt to instruct others revealed, precisely, their own comical limitations.[111]

There was much more to these plays than simple stereotypes. Playwrights often used blackface figures allegorically to make criticisms of the white creole elites (who fancied themselves aristocrats) or the colonial government. But there is no escaping the fact that the roles that Serra and Morúa adopted in their first forays into public life were exactly those that Cuban popular culture ridiculed. Men who "came from nothing" and hoped to become "something" had to take care because their rhetorical flourishes, their use of classical references, and their use of erudite vocabulary were all potential grounds for mockery as well as admiration. Perhaps this backdrop helps to explain the strategy of self-effacement employed by writers in *El Pueblo.* "A humble artisan, and in addition a member of the race of color," began a speech republished in *El Pueblo*, "I hope for the benevolence of the persons with better judgement than I, who make up this audience."[112] Serra frequently began articles and speeches with a similar rhetorical device. He also wrote, "Presumption is one of the ills suffered by the class of color," which should start with the humble task of self-transformation and only then make a claim to full recognition.[113] This was quite different from the tone that Figueroa developed in his first publications as a defender of progress, an arbiter of taste and beauty, and a humorous critic of conservative politicians.

As if the specter of the presumptuous black professor were not challenge enough, Serra and his colleagues contended with a mounting scandal in the Cuban press over the rising popularity of *danzón*. Danzón was a near-exact analogue of the Puerto Rican danza: a partner dance associated with urban people of color, and especially with Miguel Failde, a tailor and musician from Matanzas. As in danza, in the second section of each musical number couples danced in close embrace, with bent knees and legs intertwined. They interpreted basic steps with swiveling movements in the hips as well as shuffling of the feet. During the war, danzón had begun to catch on with young men of "the very best society" in Matanzas and Havana. Wealthy young men—men like the medical students imprisoned by the Voluntarios in 1871— hired Failde to play private parties (to which they also invited pretty brown women as dance partners). There was nothing particularly new in this kind of erotic encounter across class and color lines. White Cubans had long been attracted to dances and dancers that they perceived as racially impure, and therefore scandalously sensual. But during the war, white creoles in Havana and Matanzas began to adopt symbols of blackness as signs of their own rebelliousness in the face of colonial oppression. Danzón parties were thus doubly attractive as transgressions because of their erotic allure and their nationalist connotations. When the Spanish government relaxed restrictions on free association after the Pact of Zanjón, Failde and his Havana counterpart, bandleader Raimundo Valenzuela, became stars in the reconstituted white social clubs of Western Cuba. In response, the Havana newspaper *El Triunfo* launched a campaign against the contagion of "that stuff that the morenos and pardos of Matanzas call danzón." Over the next several years, white journalists kept up a steady stream of denunciations of danzón as indecent and uncivilized, a form of African witchcraft, "a tempting demon, that unsettles even the most prudent and quiet spirits." Some of these articles probably had the opposite of their intended effect, advertising precisely the aspects of the dance that made it most alluring to audiences of all colors.[114]

The increasing popularity of danzón as well as the wave of opposition by white journalists presented a dilemma for Matanzas club leaders and journalists of color. Failde and Valenzuela represented the widespread acceptance of danzón as a triumph for people of color, something to be celebrated, and a step in the direction of a desegregated popular social life.[115] They also supported the emerging sociedades de color by playing benefit concerts and dances.[116] Valenzuela even traveled to Key West to headline benefit concerts at the San Carlos.[117] There is ample evidence that Serra knew and moved in the same circles as Failde, though the relationship was not as close as Figueroa's partnership with Morel Campos.[118] So the popularity of the danzón must have presented a dilemma for Serra and Heredia. Maybe they personally loved the music and were proud of Failde's success. The sum total of journalistic attention to danzón, however, cemented the image of morenos and pardos as purveyors of bewitching rhythms, and their daughters as beguiling dance partners. The arrival of white men, seeking out such dance partners, at dances thrown by the sociedades de color in Matanzas was an awkward kind of racial integration, to say the least. One sociedad made a rule that white members were not allowed to come to dances unless accompanied by their spouses. Another announced that only members were invited to a dance headlined by Failde: "no transients."[119]

As journalists who placed themselves in the "public domain," and were deeply concerned that an unfavorable public perception of the sociedades would undermine their calls for civil and political rights, Serra and Morúa ended up taking a hard line against this sort of recreation. Serra wrote that the prevalence of gambling in the sociedades was "ridiculous," and dances attended by both men and women "are the seed of corruption and disorder." The sociedades should focus exclusively on education to close the cultural gap between whites and blacks because "enlightenment will be the brightest ray of liberty that will illuminate our frustrated path."[120] Morúa likewise argued for limiting recreation in the societies to literary readings. Sitting quietly in an audience, listening to poetry, speeches, and music, was a kind of activity, he wrote, that could elevate rather than degrade, and could "teach us the good manners of society, and about the treatment we owe to ladies."[121]

These publications offer a glimpse of the public persona that Serra began to cultivate in his early twenties as he made the transition from worker to intellectual, and would carry with him to the foundation of La Liga in New York: an unpretentious, austere, and sober advocate for black morality and self-improvement. Morality, he wrote in one of his first published poems, is "the science of duty," which instructs people how to "order their conduct," helping them to measure their actions and causing "their miserable passions to disappear."[122] It is tempting to imagine that this somber attitude was in part for show, that he would allow himself a few minutes to clap along to a rumba played by musicians in his neighborhood, or chuckle at one of Failde's clever lyrical and musical references to Afro-Cuban secret societies, before shaking his head and returning to his desk to denounce the cultural morass plaguing the class of color. It is tempting to imagine that Serra was able to accommodate restrictive social norms without internalizing them, to manage the pitfalls of building a public reputation without making a painful break with his own vernacular. But any such idea remains in the realm of speculation. There no evidence that his private attitudes to social dancing diverged from the stern opposition he expressed in print.

Developing an impeccable reputation for morality was also essential because exercising leadership in institutions that could dispose of resources gathered from members was an extremely delicate matter. The names given to the sociedades de color, La Concordia, La Armonía, and La Unión, emphasized the philosophy that free association had the power to neutralize social conflict, but in fact the sociedades were often beset with interpersonal struggles. These began at La Armonía almost as soon as it was founded, "with each struggling for his own benefit and sweeping away in quick measure our humanitarian aims." As various candidates for leadership competed for the right to manage resources and collect small stipends, they were vulnerable to (and frequently resorted to) rumors and accusations of self-dealing. Serra seems to have been victim of this kind of public denunciation. In response to "murmurings," Serra published an accounting of the amount that he collected each month from paying students and from the charitable fund established for poor students. He also published the results of his fund-raising campaign. He then challenged critics to do the sums. Given the costs of materials and renting the schoolroom as well as his donation of his own time, could they really say that he was not in fact operating the school at a personal loss? These were treacherous waters, and it is small wonder that Serra, years later, would appeal to Martí to take on the role of "Inspector" at La Liga, with responsibility for reviewing all the accounts and receiving reports of any "infraction, negligence, or suspicion."[123]

At the same time that he created this reputation as an austere moralist and unassuming advocate of humble self-improvement, Serra planted the seeds of a political strategy that he would pursue throughout his career: his school accepted white students. The figure of the upright black teacher demonstrating Christian charity to poor white children had a long tradition in the Spanish-speaking Caribbean, most notably in the figure of Rafael Cordero in Puerto Rico. As the Cuban labor movement and Cuban liberals began espousing racial unity, without creating adequate multiracial institutions, and as white Cubans of all political perspectives expressed concerns about independent black organizations, which might plot a racial rebellion to avenge slavery, Serra helped develop a new kind of institution. La Armonía was independent enough and shaped enough like a sociedad de color in its basic functioning to allow him a leadership role, and to provide benefits to constituents of African descent. Yet it did not exclude anyone on the basis of race. Serra presented La Armonía (and his allies would continue to celebrate it time and again in the coming decades) as one of the first institutions in Western Cuba to put into practice the ideals of equal treatment and racial integration.[124] Years later, he and his allies would make the same arguments about La Liga.

EXILE

Serra's first forays into the "imposing debates of the public plaza" thus differed in dramatic ways from Figueroa's—despite the fact that the two islands they called home operated under the same colonial political structure, and despite the extensive circulation of ideas and popular culture between them. Both men had experienced the fear of racial violence at the hands of Voluntarios, both negotiated the racial overtones in debates about scandalous partner dancing, both suffered through the popularity of blackface stereotypes onstage, and by the end of the 1870s, both were excluded from suffrage under the same electoral law. Yet in Ponce, Figueroa adopted the voice of an author unmarked by race or class, a defender of industry and progress, a fearless mocker of craven politicians, and an arbiter of good taste. Perhaps not all readers accepted his right to be unmarked in this way. But it was in this direction that his ambition sought and found room to maneuver. At almost exactly the same moment, in Cuba, Serra took on the role of the carefully unpretentious spokesman for the class of color and charitable teacher of children of all colors.

This reflects both the differences in the systems of racial classification and exclusion in the two settings in the wake of the massive importation of captives from Africa to Cuba in the early part of the century, and the differences in the ways that liberal politics evolved in the different parts of the Spanish Caribbean, creating different kinds of opportunities for literary self-making, and a different relationship between that project of self-making and antiracist politics. The way that race and politics worked in Cuba had led to the emergence of separate institutions for the class of color, which encouraged (or required) ambitious men of African descent to identify with and write on behalf of all members of that group. This allowed for formal civil rights activism, but it often meant that the most vehement interventions that writers of color made in the public plaza consisted of stern admonitions directed at the class of color for its ostensible failings of morality and civilization. The way that race and politics worked in the small cities of Puerto Rico, in contrast, created the possibility of social identities that modified or cut across racial status. Urban workers of African descent could participate in integrated artisan institutions and even—briefly—in electoral politics. Men of African descent who became writers could participate in liberal literary institutions and newspapers. Figueroa's mentors were, in more than a few cases, men of pardo origins whose upward social mobility had allowed them to acquire the privileges of whiteness. This encouraged and allowed Figueroa to express an identity as a writer that was not explicitly shaped by his status as black or brown. This was neither obviously more em-powering nor obviously less so. Although the context in San Juan and Ponce did not afford him race-based institutions in which to defend the interests of people of color, it provided him space to embed his antiracist politics within a broader defense of men of merit against the interlocking injustices of colonial tyranny, political corruption, privilege, and preju-dice. Each of these trajectories as writers would adapt when Serra and Figueroa became migrants, moving into the different political and intel-lectual contexts that had emerged in exile communities, including the one that was home to Gerónimo and Juan Bonilla.

Serra moved to the United States first. In spring and early summer 1880, the second insurgency in Oriente, the Little War, began to weaken. The Liberal Party, including many former revolutionaries, continued to disavow the movement. The white separatist leadership in New York, afraid of the accusation that they were fomenting a race war, refused to support Maceo's efforts to return to Cuba to lead the fighting. Spanish au-thorities made a wave of arrests of suspected separatists in Western Cuba, specifically targeting black and brown leadership. Morúa was caught up in this dragnet, though eventually released. In Havana, authorities arrested Gómez in March 1880, sending him into exile. By June, the insurgents fighting under José Maceo and Moncada surrendered to Spanish authori-ties. In August, a second group of insurgents surrendered, and Antonio Maceo abandoned his efforts to reach Cuba and join the fighting. The last isolated bands of fighters surrendered in the months that followed. Morúa and Serra produced the last issue of *El Pueblo* on August 15, then closed up shop and departed for Key West. According to Morúa, he and Serra fled to Key West in order escape imprisonment for their separatist activi-ties. Serra, in contrast, said that the two journalists fled when the colonel of the local fire brigade tried to forcibly enlist them.[125]

Relocating to Key West, Serra parted ways with Heredia (the two re-mained married yet lived separately for the better part of two decades), but crossed paths for the first time with the Bonillas and the other mi-grants who had been developing social and political institutions in Key West for more than a decade. Having been in Key West for only a few months, he likely attended the meeting called by the "émigrés of color" who gathered at the San Carlos to protest the rumors spread by the Span-ish government that the recent war was "a cry of vengeance raised by the black race against the white race." The intent of Spanish propagandists, a group of writers chosen to represent the assembly concluded, was "to dishonor our race before the severe justice of posterity" and to justify the savage repression underway in Cuba. To the contrary, they argued, the men of color were in perfect agreement with the separatist movement: "its ideas are our ideas." They then laid out a set of values that while perhaps shared by some separatists, was unfortunately not shared by all. They professed their commitment to unity and love among all Cubans in a free republic, with "all of the freedoms and all of the civil and political rights." The group favored a system of public offices based on merit, free universal public education, and the disappearance of social inequality "by means of education."[126]

In Key West, Serra quickly shifted his own literary work from stern admonitions about the evils of social dancing to full-throated separatism. Either he had been developing a complex vision of the relationship between liberalism, racial equality, social class, and independence before leaving Cuba—sotto voce—or he was an exceptionally quick study. He published his first pamphlet, a long-form poem titled *Laments of an Exile*, shortly after the gathering of the "émigrés of color" at the San Carlos. Introducing himself to a new audience, he began, of course, with an apology for his own "meager" abilities: "Forgive me, oh fatherland, if I am impertinent / directing my voice to you." Independence, Serra then explained, meant freedom of the press, freedom of religion, and the abolition of "privilege"—a notion drawn from the black civil rights movement and labor struggles. He wrote,

> In an independent Cuba
> The unjust owner will succumb
> And the oppressor of the proletariat
> Will lie forgotten in his tomb.

In this poem, Serra adopted a new voice, a nostalgic exile steeped in the great literary classics of the nationalist canon. This was frequently the voice of a Cuban, a man whose race did not condition his ability to speak for the nation. But it was also a voice—like that of the émigrés of color who had drafted their protest against Spain a few months earlier—that noted the special cruelty of the Spanish regime toward black people.

Fatherland, balsam of my soul,
Why does this path lead me toward exile,
Denying me your sweet essence,
Only because I descend from the black race?
Why have you shut with limitless strength,
Those doors that I ask you to open?
Why do your despots call me guilty
Before I have committed any crime?[127]

A year later, he published a second, longer canto of the poem *Lament of an Exile*, dedicated to the Cuban Independence Center in Key West, where he had recently read his verses in public, and providing an extensive primer (supported by five pages of footnotes) on historical and political topics. This work seems to reveal his own diligent research, his increasing comfort at presenting himself as a well-informed observer of contemporary affairs, and a desire to provide cigar makers who had dedicated less time to study with crucial information about Cuban politics.[128]

Serra continued to develop his voice as an author and a political leader in ways that drew on the understanding of racial identity that he had developed in Havana, and on his first experiences as a poet and journalist in Matanzas. For instance, he read his verses at gatherings of the local *sociedad de color*, El Progreso, and surely interacted with the men who drafted the protest of the "Cubans of color" in response to Spanish propaganda. But he also began his long trajectory as a migrant of color, with ties to both white Cubans and African Americans, in the United States. In Key West, for example, he encountered local institutions established by nationalist intellectuals and by cigar workers that had no analogues in Havana or Matanzas. He became an officer in the racially mixed San Carlos Club.[129] At the same time, he probably met the Bonillas, and certainly met other migrants of African descent who had participated in Republican politics and interacted with African American neighbors for more than a decade. He likely met some of those neighbors as well, for the first time interacting with teachers and journalists of African descent from outside Cuba. Yet Key West was only a jumping-off place before Serra relocated to New York around 1882. The Bonillas moved there at about the same time. It was their experience in that city, with its unfamiliar and unpredictable landscapes of race and politics, that would ultimately shape their careers as writers and political activists. But what was it like to be a black immigrant in New York in 1882? How did that experience shift or reinforce certain kinds of politics or literary efforts? The answer requires turning to several new characters: the Cubans of color who first settled in New York City and created the community within which Serra and the Bonillas eventually built La Liga.

∎ *3* ∎

Community

You arrive at one of New York City's great piers with no resources of any kind; as clever and agile as a student and as hungry as a school teacher.... What?! You do not understand English? You are intimidated by the incessant howl of the locomotives, the dizzying agitation of the factories, and the presence of a million persons who trample one another as they pass, then continue walking as if taking no notice? ... Go as fast as you can, as if you had urgent business. You must find a friend, as soon as possible a friend, or a countryman.

—Francisco Gonzalo Marín, "Nueva York por dentro," 1892

On a Monday night in 1892 in New York City, a group of immigrants from Cuba and Puerto Rico, most of whom were women and men of color, crowded into the two-room apartment on the first floor of 74 West Third Street, the headquarters of the educational and recreational society known as La Liga.[1] By this time, the special relationship between the leadership of La Liga and José Martí, the famous poet and journalist who had emerged as the leader of the Cuban nationalist movement in New York, was firmly established. On most nights of the week, only the male members of the club gathered for classes in geography, history, politics, and composition. They pursued the primary purpose of the society: the "advancement of the intellect and elevation of the character" of "men of color, born in Cuba and Puerto Rico," and especially their own ascent into "careers or occupations that are not commonly held by members of the class of color."[2] Men from humble backgrounds, they came to the club after long days working as cooks or cigar rollers in order to refashion themselves into professionals—an aspiration that many brought with them from Havana, Matanzas, and Key West. Martí taught classes each Thursday at the club, helping the men to polish their writing and speaking, and engaging them in discussions of his evolving political ideology. In response, the men of La Liga were the first to put their votes, their contributions, and their reputations on the line to help Martí consolidate the Cuban Revolutionary Party, founded at the beginning of the year. They mobilized to help him secure the powerful position of delegate in the party. Together, in speeches and in his newspaper, *Patria*, Martí and the most vocal spokesmen from La Liga—among them Serra, Figueroa, and Juan Bonilla—promoted the idea that the love and caring among men of different social classes and races, put into practice at La Liga, was the model of social interaction that should be adopted by the revolutionary movement as a whole.

This was a Monday, though. And on Mondays, another, more basic set of activities took place at 74 West Third Street—activities related to the club's secondary mission of "creating pleasant and respectable gatherings for the families of the members." On Mondays, La Liga was an immigrant social club, where women and men gathered to listen to music, recite poetry, see friends and relatives, meet up with sweethearts, and eat ice cream. Members' children were there too, including older children who had grown up in the United States, but who "speak our language and who incline toward our customs."[3] The members were careful that these events should be, above all, cultured and dignified. They were, of course, familiar with the admonitions of their abstemious leader, Rafael Serra, a veteran of the controversies over dancing in the social clubs of Matanzas and Havana, to beware of the enervating influences of the "narcotic of danzón."[4] They were also aware that accounts of their social activities were likely to become public because of the relationship that existed between club leaders and Martí.

Martí sometimes attended the social evenings held by the club on Mondays, and was cordial and attentive to all. He relied on the leadership of the club to help him remember and recognize the names of the men and women who attended. After one Monday gathering, he wrote two urgent notes to Juan and Gerónimo Bonilla, asking for "the names of the young ladies who sang and recited . . . and of any other person, outside of our intimate friends, whom I should not forget."[5] He then inserted the names of otherwise-anonymous immigrants into the public record through the transcendental power of typography (courtesy of Figueroa, who set the type and oversaw production for *Patria*). He etched the beautiful singing

of a Miss América Fernández and the performance of the poem "Amalia"
by a Miss Petrona Calderín, and others, into the nationalist public sphere
as the paper circulated and was read aloud in workshops across the city.[6]
Their names became part of the generalized celebration of La Liga, where
the people who gathered "after the exhaustion of the workday, are those
who know that the only true good fortune lies in friendship and culture;
those who feel or see for themselves that being of one color or another
does not limit a man in his sublime aspiration; those who do not believe
that earning his bread in one trade gives a man fewer rights or obligations
than those who earn theirs in any other."[7] Later their names became visible to history, as scholars assembled the vast printed corpus of the movement in Martí's *Collected Works.*[8]

Even immortalized in this fashion, these accounts of Mondays at La
Liga offer only a hint of a dense social world that the immigrant members
of the club created and maintained in New York. We read that Gerónimo
Bonilla and the woman he had recently married, a widow named Isabel
Acosta, both recited poetry at a Monday gathering. But we can only imagine that they were among the sweethearts who met and courted at other
such community gatherings. Gerónimo's younger brother Juan also may
have met his young wife, Dionisa Apodaca, at this kind of event. Her father
was a cigar maker and a founding member of La Liga. Her mother was the
midwife Josefa Blanco, who along with another midwife Gertrudis Heredia,
served as the president and vice president of the women's groups that operated out of La Liga. The two midwives delivered the babies born to the
women who gathered on Monday nights at La Liga to take part, children
on their laps, in evenings of music and poetry. They would soon deliver
the baby that Dionisia was, on this particular Monday in 1892, carrying
in her womb. When the two Bonilla brothers married Isabel and Dionisia,
when their children were born, did their families, along with the Apodacas,
the Serras, and others, celebrate together? Gerónimo and Isabel's marriage
certificate offers only a hint. The witnesses to the certificate were a married couple, Magín Coroneau and Lorenza Geli. He was a member of La
Liga, and she a member of the women's groups led by the two midwives.
Along with Blanco, Apodaca, and Acosta, she was part of the photograph
album of the women of La Liga that Serra published in 1899.

Already this series of names is dizzying, but these are just a few examples of the kind of evidence that exists, hinting at the immigrant social

network—the community—within which the unusual intellectual projects and political alliances created by Serra, the Bonillas, Figueroa, and
Martí took shape. But how did this community come into being? And how
might one hope to imagine and recount its emergence without devolving
into paragraph after paragraph listing dozens of names and relationships,
the many fragments and interconnections that constitute something as
unwieldy as a social network? We can begin by taking up more of the radial lines that intersected at La Liga, particularly the story of a man named
Germán Sandoval. Sandoval was a cornerstone of the community out of
which La Liga emerged. Indeed, when the members of La Liga first met at
74 West Third Street to inaugurate their new club, they elected Sandoval,
not Serra, to be their president. Sandoval's leadership did not reflect the
kind of literary self-making attained by Serra, Figueroa, and the Bonillas.
Serra wrote of him, "He is neither a politician nor does he aspire to be one;
he is not a rich man, nor a man of letters, nor a man of science." Sandoval represented something else entirely. As Serra observed, "Through the
correctness of his character, through his constancy, and conscientiousness
in all the obligations that he takes on, he has been the moral leader of our
community for a space of twenty-nine years."[9] Politicians and intellectuals, men like Serra, later relied on this community, but it was built by
immigrants like Sandoval, who were "ordinary" in the sense that they did
not write and publish their own works, and that little was written about
them. But as we will see, there was nothing ordinary about them.

Sandoval and other Cubans of African descent faced a set of problems
common to all newcomers: how to pay for travel, where to live in a new
city, where to work, where to find familiar foods, where to worship, whom
to marry, how to resolve unexpected legal, health, or financial problems,
where to bury their dead, and perhaps most important, whom to trust. Yet
each of these questions produced different answers for them than for Cubans who were seen as white. Amid the noise, bustle, and babel of incom-
prehensible languages, migrants had to decode under what circumstances
they would be subjected to insults to their dignity because of their physical appearance. They had to determine if frequenting certain spaces in the
city, moving their bodies in certain ways, or speaking to certain people
would provoke violence or harassment by authorities or everyday citizens.
They needed to know when and where women and girls faced risks of
sexual harassment and violence, and from whom.[10] Migrants who, in the

context of the Caribbean, understood themselves to be brown rather than black, or whose social reputations had improved to the point where African ancestors or features were no longer mentioned in polite company, faced the special challenge of accommodating themselves to the potentially unfamiliar ways that New Yorkers perceived them.[11]

These questions were central to an experience we might call "migrating while black." They could never be far from the minds of the first wave of Cuban and Puerto Rican migrants who looked black to other New Yorkers, or whose color might be called into question, when they set out to rent an apartment, find work, get a haircut, order a glass of beer, enroll a child in school, attend church, go to the theater, or sit on a park bench. And although the questions were by no means unfamiliar—these immigrants had long experience of tense racial politics in their own societies—the answers were potentially unpredictable. For Pachín Marín, a Puerto Rican writer who arrived in New York decades later, and joined forces with Serra, Figueroa, and the Bonillas, the solution to the problems of newly arriving in New York was obvious: "You must find a friend, as soon as possible a friend, or a countryman."[12] But in the 1870s, Cubans came from a society where hundreds of thousands of people were still held as property, and where the question of race permeated debates around colonial reform and independence. They settled in a city with an additional set of rules and hazards organized around color. The challenge for the Sandovals and other early settlers lay precisely in determining who was a friend and who was a countryman. The solutions that they found to this problem—including turning sometimes to African Americans, sometimes to white Cubans, and sometimes only to one another—are crucial to understanding the emergence of the community that would later coalesce around Serra, the Bonillas, and Martí in the evening activities at La Liga.

THE COLOR LINE

The couple that would appear as witnesses on the marriage certificate of Gerónimo Bonilla and Isabel Acosta in the late 1880s were, as noted above, Lorenza Geli and Magín Coroneau. She was a Cuban woman of African descent who arrived in New York in the early 1870s as part of a household headed by a British sugar merchant named Henry Brooks.[13] She rode in a first-class compartment on the steamer from Havana to

New York, probably in order to care for the couple's three-year-old and infant daughters. She then lived and worked as a domestic servant in their home on West Thirty-Third Street, near Fifth Avenue. (If this house were still standing today, it would be overshadowed by the hulking mass of the Empire State Building, later built directly across Thirty-Third Street.) She remained in service to the Brooks family even after, in 1878, she married Coroneau, a man of African descent who had arrived in New York from Santiago in 1870. Port officials recorded that Coroneau was a servant too, traveling in the company of a French widow and her Cuban daughter. He seems to have worked as a cook in the rooming house that the two women established, serving the wealthy Cubans and Puerto Ricans who stayed there.[14]

At the beginning of the Ten Years' War, New York had no large community of Cuban artisans like the one already forming in Key West. The Cuban population, though numbering in the thousands, was a tiny drop in a vast ocean of humanity, far too small to constitute an ethnic neighborhood of any kind.[15] In contrast to Key West, the émigré community in New York was disproportionately made up of wealthy and highly educated Cubans—merchants, planters, brokers, and professionals—who moved to the city to conduct business and to educate their children, and in some instances to escape political repression.[16] This panorama dramatically shaped the experience of early black and brown migrants from Cuba, nearly half of whom lived and worked as domestic servants in the homes of wealthy white Cubans.[17]

Wealthy Cubans thus provided an important social network for their nonwhite dependents, though not one predicated on their equality or autonomy. The Brooks family, for instance, probably resolved many of the practicalities of immigration, arranging for Geli's passage, lodging, and travel documents, even as they relied on her to resolve the challenge of traveling for four days and nights with two small children.[18] This pattern of domestic service helps situate some of the conversations about racial and class equality that took place in nationalist circles. Many members and supporters of the Cuban Junta, the body that represented the Cuban insurgency in the United States during the Ten Years' War, were former members of the slave-owning class or veterans of the Economic Society in Havana. It is not surprising to find that they often had black or brown Cubans living as servants in their households. In some instances, the servants used the same surname as their employers, suggesting that they or their parents had formerly been enslaved by the families with which they emigrated.[19]

When Lorenza Geli and Magín Coroneau arrived in New York, a small contingent of Cubans of color had also begun to settle in independent lodgings, outside homes headed by whites. Most of these independent settlers did work similar to that performed by domestic servants. They were waiters, cooks, porters, laundresses, and seamstresses. Most appear only fleetingly in the historical record so it is difficult to know for whom they performed these services, or exactly how they came to emigrate and settle in New York. But Geli and Coroneau, for instance, eventually settled out of domestic service and into their own household. They became entrepreneurs and seem to have done quite well. When Coroneau died in 1909, he left property including real estate in New York and Santiago, money in the bank, and twenty shares of stock to Geli's niece and to his two sisters in Cuba.[20] This kind of dramatic upward trajectory was likely quite rare among migrants who arrived in the context of domestic service. Judging from the death certificates of Cubans in New York in this period, it was more common for such migrants to die penniless of tuberculosis, of dysentery, or in childbirth, and to be buried in one of the city's potters' fields. But there are other, more modest instances that also clearly show that some servants settled out of homes headed by wealthy Cubans into independent lodgings in the city.[21] Coroneau and Geli's story also points to some of the ways that early settlers of color, even those working in the households of wealthy Cubans, formed horizontal networks, marrying one another and relying on one another as witnesses in administrative transactions, to find housing, or to organize the migration of friends or relatives.[22]

In addition to vertical social ties with wealthy Cubans and horizontal ties with one another, the first black and brown Cubans who settled in the city seem quickly to have developed important ties with African Americans. Lafayette Marcus, who arrived from Havana at the beginning of the Ten Years' War, may first have made the trip to New York not as a member of a wealthy Cuban household but instead as part of the crew of one of the many vessels that linked the city with Cuba. The shipping lines that provided passenger service between Havana and New York offered elegant accommodations and meals to first-class travelers on a journey that typically lasted at least four days and nights. Steamship companies therefore employed a full contingent of service staff, which might explain why Marcus sometimes appears in historical documents as a waiter and sometimes as a seaman. Perhaps he was both.[23] Marcus married an African American woman from Connecticut named Fredericka. In 1870, the couple shared an apartment on Wooster Street with their young daughter and two other African American couples, who may have been Fredericka's kin.[24] This too was by no means an isolated case. At the time, one out of four Cubans of color in New York who lived in households of their own was married to an African American.

The stories of the Coroneau and Marcus families reflect the experience of the approximately two hundred Cubans of color in New York at the beginning of the 1870s. This panorama started to change, however, when manufacturers began hiring Cuban workers to turn imported tobacco into "Clear Havana" cigars in the city. By the early 1870s, two steamboat companies offered weekly passenger service between New York, Philadelphia, Key West, Mobile, and New Orleans. In 1875, a strike in Key West failed, leaving many workers penniless and disillusioned.[25] News of higher wages available in New York brought the first wave of black and brown cigar makers to the city, including Sandoval, originally from Havana, who moved to New York with his wife, Magdalena, by about 1875. They soon became the leaders of an emerging community that included newly arriving cigar makers of color and many of the cooks, porters, and waiters who preceded them, such as both Marcus and the Coroneaus.

The first black and brown cigar workers who settled in New York found housing almost exclusively in African American enclaves, especially in the southern part of Greenwich Village and the Tenderloin, the blocks between Sixth and Eighth Avenues north of Twentieth Street. These African American enclaves were not the sprawling and densely settled black neighborhoods of the kind that would become so familiar in northern cities after the turn of the twentieth century. African Americans constituted about 2 percent of New York's population counted on 1870 and 1880 censuses. They lived, for the most part, in neighborhoods that were between 5 and 10 percent black, though many were scattered in neighborhoods that were whiter still. Yet this relatively low level of racial isolation did not mean that black people could live anywhere they wanted. The journalist Jacob Riis, famous for his muckraking account of New York's working-class districts, wrote, "The color line must be drawn through the tenements to give the picture its proper shading. The land-lord does the drawing, does it with an absence of pretense, a frankness of despotism, that is nothing if not brutal."[26] White renters, he noted, typically preferred not to rent apartments that had previously been occupied by black renters. Landlords took advantage of these prejudices to charge black renters higher rates for inferior housing. Lines of residential segregation, while minimal at the scale of neighborhoods, were stronger at the scale of city blocks, and extremely stark on the scale of multifamily apartment buildings. Black New Yorkers (those who were not live-in servants in white households) lived in buildings that were, on average, 70 percent black. They lived in households that were, on average, 90 percent black. For Greenwich Village, this pattern can be seen on map 4. The Tenderloin and surrounding area, shown on map 5, demonstrates another wrinkle in this pattern of segregation. East of Sixth Avenue and west of Eight Avenue, African Americans were present in many buildings, but typically only as live-in servants in households headed by whites.[27]

Generally speaking, Cubans whom census takers identified as black or brown were limited to the same inferior and more expensive housing reserved for black New Yorkers, while it was extremely rare for Cubans identified as white to live in such buildings.[28] Serra later explained, "They will not rent to us in almost any decent area. And when they 'do us the favor' they charge us a higher rent."[29] The segregated housing market, with its network of oppressive social relations dominated by rental agents and collectors, thus encouraged black and brown cigar makers to turn principally to one another in resolving the question of housing rather than to the white Cubans among whom they had lived in Key West. The Sandovals settled in an apartment building at 89 Thompson Street, one of two on that block occupied almost entirely by African Americans. Over the next decade, the Sandovals offered temporary lodging to a steady stream of black and brown cigar makers arriving from Cuba and Key West, including the Bonillas.[30] The apartment at 89 Thompson served as a resource for migrants of color as they first navigated the segregated rental market in an unfamiliar city. When they looked for a friend or a countryman to resolve this problem, many turned to the Sandovals.

Because of the highly localized system of racial segregation, the Sandovals and their lodgers lived in close proximity to white Cubans, including many cigar makers who lived in white-only tenements on nearby blocks.

But the reigning system of housing segregation ensured that they were in closest day-to-day contact with the non-Cuban residents of the building at 89 Thompson, all of whom were African Americans. These residents included a whitewasher, a barber who was also a musician, a hotel porter, several women who "kept house," and several others who took in laundry.[31] The Sandovals and their many lodgers and houseguests would have shared a privy or a bathroom with these neighbors. They would have overheard neighbors' arguments through shoddily constructed walls. They would have smelled the foods that their neighbors cooked, and heard the music that they played and sang. All the residents of the building likely sat on the front stoop on sweltering summer evenings in the hopes of a breeze.[32] Once the Cubans began to learn English, they may have complained together of the abuses of a landlord, discussed baseball, or played the informal lottery known as "policy." The Cubans may have heard stories of the terrifying violence that white neighbors had unleashed against African Americans in New York City in 1863, the notorious Draft Riots. They may have shared their own accounts of the horrors of slavery in Cuba and of the unfolding revolution in Oriente. The children who lived in the Sandoval apartment may have played together with the other children in the building in the hallways or on the stoop.

It is difficult to know what the Spanish-speaking people who settled on Thompson Street, and in other African American enclaves on Greene Street, Sullivan Street, Minetta Lane, and East Twenty-Seventh Street, thought of the smells, sounds, and personalities that they encountered in their new buildings. Anyone who has lived in a tightly packed apartment, trying to sleep through the heavy footsteps of upstairs neighbors, knows that this kind of close contact is as likely to breed animosity as warm feelings of friendship. In fact, the *New York Times* produced a surprising number of reports about "Cuban Negroes" in this period, almost always highlighting the more violent and salacious details of this kind of everyday intimacy with African Americans. In 1876, for instance, the *New York Times* reported that a "Cuban negro and waiter" had attacked his lover, a "young colored woman," and another man, a "Cuban negro, cigar maker" who lived at 21 Thompson Street, because the woman planned to marry the second man. A few years later, the paper wrote that a "Cuban negro" of "bad reputation" reportedly threatened a "colored woman" living on Minetta Lane because she did not accept his proposal that she leave her husband and run away with him. Even allowing for the considerable racism and sensationalism of these stories, they hint at some of the everyday texture of this shared social world.[33]

It is also difficult to know what the Cuban settlers thought about the high levels of poverty and social distress, and the extremely negative reputation, of the spaces they were forced to inhabit. The "moral turpitude" of Thompson Street (where the Sandovals lived), Jacob Riis wrote in 1890, "has been notorious for years," a kind of "border-land where the white and black races meet in common debauch."[34] In an extended and shockingly racist exposé on life in the tenements of Greenwich Village, Stephen Crane called Minetta Lane (where Lafayette Marcus and many other well-respected Cubans of color lived) one of the most "enthusiastically murderous thoroughfares in New York." He noted that "nearly all the streets thereabouts were unmistakably bad" on account of the district's "negro" residents, who were "among the worst element of their race."[35] Whether or not they agreed with these assessments, Cuban cigar makers of African descent seem to have hoped to construct respectable living quarters within the constraints of the segregated housing market. Serra, for instance, explained that part of the problem of the segregated housing market was precisely that "I want to keep my family far from any dangerous contact."[36] In doing so, they found common cause with more affluent African Americans in the city, often settling in the same more acceptable corners available behind the color line. The most dramatic example is the case of Sarah and Carlos Crespo, a Cuban couple who, in 1876, became lodgers in the Brooklyn home of Philip White and Elizabeth Guignon, prominent figures in African American social life in New York City and in local civil rights activism. Philip owned a pharmacy and was a member of the Brooklyn Board of Education. The Crespos lived with White and Guignon for at least eight years.[37]

This tendency of some Cuban immigrants of African descent to seek out lodgings in residential spaces owned or occupied by relatively well-situated African Americans has a clear consequence for our story. After staying for a time with the Sandovals at 89 Thompson Street, Juan and Gerónimo Bonilla rented a pair of rooms from an African American couple named Charles and Harriet Reason. Charles A. Reason was an engraver and jeweler, from a family well established among New York's African American elite. He was a leader in a prominent African American social club.[38] The rented downstairs apartment, in the Reasons' two-family row house at 74 West Third Street, is where Serra, Martí, the Bonillas, and others gathered to found La Liga in 1889. It is where Martí's famous speeches and composition classes took place, and where the community gathered for Monday evening social events. Several chroniclers of events at La Liga mentioned the plaque on the front door of the building reading, "Reason." One even noted, poetically, that Reason was the name of the "mistress of the house." But none explained that this mistress was an actual person, Harriet Reason, or took the time to mention who she was. Only by connecting these dots do we see something that must have been obvious to everyone who attended gatherings at La Liga: the "central point" where all the radial lines of the "vast sphere of resurgent nationalism" converged was located in a residential space shared with African Americans of comparatively high economic status. The Reasons and their children mingled with the crowds that gathered at La Liga, frequently finding opportunities to chat with Martí. A decade later, then widowed, Harriet Reason married Alfredo Vialet, a Cuban violinist and a member of La Liga. (74 West Third Street is on map 4. Note that at the time of the 1880 census, the Reasons had not yet moved there, and the building's residents were all enumerated as white.)[39]

At the same time that early Cuban settlers began to live in spaces shared with African Americans, some started to participate in elite African American social institutions. The Crespos and the Sandovals, for instance, joined the Saint Philip's Church, the congregation that comprised, in Serra's words, "the most aristocratic element of the class of color in New York," including the Reasons, the Guignons, and the Whites.[40] The members of Saint Philip's congregation shared the Cubans' desire for dignified treatment and comfortable housing as well as some political concerns. Many at St. Philip's were active, for example, in the New York Anti-Slavery Society, which now that slavery had been abolished in the United States, organized events to express support for the "interests of the Cuban negroes."[41] Notably, African American members of the Anti-Slavery Society hosted a banquet to honor the Cuban general Antonio Maceo when he arrived in the city for a brief visit in 1878. This gathering was held at the home of noted black abolitionist and civil rights leader, Reverend Henry Highland Garnett, at 102 West Third Street.[42] It is not clear if the Sandovals or their many houseguests participated in any of these events. But it would surely have been a thrill to know that the general was in their city and neighborhood.

The Cubans and New Yorkers who shared residential spaces also faced similar constraints on their efforts to educate their children. New York City did not begin to desegregate its public schools until 1883. So up until that year, the residents of the Sandoval household and African American residents of the building at 89 Thompson Street most likely all sent their children to the school for children of African descent that was located nearby on South Fifth Avenue.[43] One remarkable story gives insight into how members of the community that the Sandovals had started to construct made use of African American institutions in order to educate their children. In 1876, a Havana couple named Bibián Peñalver and Carolina Roger sent their eleven-year-old son Pastor to New York to pursue an education. Pastor lived in the city for two years, studying at the grammar school of Principal Charles L. Reason (on West Forty-Seventh Street), before his parents and siblings joined him.[44] Reason was a university-trained mathematician, a close political ally of Philip White, a pharmacist, and a member of the Brooklyn Board of Education in whose home the Crespos lived. He was also the uncle of the engraver Charles A. Reason, in whose house La Liga would later hold its functions.[45]

How did news of the school reach the Peñalver family? Which friends or countrymen were available to help the boy find his way in the immense din and relentless bustle of New York City? The answer to these questions may lie in a ship's manifest showing that Pastor arrived on the same steamer that carried a cigar maker well known to the Sandovals, Cándido Olivo.[46] Olivo was a man of color who had arrived in New York in the early 1870s, had become a US citizen, and had traveled back to Cuba on his US passport. Perhaps it was merely a coincidence that he returned home to New York on the ship that carried young Pastor. Or maybe he was one of those who, on visits from New York, brought news of the free public school run by a man of Reason's renown to the artisan clubs and sociedades de color in Havana. Maybe the Peñalver family entrusted their son to him to help the boy manage the journey, and to get settled in safe and respectable lodgings. All this is a bit speculative, to be sure. But we know for certain that Pastor, after completing school, would become an accomplished musician as well as an important bridge between elite African American social circles and the emerging social network organized by

Germán Sandoval and other Cubans of color. Later still, he would be one of the founding members of La Liga.

Ties with African Americans—created through residential arrange-ments, intermarriage, segregated churches and schools, or shared political concerns—proved to be a crucial resource when black and brown Cuban settlers created their own formal social institutions, which they began to do more than a decade before founding La Liga. In 1877, Germán San-doval founded the Logia San Manuel, a fraternal lodge and mutual aid association for Cuban men of color. Many of the men who lived at 89 Thompson joined the lodge, as did both Pastor Peñalver, when he came of age, and Magín Coroneau. The men received a charter for the lodge from an African American institution, the Grand United Order of the Odd Fellows (an organization that also figured in my earlier account of Key West). The most "aristocratic element of the class of color" in New York had created the first Grand United Order lodge three decades earlier, after the white Independent Order of the Odd Fellows rejected its application for a charter. After the Civil War, groups of African American men had es-tablished lodges in towns and cities across the United States, all linked to the emerging national institution of the Grand United Order. Along with black churches, black fraternal lodges became the backbone of an emerg-ing African American civil society in these years. Sandoval worked with members of the Order in New York to translate its rites and texts into Spanish. His translations became the basis for the San Manuel lodge in New York, and for the creation of Spanish-speaking Grand United Order lodges in Key West and Cuba soon thereafter.[47]

Cuban New Yorkers also joined a second major institution of African American civil society in this period, the Prince Hall Grand Lodge, an independent Masonic order tracing its roots to the period of the Revo-lutionary War.[48] Three years after the creation of the Logia San Manuel, Abraham Seino (who had also lived for a time at 89 Thompson), Lafay-ette Marcus (whom we met earlier, sometimes a seaman and sometimes a waiter, married to a woman from Connecticut), and several of the cigar makers living on Minetta Lane created a lodge affiliated with Prince Hall Masonry, the Logia Sol de Cuba No. 38. This was more than just a matter of convenience, although it is true that white Freemasons in the United States would never have considered their petition. The founding mem-bers seem to have been deeply integrated into African American social life prior to creating the lodge. Seino, Marcus, and at least four other founding members of the lodge were already married to African American or Afro-Canadian women at the time.[49] The founders were also already initiated into African American Freemasonry as members of existing English-speaking lodges in New York. Indeed, Marcus had not only become a member of the Mt. Olive Lodge but he actually held the post of "Master," the leader in the lodge, before spearheading the effort to translate the lodge rites and apply for a charter to create an independent lodge operating in Spanish.[50]

Deep connections between Cuban migrants and African Americans, built in residential settings, in mixed marriages, in political gatherings, and in churches and lodges, made it possible to create these two lodges for Cubans of color. At the same time, the effort to establish separate lodges seems to reveal a desire for some distance from English-speaking neighbors, landlords, fathers, and brothers-in-law—a desire for a community defined by Spanish language and Cuban origin as well as by color.

The two lodges nevertheless provided an avenue for continued contact with elite African American social life. Most notably, lodge activity put Sandoval, Marcus, and their brothers in contact with members of other lodges, with leaders in the broader Masonic and Odd Fellows orders, and with African American newspaper readers and writers, who were frequently also Odd Fellows and Masons. As early as 1880, the African American newspaper the *People's Advocate* reported on an anniversary reception organized by the San Manuel lodge: "After the usual ceremony by the Order, all joined in the Union March, until the coronet sounded for the first quadrille. The Lodge was organized about two years ago, and is composed exclusively of our Cuban American friends, and is now in a prosperous condition."[51] Several years later, a second African American newspaper, the *New York Globe*, reported that the leadership of the St. Johns and Covenant lodges attended a meeting at the Sol de Cuba headquarters on South Sixth Avenue. These brothers assisted Marcus in the rituals necessary to induct new officers: "After the installation a grand collation was given which was enjoyed by all present, and the small hours were having their being before the participants felt it incumbent upon them to leave the mystic haunt of the El Sol de Cuba."[52] The following year, the grand master of the Prince Hall Order in the United States was in New York making his rounds of the local lodges. He visited Sol de Cuba, where, according to the *New York Freeman*, he was "received royally."[53]

Social ties between Cubans of color and African Americans also frequently spilled out of "mystic" and secretive lodge activities into larger gatherings that included women and the uninitiated. Such gatherings probably began at about the same time that the first lodges were created. The Crespos, at least, would likely have attended the many elegant soirees organized by White and Guignon in their Brooklyn home. But the first reporting on this kind of contact appears in 1883, when Sandoval and the Logia San Manuel started organizing annual "Cuban American picnics," designed to bring together African Americans and Cubans of color. Unlike lodge meetings, these picnics included women and dancing. An advertisement for the third of the Cuban American picnics, held in 1885, shows how densely interconnected this social world was. The organizing committee included Pantaleón Pons, formerly a resident of 89 Thompson Street, as well as several other men who were members of *both* San Manuel and Sol de Cuba. The advertisement also announced that the young violinist Pastor Peñalver, now recently graduated from Charles Reason's school, would provide entertainment.[54]

Peñalver was, by then, a well-regarded musician in the city, and an important bridge between the Cuban and African American social worlds. He advertised his services regularly in the *New York Freeman*, and played concerts for English-speaking Odd Fellows lodges, the Bethel AME Church, and a range of other societies and clubs. Notices of his performances in the local African American press suggest that he was a versatile violinist who offered solo performances of classical music (Richard Wagner seems to have been a specialty) and also led a ten-piece orchestra able to perform at functions where "dancing was heartily indulged in."[55] This suggests a tantalizing question. What kind of music did Peñalver's band perform at the Cuban American picnics? Did he introduce African Americans in New York to the danzón, the syncopated partner dance that was taking Cuba by storm—risking rebuke from men like Serra? Did he, who had grown up with African American classmates and teachers, introduce the Cubans to the African American dance music that a decade later would come to be known as "ragtime"? One way or the other, his performances at these Cuban American dances represented an early exchange between Afro-Cuban and African American musical cultures. Scholars have long seen this kind of mutual influence, described by pianist Jelly Roll Morton as the "Spanish tinge," as deeply influential in the early development of jazz.[56] How remarkable that this musical mixture took shape, at least partly, in the same social context that eventually served as a backdrop to the singular political coalition built by Serra and Martí.

ETHNIC TIES

We might stop here, concluding that when Cubans of color arrived at the docks in New York, when they faced the task of finding a friend or a countryman, what most shaped the choices they made was race. Yet as illuminating as evidence of extensive residential, kinship, social, and even musical ties with African Americans may be, it is not the whole story. Black and brown cooks, cigar makers, and even laundresses and house-wives were also deeply embedded in social networks and spaces in the city that linked them to white Cubans, especially the area of the city where the Cuban cigar factories were located. We know, for instance, that San-doval lived in an apartment in Greenwich Village that became a hub for newly arriving migrants of color, and that put him in close contact with African Americans. We know that he joined an African American church. We know that he participated in African American fraternal life and orga-nized Cuban American picnics. But it is also true that Sandoval spent his working hours in another part of the city entirely. He and two other cigar makers, Salomé Rencurrel and Pantaleón Pons, traveled every day from the apartment that they shared at 89 Thompson Street to the workshop of Federico Knudsen, a Cuban importer and manufacturer whose shop was located in a building on Maiden Lane, in the heart of the Cuban cigar district (see map 3).

Since cigar workers typically worked up to ten hours a day, six days a week, where they worked is as crucial as where they lived to their experi-ence of the color line in New York. Just as the residential color line shaped the social world they shared with African Americans, their integration into the Cuban cigar enclave shaped the social world they shared with other Cubans.[57] Unfortunately, historians do not have a thorough picture of the Cuban cigar district, and little to go on to determine how workers of color experienced it. It is clear that cigar manufacturing was one of the largest industries in New York by the end of the 1870s, with thousands of factories employing tens of thousands of workers, most of them German and Bohemian immigrants. Most New York manufacturers introduced mechanized processes in this decade to reduce the skill necessary for cigar production. They began to incorporate women into the workforce and to speed up the process. This led to a rapid erosion of wages and to rising labor tensions, including a major strike involving more than ten thousand workers in 1877. New York's cigar factories became an incubator for the new trade union movement, especially the American Federation of Labor, which defended the prerogatives of white, male workers.[58]

Sandoval and other Cuban rollers surely watched the unfolding of these events with great interest. But they were largely removed from the massive and increasingly mechanized cigar industry in the city. Cuban and Spanish manufacturers developed a highly specialized niche in the cigar industry. They got higher prices for cigars made with imported Cuban tobacco and produced through the traditional hand-rolling method. They eschewed the mechanization adopted by their local competitors, and typically hired only Spanish, Cuban, or Puerto Rican workers, who knew how to hand roll perfectly shaped cigars.[59] This relatively privileged niche in the cigar trade was where the men who created the San Manuel and Sol de Cuba lodges, and where eventually hundreds of other black and brown cigar makers, spent most of their waking hours, quietly rolling cigars while listening to comrades or itinerant lectores read aloud from newspapers, novels, and social theory.[60] In 1880, Sandoval and the others at the Knudsen factory were better paid than most white cigar workers in the city, although they earned less than skilled workers at the most prestigious Cuban workshops. Their effective income was also depressed compared to those of white workers by the fact that they had to pay higher rents for inferior apartments—a kind of tax on color.[61] Still, they were not subject to mechanization and replacement with lower-paid women and child workers. They were responsible for their own time, and their incomes depended on the quality and number of cigars that they were able to produce—a combination of skill and work habits. This was a kind of work from which most of their African American neighbors were excluded. A few black and brown Cubans even made the jump from artisan to small manufacturer.[62]

None of this suggests that race had ceased to matter in shaping the opportunities available to cigar makers of color or their experience in the workshops. Indeed, in his first years in New York, Sandoval worked in a tiny factory that only regularly employed two other men, both men of color who also lived in his apartment. It is possible that the one or two other men who sometimes worked there were white. But it is also possible that his working hours, at least in these early years, did not offer substantially more contact with white Cubans than his domestic life. It is not clear if this kind of clustering by color was typical of the first Cuban and Spanish workshops opened in the 1870s. Were some shops more hospitable to black workers, and others more hostile, either because of the prejudices of employers or pressure from white workers wary of competition? Were cigar workers of African descent in New York more likely to end up in lower-status shops or working on lower-quality tobacco, and therefore for lower piece rates, because some employers imagined them to be less skillful? Given what we know about Cuban society—in Havana, after all, many factories still employed slaves—the emergence of perfect racial equity in New York cigar factories would be surprising. We can imagine at least that the first generation of workers of color to break into the New York workshops felt the constant need to vindicate themselves through the quality of their craftsmanship, the careful exercise of thrift, and the dignity of their comportment. Something of this is visible in Serra's account of one of these early settlers, José C. López, a man who would be elected vice president of La Liga and would later become a colonel in the Liberation Army and a politician. A child of "humble parents," this López was distinguished not only "for his industriousness, for his culture, and for his inexhaustible patriotism" but also for "the comforts with which he surrounded himself and the elegance with which he dressed, owing to his notable agility in the profession to which he dedicated himself, and to his admirable economic administration."[63]

Over time, some, and possibly even most, Cuban employers and workers became enthusiastic defenders of exemplary men of color, seeing their support for men like Sandoval and López—self-made, upright, and skilled—as evidence of their own commitments to class solidarity, meritocracy, or national unity. So it is not surprising to learn that in 1885, when New York City detectives scoured the city for a black cigar worker who was a suspect in the murder of Chang Ong, a Chinese Cuban man known in Spanish as Antonio Soloa, they brought their witness to "all of the cigar factories where Cubans are employed," asking him to cast his eyes over the faces of more than one thousand men. This episode gives a glimpse of an early experience of racial profiling. On that day, every one of the cigar workers who belonged to the Logia San Manuel and Logia Sol de Cuba, and many future members of La Liga, would have been called out in front of workmates as a criminal suspect. But it also demonstrates that these men were, by the mid-1880s, widely dispersed in the Cuban cigar factories. Otherwise, the detectives could have conducted a much more efficient operation, searching only those shops employing black and brown Cubans.[64]

The same was likely true of the broader worker culture that grew up around the Clear Havana workshops. Most of these factories clustered in the area around Pearl Street and Maiden Lane, within a few blocks of the steamship lines that connected New York to Cuba and Key West.[65] The area was a dense commercial district, marked by many kinds of economic activity. For instance, Sandoval, Pons, and Rencurrel worked in a building that housed several Cuban cigar workshops, but also a wholesale paint shop, a liquor distributor, a house painter, and a druggist, none of which was even remotely connected to the Cuban émigrés.[66] Even at the peak of Havana cigar production, when hundreds of operatives spent their working days in the Cuban workshops, it would have been hard for an outsider to recognize the area as a Cuban enclave. Yet the fact that the Cuban cigar shops were clustered in one part of the city provided opportunities for workers to build relationships across the many large and small factories where they worked. There were other Cuban workers in other workshops in the same building, on the same block, and in the same neighborhood— men with whom they crossed paths each day. However they chose to represent their industriousness, culture, agility, and careful economic administration as they moved through the streets, it was likely that some white Cubans, starting with their employers, were nearby to observe them.

The most important moment for this kind of contact was lunchtime, when all the factories emptied, and men crowded into informal dining rooms in the cigar district to converse over plates of sautéed salt cod or chopped kidneys alongside a "salad" of rice and beans. This food was typically prepared and served by "negro cook[s] and waiters," including, probably, some of the cooks and waiters who were members of the San Manuel and Sol de Cuba lodges. According to a report in the *New York Times*, the clientele in these establishments was, likewise, heterogeneous to a fault. There one could find "gabbling" Cubans with "beautiful eyes and teeth," to whom the reporter attributed the "look somehow of a tributary race," as well as Filipinos, Chinese, Brazilians, and "all of the motley people, including Mexicans, who live to the south of us." It is notable that the reporter did not mention black Cubans among this "motley crew." Yet from what the broader historical record shows about the evolving culture of cigar workers in the city, it is highly unlikely that these restaurants excluded black and brown diners.[67] The proprietors of these dining rooms were sometimes Cubans of African or Chinese descent too; by the early 1880s, José Chacón and Chang Ong, who was murdered in 1885, both operated eating houses in southern Greenwich Village. By the early 1890s, Pedro Calderín, an officer of La Liga, had opened a restaurant on Sullivan Street.[68]

Eating in the Cuban dining rooms, near the factories or in Greenwich Village, would have allowed men like Sandoval to build a broader set of relationships with workers in other shops, some of whom they probably knew from Key West, participating in the extensive exchange and comparison of cigars that ended every meal.[69] These transactions would have allowed them to build reputations as connoisseurs and expert craftsmen outside the boundaries of their individual workshop and across racial lines. Dining rooms and other shared spaces in the cigar district also provided an opportunity for workers in different shops to engage in labor organizing. While in New York, many workers shifted from mutualism to various forms of socialism and anarchism. Some made contact with recently arrived participants in the Paris Commune or joined the Second International. They developed a shared worldview that, in the words of historian Evan Daniel, "honest (nonexploitative) work was the source of all wealth and the centerpiece of human existence." They shared the view that the manufacturers kept too much of this wealth for themselves as well, and increasingly, a belief that workers ought to unify across divisions of race and nationality. By the early 1880s, male workers of African descent not only had access to well-paying skilled labor in New York's workshops but they also were included in the multiracial and increasingly radical labor organizations created by Spanish-speaking workers in the Clear Havana district.[70]

Finally, the fact that they spent their days in the Cuban cigar district meant that black and brown cigar rollers, cooks, and waiters had the opportunity to participate in conversations with white Cubans about the nationalist cause. Most of the leading merchant houses, the offices of many Cuban

professionals, and the editorial offices of the Spanish-language newspapers
were in close proximity to the Havana steamship piers, and therefore the
cigar workshops.[71] Because of the highly localized patterns of class and
racial segregation in the New York housing market, these wealthier exiles
often lived within a few blocks of cigar makers, black and white. This pattern can be seen especially clearly on map 5. The wealthier Cubans who
occupied these offices, including the men who owned the cigar factories,
who held official positions on the Cuban Junta in New York, and who published several of the Spanish-language newspapers in the city, were not
necessarily reliable allies. The leaders of the Junta, appointed by the government in arms in Cuba, hedged in their support for independence. Many
openly worked for annexation to the United States. Others remained hope-
ful for reforms to Spanish rule that might grant a greater role in Cuban
government to wealthy creoles while preserving the existing economic
order. By the mid-1870s, some members of the Junta, including its leader,
a wealthy planter named Miguel de Aldama, supported the Democratic
Party. Aldama and his supporters also tried to hold back the insurgent military from its strategy of attacks on sugar plantations and began to express
concerns about Antonio Maceo, the free man of color from Oriente who
was rapidly rising in the ranks of the insurgent military. They warned that
he sought to impose himself as a dictator, that he disobeyed orders, and that
he favored black soldiers over white. They eventually undermined his attempts to return to Cuba to join the Guerra Chiquita, leaving him stranded
in Saint Thomas. Aldama and his supporters frequently supported cigar
manufacturers in their conflicts with workers.[72]

At the same time, however, a second group of wealthy and highly educated exiles opposed the annexationists and reformists who controlled
the Junta as well as the government in arms. This radical faction began
reaching out to workers, going so far as to call their organization the Society of Cuban Artisans, though they were in fact professionals, writers,
and businessmen. True to their roots in the liberal traditions of Spanish
Republicanism, the radical nationalists encouraged the creation of mutual
aid societies and donated their time to worker education organizations—
decades before the creation of La Liga. Their publications expressed support for striking workers and even sympathy for the much-reviled Paris
Commune. Some in this faction also adopted the antiracist values that had

emerged in the populist wing of the nationalist movement, reaching out specifically to émigrés of color.[73] We can catch a glimpse of this in the funeral of Francisco Vicente Aguilera. Aguilera was the Cuban planter, readers may remember, who freed hundreds of his own slaves at the beginning of the Ten Years' War. Having risked his life and lost his fortune, he lived modestly in New York where he became a favorite of the radical and populist faction. He later assembled Cubans of color in Key West to resolve their differences with white nationalists. Then he befriended the young journalist Juan Gualberto Gómez, who served as his translator on a trip to Paris in 1876. When Aguilera died in New York in 1877, a group of black and brown Cubans living in New York claimed the honor of carrying his coffin fifteen blocks from the Church of St. Francis Xavier to its resting place in Marble Cemetery. José Chacón, the restaurateur who had recently opened his first eating house on Greene Street, was among the pallbearers. So were Abraham Seino, then living at 89 Thompson Street, and Manuel Coronado, a resident of Minetta Lane. Both were cigar makers who would help to create the Sol de Cuba lodge three years later.[74]

Another glimpse of the institutions that linked black and white Cubans in New York comes from a report by a Spanish informant that a Masonic movement, centered in New York, espoused "the union of all the elements against Spain" and "equality of conditions of color." According to the report, witnesses had seen "gentlemen, or so they seemed, sitting among blacks and mulattoes, fraternizing."[75] This account, similar to many produced by Spanish spies, was likely unreliable on many grounds, yet it was not completely fanciful. Other sources confirm, for instance, that a physician named Ramón Ylla, a veteran of the worker education efforts, created the J. M. Céspedes lodge in New York early in 1878.[76] The members of this lodge did, in fact, espouse racial equality. The ritual that lodge members used for the promotion of a member to "disciple of honor," for instance, required an officer of the lodge to raise an object (not identified in the liturgy) and explain that it symbolized the "equality of all men." He then recited,

It is true that inequalities exist in society, but these have been created by man and will disappear as we begin to extirpate pride and selfishness. Each day it will become clearer that any inequality not based on merit,

not acquired according to the works of each person, is contrary to justice, and the day will come in which the members of the great human
family will no longer divide themselves along lines of purer or less pure
blood, of one race or another, or of this or that social hierarchy."[77]

These ideas clearly prefigure Martí's later stance on race, although it
is not apparent how frequently the lodge lived up to its ideals by initiat-
ing black or brown aspirants. And as might be expected, given the deep
divisions among Cubans in exile, the wealthier men in the Order of the
Caballeros de la Luz, to which the lodge was affiliated, were not necessarily in agreement over how or whether to put into effect the principles
of equality. They did not follow the example of the Masonic lodge in Key
West in barring pardos and morenos from membership and prohibiting
discussion of race. But at one meeting of a sister lodge in Philadelphia, a
member expressed concern about "how many mistakes have been made,
through carelessness in easily admitting persons who were not well
known to us, and without confirming what sort of work they did or their
occupation."[78] In 1877, the year of the great labor mobilization in the
cigar industry, some members sought to use lodge funds to create night
classes for workers, but the proposal was voted down.[79] By 1879, as the
insurgency split over the Pact of Zanjón and the Guerra Chiquita, it was
evident that lodge members were anything but united on the question
of racial equality. One member complained that the "lodge resembled a
Messalina, occupying herself in gathering up sons of all the classes and
all colors." Messalina was a Roman empress famous for her voracious
sexual appetite. The reference here means not just a dissolute woman but
specifically an aristocratic woman who prostitutes herself with men of
low rank. Another man, objecting to the constitutional clause declaring
the equality of all men and universal fraternity, withdrew his candidacy
to the lodge.[80]

The records of lodge meetings in New York are lost, but it seems likely
that similar conversations took place in lodges, mutual aid societies, revolutionary clubs, eating houses, and workshops in that city too, and in other
spaces where Cuban nationalists interacted across lines of race and class.
By consolidating ties with the "friends" who were sometimes available
among wealthier exiles, working-class exiles might secure help in time of
crisis and might push the nationalist movement toward a more inclusive

view of who was a "countryman." But even the merchants, doctors, and manufacturers who most openly espoused racial equality had not necessarily shed, as historian Ada Ferrer has put it, the deeply ingrained "personal habits of mastership" that led them to expect deference from workers and people of color.[81] The failures of wealthy émigrés in this regard may have soured men like Sandoval on the possibilities of meaningful inclusion in institutions controlled by wealthier men, such as the Céspedes lodge. Even if those lodges were not technically segregated, such disappointments may have helped to inspire the creation of separate lodges like the Logia San Manuel and the Logia Sol de Cuba, where men like Sandoval would be in control of membership committees, where they could determine whose moral and physical qualities were suitable, and whose were unsuitable. Yet these same disaffections probably helped draw clear lines as to which white journalists, politicians, professionals, and especially workers, among all those who claimed to be racially egalitarian, were actually the most trustworthy and the most likely to repress deeply held prejudices in order to treat less fortunate or differently colored comrades with dignity.[82]

What is more, a shared distaste for the judgment, condescension, and political conservatism of certain merchants, planters, and manufacturers seems to have helped to solidify relationships between men like Sandoval and white Cuban workers across racial lines. The clearest evidence of this kind of multiracial social network comes from 1876, when some members of the Cuban Junta aligned with the Democratic Party, supporting the presidential campaign of New York governor Samuel Tilden. Tilden was an opponent of African American voting and civil rights, and a proponent of "states' rights"—positions that must have been deeply troubling to Cubans of color who knew about the rise of the Democratic Party in the South. He was also the leader of a municipal reform movement that sought to restrict suffrage for working-class whites in northern cities. The defection of leading Cubans to the Democrats owed, in large part, to frustration with the incumbent Republican, Ulysses S. Grant, who had declined to support the Cuban insurgency. But Tilden's message that government should be in the hands of a "better class" of citizens appealed broadly to wealthy and educated New Yorkers, Cubans among them. Tilden's project was anathema to many working-class New Yorkers, of course, leading to mass protest rallies in summer 1877, the months immediately leading up to the great cigar makers' strike.[83]

The support of the Cuban Junta for this profoundly undemocratic Democratic candidate was, likewise, anathema to the populist faction in the exile movement in New York, which began for the first time to recruit Cuban cigar workers into electoral politics in October 1876. A white cigar maker named Agustín Yorca took the lead, personally escorting fifty-seven men to the courthouse in October 1876 to become citizens in time for the presidential election in November. He helped nearly sixty more to naturalize in time for the 1880 election. Nearly all these men were cigar makers or cooks, and (as was the case in earlier electoral mobilizations in Key West) many were men of color, including Rencurrel, Pons, and the others who, shortly thereafter, created the Logia San Manuel and Lógia Sol de Cuba.[84] The nationalist journalist and factory reader Ramón Rubiera de Armas was witness for a smaller number of cigar makers as well as for some wealthier exiles. The black cigar maker, Cándido Olivo, whom we met earlier returning to New York in the company of the eleven-year-old Peñalver, also helped in the effort to bring artisans to the courthouse to naturalize. Meanwhile, merchants, manufacturers, and professionals continued to naturalize in large numbers, relying on a different set of witnesses from their own social circles. The naturalization records seem to indicate two distinct political networks within Cuban New York—distinct communities of friends and countrymen mobilizing to bring one another to the polls. One of these networks, which had begun to form in previous elections, linked together the wealthier and more educated exiles in the city. The other, started by Yorca, Rubiera, and Olivo in 1876, linked together Cuban workers and a handful of intellectuals, drawing them together across the idiosyncratic color line in Greenwich Village. Yorca lived, at the time, in an all-white building at 221 Thompson Street. Olivo lived in a "colored" building directly across the street, at 220 Thompson.[85]

The primary motivation for the men who naturalized with Yorca in the month before the 1876 election seems to have been voting, an act of manly citizenship denied by Spanish law at the time to most Cubans, white or black.[86] Quite apart from the deepening class and political divisions within the nationalist movement, and the repudiation of Tilden's proposal to restrict suffrage, the experience of voting in New York was intense. Voting took place in public, with party officials stationed to recruit, cajole, bribe, or intimidate voters at the last minute. Electors frequently arrived in groups, demonstrating their loyalty to particular party or club leaders.[87] The tumults that ensued were especially tense for black voters. In 1863, New York had seen the worst urban race riot in US history, a bloody pogrom waged by white New Yorkers against African American neighbors. As recently as 1869, white voters in Greenwich Village had overwhelmingly opposed and successfully blocked a state referendum to extend suffrage to black neighbors. After the ratification of the Fifteenth Amendment, the state of New York finally extended the right to vote to African American residents. Still, armed federal marshals oversaw federal elections in the city throughout the 1870s to protect black voters and crack down on alleged voter fraud in Democratic precincts. Democrats accused the marshals of voter intimidation and responded by stationing New York Police Department officers at polling stations as well. So in addition to a free-for-all of white voters and party operatives at polling stations in Greenwich Village, the black and brown Cubans who voted for the first time walked into the middle of a tense standoff between federal marshals (some of whom were African American) and the New York City police.[88]

Does the fact that the founders of the Sol de Cuba and San Manuel lodges chose to become US citizens within social networks shared with white Cuban workers and populist nationalists mean that they also gathered on Election Day and went to the polls with these men? Or did they naturalize with other Cubans but go to the polls with the African American religious and civil rights leaders with whom they lived and socialized? Or was the intersection among these distinct groups of friends and countrymen relatively fluid, allowing for multiple kinds of affiliation and coalition within the umbrella of the Republican Party? Whichever the case, it seems significant that male exiles spent their days in the racially integrated work spaces and dining rooms of the Cuban cigar district, taking part in the evolving discourses of racial inclusion that circulated among one faction of the Cuban nationalists and workers who gathered there. The idiosyncratic color line in neighborhoods like Greenwich Village meant, too, that white exiles like Yorca often settled on the same block, and in the same election district, as black and brown exiles like Olivo and Sandoval. This allowed for the emergence of neighborhood-based alliances among groups of migrants who hardly ever lived in the same buildings.

GENDER LINES

This movement back and forth between the racially segregated residential spaces of Greenwich Village and racially mixed public spaces in the Cuban cigar district (or spaces that straddled the color line in Greenwich Village) is still only half the story of the community that the Sandovals and others began to build. Daily movement out of apartment buildings shared with African Americans into the workshops and eating houses, participation in labor mobilization, and voting were all experiences limited only to men. Women's experience of migration, and of building community in relation to Cuban social hierarchies and the local color line, was quite distinct. Magdalena Sandoval, for instance, lived at 89 Thompson Street with her husband, Germán, her son, Enrique, and a wide assortment of lodgers. In 1880, she reported to census takers that she was "keeping house," as did most Cuban women in New York, independent of race. In this role, Magdalena probably did many of the same day-to-day tasks performed by women who worked for wages: cooking, cleaning, washing, and childcare. But she enjoyed the far-higher symbolic status associated with performing domestic labor in one's own home and of being a married woman. And while she did not receive wages for domestic work performed for her husband and son, the family probably received money from their many lodgers in exchange for her labor. She may also have been able to direct the work of the other women and girls in her household.[89]

Still, while Germán and his male companions spent ten-hour days, six days a week, in the cigar factories and evenings at lodge meetings, Magdalena likely spent her mornings, afternoons, and evenings in or near their Greenwich Village apartment. Although her labor was crucial to the domestic space occupied by the men who created the first lodges for migrants of color, she could not have shared the cross-racial camaraderie of the cigar workshops or eating houses. Yorca did not come collect Magdalena to walk to the courthouse. Instead, according to the laws of the time, she received "derivative" citizenship when her husband naturalized.[90] Even after becoming a citizen, she did not apply for a passport. Like children and servants, wives were expected to travel on passports granted to their husbands. And of course, Yorca did not come looking for Magdalena and the other women in her household to go to the polls on Election Day. It did not matter that federal marshals had been sent to enforce African American citizenship rights and New York City police officers had been stationed to defend the voting rights of immigrants; women had no right to vote.

This does not mean that these women were literally confined to their apartments, dutifully attending only to the domestic sphere, but it does serve as a reminder that Cuban women experienced the city differently from men. Because the nature of this difference also tends to minimize their presence in the historical record—they generally do not appear in city directories, lodge membership lists, voter registration lists, naturalization records, and so on—reconstructing their experiences requires some imagination. We can begin with the case of Mary Costello, a schoolgirl who lived at 89 Thompson. Available records show that Mary was born in New York around 1868, the daughter of a black Cuban cigar worker, one of the first to come to the city, and his wife, a woman from Scotland. It is not clear what happened to Mary's parents, but by the time she was twelve, they were out of the picture. The girl lived under the care of Magdalena. Because she attended school, Mary ventured out of the apartment into the city on a daily basis. She and other Cuban children who grew up going to New York City schools likely served as resources for adult women in their households, who had less fluency with English and less experience moving through the city. In getting to and from school, or running errands for Magdalena, Mary also probably faced the challenge of unwanted sexual attention from men in public spaces. While this was not unique to black girls, Historian Lakisha Simmons has noted that "coming of age" for black girls was made difficult or even dangerous by the presumption that they were sexually available at a young age. Perhaps as young as twelve, Mary would have known which public spaces put her at greatest risk for "meddling" and how safely to respond to verbal assault.[91]

The threat of unwanted attention was probably a challenge in encounters with Cuban men as well, should Mary venture into the Cuban cigar district during working hours. According to the *New York Times* account of the Cuban restaurants of Maiden and Pearl, "Sometimes a woman, with the dark skin, the massy, jetty hair, the flaming melting eyes of the Spanish race, daintily enters. She is the wife, the sister, the daughter, the sweetheart of one of them. Instantly the scene is tremulous with a gigantic bustle. . . . Every man is on his feet, bowing."[92] This may be a literary flourish, based on generalized stereotypes about the exotic attractions of the women of the "Spanish race" and the baroque chivalry of Latin

American men. Yet it highlights the relative absence of women from these spaces, and raises the question of whether the wives and daughters of black and brown cigar makers received the same kind of chivalrous attention. What kind of response would Mary, a young woman of mixed race, elicit given the consistent representation in Cuban popular culture—from cigarette packages to bufos—of mixed-race women as sexually attractive and available? Was the workshop where a husband or father (or in Mary's case, surrogate father) worked, or a restaurant where he took his meals, a space reliably free of disrespectful male treatment? Perhaps occasional encounters with the wives and daughters of their black and brown comrades provided a way for white comrades to put into action their expressed commitment to racial equality.

Another way to understand the different relationship that women had to space in segregated New York, and thus their different relationship to community, is to consider the different but equally urgent set of problems immigrant women had to resolve in their capacity as mothers and homemakers. The case of Carolina Roger, a seamstress from Havana, provides a view of this. Carolina had sent her eleven-year-old son Pastor to New York in 1876. Several years later, her husband, Bibián, a confectioner, joined the boy in the city.[93] Finally, Carolina made the long voyage in a steerage compartment on a steamer, along with her four other children, aged five to fourteen.[94] Carolina was, at the time, eight-months pregnant. Her experience of arriving at the docks, her need to find a friend or a countryman as quickly as possible, surely was quite different from the urgency felt by the character described by the poet Marín, the unattached male bohemian. She would give birth to another son three weeks after arriving in New York.[95]

Childbirth presented an especially pressing problem for immigrant women, and although many births still went unregistered at the time, this was one of the few moments when the details of their lives were sometimes copied into the historical record. At no time would the need to "find a friend" have seemed quite so acute as when the first pains of labor began. In fact, finding "a friend" was probably not sufficient. From what scholars are able surmise about childbirth and parenting practices in Cuba, it seems more likely that immigrant women preferred, if possible, to gather together in groups to accompany an expectant mother in her confinement and to share in the care of small children. Domestic labor was no less social than cigar making. If possible, these groups should include women with experience with labor, practical skill as midwives, and the necessary spiritual gifts to mediate the will of God, the saints, or the ancestors. It would also be particularly helpful in the case of a difficult birth or childhood illness if some of these women knew how to find a physician, and had (either directly or through the men in their families) the resources to pay a doctor or the necessary social ties to engage physicians with or without the promise of immediate payment.[96] It is not possible to know if Carolina had become acquainted with any women in New York yet, after only three weeks, or who may have gathered at the apartment on West Forty-Seventh Street for her lying-in. But it is clear from the baby's birth certificate that Julio J. Henna, an eminent physician from Ponce, Puerto Rico, and a prominent figure in the independence movement, attended her birth.[97] This was by no means an isolated instance. Birth certificates reveal that in a surprising number of cases, Cuban or Puerto Rican doctors made their way into the segregated buildings of Greenwich Village to deliver the babies of African-descended women.[98]

It is impossible to unravel with certainty the social network that linked these men of high social status to the working-class women of color whom they attended in childbirth. Historians know that many doctors in New York saw great economic potential in promoting their own participation in childbirth and actively competed for this business. Some of these Spanish-speaking doctors (most notably Henna) were participants in the liberal and nationalist movements, which likely put them in contact with working-class men. It is possible that they arrived at the homes of women like Carolina through the intervention of husbands who approached them in the male public spaces of the cigar district, drawing on bonds of obligation strengthened by nationalist sentiments or by old-fashioned patron-client relationships. But it is also possible that these doctors built relationships specifically with immigrant midwives, who almost certainly attended most of the births in this community. These women likely attended labor, supervised the social activities around lying-in, provided postpartum care, and instructed new mothers on breastfeeding and infant health. If everything went well, no report was made to civil authorities. In difficult cases, they brought doctors in for specific interventions, especially the use of forceps and the administration of chloroform, while continuing to control all other aspects of the birth. In these cases, doctors diligently submitted the paperwork for birth certificates.[99] Such encounters would have been laden with meaning. The arrival of a baby allowed for a symbolic expression of national community, united across class and racial lines in joy over the arrival of a new Cuban. Perhaps such events also allowed doctors, midwives, and parents to confirm their shared belief in the capacity of black women to be modern, hygienic mothers under the steady supervision of breadwinning husbands and enlightened medical professionals, at a moment when many in Cuba and the United States opposed black citizenship based on the claim that black women were not capable of civilized motherhood.[100]

The pressing need to resolve the challenges of childbirth thus simultaneously created connections among working-class women of color and, in not a few cases, to male exiles of much higher social status. The labor and expertise of midwives, and possibly also their ability to build and manage ties with physicians, made them central actors in the formation of this immigrant community, helping to explain the prominence of two midwives, Heredia and Blanco, in the women's groups later formed at La Liga. As the Cuban and Puerto Rican women of La Liga gathered, with children on their laps, to create their first charitable society and their first political club, they elected as their leaders the women who had delivered those children, who had seen them safely through the most joyful, painful, and perilous events in their lives.

REVOLUTION AND COMMUNITY

Thus when Serra and the brothers Bonilla first arrived in New York in the early 1880s, they, similar to other migrants who looked like them, depended on the multiple, overlapping social networks that Cubans of color had created in the city since the mid-1870s. But how does the new evidence about the emergence of this community, about the institutions that Cubans created in response to their experience of migrating while black, change the more familiar story of exile and revolution that has been told about these men, their fervent patriotism, and their remarkable alliance with Martí? Through the mid-1880s, the available record provides only hints. In the case of Serra, there is little to indicate exactly where he lived during his first period of residence in the city, between 1882 and the middle of 1885. These were the years of the first Cuban American picnics, but it is not clear what contact Serra had with Sandoval, Marcus, or the two fraternal lodges. Similarly, it is not apparent what relationships, if any, he created with African Americans in the city. It seems relatively certain that Gertrudis arrived in New York during this period, to be reunited with her husband temporarily. Still, there is no evidence that she practiced as a midwife during this period in New York, or participated in the social networks created by women and physicians. These months together seem to have been when the couple conceived their daughter, Consuelo. It was also probably when they planned out the next phase of their separation. Heredia returned to Cuba to enroll in the certification course for midwives at the University of Havana a short time later. Consuelo was born in Matanzas soon after.[101]

There is more evidence linking Serra to attempts to reorganize the nationalist insurgency during his first stay in New York. In 1882, he met Flor Crombet, a brigadier of mixed racial ancestry who was a veteran of both the Ten Years' War and the Little War.[102] This is probably when he first encountered Martí, who was also a relative newcomer to nationalist circles in New York. Serra was almost certainly in attendance when the "Independencia Club" met in a "dark basement room" in Clarendon Hall in 1883. Reporters noted that the company consisted mainly of cigar makers, "many of whom [were] negroes." The group began raising money to help free José Maceo and other officers imprisoned by the Spanish government at the end of the Little War. With a promise of backing from several wealthy Cuban New Yorkers, they also issued invitations to the commanders of the previous insurgent campaigns in Oriente—Antonio Maceo, Crombet, and Agustín Cebreco, who were all men of color, and Máximo Gómez, who was generally recognized as white—to return to the field.[103] By fall 1884, there is strong evidence that Serra was absorbed in these efforts. When the generals arrived in the city, they summoned him to the Griffou Hotel, where they had set up their headquarters. Shortly thereafter he volunteered for the expedition, receiving a commission as a lieutenant and shipping out to Jamaica in June 1885.[104]

The details of meetings between the military officers and prominent civilian exiles at the Griffou Hotel, on West Ninth Street, are part of the classic narrative of Cuban nationalism. The wealthy Cuban New Yorkers who had backed the invitation to the generals, unwilling to jeopardize negotiations with Spanish authorities in order to recover property in Cuba, withdrew the promise of financial support.[105] Then Gómez, famous for his prickly and authoritarian character, insulted the young poet who had been elected to lead the fund-raising campaign for the expedition, José Martí. Martí, in turn, withdrew his support for the expedition, arguing that as a democratic principle, the military leadership should be under firm civilian control. At a public meeting, a supporter of the generals accused Martí of "wearing a skirt." The poet is famously said to have replied, "I am so much a man, that not only cannot I not wear a skirt, I cannot fit into my underwear," volunteering to demonstrate his manhood at any moment that his opponents chose. Martí was then removed from all his positions in the movement and withdrew almost completely from nationalist activity for several years. Though already a well-known writer, Martí was not yet the central nationalist figure he would later become. His participation was not vital to the expedition. But this break was representative of a bigger problem. The revolutionaries had arrived in New York with the understanding that they would have the backing of wealthy and distinguished members of the émigré community but were now in the awkward position of having to raise funds themselves. They did not even have the money to pay their hotel tab at the Hotel Griffou.[106]

The lack of support from wealthier exiles led to a change in strategy. The generals and their representatives traveled to Paris, Mexico, New Orleans, Philadelphia, Kingston, and Key West in search of support for their plan of multiple, coordinated expeditions. Finding little support from wealthier exiles, they turned to cigar workers whose many small contributions might make up for the few larger ones that had been lost. Still unable to raise sufficient support, they scaled back their planning. They would raise the minimal funds necessary to launch a first expedition, under the command of Antonio Maceo. Once Maceo was in Oriente, according to this strategy, the people of the region would rise up. Then, once Oriente was in arms, fund-raising among exiles would become easier, or so they hoped. Although in the end this strategy did not work, it is clear that this was the moment when Maceo emerged as a featured public speaker in fund-raising events among cigar workers in Veracruz, New York, and Key West, and that the contributions of these workers provided the bulk of support for the expedition.[107] Men like Serra—and if the generals had any sense, men like Sandoval, Marcus, and the brothers Bonilla—must have become crucial to the enterprise.

The documents produced at the time give only hints in this direction. There is one report, impossible to confirm, that both José and Antonio Maceo were initiated into the Sol de Cuba lodge in fall 1884.[108] And when Antonio Maceo scheduled an appearance at Clarendon Hall in July 1885 at a fund-raising event for the expedition, the Spanish consul appealed to the district attorney in New York to prevent the gathering on the grounds that "it was a meeting of *blacks*, and it would disturb the peace."[109] This accusation is surely suspect. Spanish authorities, of course, did their best to portray organizing among revolutionaries in New York, like the revolution as a whole, as a black conspiracy. Yet if the Spanish government had reasons to exaggerate the role of black and brown immigrants in supporting the expedition, organizers of the expedition had equally strong reasons for downplaying their dependence on black and brown supporters. It would not be surprising at all if the audience that gathered to see Maceo on this visit to New York actually was considerably "blacker" than nationalist gatherings in the city a decade earlier because exiles of color were especially enthusiastic about Maceo's leadership, because wealthier allies had removed their support, and because some white workers had moved away from separatism in favor of labor radicalism. It seems highly probable that the Maceos turned to the leaders of the Sol de Cuba and San Manuel lodges for help in recruiting volunteers and raising funds among their own members, among African American neighbors, and in the multiracial workshops and eating houses. And it seems extremely likely that the members of these lodges, along with their most reliable white Cuban friends, *and* their African American friends and relations, were in the audience for the all the events featuring Maceo. It seems likely, too, that the general was the topic of conversation at the third annual Cuban American picnic, which took place two weeks after his appearance at Clarendon Hall.

Yet if it is impossible to be certain about links between Serra and the migrant community led by Sandoval, the record is much clearer in the case of Juan and Gerónimo Bonilla. The Bonillas arrived in New York around 1881, and could be found, shortly thereafter, living in the Sandoval apartment at 89 Thompson Street. There they were reunited with Rencurrel, who had been their next-door neighbor more than a decade before in Key West. They both became active in the Logia San Manuel, eventually taking over leadership of the lodge from Sandoval and Rencurrel. Juan rose to leadership in the Sol de Cuba lodge as well (as did their third brother, Francisco). As residents of these buildings and members of these lodges, the Bonillas came into frequent and intimate contact with African American social, political, and religious leaders. They had grown up within the multiracial coalitions of Reconstruction era politics in Key West. But they were living in segregated buildings in Greenwich Village in 1883 when the Supreme Court overturned the Civil Rights Act, determining that Congress had no right to prohibit private acts of racial discrimination in the United States.[110] The following year, Gerónimo would go to the courthouse to declare his intention to naturalize as a US citizen in the company of an African American political activist who also lived at 89 Thompson. Eventually the Bonillas found new lodgings in the home of the Reasons at 74 West Third Street.[111]

The Bonillas were also probably deeply involved in multiracial Cuban labor politics. But they are more difficult to situate among the supporters of the Maceo-Gómez expedition. Serra was clearly involved in the revolutionary politics in the early 1880s and the Bonillas are easy to situate in the community building. But it is not possible to prove that they even knew one another. When Serra returned from Kingston in 1887, however, the Bonillas and Sandoval would become his closest allies. The lodges created by early immigrants hoping to "find a friend" in order to resolve the problems of settling in a segregated city became Serra's most important constituents. They provided the base of support to create La Liga and to become important figures in the Cuban Revolutionary Party. At the same time, Heredia and Josefa Blanco (Juan Bonilla's mother-in-law) would work to integrate the community of women whose babies they delivered into the activities and politics at La Liga. It is to this transformation of an immigrant community into a political movement that we now turn.

· 4 ·

Convergence

A man, materially exhausted, but exuberant in spirit and virtues, dropped
suddenly upon us, opened his wings, white and divine, to shelter and care
for us, and even to bring us to complete salvation. This man, gentlemen,
was an archangel in the heaven that is the fatherland: it was José Martí.

—Rafael Serra, "Speech delivered at the inauguration of La Liga," 1890

I have lived at [Serra's] side. . . . I saw him submit himself, cultivate himself, control himself, I saw him forgive and build from the ground up. . . .
The world bleeds without pause, from crimes that are committed against
nature, and when a man, with his heart pierced by thorns, loves the same
men who deny him, that man is epic.

—José Martí, "Rafael Serra: para un libro," 1892

October 10, 1888, was the twentieth anniversary of the uprising in Cuba
at the beginning of the Ten Years' War, the most sacred day in the nationalist calendar. That day, Rafael Serra and Gerónimo Bonilla made their
way to the New York County Courthouse, along with three other men:
two cigar makers and a cook. Serra and the others petitioned to be naturalized as citizens of the United States; Bonilla, already a citizen, served
as their witness. Serra had recently returned from a failed military expedition in the company of Generals Antonio Maceo and Crombet, and Brigadier Cebreco. Traditionally, close ties to military figures were the key to
successful bids for leadership among exiles in New York, and indeed since
returning Serra had been selected as the secretary of the one remaining
separatist club in the city. He also maintained close ties with the leading
civil rights activists on the island of Cuba. In fact, that very day, an article
he had written appeared in *La Fraternidad*, the leading newspaper for the

class of color in Havana, although copies could not yet have reached New York. Viewed from this angle, the trip to the courthouse was a fitting gesture for the anniversary of the insurgency. The men each declared, under oath, that they permanently disavowed any loyalty to the king of Spain. And they asserted their capacity, as black men, to become citizens of a republic—something that many in Cuban and Spanish politics (not to mention the United States) openly questioned.[1]

But the trip to the courthouse was part of a new kind of bid for leadership as well. Over the previous month, Bonilla and Serra had created something called the Cuban Republican Club, through which they began organizing Cuban men of African descent to support Benjamin Harrison and Levi Morton in the coming presidential election, scheduled for early November. The Cuban Republican Club was one of many "colored" political clubs in the various wards of the city that helped mobilize black support for the Republican Party. The leaders of these clubs also advocated within the party for patronage positions for black men, and much less successfully, for a strong defense of civil rights in the party platform and for the nomination of black men as candidates or electors. The men who went to the courthouse with Bonilla that day—participants in the social networks created by Sandoval and Marcus over more than a decade, and supporters from afar of *La Fraternidad*—were the club's constituents.[2] From this point forward, Serra's political career, which culminated in his election to the Cuban House of Representatives, would no longer depend only on his relationships to more powerful men—although those relationships would continue to be crucial. It would depend on his relationship to voters, and on a larger project to expand and defend the right of men of color and other working-class Cubans to be voters, in both the United States and Cuba.

Serra's efforts to mobilize voters for the presidential election in 1888, even as he participated actively in civil rights struggles in Cuba, provide a wholly unexpected backdrop to the more familiar story of his support for José Martí. It is impossible to locate the precise moment when Serra and Martí initiated their political partnership. But the evening of that same day, October 10, 1888, is as good a moment as any to mark the beginning of the convergence. Martí had arrived in New York during the Guerra Chiquita, as a veteran of the secret revolutionary clubs of Havana. He had made a splash within the broader exile community with soaring speeches and had quickly integrated himself into the key nationalist institutions. Still, he had drifted away from the nationalist cause after he quarreled with Generals Gómez and Maceo, and withdrew his support for the expedition they led in 1885—an expedition for which Serra volunteered. When the expedition collapsed, Martí had returned to the nationalist fold, once again capturing attention with speeches of startling eloquence. By fall 1888, he had gathered a small group of supporters, arguing that it was almost time to restart the armed insurgency. The first step in preparing for war, he had contended, was the creation of a single democratic structure, encompassing all the different exile communities and coordinating the efforts of all the military chiefs. Only a single democratic movement could "knead the dough" of the new republic by repairing relations among what he called the "mistrusting" and "varied elements" of the national community.[3]

The twentieth-anniversary celebration was the first major event organized under his leadership, and his first opportunity to create a public forum in which to enact and perform the unity that he had begun to describe. With this in mind, several weeks before the event, Martí started to reach out to elements who might, reasonably, mistrust Martí himself. He sent a letter to Serra—a man with ties to the military leadership, a journalist read by Cubans of color in exile and on the island, and now the leader of a political club that was mobilizing Cuban men of color as US citizens and voters—explaining his conviction that the event "should be born from all and should belong equally to all." On this principle, he implored Serra to participate in planning the commemoration and subsequently offered him a place among the speakers at the event.[4] For this reason, on the evening of the same day that he walked to the courthouse to forswear his loyalty to the Spanish monarchy, to become a citizen in a republic, and to participate in the Republican campaign, Serra gave his first major speech to an assembly composed of Cuban merchants, manufacturers, professionals, writers, and workers. It was the first time that he would stand on such a stage alongside Martí. One radial line, that of a worker intellectual who had made his way through Havana, Matanzas, and Key West to become the leader of a group of migrants who, facing the challenges of migrating while black, created their own community institutions in New York, crossed with another, that of the poet, journalist, and diplomat, to create a "nationalist resurgence."

In the months that followed, Serra and the Bonillas used their reputations, their organizational skills, and their social networks in an effort to turn a long-standing ideology of racial solidarity into a new kind of political relationship. They became the hinge that connected their constituents, whom they had previously mobilized in support of Harrison and Morton, to Martí, a man who did not yet have a political constituency of his own. Martí's concern with creating "equilibrium" among the various "elements" of Cuban society required, in his eyes, a man like Serra to "submit himself, cultivate himself, [and] control himself," to "forgive and build from the ground up."[5] Martí celebrated Serra and the Bonillas as part of his broader effort to direct black political activity toward a posture of forgiveness, and toward nonthreatening participation in his coalition. Serra and the Bonillas adopted this posture. At the same time, they worked with Martí to articulate a democratic and even radical set of political values: a nation "with all and for the good of all," a nation that would ensure social harmony through equal citizenship and popular democracy. Martí was able to articulate those values convincingly in no small part because of his relationship with Serra and the Bonillas, who helped him advertise this message to their friends and allies in New York, Cuba, Key West, Kingston, Port-au-Prince, and Tampa. Then they helped him to create, and secure a leadership role in, a new political organization, the Cuban Revolutionary Party.

Here, then, we can return to the questions posed at the beginning of this book: Why did Serra and the others accept the call to demonstrate patience and forgiveness in the name of national unity? Why did they choose to promote the idea of a nation for all and with all as if it were Martí's idea rather than their own? How did they manage to assert themselves in the nationalist struggle without giving up their right to form independent associations or to demand equal treatment as people of color? The answers to these questions are not to be found in the intricacies of Martí's writings, in the varied and evolving influences on his philosophy, or in the many accounts of his personal brilliance but instead in the social worlds built by artisan intellectuals and black migrants over the previous two decades. Men and women in this social world did not just support Martí; they helped to create him, drawing on a complex terrain of interconnected political commitments that were in play on this single extraordinary day—a day when Serra led a group of black and brown constituents to naturalize as US citizens and become Republican voters, published an article in the most important Havana newspaper for the "race of color," and stood for the first time beside Martí as the only black speaker at the patriotic gathering at Clarendon Hall.

TO STRUM HIS LYRE ON THE FIELD OF BATTLE

How did Serra, who had scarcely left an impression in Cuban public life during his first years in New York City, become the political and intellectual leader of the community forged by Germán Sandoval, Lafayette Marcus, and others in the segregated apartment buildings in New York? This rise to prominence began with his participation in the military expedition organized in New York, Key West, and New Orleans in 1884 and 1885. As an attempt to rekindle the revolution in Cuba, the expedition was a resounding failure. But it provided a platform from which Serra earned bona fides as both a soldier and an intellectual. Most participants in the independence movement believed that only men prepared to sacrifice their lives (or at least their scarce resources) for the fatherland could claim the moral authority to speak for the national community.[6] From the beginning, however, Serra's role in the expedition seems to have hinged on his abilities as a writer rather than as a warrior. The military commanders needed the services of men with the skills and temperament to serve as secretaries and record keepers. Although he had no previous military experience, he received the rank of lieutenant, joining the staff of Brigadier Cebreco—one of the most prominent men of color among the veterans of the previous insurgencies.[7] Serra was critical of men who jockeyed for such positions in the hopes that service to high-ranking generals would promote their own political importance.[8] But his own career clearly benefited from the two years that he spent in close quarters with Cebreco, the Maceos, and other top military figures.[9]

In addition to Serra's help with practical matters such as correspondence and record keeping, the military leadership also seems to have valued his skills as a poet and essayist. Indeed, contemporaries seemed generally to understand that Serra's military career was a natural part of his continued efforts at literary self-making. One of his comrades noted that the young poet enlisted because he "wished to strum his lyre on the field of battle."

This was a reference, easily understood by contemporaries, to other nationalist poets who modeled their verses on the ancient victory odes.[10] In a letter praising one of Serra's poems, General Flor Crombet, one of the leaders of the expedition, quoted Lamartine, "Poets and heroes are of the same breed: the latter do what the former conceive." The General cast Serra as a poet, writing, "Keep singing your verses—this is the high mission that nature has put in your hands . . . the bard of the fatherland!"[11]

Serra took up this role with enthusiasm. He never saw battle, but he published a pamphlet titled *Echoes of the Soul* during his first months after shipping out to Kingston, where the company awaited orders to depart for Cuba. In this text, written in verse, Serra dispensed with his typical preamble about being an unworthy speaker to address such a weighty topic. He adopted instead the voice, familiar in the poetry of the nationalist movement, of a poet driven to take up his lyre because of the agitation of his soul. His happy remembrance of natural landscapes and beautiful women in Cuba had been cruelly interrupted by the harsh experience of exile in the "north," and the bitter recollection of colonial oppression and slavery. "I feel a burning desire," he wrote, "my soul is oppressed." Unable to remain indifferent to the rush of sentiment, he undertook to represent his feelings in verse. Under cover of this literary device, he offered an effusive rallying cry for the fifty or so men who had agreed to serve under Antonio Maceo, and who had begun to gather in Kingston, where they awaited supplies and orders to embark to Cuba. This was an "enthusiastic host" compelled toward selfless acts of manly sacrifice by the same deep agitation of the soul that drove the poet to write his verses.[12]

Serra made it clear, however, that the men were not engaged in a purely emotional rebellion. And the poem itself, while impassioned, also functioned as a "literary essay," offering a carefully reasoned and coherent political philosophy. Serra, the "bard" assigned the task of conceiving the ideals for which the military heroes made their sacrifice, explained that the men fought for republican government, for freedom of conscience, for free and universal education, and of course, against the evils of excessive social dancing. As he had done since his first publications in Matanzas, Serra expressed a firm commitment to social harmony. The Cuban flag was the enemy of "hatred and discord," and would provide shelter to "all of the elements" who, in the spirit of peace and concord, contributed their labor to the cause of national progress. Yet as he had argued in his previous writings, the revolution could not hope to produce a harmonious society unless it also guaranteed justice.

> Liberty does not consist in bequeathing that privilege to one class
> Which harms another with its sumptuous absolutism, sorrowful and
> devastating.

The revolution was a means of achieving a new kind of prosperity that, according to Serra, would exchange the luck of "exploited" and "exploiters."[13]

Serra did not directly address the accusation, which had proved such a potent weapon for the Spanish government, that the expedition was a racial rebellion, seeking black supremacy and vengeance against whites. Yet he made a careful argument that demands for equality were not particularistic acts but rather part of a universal goal of national fulfillment. The "rancid aristocracy," he explained, not only threatened national unity by inciting resentments among the poor; it was a "vestige of the past," a dark shadow across society that will not survive "the light of our century." The elimination of unfair and antiquated privileges was not a matter of revenge or supremacy; it was a crucial step toward the triumph of universal enlightenment values. To drive home the connection between the abolition of racial and class privileges and universal ideals of political freedom, Serra concluded his poem with a Spanish translation of the "Declaration of the Rights of Man."[14]

Echoes of the Soul offers evidence of Serra's emerging role as spokesman for the faction of the movement that—despite the defections of men like Martí—followed the Maceos and Gómez into the field. It shows that he was already quite adept at balancing his staunch rejection of class and racial privilege against a concern for unity and harmony among all classes— what Martí would call "equilibrium." Serra would later play the role of disciple who had learned the gospel of unity through social justice from Martí, the apostle. But long before he came to know Martí, Serra, like many other nationalist authors, imagined that men who faced death together would create a shared self-awareness as Cubans. This national sentiment would then eliminate the possibility that any would place narrowly defined self-interest ahead of shared and universal goals. He called on his comrades to discard "clumsy pride," "self-love," and "revenge which will make the world narrow." Wealthy Cubans must give up their privilege, workers should give up their class hatred, and—once the apprentice system was abolished—former slaves must renounce resentment and retaliation. For Serra, the poetic simile that explained this loss of the self in the collective, the common essence and the shared ideal of the *patria*, was romantic love. He wrote,

> Two lives bound together with the ribbon
> Of unity, of friendship. Like turtledoves
> Who in caring and fraternal embrace
> Flutter their wings
> Their gazes aligned in pure faith
> Aflame with pleasing affections
> And tender caresses which run along their wings
> Feeding our passions.
> The collision of two souls who with a kiss
> Condense the deep and virtuous love
> Which works its enthralling magic
> To widen their existence in this world.[15]

The idea of a political coalition built on love and tenderness among men, rather than shared military experience, would become Serra's trademark in his subsequent alliance with Martí. At the time that Serra published this poem, however, Martí was still persona non grata in the nationalist movement.[16]

THE COLLAPSE OF THE EXPEDITION

In *Echoes of the Soul*, Serra managed to craft a heroic narrative, a groundswell of lyricism and fervor, and a carefully articulated set of political values for an expedition that was swiftly running aground. Even as Serra began working on the poem, the company experienced the first in a long series of disappointments. After losing the support of wealthy New York exiles, the leaders of the expedition had managed to raise a minimum of funds at gatherings of workers in New York, Key West, and New Orleans, where the generals had settled their wives and children. General Gómez, relying on family ties with the president of the Dominican Republic, used the money to purchase rifles and ammunition, and then transport them to Santo Domingo. In May 1885, just as Serra prepared to depart for Kingston, Gómez's allies lost power and the new Dominican government took possession of these supplies. Gómez spent the rest of the year trying, unsuccessfully, to recover the lost matériel. This left General Antonio Maceo at the head of a movement that was almost entirely without resources.[17]

Leaving the volunteers in Kingston, Maceo returned to New York, Philadelphia, and Key West to ask exiles for a second chance with their money. It was a delicate matter to ask for continued contributions from workers when funds already collected had been lost through such a terrible blunder. Self-styled commanders passed through the exile communities on a regular basis, mobilizing their retinues of allied civilian leaders and collecting money for expeditions that never took shape. The line between sublime hero, well-meaning but tragically mistaken patriot, and self-serving charlatan was often a matter of debate. Only Maceo's extraordinary popularity among cigar workers—and almost certainly, though nobody but the Spanish consul would say so, within the particular social networks built by Cubans of color—was sufficient to inspire enthusiastic patriotic gatherings at Clarendon Hall in New York, at the Club San Carlos in Key West, and on a tour of cigar workshops in both cities. Nevertheless, Maceo managed the embarrassment of asking for the same money twice by promising not to ask again. On receiving a Cuban flag as a present from a group of supporters in Key West, he brought the assembly to tears by declaring that he would raise the banner on the island of Cuba or have his body wrapped in it for burial.[18] When the expedition eventually collapsed, Cuban workers had had enough. For the next seven years, when nationalist leaders called meetings, attendance was generally anemic.[19]

While Maceo toured the exile communities on this fund-raising trip, Serra and the rest of the company lived in Kingston, mingling with the community of Cuban exiles that had settled there, including merchants, cigar workers, and a contingent of small tobacco farmers who had settled in an agricultural colony near Kingston at the end of the Ten Years' War. Serra and his comrades also would have noticed the deep economic crisis in the British colony and the massive exodus of black workers on the new steamship routes to the Colombian province of Panama, especially to Colón, the terminus of the Panama Railroad and the staging ground where the French had recently begun a massive effort to construct a canal.[20] Indeed, they could not have missed the flow of migrants to Panama because soon the Cuban volunteers would file onto the same steamships. Serra relocated from Kingston to Colón, probably traveling on a ship like the one that, according to a local paper, "left here for Colon, taking freight, also several Cubans and deck passengers, and 432 Canal laborers."[21] Serra and his comrades had embarked on an expedition to Cuba to make a revolution; instead they had left the immigrant communities of New York and Key West only to find themselves in the midst of a mass migration of West Indian laborers—the first mass migration of free black workers in the Americas after abolition. We can only imagine what the Cubans thought of the workers among whom they traveled. Did they see an affinity between themselves and the canal workers, based on shared racial identity and experiences of migration? Or did they see themselves as fundamentally distinct from the bulk of migrants—who were laborers rather than artisans—for reasons of language, class, or culture? Did they consider how Cuba, in its transition to free labor, might make land available to former slaves, avoiding the crisis that now beset the English colony?

Serra and his comrades also found themselves in the middle of a Caribbean region that was a crossroads for a diverse collection of black and brown reformists and revolutionaries. While in Kingston, Serra and his comrades would have observed that colonial reforms, instituted the prior year, used property requirements to exclude black and brown majorities from the limited right to elect local officials. They surely noted that men of color who called for a more inclusive suffrage were met with accusations that they sought to use the ballot to create a black republic on the model of Haiti. They almost certainly also crossed paths with Haitian exiles living in Kingston. Indeed, only a few years before, the Spanish consul in Kingston reported that Maceo's supporters regularly socialized and discussed politics with Haitian exiles in one of that city's drinking establishments. Some of the Cubans in Kingston had subsequently joined a failed expedition to Haiti, seeking to unseat the National Party in Port-au-Prince in 1883. The Cubans who gathered in Kingston in 1885 probably pondered the accounts of that conflict that circulated in Jamaica at the time, which portrayed it as a race war between Haitian blacks (the National Party) and mulattoes (Maceo's allies in the Liberal Party). The Cubans also likely knew of the difficulties that a group of Venezuelan revolutionaries had experienced in transporting weapons and munitions through the British colony as the embargo of this shipment gave rise to one of the most important legal cases of the day: a private suit by a British subject against the colonial governor.[22]

Then, when the company landed in Colón, it encountered a city that lay in charred ruins. Liberal forces on the Caribbean coast of Colombia had risen up against the government in spring 1885, just as Serra was embarking for Jamaica. The leader of the local Liberal faction in Colón, a man named Pedro Prestán, was a man of mixed African ancestry, a prominent lawyer, a property owner, and an acquaintance of some of the Cubans on the expedition.[23] Like the Venezuelans whose attempt to ship their weapons through Jamaica had been thwarted, Prestán saw his efforts foiled by local officials who prevented him from unloading a shipment of arms. When he tried to take the ship by force, the United States landed troops to help the Colombians capture and hang Prestán and his followers. During the fighting, the city of Colón burned to the ground. Liberals noted that the fire wiped out Prestán's properties and suspected it had been set by his enemies. The authorities blamed Prestán for the fire, representing the Liberals as "riffraff" and arsonists drawn from among the various black Caribbean migrants in the city. As Serra and the other Cubans disembarked from their ship to find the city in ashes, what lessons did they draw from each of these failed projects at reform and revolution? Did British rule in Jamaica provide an enlightened alternative to Spanish colonialism or further proof that only independence would bring social equality? What logistical challenges would they face in moving arms and men through Kingston and Colón? What were they to make of the extraordinary violence and the familiar accusations of race warfare that various governments in the region, including that of the United States, had used to suppress black and brown liberals?

Any such conversations likely faded quickly in the face of more immediate concerns. Like almost everyone else who arrived in Panama in those years, the Cubans immediately fell ill with yellow fever and malaria. Several comrades died in the first weeks. The rest of the "enthusiastic host," perhaps with enthusiasm waning, settled in to wait for the moment of heroic sacrifice while suffering the decidedly unheroic torments of fevers and biting insects. As funds ran short, their daily rations were cut. Many were sent to live with Cuban settlers in various towns and camps along the canal line. With each delay, with each day they spent waiting rather than fighting, the soldiers took one step further from the virile enterprise of soldiering, and one step closer to a violation of what they understood to be the most basic norm of manliness: self-sufficiency through productive labor. One participant in the expedition called this "the shame of eating the bread that someone else earned to feed his family."[24] When finally a new shipment of arms—purchased with the proceeds of Maceo's second round of fund-raising—arrived, the Colombian authorities, bowing to Spanish pressure, refused to allow the Cubans to unload any of the weapons—a nearly identical repetition of Prestán's difficulties. The ship had to be sent back to New York, and the expedition was delayed.[25]

After eight debilitating months in the Canal Zone, the volunteers returned to Jamaica to await a second attempt to deliver the shipment. With dwindling funds and little hope of raising more in Kingston, Maceo sent them to live with the Cuban families on the tobacco farms outside the city. They adapted to a rudimentary rural lifestyle, going barefoot, gathering on nearby farms each night for music and dancing, and surviving on the "yuccas, malangas, sweet potatoes, and plantains that we could find."[26] In July, slightly more than a year into the expedition, more bad news arrived. General Crombet had arrived from New York on a hired ship loaded with the long-awaited supplies but had found no one at the rendezvous point on the coast of Jamaica. The captain of the ship, concerned that British authorities would find the weapons, had dumped the shipment overboard. For a second time the military commanders had lost matériel purchased with donations wrung from workers in Key West and New York. Tensions ran high among the generals. Maceo and Crombet exchanged insults in public, and nearly fought a duel. After fifteen grueling months, in August 1886, the expedition ended with a disheartening whimper. Serra, like many in the company, returned to Panama, where some of the men found opportunities as contractors on canal projects. From there he made his way back to New York.[27] He still had no real military experience. But he returned from the expedition with new literary accomplishments, a familiarity with racial politics in Jamaica and Panama, and a new set of relationships with civilian and military leaders scattered in Cuban communities around the greater Caribbean.[28]

SERRA, SANDOVAL, AND THE BONILLAS

When he returned to New York, Serra's relationships with Crombet and the Maceos as well as his growing literary reputation contributed crucially to his rising political status, including his selection as secretary of a new separatist club formed by a few die-hard nationalists in New York, the Club Los Independientes. At meetings of the club, he witnessed and perhaps took part in another round of angry confrontations between the veterans of the expedition and Martí.[29] Yet his relationships within the already-dynamic community created by Cubans of color in New York were even more important, especially his partnership with Sandoval and the Bonillas, who had not taken part in the failed expedition. During the time that Serra had been in Kingston and Panama, they remained in New York, where the already-strained relations between workers and wealthier exiles had reached a breaking point. When a group of cigar workers in New York went out on strike early in 1886, both of the Cuban newspapers in the city, the *Avisador Cubano* (edited by conservative Enrique Trujillo) and *La República* (edited by the populist Ramón Rubiera de Armas) denounced the strikers for their lack of patriotic commitment. Cuban labor radicals responded by denouncing the separatist leadership as compromised by its relationship with employers and calling on workers to stop contributing to both newspapers. Similar conflicts had emerged in the exile settlement in Key West, where a fire that same year destroyed the San Carlos and hundreds of other buildings, leaving thousands of workers without homes or employment. Nationalists in Key West denounced workers for accepting help from the Spanish consul in the city. But at the same time, many manufacturers began relocating to Tampa in an effort to undermine the power of local unions. Factory owners also worked with US officials to identify and deport Cuban and Spanish anarchists who worked to organize the cigar makers. Nationalist leaders found it increasingly hard, therefore, to mobilize support from workers. There were no more large rallies like the ones that had gathered for Maceo's speeches in 1884 and 1885.[30]

Like many workers in New York City and across the world, working-class Cuban exiles understood their relationship to employers and the extreme class divisions in the city around them through the lens of the simmering debate over the murder trial of the Haymarket defendants. In summer 1886, shortly after a steamboat captain delivered Maceo's second shipment of arms into the depths of Kingston harbor and only a month after the devastating fire in Key West destroyed the San Carlos, a jury in Chicago convicted eight men for the murder of a policeman by means of a bomb thrown during a demonstration of workers in Haymarket Square. The demonstrations had begun as a protest of police violence against workers rallying in favor of the eight-hour day. Except for one man, who may have been the bomb maker, the defendants were convicted primarily on the basis of their published writings and reports of their speeches, which advocated worker militancy, including preparation for armed class conflict.[31] For Cuban workers in New York, as for so many around the world, the trial and conviction of the Haymarket defendants became symbols of a society in which the legal and political systems were rigged in favor of the wealthy and against workers. Calls for solidarity with the Chicago martyrs, as the Haymarket defendants were known, became an effective tool for mobilizing workers as Cuban labor activists in New York, Key West, and Havana organized a wave of strikes over wages and issues of "worker dignity," including the right not to be physically abused by bosses, and the rights of black and brown workers to be employed in any workshop. Workers continued to move among these cities and often collaborated to provide funds for strikers from afar. They increasingly understood their fight for a greater share of the wealth created through their labor, for autonomy as craftsmen, and for respectful treatment from employers to be part of an international workingmen's movement rather than a component of a nationalist struggle.[32]

Anarchist labor organizations were typically racially inclusive, and attracted many Cubans of color in Havana, Key West, New York, and Tampa. Yet as working-class comrades broke with nationalist groups to create racially mixed labor organizations, the Bonillas, the Sandovals, and other Cubans of African descent continued developing their own independent social networks in New York as well. These networks continued to bring them into close contact with African American leaders in the city. Their activities, for instance, appeared regularly in the "Local Gossip" column of the *New York Freeman*, the primary African American newspaper in the city. Such notices included the annual Cuban American picnic and other activities organized by "Germie Sandoval," the graduation of Francisco Peñalver (brother of the well-known Cuban musician Pastor) from Charles Reason's Grammar School, and the comings and goings of distinguished men of color from Cuba.[33] Through Masonic activities, Cubans of color also developed a new relationship with a man named William Derrick, the pastor at the Bethel AME Church on Sullivan Street, the largest African American congregation in the city. Derrick was an immigrant from the West Indies and a veteran of the Civil War. He had been arguing for years that African

American leaders ought to "open up a closer communication with our Jamaican, Haytian, and Cuban friends," and to "make ourselves the medium" for trade between the United States and the West Indies.[34] By December 1886, Derrick opened Bethel Church to the Sol de Cuba lodge, which organized a funeral service for three brothers who died that month.[35]

Derrick was also a local political boss, the main link between African American voters in the city and the Republican Party. "He never hesitates to tell his people, singly or collectively, how to vote," one critic noted. "He considers himself the guardian and guide of his flock, and far from having cause to regret his course, is rated as a man no politician can afford to ruffle, for he controls thousands of votes."[36] Expanding his base of supporters was probably part of Derrick's goal when he organized a lecture at the end of 1886 for "the resident Cubans" of New York and Brooklyn at his church, covering the recent emancipation of slaves in Cuba as well as the Cubans' "acceptance as citizens in America and their advancement and thrift as active, busy people since their exile."[37] A few months later, several Cuban "societies" organized a celebration at Bethel Church to mark the end of slavery in their homeland, inviting African American veterans of the Civil War, seen as a parallel to the Cuban struggle, to take part.[38]

Although Serra missed many of these developments during his time in Kingston and Colón, he surely learned of them from afar or shortly after returning to the city. When he arrived for a second time at the docks in Manhattan, and made his way from the East River through the familiar dizzying bustle to find his friends and countrymen, he soon found Sandoval and the Bonillas, and immediately began transforming the social networks that they had built into a new kind of political movement.[39] Their first collaboration, which they initiated in the months after the execution of the Haymarket defendants, was a project to support the Cuban journalist and civil rights leader Juan Gualberto Gómez and to breathe new life into his newspaper, *La Fraternidad*, in Havana. Gómez, readers may recall, was born to enslaved parents on a plantation in Matanzas. His parents purchased his freedom with savings earned with their labors as a seamstress and a seller of fruits and vegetables, and educated him in one of the few private schools that accepted students of color in Havana. He then departed for France where rather than learning the craft of carriage making as planned, he became a journalist. During the Ten Years' War, he crossed paths with insurgent leader Francisco Vicente Aguilera in Paris and with liberal intellectual Nicolás Azcárate in Mexico. He returned to Cuba in 1878, where he joined Azcárate's literary circles, which also included a young lawyer named Martí.[40]

When Gómez founded the newspaper *La Fraternidad* in Havana in 1879, he became, along with Serra's mentor, Martín Morúa Delgado, the most prominent of the new journalists who took up the cause of the class of color in the aftermath of the Ten Years' War. Gómez was arrested and forced into exile in 1880, a few months before Serra and Morúa closed *El Pueblo* and departed Matanzas. After two years in the penal colony in Ceuta, he settled in Madrid, where he developed an alliance with Spanish liberals and abolitionists. Working together with a group of younger writers and allies in Cuba, Gómez used his ties in Spain to pressure peninsular officials to issue decrees in favor of equal civil rights in Cuba and Puerto Rico, including access to cafés, theaters, parks, and other public accommodations. Creole politicians and petty officials undermined these decrees, however, by declining to abide by or enforce them. Gómez and his allies responded with lawsuits, seeking the enforcement of civil rights statutes.[41] The group of Gómez supporters that remained in Cuba also created a project to unify all the sociedades de color into a single network, a "Directorio" representing all the class of color on the island in negotiations with political parties and the government.[42] In 1887, this group reopened *La Fraternidad*, an "independent political newspaper dedicated to the defense of the interests of the race of color." *La Fraternidad* allowed Cubans of color in different towns and cities on the island and in multiple exile settlements to participate in and imagine themselves as a single community of writers and readers.[43]

It was this project that Serra and his new allies took up in the first months after he returned from Kingston. In New York, issues of the newspaper reached subscribers, and subscription fees reached the editors, "owing to the activity and zeal of our particular friend Señor [Germán] Sandoval." By the end of 1887, Sandoval, Serra, and the Bonillas had begun a broader fund-raising campaign, with the idea of collecting donations to purchase a printing press for *La Fraternidad* and for Gómez, when he should return from exile. Their fund-raising relied heavily on the migrant institutions that Sandoval and the Bonillas had built over the previous decade, especially the Odd Fellows lodges operating in New York, Key West, and Havana. Sandoval also returned to his long practice of organizing annual picnics bringing together Cubans and African Americans in

New York. By February 1888, Sandoval had developed a plan to "celebrate a Cuban-American (which is to say Anglo-Hispanic) reception to benefit the press . . . without receiving any of the funds for payment of expenses." According to the organizers, "The enthusiasm seems to have reached even the American people," by which they meant African Americans, especially a group of eighteen women and girls that volunteered for the organizing committee for the event to raise funds for *La Fraternidad*.[44]

At the same time that Gómez used his ties with liberal politicians in Madrid to push forward the cause of civil and political equality in the colonies, the New Yorkers used their relative economic security, freedom of association, and ties with African Americans to the same ends. *La Fraternidad*, in turn, functioned as a means of communication between the New Yorkers and counterparts in Cuba and elsewhere, helping to create a community of writers and readers across considerable distances. For instance, Abraham Seino, a founding member of the Sol de Cuba lodge and at one time a resident of the Sandoval apartment at 89 Thompson Street, sent a request from New York for information about the whereabouts of his father. *La Fraternidad* published the query, with the request that information be directed to the editorial office in Havana. Several weeks later the newspaper published news that the older man was alive and the details of his whereabouts.[45] In another issue, Serra, in New York, sent thanks for the good wishes that he had received on his birthday from friends in San Juan, Boston, and Kingston.[46] That Serra had friends in so many locations probably reflected his own itinerary over the previous years and the high degree of mobility among the people he encountered on his travels. But the announcement only makes sense if Serra and the editors also had reason to believe that *La Fraternidad* was a means of getting a message to this broad network. Apparently his friends in San Juan, Boston, and Kingston were likely to receive and read the newspaper as well. The editors in Havana knew, too, that Serra and other New Yorkers would read the note that they published about Gertrudis Heredia's efforts, in the company of a white doctor and a white midwife, in delivering a baby to the wife of the newspaper's editor, Miguel Gualba.[47]

Though Sandoval continued to take on important ceremonial and organizational roles, serving as president of the fund-raising committee, handling subscriptions, and collecting funds from allies in Florida to put toward the purchase of the press, Sandoval was "not a man of science." Serra took on the tasks most suited to a writer. He was secretary of the fund-raising committee and New York correspondent for *La Fraternidad*—tasks that he gradually shared with another aspiring writer, the teenage Juan Bonilla. Their contributions make it clear that the New Yorkers, even after many years in exile, were well apprised of the major issues that concerned the editors of *La Fraternidad*. For instance, Serra joined in the chorus of objections to the racist conclusions of the book *Prostitution in the City of Havana* when it appeared in 1888. He reported that the "Cubans residing here protest this work deeply and energetically." He then rebuked journalist and publisher Enrique Trujillo, a prominent Cuban New Yorker (and a man who would emerge as a political enemy of Martí, Serra, and Figueroa over subsequent years), for his positive review of the book. Serra chided Trujillo, "We can see through your disguise!" Serra also sent *La Fraternidad* a repudiation of another well-known exile, a wealthy businessman named Fidel Pierra, who had recently published a series of articles making the case against revolution and in favor of efforts to reform Spanish colonialism through participation in the limited political arena. Pierra warned that white Cubans were not strong enough to withstand the "innovations and excesses" of the blacks. Serra took him to task for the "unjust estimation that he makes of the long-suffering class to which we have the honor of belonging."[48]

In addition to reports on the dubious opinions of certain prominent Cuban exiles in New York, Serra offered readers of *La Fraternidad* observations on social conditions in the United States. As "the legitimate sons that we are of the unfortunate fatherland known as Cuba," the New Yorkers desired to present "tangible facts" about events in the North American city that might be helpful to readers back home.[49] These "facts" could include small matters such as a heat wave buffeting the city or the visit of a Haitian general as well as larger ones: "The strike by the operatives who work in the elaboration of Havana cigars in this city has ended satisfactorily; the workers having succeeded in obtaining the increase of two dollars [per thousand cigars] that they, in all justice, had demanded."[50] A cheer probably went up in the workshops of Havana, Key West, and Kingston—not to mention New York— when the lectores read this news aloud. Serra's reports in *La Fraternidad* also reveal the New Yorkers' deep engagement with local politics and their consequences for debates in Cuba. Serra summarized the rise of widespread anti-Chinese sentiment in the United States and explained the workings of Chinese exclusion. These served as a warning to Cubans against false admiration for the United States, to dispel any hope that annexation would bring desired social change to the island and to criticize Cuban politicians—especially the former insurgents who now supported the Autonomista Party and resisted calls for equal civil and political rights—for their own "ethnographic intransigence."[51]

Above all, Serra sought to provide the class of color in Cuba, which is to say, the network of writers and readers among whom *La Fraternidad* circulated, special insight into one particular aspect of life in the United States. "The readers of *La Fraternidad* will have noticed that it has always been our practice to introduce, in our dispatches, as far as our feeble talents allow, the degree of advancement and culture attained by the class of color in the United States," he wrote, as well as the "countless abuses committed daily against the great majority."[52] In this effort Juan Bonilla, who had been born in the United States and spoke fluent English, was probably a crucial resource, helping to translate African American newspapers and other sources. Serra and Bonilla, from the perspective of the particular kinds of segregation and sociability that they experienced in Greenwich Village, provided readers in Cuba and in other exile communities details about the life of Frederick Douglass, accounts of violence against African Americans in the southern states, statistics on educational opportunities enjoyed by African Americans, and information about the gatherings and speeches of prominent African Americans. They also offered news of cases won by T. McCants Stewart, a leading African American lawyer and the coeditor, along with a transplanted Floridian named T. Thomas Fortune, of the local African American newspaper, the *New York Age*. The *New York Age* had become the principle news outlet reporting on the club and lodge activities organized by Sandoval and the others. From the reports sent to *La Fraternidad*, it is also clear that the Cubans became readers of the *New York Age*, and depended on it as a source for the news that they transmitted to Spanish-speaking readers in Cuba and the migrant communities.[53]

Serra, Sandoval, and the Bonillas were thus able to count on coverage in both *La Fraternidad* and the *New York Age* when they undertook their second major project, the Cuban Republican Club. Beginning in August 1888, they mobilized the men in the Sol de Cuba and San Manuel lodges—whom they had already organized as supporters of *La Fraternidad*—to participate in the upcoming presidential elections in the United States. Cuban workers in New York had been naturalizing and registering to vote for more than a decade. The club's secretary, Gerónimo Bonilla, was the son of one of the first Cubans of color to naturalize as a US citizen in 1870 and a veteran of Key West Republican politics. And many of the members had naturalized as part of the network organized by Agustín Yorca over the three preceding election cycles. But the coverage in the *New York Age* makes it clear that the Cuban Republican Club was something different— one of many political clubs that operated within the African American wing of the Republican Party. This suggests that it was part of the political network built by Reverend Derrick, the man who for several years had been hosting events organized by and for Cubans at the Bethel Church.[54] The club seems also to be the first Cuban political organization in New York in which all the officers were men of color.

The effort to create the Cuban Republican Club was distantly removed from the lives of those readers of *La Fraternidad* who lived in Cuba. Yet this project was clearly one of those "tangible facts" gleaned from the experience of exile that might have relevance to readers on the island. Indeed, the activities of the Cuban Republican Club had direct implications for one of the main topics taken up in the newspaper, as representatives in the Spanish Cortes debated the question of universal suffrage. Since 1876, Spanish law had restricted suffrage to men who paid a minimum tax contribution or who were eligible based on "capacity." In the colonies, the minimum tax required to participate in elections for representatives to the Cortes was steeply prohibitive at twenty-five pesos. Writers in *La Fraternidad* criticized Cuban politicians for their inconsistent support for the principle of universal suffrage. They also called on the "black race" to seek inclusion in the broader electoral lists compiled for municipal and provincial elections, for which the minimum tax contribution to be eligible to vote was only five pesos. In small towns, all male heads of household were eligible to vote in local contests. This meant that many men of African descent had access to the franchise. If "our brothers" would make the effort to participate, the writers in *La Fraternidad* argued as part of a campaign to encourage readers to enroll in electoral lists, this would put pressure on parties to compete for the sympathies of black voters and would help to defeat the argument that they were not yet prepared to be trusted with the vote.[55] In organizing the Cuban Republican Club, the

New Yorkers were answering this call for all who were eligible to make use of the right to vote and demonstrating the capacity of black men to participate in electoral politics.

More than that, the club offered a model of dignified, orderly activity that proved the capacity of black men to be responsible participants in political life. This evidence might influence the thinking of politicians in Cuba and Madrid as well as exiles like Martí, who was fascinated and repelled by the workings of mass urban democracy in his adopted city. In his reports to *La Fraternidad*, Serra highlighted a parade organized by the club, with the participation of five hundred persons of both sexes and "all classes." Cubans of color participated in electoral politics *together* with white Cubans without any irregularities or unrest. They gathered and paraded in orderly fashion. It was a great pleasure, Serra wrote, to paint a picture for readers in *La Fraternidad* of "the elegance and good taste with which they were attired, and the order and composure of the subordinates with their superiors, and the striking, surprising image they presented along the whole trajectory." This hierarchy of superiors and subordinates presumably referred to elected positions rather than social rank. The "superiors" were Sandoval, Serra, Bonilla, and the other officers of the club—a point that would not likely have been lost on readers of *La Fraternidad*. Still, the message of social order was clear. These accounts allowed Serra the opportunity to bask in and perhaps embellish the glow of a successful event that he and his constituents had organized, highlighting their contribution to the sparkling ethnic reputation Cubans of color enjoyed in the city. He noted that the "press has spoken two or three times of the good conduct that the Cubans observe, etc."[56]

The third major project that Serra, the Bonillas, and Sandoval undertook together was the creation of a new sociedad de color in New York, which in early 1888, began to meet at the apartment that the Bonillas rented on West Third Street. Serra appealed to the readership of *La Fraternidad* for support in building an institution that—as the editors of newspaper so often implored—would forgo recreation in order to focus almost exclusively on instruction.[57] Unfortunately, no copy of this appeal survives. But it was probably similar in tone to an essay he wrote, soon thereafter, in which he explained that the purpose of the society was "to lighten the insufferable burden of a servile condition" and to move beyond what he called "a precarious dignity." In close agreement with the editorial position regularly expressed in *La Fraternidad*, he noted that "the oppressed classes, far from considering the reason for their misfortune, which is the lack of enlightenment, prefer to take pleasure in their vices. They might someday seek redemption through violence, but they will be undone by their own failings, weak and defeated." Education, however, could serve as a tool for improving the standing of the oppressed classes and for creating equilibrium among the "elements" of Cuban society. "We see no better means for harmonizing the classes who will have to mix in the future, than, with pure hands, raising the class that is now prostrate out of its inertia."[58] This would not be a single club but rather the first in a planned network of societies, sustained by its own members, taking responsibility for the destiny of the class of color.

Perhaps this idea of a network is one of the reasons why Serra, Sandoval, and the Bonillas chose to avoid the names typically employed by sociedades de color in Cuba and in exile communities: Harmony, Equality, Fraternity, Progress, and so on. They proposed instead to call it La Liga (the League). The name may have been a reference as well to the long-standing ideal of an Antillean League, a confederation that would, proponents hoped, unite Cuba, Puerto Rico, and other Caribbean islands into a confederation of independent states. Finally, La Liga may have been a nod to the Afro-American League, founded in New York only months earlier by the editors of the *New York Age*. Serra and Sandoval knew of the campaign, which filled the pages of the *New York Age*, to create a national network of African American societies dedicated to the "manly" defense of civil rights outside the constraints of the patronage systems of the political parties.[59] The organizers of the Afro-American League may also have been aware of the nearly identical project that the editors of *La Fraternidad* had proposed in Cuba two years before, the Directorio de Sociedades de Color. The similarities in these names, Antillean League, the League, and the Afro-American League, hint at the ideas and strategies that flowed in both directions between Cuban and African American journalists, and between New York and Havana.

MARTÍ

This was exactly the moment when, as Serra would later describe it, José Martí "dropped suddenly upon us." Suddenly, because it was not at all obvious before the end of 1888 that Martí would become a major supporter of the project to create La Liga, or that Martí's involvement in the educational society would so effectively build the men of the Sol de Cuba and San Manuel lodges into his first reliable constituency. Martí had been a well-known figure among exiles since he had arrived in New York in 1880. A speech that he made shortly after arriving earned him a reputation as a scintillating orator and quite possibly identified him to exile audiences as a racial liberal, in the mode of Azcárate and others in Havana and Matanzas. He addressed rumors that slaves were beginning to set fires on cane plantations—acts of violence that adopted, as he called it, "the terrorizing language taught by our cruelty and their misfortune." He believed, however, that abolition would put an end to these frightening episodes. Martí dismissed Spanish accusations of race war. There was no reason to fear that "men, most of whom are submissive, a few of whom are restless, and a good number of whom are intelligent, will pursue barbaric purposes, the mere suspicion of which causes honorable blacks and honorable mulattoes to blush." He noted that Cuban men of color continued to feel bitter toward "we who have oppressed them" and who "absolutely" do not yet "deserve their trust." Cubans of color, he said, distanced themselves from "those who scorn them, or who pretend to fear them," and that they felt disdain for "those who seek their applause with improper flattery." But, Martí observed, it would be an offense to conclude that "they" have not conducted a revolution for "our freedom" when we have made a revolution "for our freedom and for theirs."[60]

Cubans of color who heard this speech likely noted that he configured himself as a participant in a conversation among "Cubans," whom he referred to using the pronoun "we," about the relative dangers posed by "blacks and mulattoes," whom he referred to as "they." His expression of sympathy, at a distance, was probably welcome. But it did not distinguish Martí from other nationalists. He was not the kind of writer who accompanied cigar workers, white and black, to the courthouse to become citizens. Martí was not the type of journalist who would visit the local prison to offer comfort to a cigar maker condemned to death for killing his African American lover. He was not the type of literary luminary who volunteered to give worker education classes, or who was in and out of cigar workshops in the capacity of shop floor reader. Rather, he could be found reporting on the city's cultural and political life or dining alongside the cream of New York society at Delmonico's restaurant on Fifth Avenue.[61] Perhaps most important, he had publicly broken with Gómez and Maceo. In doing so, he had established himself as a leading proponent of civilian control over the independence movement. This had the effect of distancing him from the wing of the movement that had propelled men of color into positions of leadership and that had most vigorously adopted a radically democratic view of social transformation, recently expressed in Serra's poetic elegy to the 1885 expedition. Supporters of Maceo and Gómez, including Crombet and Morúa, regularly attacked and impugned Martí's patriotism.[62]

So how to explain his sudden appearance at La Liga? For one thing, Martí's extensive writings in the Latin American press in this period demonstrate a gradual evolution in his thinking. From the mid-1870s, he had expressed sympathy for the plight of workers, and since his arrival in the United States, he had described his distaste for the extreme class divisions that he observed in Gilded Age New York. His social positions showed clear affinities with various forms of socialist thought, including the ideal of social harmony through education and free association so influential among Spanish, Puerto Rican, and Cuban liberals.[63] Yet through the mid-1880s, Martí tended to approach these inequities from a distance and to express an overriding concern with the need to find ways to limit the dangers of class division. He described the frightening power of the teeming mass of workers in the city during a demonstration, and the "ignorance and excess" of worker activism.[64] On US elections, he wrote, "The ignorant masses in the hands of professional politicians are terrible. They do not know how to see past the mask of justice worn by those who exploit their resentments." He thought black voters in the South, especially, were "easily incited and habitually embittered."[65] In 1886, as Cuban workers took up the cause of the Chicago martyrs, Martí strongly supported the arrest and conviction of the Haymarket defendants. His account of the incident, like much of his reporting on the United States in the period, echoed the xenophobic perspective of the leading newspapers in the United States.[66]

As Cuban workers turned increasingly toward anarchism, however, Martí's views on worker politics also began to evolve. He became an ardent admirer of the social theories of Henry George, whose 1879 book *Poverty and Progress*, which analyzed the causes of industrial depressions, was one of the most widely read books of the era. Martí came to share George's view that ensuring the availability of land to smallholders was crucial to preventing the growth and suffering of the urban masses. This led him circuitously to a position that was popular among supporters of Maceo and Gómez. He also celebrated George's campaign for mayor of New York as part of the Labor Party in 1886. He admired the alliance between "healthy, daring and clean" thinkers and laboring men, including black men, "united for the first time in serious political endeavor"—a movement that he qualified as the "baptism of a new race."[67] Martí remained constitutionally opposed to destabilizing class "hatreds" and disharmony, as he would for the rest of his life. But by 1887, he held the imperfections of the United States responsible for social disorder rather than "embittered" black voters or murderous immigrant "fanatics." The key to preventing both racial conflict and worker excesses, Martí argued, was not repression but instead the establishment of a just and inclusive political order built on popular education and effective leadership.[68] Following George's example, Martí would create the Cuban Revolutionary Party as a workingman's party, reconfiguring the symbolic inclusion that the Cuban leadership had long offered "our blacks" and "our workers" into a new set of democratic political institutions. He continued, though, to share George's animosity toward Chinese immigrants.

It is not clear to what degree Martí had already imagined this new kind of political movement when he first invited Serra to speak at the anniversary event on October 10, 1888. Was this invitation a recognition of Serra's roles as "bard" of the 1885 expedition, secretary of the Club Los Independientes, and correspondent for *La Fraternidad*, or did Martí understand that Serra, as the leader of the Cuban Republican Club, had already begun to unite the exiles of color in New York in "serious political endeavor"? To what extent did Martí's plan to create a workingman's party precede his encounter with Serra and the other men of La Liga, and to what degree did the plan grow out of this encounter? We can only imagine Martí's thoughts, on the night of October 10, when Serra stood before an audience that included professionals, writers, merchants, bankers, "ladies," cigar makers, seamstresses, waiters, housewives, and perhaps even domestic servants. Some of the workers in the audience and all the members of the Cuban Republican Club had surely heard Serra speak before. But he was a novel figure for many in the assembled crowd. His performance would have to negotiate the unspoken prejudices, expectations, and curiosities of the audience. It might vindicate his own status as an intellectual and, by extension, the merits of the "class" that he had been put in the position of representing. Or it might simply confirm the low expectations of the least generous members of the assembly. It might energize the men of color in the audience and some white workers, allowing them to believe in a nationalist movement whose ideals were their ideals. Yet could it do so without frightening the merchants, manufacturers, planters, and doctors, who feared any expression of black empowerment?

Serra began his address with a familiar gesture of self-deprecation. "It is embarrassing, very embarrassing, when someone lacking the advantageous faculties to make himself heard, to make himself understood, embargoes the attention of those who know how to think, who know how to speak, who know how to judge." Yet even as he downplayed his own abilities, Serra disarmed listeners who might be tempted to focus on his limitations as a speaker. A speech at a patriotic gathering in Masonic Hall, he chided, should not be treated as a test "where exacting academicians ought to abuse, with pitiless criticism, the people of simple dress, those who are modest but are devoted to freedom."[69] Here we see the contours of Serra's long path from an artisan of humble origins to a participant in the public plaza, including the heavy weight of expectations, the constraints imposed by stereotypes, and the opportunities made available by certain kinds of liberal politics.

Serra then returned to the familiar metaphors of family, exile, and remembrance that he had developed in *Echoes of the Soul*. The Cubans present were a group of migratory swallows united by the powerful memories of a distant *patria*, by a shared sense of mourning for fallen martyrs, and by a common hope for the future. It was in the name of this shared vision that Serra introduced an explicit project of social justice. He had no wish, he said, to disrupt the spirit of unity by inciting "selfish passions." Nevertheless, he considered it a "patriotic duty" to speak out against those who thought that the success of a republic depended only on establishing public order. It was painful to see the country divided by "the venomous and vainglorious waves of ethnographic prejudices." Such ideas, he said, were never introduced by the "popular elements," but by "the elements that preen over their own wisdom."[70] Members of the audience who had been reading Serra's reports in *La Fraternidad* would probably know that this barb was directed at several prominent Cuban exiles, Trujillo and Pierra—as well as the Autonomista Party in Cuba. For Serra, there was no threat of social disorder in the prospect of revolution. It was rather the specter of a "tyrannical Republic," reproducing the vices of colonial government, which posed a danger to popular liberties. Yet the Cuban people were not so childish or gullible as to be duped into this sort of independence. As if to prove the point, he closed with a flourish of historical and literary references to Moses, Demosthenes, Tyrtaeus, Saint John, the Count of Mirabeau, Thomas Jefferson, Benjamin Franklin, and Simón Bolívar.[71] Serra had begun his speech with protestations of his own lack of "advantageous faculties." He concluded with an impeccable demonstration of his familiarity with classical and modern political history.

Whether Martí could have anticipated the content of this speech or not, he had put Serra in a position to express what intellectuals of color had been arguing for a decade, that the ideals of the movement were "our ideals," while also carefully spelling out exactly what those ideals were. This did little to help Martí fend off the regular attacks of the established nationalist leadership. But it set in motion a remarkable political alliance through which Martí would reframe his vision of nationalist struggle as an attempt to find equilibrium among various elements that was inseparable from a basic project of class and racial justice, and would use this message to sidestep political opponents by appealing directly to working-class exiles. Shortly after the October speech, Serra went to see Martí, seeking support for the project to create La Liga. This kind of request for patronage would have been a familiar exercise, and Serra was probably not surprised when he received no immediate answer from Martí. Then Serra published a favorable report on Martí in *La Fraternidad*. Martí responded with a personal letter to Serra acknowledging the "kindness" and the "honor that you do me in what you say about me." Martí also acknowledged Serra's request for help in starting La Liga. He wrote, "I desire its success, and that it should be established immediately, as if it were my own." He explained his support with a remarkable expression of precisely the political position that Serra had been articulating for most of the decade. La Liga would be a starting point for a movement that sought "not simply political change but rather a good, healthy, just, and equitable social structure, without flattery nor demagogues nor the excessive pride of potentates, without ever forgetting that those whose suffering is greatest have a sublime right to justice, and that men's prejudices, and impermanent social inequalities, cannot overcome the equality that nature has created."[72]

Martí also acknowledged with startling frankness that his decision to extend an offer of friendship might easily be mistaken as insincere populism, an established tradition in the movement. He feared, he wrote, "that those who have suffered so much at the hands of false friends, will take my enthusiasm, and the secret oath that I have taken to live in order to serve you, as interference and adulation, or a desire to seek popularity. This idea is hateful to me. . . . I, who ask for nothing, would have the honor of asking to be useful, really useful to your *Sociedad La Liga*."[73] Serra and his allies probably did wonder about this very question. But Martí eventually won them over. He tried, unsuccessfully, to help them find a place to locate the society, most likely aware of the relatively few options open to them in the segregated rental market.[74] Martí started regularly to attend the literary gatherings that Serra and the Bonillas organized in the rooms that the Bonillas rented from the Reasons over spring and summer 1889. He also began to bring other men from his own social world to events at 74 West Third Street. Two wealthy cigar manufacturers, Manuel Barranco and Benjamín Guerra, as well as a young doctor named Buenaventura Portuondo and a young lawyer, Gonzalo de Quesada, eventually became founding members of La Liga and volunteer teachers.[75] Along with the Bonillas, Serra, and Figueroa (who arrived in New York in 1889), these four men became Martí's inner circle over the next several years, helping him to develop his strategy for rebuilding the movement under his leadership.

The best view of the dynamics of this emerging set of relationships comes from the letters that Martí wrote to Serra, Juan Bonilla, and the man who was treasurer of La Liga, Manuel de Jesús González. It is perhaps not surprising, given Serra's own image of a movement unified by "deep and virtuous love" among men of distinct social backgrounds, that these letters resemble, more than anything, the artifacts of a tentative courtship. As he often did in his speeches, Martí presented himself in his letters as a man overcome by fatigue, by illness, and by the horrors of the world. He worked feverishly in tortured solitude, and never had enough time or energy to accomplish tasks that were desperately urgent. He was also beset by enemies who spoke ill of him, "evil men, and rogues who feed on the credulity and ignorance of good men." In the gloom of the dark room where he sat among mountains of papers, only his sincere and growing love for Serra and Bonilla, and theirs for him, offered him a bright ray of hope. Serra's kindness, he wrote, was "excellent medicine" when it found him prostrate one afternoon.[76] In one letter, Martí described his heart as a flower that had been trodden. Serra's friendship was the dew and sunshine that would reanimate it.[77] In another letter, he told Juan Bonilla, "My discouragement is great, and I stumble along like one who falls apart on the path, and walks along picking up his own pieces from the ground." He added, "As I struggle, those who console me, through their honor and nobility, are always on my mind. . . . Remain as good and unassuming as you are, and as I would wish to be, and love, without eclipses, your friend José Martí."[78] He wrote to Serra, "Yes. I want to come Sunday, to be with you all. I am sick, but I know I will be able to go. Coming to see you this Sunday will be the only reason I will leave this little corner where my work distracts me from my sadness."[79]

These letters were also sometimes slightly defensive, since Martí's attention was divided. Frequently he disappeared, canceled appointments, or delayed in responding to messages. This is understandable. In 1889, in addition to helping to create La Liga, Martí participated in the first International Conference of American States. He represented several Latin American countries as a diplomat and was a correspondent for multiple Latin American newspapers. In each of these capacities, he led an effort to organize public opinion in Latin America against what he saw as a rising threat from US imperialism. He also taught in the evenings at a New York City high school and suffered from sarcoidosis, a serious chronic illness. He experienced recurring painful infections in his groin, fevers, and bouts of fatigue, which frequently left him indisposed. Serra and the Bonillas knew this, and it is not clear whether they were actually sensitive about his tendency to disappear suddenly from view. But he was at pains to explain that his periodic inattention was not a measure of his esteem for them, not the inevitable result of the fact that they were men of relatively low status and he was a famous poet and diplomat. "What must you have thought of me, when you saw that I did not answer as quickly as I should have," he wrote to Juan Bonilla. "You have no reason to know that after so much writing paper has come to seem a poor vehicle for the better sentiments of my heart." Martí hoped that Bonilla "will have seen in my eyes that which I hold in my heart for you, who seem to me a heart of gold and a man of flawless character." He urged Bonilla to believe that "although I delay more than is fair in answering one of your letters, it can only be great sorrows or arduous labors, never any coolness in the certain affection of your friend, José Martí."[80]

The letters that Serra and Bonilla wrote back to Martí are lost. But we can see something of the language that they began to adopt as part of this evolving relationship in several speeches that Serra gave in this period. At the inauguration of La Liga, Serra described Martí as "a man, materially exhausted, but exuberant in spirit and virtues, who dropped suddenly upon us, who opened his wings, white and divine, to shelter and care for us, and even to bring us to complete salvation. This man, gentlemen, was an archangel in the heaven that is the fatherland: it was José Martí." Several months later, at meeting of the Club Los Independientes, he said, "And you, Martí, sincere philanthropist; initiator of all that is sublime, against you fight only those who are envious or who do not know how to understand you. Continue your struggle, continue without pause, continue on with your soul of a prophet lifted high, for on your path you will never be without manly arms and generous hearts, to help you make Cuba blossom with justice."[81]

Perhaps the most revealing exchange during this period of courtship involved an incident in one of Martí's Thursday night classes at La Liga, which he referred to in his letters as "our Thursdays" and "the best night of the week."[82] As noted earlier, the men who attended the Thursday classes typically arrived at around eight o'clock, and spent part of the next hour writing short essays or questions, which they then placed unsigned on a table before Martí arrived. On this particular Thursday, one of the essays on the table posed a question that touched a nerve. "Can an intimate friendship between two persons of different social status be possible? Would there not be doubts about the sincerity of the man who is above and the man who is below? Would not the former suspect the sentiments of the latter, guessing that they reflect the necessities of his low status? Would not the humbler man doubt too, inferring that the former seeks to exercise authority?"[83]

Martí had, in fact, been trying to answer this question in many ways since his first letters to Serra. He implored them to look in his eyes to see his sincerity. He explained that his alliance with them stemmed not just from an abstract commitment to justice but from a theory that liberals must build alliances with "the people" or risk, as had happened so often in Latin America, the victory of conservative dictators backed by popular support. Time and again he reminded them that any inattention on his part owed only to his busy schedule, his illness, his depression, and the dreary solitude of his writing. He pointed out that he, like them, was forced to work in order to earn his daily bread. We workers, he told them, have no choice but to "make excuses to one another and to understand one another."[84] He demonstrated his sincere affection through greeting them warmly and respectfully, remembering details of their lives and family relations, holding the door for them on the way in or out of the apartment at 74 West Third Street, and bringing candy to their children. But when faced with a direct challenge to the possibility of sincere friendships between men of different social status, he was taken aback. He paused. He lost his composure, or so it seemed to both Serra and González.

After the meeting, both men wrote to Martí. They expressed concern that he may have misinterpreted these questions as a reference to himself. They assured him that they were not the individuals responsible for the impertinent questions. They asked if his feelings were hurt, if he was willing to forgive.[85] Perhaps they intended these questions as a test. Could this question, reasonably posed, really have upset Martí? Was he the kind of politician who expected deference and obsequiousness from those he called his friends? They could not ask such things directly, so perhaps they rushed to apologize instead, playing the part of dutiful clients to a thin-skinned patron. In his reply, Martí recognized the implicit question, turning it back at them. "But what kind of man do you suppose that I am?" he responded. "Merely a talented dancer, who performs pirouettes of teaching and love, so that gullible persons will applaud my steps?" Far from making him uncomfortable, he assured them, the questions gave him great pleasure, the "pleasure of being among men."[86]

This expression, the "pleasure of being among men," may well have been the key to Martí's efforts at courtship among this new group of constituents. Martí asked them to play the part of men of exemplary self-restraint, lack of pretention, tenderness, and forgiveness. This would allow him to incorporate them into the movement without frightening wealthier and more educated Cubans, while also satisfying his own concerns about equilibrium among the elements of a diverse society. They were willing, for reasons of their own, to present themselves in these ways. Serra and the Bonillas volunteered to be exemplars of disciplined, enlightened, and nonthreatening manliness, to be in living contradiction

to long-standing prejudices about the dangers of unrestrained black masculinity.[87] Yet this was not always a comfortable balance. Both the Cuban
separatist movement and the anarchist labor movement placed a high
value on the more assertive elements of manhood, including a man's willingness to stand up for his ideas and his dignity. So working-class participants were highly sensitive to any sign that they were expected to
defer, as would be expected in Cuban society, to those who considered
themselves social superiors. In his letters, Martí assured them that when
he read the *papelito*, he was aware that the man who wrote it was "a man
like myself, a sincere asker of questions."[88] He wrote that he became aware
that "I am among men who are whole."[89] And it was this kind of "whole"
man that excited his particular affections. "We are men and we are making
men," he wrote to Serra, and in another passage, he explained, "I do not
want castrated men."[90] This ideal of shared manhood became one of the
central elements of Martí's subsequent appeals to working-class constituents outside La Liga, nearly as powerful as—or perhaps more accurately,
inseparable from—the ideal of shared Cubanness.

A WORKINGMAN'S PARTY

By 1891, Martí's unusual relationship with the leaders at La Liga had not
only cemented his popularity among Cubans of color in New York; it had
begun to pave the way for a broader political appeal to the thousands of
radical cigar makers in Tampa and Key West. For three years Martí had
built a base of support among the members of the Logia San Manuel, the
Logia Sol de Cuba, the Committee to Support *La Fraternidad*, and the
now-inactive Cuban Republican Club. He also had close allies among white
cigar makers and labor leaders in New York. He still faced stiff opposition, though, from established nationalist leaders, who had not forgiven his
break with Gómez and Maceo. Then, in fall 1891, Martí's emergence as the
leader of a newly resurgent democratic wing of the nationalist movement
entered its next phase. This began in Tampa, a new cigar enclave built by
Cuban manufacturers in the wake of the fire in Key West and the wave
of strikes that followed. By 1888 and 1889, thousands of workers started
moving to Tampa from Key West, Havana, and New York, bringing with
them their traditions of multiracial labor organizing and self-education.
Nationalists in Key West and New York had grown increasingly estranged

from labor causes in these years, seeing worker radicalism as incompatible with nationalism. But in Tampa, veteran factory readers who were sympathetic to labor led the two primary nationalist organizations. One of the two was a socialist. These lectores created worker education centers, translated and circulated reading material to the factories, and along with several black Cuban writers, published local newspapers.[91]

Tampa was, in short, ideal territory into which to expand the project that Martí had launched at La Liga in New York. In November 1891, the Tampa lectores, along with a prominent businessman of color, invited Martí to participate in a night of speeches and poetry. How much did they know about Martí's evolution into a populist? This is hard to say. One of the organizers had seen him speak in Philadelphia. Another had been an active member of the fund-raising committee for *La Fraternidad* and had corresponded with Sandoval in this capacity. Quite a few had probably read (or heard a lector read) Martí's invitations to anniversary events, published in leading New York papers. They probably also knew of his letter to the *New York Evening Post*, which had been republished as a pamphlet and circulated among exiles. They had surely read Serra's account of Martí in *La Fraternidad*, and a collection of speeches that Serra had published as a pamphlet, including his praise for Martí at the Club Los Independientes and La Liga. As a result, they knew something about Martí's role at La Liga. They knew as well that nationalists in Key West still saw Martí as an inspiring writer, but a tepid revolutionary, and that the military leadership saw him as a typical New York "aristocrat." Based on all this, they likely expected a great orator who might possibly be a convincing and sincere man of the people too. But as Cuban scholar Jorge Mañach notes, these high expectations were matched by "a certain subtle distrust" because of Martí's reputation as a "deserter of Maceo and Gómez."[92]

Martí addressed himself directly to this audience. He borrowed freely from the language of working-class struggle, describing Cuba as a "hardworking fatherland," a nation that "has raised itself face to face with the greedy boss who lies in wait for us, who divides us." In a nod to the practice of shop floor reading in cigar factories and artisan intellectual life more broadly, he called Cubans a "cultured people, with the table for thinking next to the table for earning one's bread . . . which is more than enough answer to the scornful of this earth." As in his earlier correspondence with the men of La Liga, he explained that the transcendental quality of Cuban identity, which had the power to unify a diverse social body and build an equitable republic, was vested simultaneously in shared nationality and shared manhood. "I do not know what mysterious tenderness I find in this sweetest of words, cubano (Cuban man)," he pondered, "nor why it has such a pure flavor, purer still than the word hombre (man) which is already so beautiful." The one thing he most wished for was that "the first law of our republic be that worshipful respect for the full dignity of men." To men who had organized strikes to protest the mistreatment of workers by bosses and who had organized campaigns to protest a legal code that punished crimes more harshly if committed by blacks against whites, Martí promised that Cuba would be a society in which "each true man will feel on his own cheek a slap on the cheek of any other man."[93]

The Martí who appeared in Tampa, after three years of meetings at La Liga, no longer described the desires, loyalties, and merits of "our blacks" as if they were distinct from those of "the Cubans." He no longer relied on stories of the bonds of loyalty between white generals and their loyal servants—Estrada Palma's profession of affection for "his black," or Ignacio Agramonte's declaration that "his mulatto" was "his brother."[94] Instead, he emphasized the knowledge that he had gained through his personal relationships with black Cubans, Serra, the Bonillas, and the others at La Liga. Because of these relationships, he told the workers in Tampa, he knew black men to be different from white men only in the "greater, more natural, and more useful intensity of their love for freedom." Others may fear the black man, he declared; "I love him." He concluded his speech by calling all Cubans to come together around the principle that the revolution in Cuba would be fought in the name of "this formula of triumphant love: with all and for the good of all." This would become the catchphrase for the idea of a revolution that would pursue independence and social justice.[95] Reportedly the speech was a resounding success. Martí spent more than an hour afterward exchanging greetings with workers who wanted to shake his hand.[96]

Having adapted his own view of the equilibrium of social elements to a language of social justice and shared male dignity, and having won the sympathies of the crowd, Martí quickly moved to constitute an inner circle in Tampa. The organizers in Tampa had invited an expert stenographer to attend and record Martí's words. They immediately published and circulated thousands of copies of the "with all and for the good of all" speech.

On his second day in Tampa, Martí gathered the most important Cubans of color in the settlement and prevailed on them to establish a local branch of La Liga.[97] This became a home base for Martí on his dozens of subsequent trips to Tampa, allowing him to build ties with aspiring black and brown writers in that city, and to put into practice his belief that they were and ought to be "whole men."[98] Already, by the time that he departed from his first visit, in fall 1891, his speeches and his new alliances had made him an extremely popular figure among workers in the city. The crowd escorting him to the train station reportedly stretched for three city blocks.

If his previous experience at La Liga in New York and the reputation it had allowed him to build helped in introducing Martí to the larger constituency in Tampa, the inner circle of supporters that he built on his first visit to Tampa was equally helpful in introducing him to the still-larger community of workers in Key West. This next phase of movement building took place in late December 1891 and early January 1892. Even after the fire and the exodus of many manufacturers to Tampa, Key West was still home to the largest number of Cuban exiles, including thousands of workers who had become estranged from the nationalist cause. Since Antonio Maceo's last visit to the city, to collect funds that would purchase weapons that, a few months later, would be dumped by a skittish steamboat captain into Kingston harbor, the seasoned nationalist leaders in the city had struggled to interest workers in their activities. Those nationalist leaders, with few exceptions, were still skeptical of Martí and reluctant to cede a prominent place in their movement to him. With help from the lector Francisco María González and several of the prominent lectores from Tampa, Martí sidestepped this opposition by appealing directly to workers. The men from Tampa, all of whom had recently relocated from Key West, brought him to speak to workers at factories, republished and disseminated his recent speeches, and introduced him to large crowds at the rebuilt San Carlos Club.[99]

Martí quickly turned his swelling popularity among workers to his advantage. He drafted the principles for a new political organization, the Cuban Revolutionary Party, and before consulting the leadership of the local separatist organizations, presented those principles directly to workers at a meeting at the San Carlos. The principles included the pursuit of absolute independence for Cuba and Puerto Rico; careful preparation of a broad coalition of forces in order to conduct, at the proper moment, a "brief and generous" war; a program to attract and welcome new supporters; and a promise to dispense with authoritarian and bureaucratic rule in order to "create a new, sincerely democratic, people through the frank and cordial exercise of the legitimate capacities of men, capable of overcoming, through orderly and real work and the equilibrium of the social forces, the dangers of sudden freedom in a society composed for slavery," and to create an independent nation "for the good of all Cubans, and in order to turn over to the whole nation a free fatherland."[100] In a deep and melodious voice, Francisco María González read these principles aloud to a mass assembly at the San Carlos, to thunderous applause. Martí had gained popularity with the mass of workers, but as important, he had won the support of worker organizers and intellectuals, including several of the men who had drafted the "Protest of the Cubans of Color" in 1881 and had subsequently emerged as the most prominent black labor activists in the city.[101] Somewhat reluctantly, the heads of the various separatist groups in Key West voted to approve the principles that Martí had proposed, and to allow him to undertake the task of writing up a set of statutes or bylaws to govern the party.[102]

Martí had likely planned out some of this with his allies in New York and Tampa. Some of it seems to have been spontaneous, a quick reaction to a sequence of events that nobody quite foresaw. Chroniclers of these events reported quick conversions in response to Martí's eloquence and charisma, putting the emphasis on his skill at presenting himself to workers. But at least part of this success had to do with the quick and effective decisions of worker organizers, factory readers, and black and brown intellectuals, who seized on Martí's charisma as an opportunity to restructure the separatist movement in a way that promoted their own political projects, and allowed them considerable power within a movement that had traditionally delegated leadership to military veterans and New York "aristocrats." Back in New York, Martí drew up a set of statutes that transformed the movement into a workingman's party, albeit one with a platform that was expressly inclusive of professionals and even manufacturers who accepted the ideals of equality and unity. Any organization or club that voted to accept the principles and statutes of the party had the right to vote, through their representatives, to elect the two officers who would run the central party: the delegate and treasurer. These clubs were required to contribute half the funds that they raised to the central party but were free to dispose of the remainder on terms of complete autonomy.[103] This was a major change; for the first time the leadership in the movement would be popularly elected. It was also a marked contrast to the existing political parties in Cuba, where voting was still restricted to taxpayers and "capacities."

The statutes allowed Martí's close supporters in New York, Tampa, and Key West to create a handful of clubs that quickly affiliated with the party, and to confirm Martí's leadership in it, while leaving little or no space for anyone to oppose him. The only way to counter Martí's bid for the post of delegate was to join the party, accepting its principles and bylaws, and granting it legitimacy as the democratic expression of the movement. And in any event, it would be difficult to succeed in such a challenge since by spring 1892, the Advisory Councils in New York, Key West, and Tampa, composed of the elected presidents of each of the clubs, were firmly in the control of Martí's allies from the labor movement and La Liga. This set up a struggle, which played out over the course of 1892, in the court of public opinion. Martí and his allies worked to translate his popularity among workers into mass membership in the party. They encouraged and cajoled workers to establish new clubs, and to affiliate with the party. Meanwhile, Martí's opponents attacked him in public, seeking to undermine his popularity. Martí had hardly returned from his first trip to Key West when a group of veterans of the Ten Years' War published a letter in a Havana newspaper denouncing him. They noted that he had never served in the military, questioned his patriotism, and accused him of living off the donations of unsuspecting workers in the émigré communities.[104]

The ensuing controversy provided an opportunity for his most enthusiastic supporters to rally around him, sending him letters of support, organizing meetings and rallies in Tampa and Key West, and eventually sending a commission to Havana to negotiate a resolution. In New York, Serra called a meeting at La Liga, where he delivered a stirring speech in defense of Martí. "He deplores and combats the existence of classes that are despised or excluded from their rights, because of his own instincts and because, as a practical politician, he knows that with the promise to make amends to the suffering masses, it will be easy to chase the tyrants from power." Martí, Serra told the men who had gathered at La Liga, "is Democracy." To offend Martí, he said, was to "kill the fatherland."[105] Opponents led by Trujillo, the editor of New York's leading Cuban newspaper, continued to criticize Martí and the party, seeing him as a civilian dictator who had arrogated full power to direct the movement to himself and as "mentally unhinged" in his fervent advocacy of social equality. To them Martí seemed to be preaching "hatred for rich, cultivated, and conservative men," and "hatred for the United States," and he seemed to be introducing fearsome elements into the Cuban movement, "which had always before emerged from the high and wealthy classes."[106]

In response, the men who had rallied around Martí launched a campaign to collect donations from workers in the cigar factories to start a newspaper. By March 1892, they had collected enough money to create *Patria*, giving Martí a platform to counter opposition from Cuban journalists, and to disseminate his message of a movement "with all and for all" directly to readers (and especially workers listening to readers) in New York, Florida, New Orleans, Jamaica, and beyond.[107] At about the same time, Serra published a collection of his speeches, including several in which he defended Martí, as well as some documents relating to La Liga in his first book, *Political Essays*. Serra and his allies also remained his point of contact with the half-dozen clubs that they had helped to create in New York. In July 1892, for instance, Martí dashed off a letter to Juan Bonilla explaining that he needed urgently to gather the presidents and secretaries of all the New York Clubs in order to "refute the willful malignancy" of a recently published article about the party. He asked Bonilla if he knew where to find several of these men "during the day."[108]

It seems unlikely that Serra and Gerónimo Bonilla could have anticipated, as they walked to the courthouse on October 10, 1888, that their relationship with Martí, who would appear onstage with Serra that evening, would have taken this shape a mere four years later. And it seems quite unlikely that Martí could have imagined that his earnestly expressed support for Serra and Bonilla in their efforts to create La Liga in 1889 would turn out to be so successful a step toward creating a party of serious workingmen, and consolidating his own status as their enlightened and irreproachable leader. Because of the mythical status that Martí obtained after his death, many accounts treat this unexpected turn of events as inevitable. They focus on Martí's sweeping oratory, his overwhelming charisma, his gentle poetic eyes, and the intrinsic patriotism of the men who became his followers. In these versions of the story, Martí was always, inevitably, an ally of the people and the Father of the Fatherland.

He was a Christlike figure, who transformed the men around him into disciples through the potency of his ideals and the force of his character. Yet the convergence of these radial lines in the great sphere of resurgent patriotism—first in La Liga in New York, then in his first speeches in Tampa, and finally at the San Carlos in Key West and in the pages of *Patria*—is better explained by tracing the lines back to their points of origin, in the experiences of "humble" artisans in Havana and Key West. It is better explained by observing them as they passed through the political openings that first introduced those artisans to the "public square." And it is better explained by reconstructing the unique experiences of "migrating while black"—experiences that created the immediate context for the collaboration with Martí. In New York, these included the apartment in the home of a prominent African American couple at 74 West Third Street, the network of writers and readers that had created the newspaper *La Fraternidad*, and the political club consisting of "sixty intelligent and well-dressed men" led by Serra, Sandoval, and Gerónimo Bonilla. Martí's manner of speaking, the sincerity of his eyes, his unpretentious friendship, and his love letters certainly swayed the leaders of these groups. But those men also chose to make him into a leader. They promoted him in order to push forward a claim on the nationalist movement that they had been making for more than a decade. Of all the accounts of Martí's emergence as a popular democrat, perhaps the most telling in this regard is the one offered by Serra in the midst of the controversies surrounding the formation of the Cuban Revolutionary Party. "We protest," he proclaimed, "the insult that is done to us by those who believe us to be the blind followers of Martí."[109] Serra and the other men of "humble" origins who had joined the party had become followers of Martí, of course. But they were anything but blind.

In this moment, in the hubbub of propaganda work and party organizing, Martí's relationship with Serra and the Bonillas would take on a second life. Martí relied on key organizers in Tampa and Key West for the heavy lifting in building the party. He relied on the handful of men in his inner circle in New York for help in drafting the newspaper. Some were the same white men that he had brought with him to become founding members and teachers at La Liga: Benjamín Guerra (who was elected as treasurer of the party) and Quesada (who became Martí's secretary). These writers came, as Serra later put it, from the "yellowest cream of the Cuban aristocracy," and they knew there was a risk that in using the newspaper to appeal to workers in Key West and Tampa, Martí would further alienate members of their own social class.[110] They paid careful attention to producing a balance between appeals to workers, white and black, and celebrations of the sacrifices and accomplishments of wealthy white Cubans, creating a newspaper that like the public meetings Martí arranged, served as a model for the ideal of integrating diverse elements under the banner of national unity. In the pages of *Patria*, the authors developed, along with Martí, the story of La Liga, "the house of love and affection," and celebrated its most famous students. This served as a form of outreach to the "wide base" of the party, through the celebration of the merits and dignity of black men and women, and as an advertisement of the equilibrium of elements that was possible in the movement. As he had done since the day that he first invited Serra to give a speech in front of the assembled Cuban émigré community, Martí continued to shape the party and *Patria* in ways that opened space for the men of La Liga to tell their own stories as well, to articulate their own politics. In the pages of *Patria* and at party meetings in New York, they became coproducers of the image of a movement composed of reformed white Cubans, willing to dispense with their privileges, and of forgiving black Cubans willing to dedicate themselves to self-improvement and the welfare of all. In these efforts, their trajectories would intersect with those of two printers from Puerto Rico, Figueroa and Marín, who arrived in New York in this period, and became two of Martí's principal collaborators in building the party and in editing *Patria*.

▪ 5 ▪

Crossing

One must live in this country for some years to understand that this race
does not tend to perfect and improve, through crossing, those races that
it believes to be inferior.
—Sotero Figueroa, Antonio Vélez Alvarado, and Francisco Gonzalo
Marín, "Al pueblo puertorriqueño," 1892

On the first Sunday in April 1892, two cigar makers named Rosendo
Rodríguez and Augusto Benech hosted a group of twenty-three men at a
meeting at an apartment on Third Avenue, near Ninety-Ninth Street (see
map 6). Both of the hosts were stalwart members of the immigrant educational society La Liga, as were many of those they invited. Rodríguez
took the floor to explain that they had called the meeting for the purpose
of creating a political club. The men responded enthusiastically. Because
some were Cuban and others Puerto Rican, they decided to call their
association the Club Las Dos Antillas (the Two Antilles). Club members then elected Benech, a Cuban, to serve as secretary and Rodríguez,
a Puerto Rican, as president. They named the Cuban general Antonio
Maceo (then living in Costa Rica) and the Puerto Rican doctor Ramón
Emeterio Betances (then living in Paris) as honorary presidents. They
collected contributions from the members, adding up to $3.40. And they
voted to approve the principles and bylaws of the Cuban Revolutionary
Party. These were the crucial steps necessary to claim membership in
the party. Rodríguez was therefore able to join the presidents of the five
other affiliated clubs in the city on the party's New York Advisory Council. He was the only black cigar maker on the council when it met, five
days later, to elect the first party delegate. He cast the vote of the Club
Las Dos Antillas for Martí.[1]

The notes of the founding meeting, copied into the club minute book by Secretary Benech, offer a glimpse at the efforts to create the Cuban Revolutionary Party over spring and summer 1892. The party grew through collaboration between working-class leaders like Rodríguez and Benech and the inner circle of "disciples" that had formed around Martí. Serra was part of this inner circle. He attended the first meeting of Las Dos Antillas, and also surely gave advice to Rodríguez and Benech and encouraged other members of La Liga to join their effort. Several prominent white members of Martí's inner circle also attended the first meeting of Las Dos Antillas or joined shortly thereafter: the wealthy lawyer Quesada, Martí's personal secretary, as well as a leading Puerto Rican publisher and a wealthy Cuban manufacturer. These were some of the same men Martí brought to La Liga to serve as teachers. They remained on the membership rolls throughout the life of the club. But having lent their support and prestige to its creation, and having promised to pay regular dues, none of them, not even Serra, would return for subsequent meetings.

None, that is, except the two Puerto Rican typographers, Figueroa and Marín. Both had recently joined Martí's inner circle, writing essays for *Patria*, making speeches at party gatherings, and circulating among the various clubs formed in New York in this period. At the first meeting of Las Dos Antillas, they were joined by a third typesetter from the smaller island, a white man named Modesto Tirado, who also participated in the exhausting effort to turn Martí's popularity among workers into a formal party structure and a resounding victory in his bid to become the delegate.[2] Figueroa, Marín, and Tirado returned to assist Rodríguez over subsequent meetings. They drafted and printed a constitution for the club, and offered guidance on how to interpret these bylaws. They probably also helped men with less experience in public life to master the particulars of running the club.[3] In particular, they may have helped Arturo Schomburg, a teenager recently arrived from San Juan, to manage the tasks of record keeping and correspondence. Schomburg, who was also a typesetter, became the secretary of the club several months after the founding meeting, when Gerónimo Bonilla and several dozen others met at the headquarters of La Liga to create the Club Guerrilla de Maceo. Benech stepped down from Las Dos Antillas to become president of this new club. Schomburg took his place.[4]

The men of La Liga created these two black (or mostly black) political clubs and promoted two black cigar makers to the Party Advisory

Council at an especially sensitive moment. In spring and summer 1892, even as Martí's supporters worked to build the Cuban Revolutionary Party in exile, in Cuba the civil rights movement picked up steam under the leadership of the journalist Juan Gualberto Gómez, now returned to Havana. Gómez and his allies toured the island, visiting and helping to revitalize the sociedades de color, seeking to resolve conflicts among local factions, and rebuilding the Directorio Central de Sociedades de Color. The Directorio worked as an island-wide civil rights organization, hosting a convention in Havana in July 1892 (a month before the founding of the Club Guerrilla de Maceo) and drafting a set of demands to submit to the colonial government. These included the expansion of public schooling, the elimination of racial discrimination in criminal sentencing, the elimination of separate birth and death registries and identity cards based on race, the right to the honorific titles don and doña, the enforcement of laws against discrimination in cafés and theaters, and an end to municipal ordinances requiring people of color to give way to white people on sidewalks and restricting access to public parks. The Directorio also applied pressure to the leadership of the Liberal Party, now known as Autonomistas, to endorse this program of civil and political equality. To support the work of the Directorio, Gómez and his allies created a new newspaper, *La Igualdad*, which took the place of their previous publication, *La Fraternidad.*[5]

These efforts touched off a bitter polemic over strategy, which reverberated among exiles in New York just as they began the work of building Martí's party. On one side of the conflict, the exile network that Sandoval and others had established in Greenwich Village—by now, beginning to relocate to the Tenderloin and the area around upper Third Avenue, participated in the activities of the Directorio. In a letter to Gómez, Juan Bonilla described this as wholehearted support for "your—I mean to say—our enterprise."[6] As a spokesman for the network, Bonilla also defended the civil rights efforts in print. One of the "greatest anomalies that the class of color faces," he wrote, paraphrasing a communication from the Directorio, "is the need to organize itself as a class, when the ardent desire of all of the thinking men of this class is to achieve a society in which men come together and associate in public and social life, not according to the color of their skin, but rather because of their affinities of ideas and thoughts." But as long as white Cubans did not fully accept this principle, guaranteeing adequate space for participation by men of color, it remained necessary to organize independent institutions.[7] To that end, exiles started creating new sociedades de color in the United States.[8] The group in New York that had previously supported the newspaper *La Fraternidad* reorganized to distribute and collect funds for *La Igualdad.* This was the same group that had begun to organize within the Cuban Revolutionary Party. Silvestre Pivaló, the treasurer of Las Dos Antillas and a founding member of Guerrilla de Maceo was on the committee to support *La Igualdad,* as was Olayo Miranda, an officer in Guerrilla de Maceo. Pedro Calderín, one of the founders of Guerrilla de Maceo, led the newly created Sociedad Los Treinta and was the agent of *La Igualdad* in New York City, handling subscriptions and all other inquiries. He also owned and operated a restaurant on Sullivan Street.[9]

On the other hand, Martín Morúa Delgado, Serra's old friend and mentor from Matanzas (and his comrade on the failed expedition to Kingston and Panama), vigorously attacked Gómez and the Directorio. Recently returned to Cuba from exile in the United States and now aligned with the Autonomistas, Morúa argued that a legal strategy to secure civil rights was nonsensical because peaceful interaction between the races could not be imposed by government dictate. The class of color, Morúa maintained, should instead focus only on its own elevation through education and correct behavior. In fall 1892, a group of journalists in Santiago, led by a man named Manuel Bergues Pruna (who would later come to New York and would join the Club Las Dos Antillas), threatened to abstain from voting in provincial elections unless the Autonomistas nominated more men of color for key positions in the party and as candidates for electoral offices. Morúa and others, including the New York publisher Enrique Trujillo, accused Bergues Pruna and the Directorio of "auctioning their political opinions to the highest bidder," of plotting to create a black political party, and of course, of seeking to inspire race warfare.[10] Writing to *La Igualdad* from New York, Serra declared himself to be "on the side of Juan Gualberto Gómez." He described the Directorio as "a necessary, legitimate, and patriotic institution."[11] Morúa then responded with a bitter personal attack against Serra, whom he called an "ingrate," a "rodent," and a "cigar maker" who "has had the audacity to strut about in the press without knowing how to write." Morúa also described Serra as "a crazed issuer of challenges, a defamer of his own virtuous wife, and an idiotic flirt." It is not possible to know whether this insult was wholly invented, or if it drew on aspects of Serra's public reputation or on episodes in the private lives of Rafael and Gertrudis during the many years that they lived apart. In any event, the personal nature of this attack sent shock waves through the network of readers and activists that spanned New York, Florida, Cuba, and Jamaica, as did Serra's comparatively restrained response, which nevertheless systematically dismantled Morúa's career as an intellectual and revolutionary, reframing every act and decision as duplicitous, craven, and self-serving.[12]

As the conflict played out, Martí sought to harmonize the diverse elements of his coalition with densely constructed paragraphs that invited contrasting interpretations. "All that divides men," he wrote in an essay titled "My Race," published in *Patria* and *La Igualdad* early in 1893, "all that specifies, separates, or encloses is a sin against humanity." He warned of the risks of "black racism," arguing that the "black who isolates himself, provokes the white to isolate himself."[13] The natural and healthy state of affairs in a just society, he wrote, was for men to gather according to shared sentiments, ideas, or interests, not race. He denounced independent black organizing on principle and imagined a world in which the "black racist" would be equally guilty as the "white racist." But that world was carefully phrased in the future tense. He admitted that the time had not yet come when racial discrimination had vanished and the "word racist will fall from the lips of the blacks who use it today in good faith."[14] And general pronouncements aside, his defense of Gómez in particular was clear. The journalist and civil rights leader did not hope to inspire anger and hatred but "rather to prevent it from arising, with the sure remedy of justice."[15] He offered a similar exception for the activities led by Serra and the Bonillas in New York. La Liga, far from being an institution that "divided men," was the institution that best combined the fundamental principle of unity with its necessary precondition, justice. There, "with neither flattery for one group, nor humiliation for the other, but rather with their gazes meeting at the same level, the children of those who committed injustice" gathered to exchange ideas with "the children of those who suffered from the injustice."[16]

This was the contradictory backdrop against which Martí's supporters constructed the party, and the party reflected those same contradictions. Together, members of the party worked to ensure that in a literal sense, there was no separation into black and white clubs, or artisan and professional clubs. Gonzalo de Quesada, a man descended from the "yellowest cream of the Cuban aristocracy," recruited young men of his social class into a club, winning a seat on the Advisory Council. *Patria* was quick to note that the membership included several cigar makers as well. Several clubs were composed mainly of white cigar makers, with almost no overlap with the membership of La Liga. These clubs typically elected white cigar makers, some of whom were artisans on the cusp of the transition to small manufacturer, to the council. The majority-white clubs often also elected at least one prominent man of color (usually Serra or Figueroa) as a lesser officer. Finally, there were the clubs associated with La Liga, led by men of color. *Patria* was scrupulous in its treatment of these clubs too, leaving unspoken the fact that the movement continued to operate against a backdrop in which racial separation, while not absolute, was a regular feature of Cuban social and now political life. Nevertheless, it seems clear that independent organizing was still necessary to mobilize these diverse constituents and to promote diverse leaders, perhaps especially men of color, to positions on the party's Advisory Councils.[17] The fact that some men of color, elected by their own supporters (ideally, including some white workers), occupied a place of honor each time that the party gathered was crucial to the argument that the movement was both unified in common purpose and sincerely democratic.

FIGUEROA AND MARÍN

Perhaps the most surprising thing about the ways that independent black social networks mobilized to support their chosen leaders and to help create a visibly democratic party leadership in New York, however, was the prominence of Puerto Rican exiles in these activities. Only weeks before they attended the meeting to create Las Dos Antillas, Sotero Figueroa, Pachín Marín, and Modesto Tirado had drawn together a diverse group of exiles in the city to organize the Club Borinquen, the indigenous name for the island of Puerto Rico. That club elected Figueroa as its president, placing him on the New York Advisory Council. He joined the Puerto Rican, Rodríguez (and several months later, the Cuban, Benech), as the only men of color on the council. The council then elected Figueroa as its secretary. This made him the highest-ranking man of color in the

New York branch of the party, though men of color held similar positions on the Advisory Councils in Florida, Haiti, and Jamaica.[18] Within the year, Figueroa became the publisher of *Patria*, and with Martí traveling for extended periods, he also sometimes served as the de facto editor of the newspaper. Marín, meanwhile, became a favored speaker at party events and in fund-raising campaigns in the factories and a noted celebrity among cigar workers. In short, Figueroa and Marín quickly became two of Martí's most visible African-descended supporters, and indispensable participants in the projection of a movement with all and for all—a movement that could accommodate the pressure not to discuss racial differences while also fostering and depending on independent black organizing and leadership.[19] Thus, in this burst of party building, a pair of artisans who had transformed themselves into writers in the print workshops of San Juan and Ponce finally crossed paths with the cigar workers who had become writers in the sociedades de color of Havana and Matanzas, and community leaders in the neighborhoods of New York. They joined the conversations among Cubans about the relationship to a national community of race, class, and shared manhood.

Yet as we have seen, the experiences of the typesetters who first became writers in Puerto Rico were quite distinct from those of the cigar makers who first became writers in Western Cuba and in exile. How did the patterns of racial classification and racial politics that operated in the small cities of Puerto Rico—where there was nothing like the Directorio Central de Sociedades de Color, New York City's patchwork color line, African American churches, or black fraternal orders—shape Figueroa's and Marín's engagement with the racial politics of the Cuban struggle? How did their experiences migrating across the varied racial landscapes of the greater Caribbean differ from those of their Cuban counterparts, and shape the ways that they asserted themselves in the Cuban movement and their particular intellectual contributions to the emerging conversation about race in the Cuban movement? Finally, how did the Cubans regard the prominence of Puerto Ricans of African descent in their movement? Answering these questions requires again tracing these lines backward from their point of intersection. The story therefore now returns to Puerto Rico to pick up the trail of Sotero Figueroa and to introduce his younger compatriot, the poet and bohemian Francisco Gonzalo Marín.

PONCE, 1887

Before coming to New York, both Figueroa and Marín lived in the southern coastal city of Ponce. Figueroa and his first wife, Manuela Aguayo, moved to Ponce in 1880. She labored as a seamstress—a skilled occupation that allowed her to work within the respectable confines of their home. He earned his living in an ink-stained apron—carefully aligning lines of type, checking and rechecking proofs, and composing pages in exchange for daily wages. Although less than one-tenth of the size of Havana and half the size of Matanzas, Ponce was one of the largest and fastest-growing urban centers on the island of Puerto Rico. A paved highway, one of the only good roads on the island, connected the small city through a series of rural barrios planted in cane, bananas, and other vegetables to the satellite town of Juana Díaz, about ten miles distant. From there, the highway continued another sixty-five miles to the north and east to San Juan. Another road led north into the mountainous coffee district, and a third went to the cane lands to the west. Regular steam service departed Ponce's port for Saint Thomas and San Juan, where connections could be made for passage to other Caribbean islands, Europe, and the United States, including the twice-monthly steamer to New York. This allowed coffee from the mountains and sugar from the surrounding coastal plain to flow through the city and out into the Atlantic market, while manufactures and consumer goods of various sorts flowed in. By the 1890s, nearly a third of all exports from Puerto Rico and a fourth of all imports moved through Ponce.[20] The newspapers produced in the city's print shops, accordingly, faced relentlessly toward the port, dominated by timetables for the various passenger lines, advertisements for imports, and news of commodity prices. The news of the world, including several publications from New York, arrived at a pace determined by the comings and goings of steamers, even after a new, highly abbreviated form of international news began arriving by telegraph cable from Havana.[21]

As in the other cities of Puerto Rico, these economic conditions produced a sharply regimented class hierarchy, visible most clearly in the electoral system. The right to vote for representatives in the Spanish Cortes was restricted to wealthy taxpayers, who tended to be the owners of sugar plantations or mills, merchants engaged in the import or export of goods, and the owners of small factories or workshops. An additional and similarly small group of men—those with academic titles, public employees who earned above a minimum salary, and members of the military—also had the right to vote as capacidades. Altogether, this added up to only a few hundred voters, a formally constituted elite that comprised about one-half of 1 percent of the male population of the district.[22] These voters and their families constituted the "first class" of citizens—a classification that actually appeared both on official identity cards and censuses. Although they were sharply divided in their political views, members of this class generally shared a basic desire for modernization in the form of infrastructure, elegant architecture, and elite cultural activities. They also shared a deep concern over the rapid and uncontrolled growth of the city in the aftermath of abolition, as rural workers, some recently freed, migrated in from the surrounding countryside. With the goal of controlling these "third-class" residents, they tended to favor measures such as stricter building codes, forced labor on public works, and public morality and hygiene campaigns.[23]

Figueroa and Aguayo were "second-class" citizens—the term given to the six hundred or so skilled workers in the city.[24] These artisans, including several dozen typographers and about sixty cigar makers, were disproportionately persons of African descent. They had begun to create mutual aid and recreational societies like the ones in Cuba. But in contrast to Cuba, where efforts to whiten the urban working class through Spanish immigration had already had a major impact, the artisans of Ponce did not segregate their social institutions by race. Indeed, it was not unusual for men of color to lead them. (This is something that likely caught the attention of migrants from Western Cuba when they met the Puerto Ricans in exile, and probably made it comparatively easy for men like Figueroa and Rodríguez to recruit white countrymen into their political clubs in New York).[25] Though he remained an artisan, little by little Figueroa built another identity as a man in print, a participant in the fierce debates of the public plaza. His efforts to launch his own newspaper failed once in 1880 and then again in 1881, but he began contributing articles to Ponce's other newspapers. His play *Don Mamerto*, which audaciously poked fun at conservative politicians, had a successful run at the city's elegant Teatro La Perla. He thus straddled the line between the journalists and intellectuals who published in the print shops of the city, and the craftsmen who earned their living in those shops, producing printed pages. This was probably aided by the fact that Aguayo, although an illegitimate child, was an acknowledged member of a prominent white family.[26]

Contact between liberal journalists and artisans—that is, contact across the very line that Figueroa and Aguayo straddled—continued to be a central and potentially explosive aspect of the politics of the city. Many of Ponce's artisans had availed themselves of the right to vote in the elections of 1873, when suffrage had been expanded to all men who could read and write. They had resoundingly supported Liberal candidates, who had briefly held local offices. Then a Conservative backlash had purged men of lower social standing from the voter rolls. As a result, the Unconditionally Spanish Party, as Conservatives were also known, controlled almost the all the levers of local political power. Liberals in the city had regrouped around the figure of Baldorioty (the abolitionist and schoolteacher whose status as a suspected mulatto had been impugned by opponents when he served as a representative in the Spanish Cortes in the early 1870s). By the beginning of the 1880s, Baldorioty edited a newspaper at the Ponce print workshop of another schoolteacher and journalist, Ramón Marín. Marín was also a man of plebeian origins. When his mother brought him to be baptized, the priest identified her as "Rosa, the slave of Vicente Marín," and Ramón as her natural child, freed at birth. The priest did not write down that Vicente was the child's father, though members of his family served as godparents. Eventually, Vicente freed Rosa too, and the couple had six more children together, none formally recognized by their father.[27] Over time, through the financial support of his father, through education, and through marriages to white women, Ramón overcame his status at birth to acquire or nearly approximate the status of a white man. His particular experience of ascending status, consolidated through advantageous marriage, likely informed his ideas about social mobility and racial identity, and those of Figueroa and the other men in Baldorioty's circle.[28]

Figueroa worked setting type at Marín's publishing house, and along with Marín and Baldorioty, participated in an emerging movement for political autonomy from Spain. Favoring colonial reforms on the model of Canada's relationship with Great Britain, the Autonomistas, as they were called, also supported free trade, universal manhood suffrage, civil and press freedoms, and republicanism. They were consistently at odds with local officials, who regularly impounded newspapers, imposed fines, and even arrested writers and publishers, including both Marín and Figueroa,

for a range of political offenses. Figueroa may have been especially useful to the Autonomistas in their continued appeals to artisans. In 1883,
he was the featured speaker at the inaugural event of the Artisan Recreational and Instructional Society in Juana Díaz, the small town ten miles
outside Ponce. During his speech in 1883, the Conservative mayor arrived
with a group of Voluntarios to force Figueroa down from the podium
and disband the workers.[29] Conservatives depicted the Autonomistas'
relationship with artisans as dangerously radical and destabilizing, and
part of the broader threat of disorder created by the stream of vagrants
and criminals into the city. It is likely that they had speeches by men like
Figueroa in mind. They certainly had the artisans of Juana Díaz in mind.
Those artisans would soon suffer much more serious abuse at the hands
of authorities.[30]

By the mid-1880s, though he continued also to set type in order to earn
a living, Figueroa had risen to the status of collaborator and "coeditor" for
several newspapers produced at Marín's shop.[31] Government officials recognized this progression by affording him status as a professional and the
honorific title don. "Don Sotero Figueroa," a "journalist," for instance, appears on the record of "Doña" Manuela Aguayo's death from tuberculosis
in 1886.[32] The honorific titles don and doña were still generally restricted
to legitimate, white persons. Indeed, a decree that persons of African descent had the right to use don and doña in Puerto Rico as well as Cuba
would be a major, and hotly contested, victory for Gómez and the Cuban
civil rights movement at the end of 1893.[33] Yet in parts of Puerto Rico, as
in Eastern Cuba, the honorific had long been applied to some persons with
African ancestry.[34] It is difficult to know on what grounds. Perhaps officials
were conscious of a policy that racial "impurity" no longer precluded individuals from honorable personhood, and applied the term don to Figueroa
because they wished to show him respect despite their belief that he was
not white and not legitimate. Or perhaps they were affording him a kind of
partial whiteness that could accommodate his darker skin tone, curly hair,
and pardo lineage in public transactions, without presuming that he would
necessarily receive honorable treatment in private interactions.

When Liberals gathered in Ponce in 1887 to reorganize their movement
as the Puerto Rican Autonomista Party, they too recognized him as "Don
Sotero Figueroa." He attended as the representative of the newspaper *El
Pueblo* (owned by Ramón Marín), and as the elected delegate representing

the Autonomista committees of the towns of Moca and Bayamón.[35] Again, it is not clear if any of those who selected him as their representative did so as a conscious gesture that artisans and pardos could have positions of responsibility in the party, or if they had begun to perceive Figueroa principally as a Liberal journalist, like Marín and others, whose standing as a writer attenuated his plebeian origins or at least required politely avoiding any mention of them. Either way, Figueroa had taken the first important steps to becoming, in New York, a collaborator and editor of *Patria*, and a man whose race politics centered on his accomplishments as a writer and politician. Baldorioty and Marín had conceded him a role as a spokesman for the general interest—a Puerto Rican writer without racial or class qualification. As would later be the case in New York, it is not likely that other artisans would have failed to notice that one of their own had been so prominently included in the Autonomista Assembly and had been successful in his efforts to remake himself into Don Sotero Figueroa.

The honorable status afforded to upwardly mobile men like Baldorioty, Ramón Marín, and Sotero Figueroa would have been particularly salient for a young typesetter named Francisco Gonzalo Marín, whose family called him Pachín. Born in 1863 in the northern city of Arecibo, he was the son of Ramón Marín's younger brother Santiago. Although both Ramón and Santiago were the natural sons of a woman held in slavery by their father, Ramón had succeeded in integrating himself into patrician society in Ponce. Santiago, however, had remained in Arecibo, where he became a small businessman and married a woman of mixed race.[36] After primary school, their oldest son, Pachín, became an apprentice typesetter. Their second child, Wenceslao, became an apprentice blacksmith. As a teenager, Pachín also became a noted musician in Arecibo, composing and performing songs at bohemian gatherings in the public squares of the city. The workings of law and custom in Puerto Rico dictated countless gestures of submission on the part of men of low rank when encountering "superiors," including Spanish soldiers and other representatives of authority. This was perhaps especially so in the Conservative bastion of Arecibo. Pachín and Wenceslao chafed at these norms. As part of their evening activities, both boys engaged in street fights with Conservative youths, and in acts of defiance against the Civil Guard and other authorities.[37]

While a teenager, Pachín also began the familiar climb from print worker to author, sending poems and articles to his uncle Ramón's newspaper in

Ponce. He started to travel to Ponce to participate in Liberal political organizing and published his first book of poetry on his uncle's presses. He
probably also joined Figueroa as a tradesman in Ramón's workshop.[38] This
highlights a significant difference between the kinds of racial mobility
that operated in Ponce and the experience of "passing" that evolved in the
United States in the last decades of the nineteenth century. While there
were several ways for persons of mixed ancestry to acquire the privileges
of whiteness in the United States, as the rise of Jim Crow foreclosed the
possibility of intermediate status, nearly all ways to become white required
steadfast secrecy, and what historian Allyson Hobbs has called "voluntary
exile" from African American kin and communities. To pass meant to sever
or scrupulously conceal relations with family members, or risk exposure
and violence. By contrast, Ramón does not seem to have felt a necessity to
distance himself from his nephew. He even wrote a play, produced to great
acclaim at the Teatro la Perla, in which the main character was a young
man of illegitimate birth and unknown lineage, recognized by his father
but unfairly precluded from marrying his true love for reasons of social
prejudice. His most famous literary accomplishment, then, called attention
to the seemingly quite-public "secret" of his own, possibly fragile, social
status. He was, though, likely careful to conceal the fact that his mother had
been enslaved. This was probably a private secret, protected by a smaller
circle of family members and confidantes.[39]

As followers of Baldorioty, the two Maríns and Figueroa supported
what they called an "eminently democratic" form of Autonomismo. They
saw full political autonomy as inseparable from a restoration of the citizenship rights of artisans, and the extension of citizenship rights to male
laborers and peasants—a project that Conservatives continued to depict
as a threat to public order and a violation of all sensible political philosophy.[40] The Conservative mayor of one small town noted with dismay that
the Partido Autonomista in his jurisdiction was "composed, in its totality,
of laborers and blacks from the artisan class, men, in conclusion, who have
no education and from whom nothing favorable can be expected. They
give credit to the malignant ideas [spread by the party], which rile them
up, flattering them and causing them to believe that they have a right, as
free men and citizens, to take part in public life."[41] Of course, this report
may have been part of a strategy to depict the Autonomistas as out-of-
control radicals. It may exaggerate the alliance between Autonomistas

and artisans, and the presence of black men among those workers. But to the extent that such an alliance existed, Figueroa and Pachín were its eager proponents, much as they were mentors, several years later, to the men of La Liga when they started creating their own political clubs and joining the Cuban Revolutionary Party. Indeed, their connection with Rodríguez, the future president of the Club Las Dos Antillas, may have begun in these years. Rodríguez was a cigar maker, the son of a San Juan carpenter, and only a few years older than Figueroa. He seems to have lived in Ponce by 1883.[42]

Figueroa and Marín were severely disappointed, therefore, when the 1887 Autonomista Constituent Assembly voted to approve a platform of political integration with Spain—a project to become an overseas province with rights equal to provinces on the peninsula . They also objected to the decision to follow in the footsteps of the Cuban Autonomista Party, limiting the official work of local party committees to organizing the tiny contingent of eligible voters in their towns instead of organizing more broadly and advocating the radical expansion of suffrage.[43] Marín, the young brawler and bohemian, joined a group that turned toward direct action. He helped to create a network of secret societies, including small peddlers, artisans, and even field hands. Modeling themselves on Irish Republicans, members of these societies swore that they would do no business in establishments run by peninsular Spaniards or members of the Unconditionally Spanish Party. In appealing to this broad constituency, the "eminently democratic" members of the Autonomista Party not only made the shocking assertion that "as free men and citizens," working-class allies had the right to participate in "the public life," but they also tapped into a deep reserve of animosity toward Spanish businessmen, who dominated retail trade in Puerto Rico and, in this role, were the main source of credit in the colony. It was not difficult to find workers and small farmers struggling to make payments to peninsular shopkeepers, and resentful of the burden of colonial taxation.[44] Conservatives accused the organizers of the boycott of "inculcating our simple country folk with hatred against Spaniards from the Peninsula" and promising relief from the burden of taxes.[45] When, over summer 1887, a series of suspicious fires struck the establishments of peninsular businessmen, the Unconditionally Spanish press accused the Autonomistas of plotting a rebellion and called for immediate response from the government "to put an end, once and for all, to this Autonomista tumult [*bayoya*] to these children of Cain, these demagogues, socialists, and arsonists."[46]

For reference, this was the very moment that Serra, Cebreco, and the other participants of the unsuccessful military expedition led by Máximo Gómez and Antonio Maceo were leaving Kingston, and finding their way back to the Panama Canal Zone and to New York. In Cuba, supporters of Juan Gualberto Gómez were just beginning their efforts to resuscitate the newspaper *La Fraternidad*, anticipating that Gómez would be permitted soon to return from exile. In Key West, Cuban settlers were rebuilding from the devastating fire that had destroyed most of the homes and factories in that city the previous year. Many had started to relocate to the newly forming settlements in Tampa. In New York, Cuban exiles were consumed by debates about the impending execution of the Haymarket defendants. The poet and diplomat Martí, having recently become an admirer of Henry George, was about to return to Cuban politics with a project to build a workingman's party. For their part, Figueroa and Marín, along with the other citizens of Ponce, watched as a detachment of Civil Guard troops departed along the road to Juana Díaz, where with assistance and encouragement from Unconditional supporters, they unleashed a wave of terrible brutality on the radical wing of the Autonomista Party. The soldiers arrested dozens of small shopkeepers, artisans, and field hands—some of whom had probably been in the audience when Figueroa was arrested there four years earlier—illegally detaining and torturing them until they confessed to participation in a conspiracy and implicated Autonomista leaders. Over the next several months, the Civil Guard employed the same methods in Ponce and other cities and towns.[47]

The treatment of a few well-to-do prisoners was, for the most part, constrained by the norms of "gentlemanly" behavior. But authorities gave the Civil Guard a free hand to submit men of lower social status to the most horrifying cruelties, in clear violation of Spanish law. Guard members hung Victor Honoré, a mulatto stonemason from Mayagüez, by his arms and legs for days, and beat him with sticks across his torso. They broke the fingers of Gil Bones, a mulatto tailor from Ponce. They hung a cobbler in Guayanilla by his feet from a telegraph post. Others suffered the torsion of their testicles or were dunked headfirst into latrines. Stripped naked, they were verbally and psychologically abused as well;

they were forced to endure insults and to bear false testimony against other men.[48] Figueroa and Marín were as attuned as worker intellectuals in Key West and New York to the question of full and unfettered manhood. They probably understood these abuses as conscious humiliations, designed to reduce artisans to something less than full men. They likely noticed that the Liberal press nevertheless reserved its greatest outrage for the relatively minor indignities suffered by the few patrician prisoners, especially a single slap to the face of the well-to-do publisher of the *Revista de Puerto Rico*, a man with whom Marín and Figueroa would spar bitterly in subsequent years.[49]

The two were also in the eye of the storm as Conservatives and colonial authorities clamped down on freedom of expression. Three guard members appeared one day at offices of the newspaper *El Pueblo*, which was published in the workshop where Figueroa and Marín spent their days. Figueroa was also a frequent contributor and had been the paper's representative at the Autonomista Assembly. The soldiers demanded, at gunpoint, that the publisher of *El Pueblo*, Ramón Marín, sign and publish a retraction of the letters from prisoners detailing their suffering. Instead, he closed down the newspaper and immediately founded a new one, under a new name, *El Popular*. Shortly thereafter, authorities imprisoned both Ramón and Baldorioty, leaving Figueroa as director and editor of *El Popular*.[50] In this role, "Don Sotero Figueroa" assisted one of the most vulnerable victims of torture, a man who did not know how to read or write, to denounce the abuses of the Civil Guard and to recant his coerced testimony.[51] Meanwhile, Pachín learned that the authorities had identified him as a conspirator. He escaped arrest by fleeing on a small boat from the western coast of Puerto Rico to the Dominican Republic.[52] This moment also seems to have helped push into exile the other Puerto Rican artisans who later joined the Cuban Revolutionary Party. The typographer Modesto Tirado was arrested and expelled from the island at around this time for his involvement in the boycott movement, and he eventually made his way to New York.[53] Silvestre Pivaló, a cigar maker from Eastern Cuba and veteran of the Ten Years' War who had resettled in San Juan, departed for New York in the wake of the repression too. There he became the treasurer of the Club Las Dos Antillas and a founding member of the Club Guerrilla de Maceo. In Puerto Rico, he had married Pilar Cazuela, the daughter of a San Juan laundress. She followed him to New York and also became an important figure in the exile community: an officer in the women's groups led by Josefa Blanco de Apodaca and Gertrudis Heredia in New York.[54]

MANLY HEARTS

These events, known colloquially as the *compontes*, the tortures, wound down by the beginning of 1888, when Liberals in Madrid managed to force the replacement of the governor-general in San Juan and most of the remaining prisoners were released. The following year the Crown issued a general pardon for political prisoners and violators of censorship laws.[55] Still, the compontes proved a turning point in the relationship of both Figueroa and Marín with the Autonomista movement, and a major factor pushing them into exile and separatist politics. Like many in the radical wing of the movement, both men saw the tortures as an escalation, which should be met with what they described as a vigorous, masculine response. Liberals ought to "save the dignity of the country," as the Puerto Rican separatist leader Ramón Emeterio Betances wrote, by abandoning the policy of "gentleness" and developing instead "manly hearts."[56] Yet by the time that Baldorioty was released, he was ailing and in no condition to continue as leader of the party. The men who emerged to take his place were the same figures who had opposed the radical platform at the party assembly. They now sought to distance themselves from the boycott movement, from the project of political autonomy, and from the risks associated with artisan radicalism.

The new leadership of the party did not wholly disavow their artisan allies. They merely sought to dampen the desire for confrontation. In the service of this strategy, they constructed a highly selective account of the history of the Liberal movement. They claimed that patrician Liberals had rallied to the cause of abolition, for which they deserved the gratitude of the working classes.[57] They also created a campaign to commemorate the black cigar maker and schoolteacher Cordero, claiming that his life symbolized the unique experience of Puerto Rican "ethnic relations." Because of their experiences in the humble classroom of el Maestro Rafael, the logic went, wealthy creoles had long since accepted "the democratic dissolution of caste privilege." Artisans, they argued, ought to be similarly restrained by the "spirit of confraternity" and "cordiality." They should emulate the humble and charitable figure of Rafael rather than "bloody the pages" of Puerto Rican history "with the names of a Toussaint or a Dessalines." These two most famous leaders of the Haitian Revolution were easily recognizable, according to the prevailing view of Haiti in Puerto Rico (as in Cuba), as symbols of race war, black supremacy, and brutal violence against whites.[58]

Figueroa and Marín dissented from the course plotted by the new leaders of the Autonomista Party. In Figueroa's case, the dissent was at first somewhat oblique. In the aftermath of the compontes he wrote a collection of short biographies, which he called a "biographical essay about those who have most contributed to the progress of Puerto Rico." Overall, the thirty biographical sketches were fairly consistent with the prevailing liberal notions of the "progress" of the island (education, publishing, cultural institutions, and infrastructure), and they won him a prize from a leading Ponce literary society. Figueroa, however, used some of the sketches pointedly to contest the idea of cordiality and social peace. His sketch of the life of Rafael Cordero, in whose classroom he had studied, acknowledged the campaign to commemorate the black schoolteacher. Yet for Figueroa, Cordero's biography did not demonstrate the absence of racism in Puerto Rico but rather the accomplishments of a man who had struggled to overcome the obstacles placed before him by a society "refractory towards all those of his race." While other writers sought to distinguish Cordero from Toussaint-Louverture, Figueroa argued that Cordero should be remembered alongside the "great Dominican." In another of his sketches, he noted that the worst violence in Haiti began with the French attempt to reenslave the Haitian people and was not a mark of a spirit of vengeance against whites. Published as a book on Ramón Marín's presses, this essay was Figueroa's last major intervention in the "fierce debates of the public plaza" in Puerto Rico—an important calling card with which he could present himself to writers and intellectuals in New York when he moved there in June 1889.[59]

Marín remained in exile in the Dominican Republic and Venezuela for nearly three years before returning to Ponce, where together with a new ally, a Colombian typesetter and journalist of African descent named Juan Coronel, he began publishing a newspaper that became a "revolutionary herald." The two men had met while working in the print shops of Caracas. Now in Puerto Rico, they pushed back against the caution of the

Autonomist leadership, seeking to "stimulate the patriotism of the lower classes." It is not clear whether Marín and Coronel also took part in a handful of violent attacks made against prominent Conservative politicians, the so-called countercompontes. Nevertheless, in retribution for these attacks, Conservatives waylaid and brutally beat both Marín and his uncle Ramón on the streets of Ponce.[60] Writing and publishing was also its own kind of "manly" response to repression. Crowds gathered at the newspaper's offices each time an issue appeared, eager to see what the two audacious typographers had dared to print. When the authorities imposed fines on the newspaper, readers donated funds to keep the presses rolling.[61]

Needless to say, the leadership of the Autonomista Party opposed the radicalism that Marín and Coronel hoped to inspire among the artisans of the city. At their most sympathetic, writers in the Autonomista Press distanced themselves from the boycott movement as "the thoughtless enthusiasm, the simple inexperience, and the hot-headed patriotism of some liberals."[62] But other writers, revealing the continued association between artisans and nonwhite racial status, argued that workers, under the "pretext" of class struggle, might "set alight a race war, as bloody as those in neighboring Antilles," and that the "poor and badly advised men of color" would end up "paying the price."[63] The Unconditionally Spanish press pointed to this widening rift with smug satisfaction: "He who ought to obey now seeks to impose his will on he who commands." This was the inevitable consequence, Conservative authors crowed, of teaching the dubious principles of democracy and the "rule of conscience" to workers, rather than the "eternal principles of good order, of healthy doctrine, and of social morality."[64]

Finally, in August 1891, the authorities impounded Marín's newspapers and confiscated his press. They brought a criminal charge for "grave injury" and published a warrant for his arrest. Even while declaring him a criminal, officials acknowledged his profession and afforded him a title that indicated honorable manhood, identifying him as "Don Francisco Gonzalo Marín," a journalist. At the same time, for the purpose of identification, officials noted that he was of "regular stature, short hair, extensive forehead . . . black eyes, wide nose, regular mouth, cinnamon color, wispy moustache, decently dressed."[65] This use of color as a physical description rather than a definitive racial classification provides another glimpse of the system of racial nomenclature that shaped the lives of these typographers before they emigrated. This was not the system that awaited them in the United States, where both the leading statistical experts at the Census Bureau and most African American writers favored the elimination of mulatto and other intermediate categories, and a clear dividing line between "white" and "Negro" races.[66]

To be sure, the project of eliminating intermediate categories in the United States was still a work in progress. But Jim Crow laws typically applied legally to a broad definition of "Negro": all persons with "any perceptible trace" of African ancestry. New York was one of the only states with a law on the books prohibiting racial discrimination in hotels, restaurants, and taverns. Yet racial discrimination persisted in ways that also drew increasingly sharp lines between white and black. In New York, the year before Marín arrived, a bartender at the Trainor Hotel refused to serve a glass of beer to newspaper editor T. Thomas Fortune. When Fortune refused to leave the establishment, protesting the illegal act of discrimination, the owner of the hotel called a New York City police sergeant, who then placed Fortune under arrest. Fortune and his coeditor, T. McCants Stewart, responded with a civil rights suit and a national publicity campaign. Fortune was a man of mixed racial ancestry and intermediate appearance—something that was sometimes a source of tension with other African American writers. Juan Bonilla, describing the case for readers in Havana, called him a "pardo." But to the employee at the Trainor Hotel and the police, and to participants in the civil rights campaign that followed his arrest, he was simply "colored."[67]

Marín's departure from Puerto Rico and arrival in New York did not end the tense back and forth with the Autonomista leadership. In December 1891, the Autonomista Party in Puerto Rico issued a formal statement denouncing the "impatience and exaggeration of some injudicious coreligionists," and the sinister work of others who only pretended to be Autonomistas in order to pursue independence. The party insisted that it "reject[ed] energetically any solidarity or communion with those insolent" comrades who pursued anything other than the narrow reforms delineated in the party platform.[68] Then, in January 1892, Martí announced the creation of the Cuban Revolutionary Party to "achieve" the absolute independence of Cuba and "aid in" that of Puerto Rico. At about the same time, Juan Gualberto Gómez and his allies began reconstructing the Directorio de Sociedades de Color in Cuba and the émigré communities. By

the end of February, Figueroa and Marín had created the Club Borinquen, and the club had approved the principles and bylaws of the Cuban
Revolutionary Party. The second week in March, the first issue of *Patria*
appeared. In it, together with the publisher Antonio Vélez Alvarado,
Figueroa and Marín issued a manifesto to the "Puerto Rican people" in the
name of the Club Borinquen. They responded to the accusation that they
were "injudicious" and "insolent," denouncing the leadership of the Partido Autonomista for its timidity and declaring themselves separatists.[69]

As in Ponce, Figueroa and Marín voiced their objections largely in
terms of class and unconstrained manhood, rather than as a tension between blacks and whites. In a speech to the members of the Cuban Revolutionary Party several weeks later, Figueroa explained, "The great struggles for rights do not give rise to leaders from the comfortable elements
of society, who are perfectly content with the established order of things."
Neither "arrogant" patricians nor "presumptuous" intellectuals, hoping to
establish themselves as the "mentors" of the simple folk, were fit to lead
the coming struggle. "True leaders come from the suffering masses, from
the disinherited who carry inspiration in their minds, tortures in their
hearts, and truth on their lips."[70] In an article in *Patria*, Marín addressed
himself directly to the Autonomista Party:

> You who, from the pontifical tripod of your ridiculous pride, issue
> certificates of *judicious and wise* liberals, and propose yourselves as
> shepherds, helping the flock to avoid the dangerous path and the high
> cliffs . . . you courtesans who are flattered by a smile from the Gover-
> nor's secretary but embarrassed by the complaints of those who are
> generous and impatient. Hear the frank and honorable voice of an out-
> cast who aspires to nothing, except perhaps to spill his blood for the
> dignity of his people, the people to which he owes all his dignity and all
> the blood in his veins.[71]

Marín titled his essay "The Slap across the Face." This was possibly an allusion to Martí's famous first speech in Tampa, in which he promised that
in the Cuban republic, "a slap on the face of any man will be felt equally
by all." In the language of manhood and honor, shared by both Cubans
and Puerto Ricans in exile, the Autonomistas had proven that they were
incapable of responding to such affronts, especially when visited on their
plebeian allies.

MEN OF TRUE MERIT

In their manifesto to the Puerto Rican people, Figueroa, Marín, and Vélez Alvarado also explained why they disagreed with Puerto Ricans who favored annexation to the United States. It was here that they engaged directly with the question of race. They did not wish, they wrote, "to resign ourselves to the complete absorption of our race by another, we cannot be seduced to the point of forgetting our language, customs, traditions, sentiments . . . everything that constitutes our physiognomy of a Latin American people." The question of race, they suggested, was central to their politics. Race, though, was not an issue of biology but rather of the conscious efforts of cultured men to construct common "language, customs, traditions, and sentiments." Furthermore, race was not a matter of divisions within the Puerto Rican national community. It was instead a hemispheric divide between a "Latin race" and Anglo-Saxons. Here, two highly visible nonwhite members of Martí's coalition, mentors and supporters for the black men who established their own political clubs in New York, presented themselves as spokesmen for a Latin American race whose definition had little to do with divisions of color or heredity. They endorsed a project of racial assimilation: the absorption of African-descended people into the Latin race. And they highlighted the contrast between such a view and the racial hostilities that they had witnessed in the United States. "One must live in this country for some years to understand that this race does not tend to perfect and improve, through crossing, those races that it believes to be inferior."[72]

This performance of racial unity drew on a view of Latin American identity that had growing purchase among wealthy and highly educated exiles. But what did they mean by it? What impact did living in the United States "for some years," at precisely the moment of the consolidation of Jim Crow, the peak of lynching, and the rise of racial explanations for empire, have on their understanding of race in Puerto Rico? This returns us to the question, posed in an earlier chapter, of migrating while black, or in this case, migrating while something that was (in the cities of Puerto Rico) other than black but also not fully white. When Figueroa, the typesetter and journalist, arrived at the piers in New York in June 1889, he was not, like the traveler Marín described in his famous vignette, "lacking resources of any kind; as clever and agile as a student and as hungry as a school teacher." He and his wife Inocencia traveled in the first-class compartment in the company of a prominent Autonomista physician from Ponce.[73] It is impossible to be certain, when he set off to find a "friend" or a "countryman," in which direction he turned. Yet it seems likely that—rather than walk to one of the cigar factories near the piers, the home of Germán and Magdalena Sandoval on Thompson Street, or the Bonillas' flat on West Third Street—he sought as quickly as possible to find the offices of the editors and publishers producing Spanish-language texts in the city in the area near Printing House Square (see map 3). Probably he started with Vélez Alvarado, the leading Puerto Rican publisher in New York and a man with close ties to the Autonomista press in Puerto Rico. Perhaps using Vélez Alvarado as a reference or using copies of his own prizewinning book as a calling card, he then introduced himself to others in the New York publishing world. The technical skills offered by an experienced Puerto Rican typesetter were likely in high demand, as producing clean Spanish copy while working with the city's mostly English-speaking or German-speaking setters could not have been easy.[74] Figueroa soon found a job setting type for *La América Ilustrada*, one of the most important literary and general interest magazines in the Spanish-speaking world at the time. Marín later helped to produce the *Revista Popular*, published by Vélez Alvarado himself. Tirado (who had participated in the boycott movement in Puerto Rico) worked setting type for the Cuban journalist and publisher Enrique Trujillo, the man who became Martí's sworn enemy in this period.[75]

The Puerto Rican typographers thus found their way from the city piers directly into an extraordinary moment of commercial activity and cultural production. New York's Spanish-language publishers did not address themselves primarily to the small population of Spanish-speaking residents in the city. Instead, they produced books, manuals, and magazines for export to Latin America. The Spanish-language magazines had begun as catalogs, which were vehicles for New York businessmen "desirous of introducing their manufactures and wares to the millions of the Spanish-American Republics."[76] The catalogs provided price lists and the contact information for agents who could export cod liver oil, public lighting, streetcars, printing presses, pianos, and books. Over time, New York advertising agents and editors started adding literary and journalistic content to these catalogs, most of which tended, understandably, to celebrate the introduction of modern industrial methods and products to the region. According to this logic, by distributing advertisements for the latest consumer goods, the publishers in New York were making a crucial contribution to the progress of Latin America. But by the time that Figueroa and Marín arrived, the tenor of the writing in these publications had shifted as New York advertisers, eager to offer the most attractive material to potential readers in the cities of Latin America, had recruited top literary figures from across the region and from among exiles in the United States. These authors used the New York magazines— magazines built on the project of expanding exports from the United States—to promote the cultural and political unity of Latin America, and to celebrate Hispanism as a response to the influence, imperial grasp, and Anglo-Saxonism of the United States.[77]

The most famous proponent of this ideal of Latin American unity within this world of New York publishing was none other than Martí, the diplomat, journalist, and rising literary star who, in 1889, was still several years away from becoming the popularly elected leader of the Cuban Revolutionary Party. Although he had worked as a correspondent for various publications produced in Buenos Aires and Mexico City for nearly a decade, Martí became increasingly active in the world of literary production for export at precisely the same time that he first began building his relationship with black and brown Cuban exiles in frequent letters and weekly visits to La Liga. He published a Spanish translation of a novel by a North American writer, and with the support of a wealthy investor, briefly edited a children's magazine, with a distinctly didactic and Hispanist tone, marketed to Latin American educators.[78] He also became president of the Hispanic American Literary Society, an organization created by the various editors, authors, and book dealers who worked in Spanish-language publishing in the city. Under Martí, the society proposed itself as a standard-bearer for the region, a mechanism for demonstrating to the United States the most accomplished face of Latin American culture, the "qualities of mental strength, and visible culture, and decorous organization that might incline them towards respect."[79]

This was no easy task. Beginning with the campaign to acquire Texas, the various currents of race science in the United States, including vernacular variants, had typically regarded Spaniards and especially Latin Americans as emblems of racial impurity, a "mongrelized" race incapable of effective self-government. By the end of the century, as one newspaper put it, the "prevailing opinion in this country" held that the majority of the natives of Cuba were "mixed breeds." Since proponents of Anglo-Saxon supremacy posited that white racial purity was a necessary condition for republican self-government, this sort of racial thinking deeply shaped opinions about whether to intervene in the Cuban independence struggle, especially proposals to annex the island. Exiles and migrants experienced these racial views from close at hand, as when a *New York Times* reporter described the Cubans he encountered in an eating house near Maiden Lane as having "the look, somehow, of a tributary race," being both under-sized and prone to "gabbling like monkeys."[80] Martí wrote about his own experience of discrimination in his private notebooks after receiving par-ticularly insulting treatment from an employee at a New York Hotel: "One lives in the United States like a boxer. These people speak, and it seems as if they are jabbing their fists under a person's eye."[81] In response to pervasive storytelling about Anglo-American superiority and expansion, Martí became the leading defender of the idea that despite a chaotic past and the confusion of racial mixture, "our America too, raises palaces, and gathers together the useful surplus of the oppressed; it also tames the jungle, bringing the book and newspaper, the town and the railway; our America too, with the sun on its brow, acquires its perfect form in cities that sprout up across the deserts."[82]

This helps to explain the racial logic at work in the 1892 manifesto from the leaders of the Club Borinquen—including Figueroa and Marín—"to the Puerto Rican people." Rafael Serra, Germán Sandoval, Silvestre Pivaló, Rosendo Rodríguez, and the brothers Bonilla spent their working days in the company of increasingly radical cigar workers, exchanging ideas about anarchism and socialism. Sotero Figueroa and Pachín Marín spent their days in the middle of commercial ventures designed to broad-cast a new vision of Latin American cultural destiny while also selling modern industrial and consumer products to the region. Indeed, it was in this world of publishing that both men made the transition from ar-tisan to author a second time. Figueroa's first contribution appeared in *La Revista Ilustrada* almost exactly a year after he arrived in New York. This, and subsequent contributions to *El Avisador Hispano-Americano* and *El album del porvenir*, marked a major milestone on his path of social mobility. For the first time, he enjoyed an audience of thousands, widely dispersed across the Spanish-speaking world. And while the handful of readers in the small cities of Puerto Rico knew him by sight, understanding the journalist and playwright to be the same man who worked in an ink-smeared apron in a local print shop, readers in Colombia or Mexico would have no reason to suspect that the man whom publishers described as "Don Sotero Figueroa, distinguished Puerto Rican writer," who appeared alongside the great poets and thinkers of his generation, was an artisan or a man of color.[83]

Figueroa's writings quickly adapted to the Hispanist literary project that had begun to take form in the world of New York publishing. His contributions to various literary magazines in New York "highlighted the individuality, and untold richness, of Hispano-American letters."[84] New York publishers also discovered that Figueroa could be counted on to oversee the content of literary magazines as well as the mechanics of production. He soon became one of the "principal editors" of *La América Ilustrada*. This means that he may well have been part of the editorial team that decided to publish Martí's most famous essay, "Our America," in January 1891. In it, Martí argued for unity "from the Rio Grande to the Straights of Magellan" in order to confront the danger posed by "the scorn of our formidable neighbor," the United States.[85] The same issue of *La América Ilustrada* also featured two contributions from Figueroa, one of which was dedicated to his "dear friend," Martí. When Marín arrived in New York in late summer 1892, he too immediately started to publish essays in *La América Ilustrada* and the *Revista Popular*. The most famous of these was the vignette (already cited many times in this book) of an immigrant arriving for the first time at the piers of New York City, and then setting off in search of a friend or a countryman—a vignette that makes no mention of race or the challenges of settling behind the color line.[86] When Marín himself arrived on the piers, it seems a good bet that he went off immediately to look for his comrades, Figueroa and Tirado.

The politics of race within the literary and publishing circles in New York were different from the politics of race in cigar workshops. Many, and possibly most, of the writers in and readers of the New York literary magazines understood that the "visible culture" that would most incline the United States to respect was the culture of Latin America's white and educated minority, to which they belonged. They imagined themselves to embody the unique promise of "our America," and to be in the best position to compel respect from the United States and Europe. They had long favored the whitening of the islands through immigration and had begun to dabble in the emerging science of eugenics, which invested the old projects of whitening with a new, ostensibly biological urgency. Martí did not necessarily disagree with the idea that Latin American culture was and should be built on classical, European foundations. He started to espouse a view of race, however, that explicitly dissented from the leading voices of race science in Europe and the United States. "Feeble thinkers" might "string together and reheat the bookshelf races," Martí wrote. But "the cordial observer" looking for evidence of race in "nature" would search in vain, finding instead "the victorious love, the turbulent appetite, and the universal identity of man. The soul emanates, equal and eternal, from bodies that are diverse in form and color."[87] To Martí, race ought to signify not a biological fact but rather a process, determined by history, geography, climate, and the transcendental efforts of great thinkers. This is what created "peoples" with distinctive shared characteristics. For this reason, it was necessary that Latin Americans resist the temptation to emulate or assimilate into the United States. Latin Americans, guided by their "bookish redeemers," must find their own route toward modern democratic society and their own literary forms, consistent with their collective essence as a people.[88]

The version of this argument that he presented to his social peers, while rejecting the scientific basis of Anglo-Saxon supremacy, was hardly egalitarian with respect to the diverse elements that constituted Latin American societies. At a function organized by the Hispanic American Literary Society to host a group of Latin American diplomats, Martí contended that "the independent creole is he who dominates and makes certain, not the Indian in spurs, marked by the whip, who puts his foot in the stirrup so he may appear taller than his master."[89] In "Nuestra América," distributed, along with advertisements for North American manufactures, to urban literary types in Latin America, he celebrated the "autochthonous mestizo," whose natural intelligence had triumphed over the false erudition of the "exotic creole." But he assured his audience that the natural man "is good, he prizes and submits to superior intelligence, as long as it does not take advantage of his submission to harm him, and does not offend him through disregard."[90] Audiences in Latin America would not necessarily have known that Martí himself had already begun to put this somewhat-condescending ideal into practice each week at La Liga, and that his ideas about natural men were already shifting from the notion that they were merely "sufficient" to something else.[91] Exiles, however, did know this. Figueroa surely watched as Martí's views, or at least his rhetoric, evolved in response to his alliance with black and brown migrants. He eventually maintained that the Cuban revolutionary project would be successful in creating a modern democratic order, where other Latin American independence struggles had failed, precisely because blacks in Cuba were no longer in a primitive state. In 1892, in one of his more radically egalitarian moments, Martí wrote, "The man of color in Cuba is already a being with full use of his reason. . . . [H]e does not need to wait for the manna of culture to fall from the white heavens, because he is honing himself and raising himself up."[92]

The men of La Liga would have recognized this metaphor as a reference to themselves. In an essay on La Liga, published only months before, Serra had called on those who "needed" an educational society to decide for themselves that they should have one "and not wait, like the ancient people of Israel in the desert, for the manna to arrive."[93] They also surely watched as Martí started to treat Figueroa as an "independent creole" and "bookish redeemer," rather than a man of "natural reason" or a "sufficient negro." In particular, he pressed the well-heeled publishers and authors of the city to accept Figueroa as a member of the Hispanic American Literary Society. Thus at exactly the same moment that Martí began to write to the founders of La Liga, declaring the sincerity of his love for them and imploring them to accept him as a true friend instead of a traditional flatterer, he started corresponding with Figueroa. These letters were simpler. He encouraged the typographer turned author to come mingle with the top publishers and literary luminaries of the city, and with distinguished literary figures from Latin America. Martí assured Figueroa that the other members, men from decidedly aristocratic families who had a high regard for their own academic degrees, considered him "a man of true merit" and that they were sincerely pleased to have him in their midst.[94] In some cases this was probably true. Figueroa later recalled, though, that he usually declined the "honor" of attending the meetings of the Hispanic American Literary Society, despite Martí's insistence, because "I had too much respect for myself to expose myself to the disdain of certain elements" within it.[95] Yet it was precisely this disdain on the part of others that turned Martí's willingness to treat Figueroa as part of the elite tasked with remaking Latin American culture into a potent expression of antiracism. The contrast between a Latin America that shunned racial division and an Anglo-America fixated on racial division was important because of the ways that it resonated with the contrast between the idealized Latin America that Martí (with all his imperfections) had begun to enact and the all-too-familiar disdain of other exiles.

Nor was the inclusion that Martí offered Figueroa merely rhetorical. In March 1892, in response to the entreaties of allies, Martí began to produce his own newspaper, *Patria*.[96] During the first months of the new venture, Figueroa was part of the editorial team that gathered each Friday evening in a small workshop on Park Row, facing Printing House Square, owned and operated by three Italian tradesmen.[97] There, Martí and his associates made final changes to the copy amid the noisy clatter of the workshop, as the typesetter dropped the small lead types into place. The team made decisions about layout while standing shoulder to shoulder with another tradesman as he composed the pages. The pressmen began to prepare the paper and ink as Martí and his collaborators reviewed the first proofs, making last-minute editorial decisions, cutting and pasting, and adding crucial phrases. At this point Figueroa took over, managing the challenges of working with "foreign" typesetters, who made inexcusable errors of Spanish orthography. After his long week of work producing *La Revista Ilustrada*, he would meticulously review the proofs, making sure that the articulations of Martí's ideas, and those of Gonzalo de Quesada, Juan Bonilla, Serra, and Marín, as well as his own, were impeccable. They were about to take final form. Once printed, they would travel across the street to the monumental post office and from there would circulate across the greater Caribbean. Thus almost immediately, they would constitute the principal historical archive of the movement. Figueroa "despairs," Martí wrote, "with the absence of accents where they are necessary, and with the prodigality of accents where they are not needed and he rebels against the arbitrary use of punctuation."[98] The same skills that had initially earned him a place in producing the literary magazines of the city now assured him a spot in Martí's inner circle.

The writers in *Patria* did not miss the opportunity to chronicle these Friday night production meetings, framing them in didactic terms. In their account, the newspaper was an institution, like *La Liga*, that put the essential national values of democracy and solidarity into practice—a model for the movement and the coming republic. After the newspapers were printed, folded, and bundled, the workers and the editorial team shared the brute labor of loading the bundles and delivering them to the post office, and then the men would go together to an Italian restaurant for a well-deserved feast. "It is important to observe," the editors of *Patria* wrote of these evenings, "the democratic spirit that predominates in the group. Editors and craftsmen form a brotherhood with only one aspiration: each one is esteemed according to his merits and none is worth more than another in the hour of mutual satisfaction. In the work, everyone has done his active part. When these moments of intimate cordiality finally arrive, it is just that everyone be applauded for his efforts, and that they enjoy, without unwarranted limitations, the equity that we preach."[99]

As had been the case over the previous two decades in San Juan and Ponce, Figueroa was at the center of this fraternity between editors and craftsmen. But on which side of the line did he reside? In some instances, he seems to be one of the "typesetter-authors" who sat around the "fraternal table" set by publisher Vélez Alvarado, conversing with tobacco workers, "revolutionary lawyers," and doctors with degrees from French universities.[100] Yet he was also possibly something else. Within a year of the appearance of the first issue of *Patria*, Figueroa established his own print shop. At this point Figueroa took over full responsibility for the typesetting, composition, proofing, and printing of *Patria*, while also commencing his own efforts to produce books and other printed material for the export trade to Latin America.[101] He became thereafter the "owner of the *Imprenta América*"—a publisher who was also "the prize-winning author of biographies and the energetic poet from Puerto Rico, our brother in hope and labor." In this instance, *Patria* noted that Figueroa, "being, still, an experienced typographer, lends all of his determination so that our newspaper has an appearance equal to the high level of the best of its class."[102] But in other cases, he appeared simply as "one of Puerto Rico's most meritorious sons, most proven characters, and most energetic and renowned writers."[103]

Figueroa's role as a publisher ensured that of all the writers in *Patria*, he was the only one who never missed the crucial hours of production after the deadline. As Martí spent more and more of his time traveling, he often left Figueroa in charge of the editorial content as well. Enemies whispered that Figueroa had become the de facto editor in chief of the newspaper. Figueroa denied the accusation, but there is good evidence that he was helping to shape the content of *Patria*. And the accusation, if offensive to some enemies, was likely seen favorably by many of the working-class and African-descended readers and factory floor listeners who formed the rank and file of the party.[104] Audiences in New York, at least, knew that the self-proclaimed defenders of Hispanic civilization were not always or indeed usually welcoming to people of African descent. They knew that Figueroa, by presenting himself as an arbiter of taste, a creator of culture, and a defender of civilization—without adjectives— exerted pressure on Martí and other allies to live up to the principles of racial equality in a way that complemented his somewhat-condescending but evolving support for the "natural" men of La Liga. Figueroa was not required to perform the role of an exemplary *black* man. He could simply be an exemplary man.

Pachín Marín offered something slightly different. He tested the limits of his status as a writer with no racial qualification by asserting a proud and indomitable masculinity, especially in his oratory. Martí wrote that his speeches were like a "gentle murmuring current when he slides over sand or between flower beds." But they became "crushing, thunderous, and impetuous, when he runs between rocks or smashes up against the dikes that seek to contain his furious course; he turns and jumps and churns and overflows them."[105] This kind of alternation between elegant control and violent eruption was apparently appealing to the crowds at party gatherings. When Marín finished speaking, immediately audiences would begin to applaud and call for him to return for an encore, and sometimes two or three. When he was reluctant to speak, crowds would call him forth. In these instances, he played the role of a man who saw speaking as insufficient and popularity as trivial. He wished only for the opportunity to fight.[106]

The image of a charismatic young man of mixed racial ancestry vowing to take to the battlefield to defend the honor of his fatherland, whipping crowds of working men into a fervor, may have been unsettling to those who worried that Martí, by courting popular support, risked unleashing uncontainable conflicts. Indeed, the editors of *Patria* came close to criticizing Marín's excesses, deploying a typically obscure subjunctive to indicate the line that the young Puerto Rican was approaching, while not actually accusing him of crossing it. If we were to believe, they wrote, that "a censurable passion for notoriety, or an excessive desire for sterile polemic" drove Marín's vigorous prose, *Patria* would offer him a warning. "It might be," they observed, "that the newspaper *Patria*—perhaps for reasons of excessive or inopportune piety—would find the caustic eloquence" with which Marín "fustigates against this sinner or that" to be "unnecessary." But regardless of whether he was actually guilty of the unnecessary excesses for which some excessively pious observers might fault him, *Patria* made the crucial move of affording Marín a status without racial or class qualification. *Patria* could raise the possibility of condemnation, but would not actually condemn Marín, who was simply the "eloquent poet, impetuous liberal, intrepid worker, who out of the poison and difficulties of the world has built, uncorrupted, a soul that is hostile to despotism and villainy."[107]

MIGRATING WHILE MIXED

All this helps to explain how Figueroa and Marín (along with Vélez Alvarado) came to present themselves as spokesmen for a Latin American race, confronting an Anglo-Saxon enemy. What, though, did they mean by the phrase, "One must live in this country for some years to understand that this race does not tend to perfect and improve, through crossing, those races that it believes to be inferior"? On the face of it, this seems to be a reference to the idea, proposed by some intellectuals in the Spanish Caribbean over several preceding decades, that the Latin race had a particular genius for assimilating Africans and native peoples, and that mixture could produce a gradual whitening of the population of the islands. The idea of perfection and improvement also hints at a variant of eugenics that began to emerge in the Spanish Caribbean at about this time. This way of thinking about race science emphasized the benefits of hybridization and considered racial characteristics to be changeable, a product of the adaptation of organisms and species to environments, rather than natural selection and the immutable laws of heredity.[108] It hints too at the vernacular appropriation of these ideals of whitening through crossing. It is not clear whether Puerto Ricans had started to use the phrase "improve the race," as they did by the end of the twentieth century, to describe a desire (typically understood to be widespread) to seek out marriage partners with lighter skin in order to achieve a higher racial status for one's children.[109]

While deeply intertwined with the notion of white superiority, the idea of racial improvement through mixture nevertheless stood in sharp contrast with the mainstream of race science in the United States. There, scholars disagreed mainly on how many racial variants existed, and whether these races constituted separate species. But they typically agreed on the idea that races were distinct, naturally occurring biological entities, on the superiority of Anglo-Saxons, and on the eugenic benefits of racial purity. This scientific consensus helped to inspire a range of laws designed to clearly define races, to keep them separate, and to justify white supremacy. For instance, many states treated interracial sex as a criminal act, and refused to permit or acknowledge interracial marriages. Federal authorities also did nothing to stop a wave of racial terrorism, which peaked in the early 1890s. Mobs of white citizens, supported by local politicians and police, subjected African Americans to violence, mutilation, and death in the name of defending white female purity, and by extension the purity of the white race. Even in states like New York, which did not prohibit interracial marriage, the specter of "miscegenation" and "mongrelization" as well as the imagined figure of the black rapist were important tools for discrediting the project of equal citizenship for black men.[110]

The emphasis on racial purity inflected African American political expressions in this period too, in ways that were likely unfamiliar to Figueroa and Marín, and perhaps unthinkable. While in the mid-nineteenth century some leading African American writers had advocated racial "amalgamation," by the 1890s, few still took this position. Nearly all African American writers opposed legal restrictions on marriage, but few advocated openly for "social equality"—a phrase that risked the same violent reaction as the less polite synonym "miscegenation." Many openly opposed intermarriages for fear of white backlash, because it reflected a lack of "race pride," or because they had developed their own ideas about heredity, fitness, and eugenics that imagined racial improvement to be threatened rather than aided by intermixture.[111] Figueroa would not have missed, during his first months in New York, the scathing headlines—in both the black and white press—over the appointment of Frederick Douglass to a diplomatic post in Haiti. Douglass was the most famous African American intellectual of the nineteenth century, a veteran of the abolitionist movement and Republican politics, and a proponent of amalgamation. In 1884, he had married Helen Pitts, a white woman, eliciting denunciation from many African American writers as well as segregationists. The simmering controversy over the match resurfaced in 1889, when several officers objected, on the ostensibly moral grounds of opposition to race mixture, to transporting the couple on a US Navy vessel.[112]

This widespread opposition to "crossing"—the belief, even among many African Americans, that it was a form of contamination and in no way an "improvement"—was of great consequence for Figueroa. He arrived in New York only weeks after having married Inocencia Martínez, a woman identified as white by Puerto Rican contemporaries. It is impossible to know whether members of Inocencia's family or others in Puerto Rico expressed reservations about the match. They probably saw his color and his illegitimacy as serious marks against him, and may well have indicated as much in private.[113] In public, however, the Martínez family and those around them treated Figueroa as a suitable alliance. Indeed, Inocencia's father served as a witness to the marriage. Ricardo Aguayo, a prominent white author, who may have been a distant relative of Figueroa's first wife, also witnessed the marriage. On the record of the marriage, the priest identified the groom as Don Sotero Figueroa—respectful treatment that he typically received in public transactions at this point in his life. The priest also consolidated Figueroa's upward mobility by creating a new account of his origins. Figueroa was now the "legitimate son of Don José Mercedes Figueroa and Doña María Rosenda Fernández."[114] The slipperiness of social and racial categories in Puerto Rico makes it difficult to know exactly what to make of this document. Perhaps the priest merely colluded with the family to create an honorable veneer for a private reality that everyone knew or suspected, and some regretted. Perhaps the priest, knowing that Figueroa was a respected journalist, seeing that a respectable white family offered no objections to the match, observing Figueroa had previously been married to an Aguayo, and recognizing a white man named Aguayo in the wedding party, asked no questions. Perhaps he merely presumed that the details of Figueroa's origins ought to match his current status

Figueroa's own writings offer a clue to how he likely understood the question of "unequal marriage." For indeed, what hostile North American commentators derisively called "miscegenation," "mongrelization," or "social equality" was, for both Figueroa and Marín, a centerpiece of their democratic politics—a politics that they configured as a defense of unfettered manhood. In a biographical sketch of the Puerto Rican painter José Campeche, Figueroa recounted—elaborating freely on what had been a minor detail in earlier biographies—that the painter fell in love with a woman of higher racial status, but believed wrongly that the "honorable name" he had already begun to build through his fame as an artist was enough to erase the "difference of position that separated him from the object of his affections." The name of the "ingrate" who spurned Campeche was forgotten rather than remembered for eternity as it would have been had she not spurned her worthy lover. This provided "a just lesson that should be remembered" by those Puerto Ricans who remained "haughty and vain."[115] Marín covered a similar theme in his autobiographical poem "Emilia," published in Venezuela in 1889. The poem tells the tale of a young man of "bronzed visage" in love with a girl with a "tidy throat, white as snow." Even after the young man, "intrepid and audacious," studies, acquires a profession, and wins widespread applause, the girl's father steadfastly opposes the match. The girl dies of sorrow, and the young man descends into madness.[116]

Like Figueroa, Marín used the story of love in vain as a platform for a broader reflection on the imperfections of what he called, with bitter sarcasm, the Puerto Rican "Garden of Eden." The first three stanzas of "Emilia" herald the march of universal progress, enlightenment, and freedom before pausing to consider the incomplete triumph of universal values:

> Yet something is still missing; a persecuted race
> Banished from the great concert
> Of human society
> Without hope, without direction, and already fading
> At the oars, steers its skiff
> Towards an uncertain port.[117]

Cuban and African American counterparts broadly shared the Puerto Ricans' belief in a right to marry across color lines, but by the early 1890s, most sought to distance claims to public and political rights from the bugbear of social equality. Attorney T. McCants Stewart did just this in his opening statement in the first civil rights case taken by the Afro-American

League—the case against the Trainor Hotel for refusing to serve the journalist Fortune. "Remember gentlemen that this is not a matter of social rights. . . . The intelligent Afro-American does not bother his head any more about social equality than you do about the man in the moon."[118] Marín and Figueroa, by contrast, paid almost no attention to the question of equal access to public accommodations. They located their most forceful critiques of racial injustice in the private sphere.

It seems likely that Sotero saw his marriage to Inocencia in these terms, as evidence that his own good name and rising fame ought to be "sufficient to erase the difference of position" that separated him from Inocencia, and as a test of the democratic values espoused in his corner of Ponce society. Perhaps all those involved, even the priest, saw matters in a similar fashion. Or maybe they stopped somewhat short of this principle. In any event, his new public identity as the legitimate son of Don José and Doña María was inscribed in formal cursive in the sacramental records, and then copied over into the newly established civil registry. It had the sanction of both church and state.

It is clear that for Sotero and Inocencia, moving to the United States meant encountering the ways that people there had begun to construe race around the principle that "any perceptible trace" of Negro blood assigned a person to a fixed biological destiny. They could not have missed the hostility in most quarters to "crossing" in the sense of sexual contact between persons of different racial status, to "passing" in the sense of the movement of persons from one racial status to another, and to intermediate categories such as mulatto. Each of these social phenomena existed in the United States. But the social and political meanings that attached to them were, at that moment, shifting in an unfamiliar, and most likely unwelcome, direction. In many parts of the United States, local officials would likely have denied the validity of their marriage and might well have arrested them for fornication. Even staying in New York did not shield them from the widespread condemnation of interracial sociability. A white Puerto Rican family that entertained nonwhite friends in their home on upper Lexington Avenue, not far from where Sotero and Inocencia lived at the time, received threats and eventually attacks for violating the norms of strict racial segregation favored by German and Irish residents. Neighbors smeared feces on their door, broke a baby carriage that they had left in the hallway to pieces, and shut off their gas line.[119]

There is no knowing whether Sotero and Inocencia encountered anything like this. Yet it is clear that the absence of laws against intermarriage in New York did nothing to prevent private citizens from refusing to rent to mixed couples, from subjecting one or both of them to brutal violence, or simply from treating them with disrespect or hostility. The problem of accommodating New York's idiosyncratic color line could not have been simple to resolve.

The couple probably also noticed the ways that the concern for scientific racial classification had filtered into the civil registration of births, marriages, and deaths in New York. When Inocencia gave birth to the couple's first child, Julita, the doctor who filed her birth certificate at the Department of Health recorded her race as "colored."[120] Back in Ponce, both sacramental and civil registers would almost certainly have inscribed her as a legitimate daughter, affording the honorific don and doña to both of her parents and all four of her grandparents. Neither doctors nor public health agencies would have had anything to do with it. Yet they probably noticed a gap between the emerging legal and scientific principle that persons were to be permanently assigned to clear racial categories, without consideration of intermediate status and the daily practice of race in social interactions, which continued to operate in much more blurry fashion. Perhaps Inocencia and Sotero were strategic in their engagement with systems of bureaucratic classification in New York, treating record keeping as an opportunity to negotiate racial status, as it had always been in Puerto Rico. Maybe they had help in this effort when Julita died two years later. The girl's death certificate, filed by a Cuban doctor who was a member of the Cuban Revolutionary Party and a friend of the family, identified the child as white.[121]

In fact, several members of La Liga, the Logia Sol de Cuba, and the Club Las Dos Antillas appeared as black or mulatto on some public documents in New York, and white on others.[122] This was not necessarily particular to them, as there is good evidence that census takers in New York counted many African Americans of intermediate appearance as white in this period, especially when they lived in white neighborhoods or households. There is no reason to believe that the classification of black New Yorkers—including Cuban and Puerto Rican exiles of African descent—as white, on any particular document, necessarily indicated that they were "passing," which is to say living in such a way as to acquire, by intentional concealment, the privileges of whiteness in public and in private, although some certainly did make such efforts. These variations in how individuals appear, rather, highlight the contingent and inconsistent nature of racial classification even in a context in which legal and scientific consensus presumed fixed racial boundaries.[123]

The situation for Cubans and Puerto Ricans of intermediate status was further complicated, however, by the widespread perception that the Latin race in general was "mongrelized." White Cubans might bristle at the "prevailing opinion in this country" that the majority of the natives of Cuba were "mixed breeds." Indeed, the wealthier and whiter faction of the Cuban Revolutionary Party would, by the end of the decade, dedicate itself assiduously to presenting the public in the United States with statistical evidence of the pure whiteness of the majority of the island's population.[124] But the widespread idea that being Cuban or Latin always implied a degree of mixture, and the understanding that this sort of mixture lay somehow outside the clear dividing lines between white and black in the United States, probably influenced the day-to-day assignations of race that exiles of partial African ancestry negotiated. There are in fact clear hints in this direction. For instance, when Cayetano Alfonso, a Cuban cigar maker, a supporter of Serra, and a member of the Cuban Revolutionary Party, married a white woman, the marriage certificate that recorded their match described Alfonso as "Cuban mixte." Similarly, a New York birth certificate filed for the child of a Cuban cigar maker married to a white New Yorker identified the baby as "almost white-Negro-mulatto."[125] Neither of these categories could make sense within the reigning view that whiteness could not be obtained by degree and that any trace of "Negro blood" made a person simply "colored." The clerks and medical professionals seem, then, to have made exceptions, probably to accommodate the particular racial status associated with Cubanness. "Cuban mixte" was an inferior status to be sure, but it implied relative privileges when compared with blackness, including the ability to sidestep the scandal of mixed marriage. African Americans knew this, and sometimes sought out this kind of exception for themselves, passing for Cuban rather than for white. For instance, the *New York Times* reported on the case in this period of a "polite and apparently well-to-do" man who "professed to be a Cuban" in order to secure a place as a boarder with a Brooklyn family, and then to marry the niece of his landlady. When the man was later found to be a "Negro," his young wife "fell fainting to the floor" and then sued for divorce.[126] Perhaps Inocencia and Sotero discovered that New Yorkers did not always perceive in their family a clear case of racial crossing. Maybe some neighbors squinted at his appearance and saw a form of mixture that was Latin instead of black. Perhaps other neighbors regarded Inocencia as unreliably white to begin with.

All these considerations might well have convinced Figueroa, Martínez, and Marín—if they needed convincing—that race was a social invention rather than a biological condition, to consider the overwhelming concern about racial purity in the United States to be a form of fanaticism, and to prefer the emerging idea of a culturally accomplished, mestizo, Latin American race. At the same time, their assertion that hostility to crossing was a fundamental characteristic of the United States and therefore antithetical to Latin American identity was still a fairly controversial claim. It was especially controversial when asserted by two men of African descent who were, in other writings, so articulate about the injustice of continued *opposition* to racial crossing in Puerto Rican family life. In case anyone in New York failed to make the connection, Marín made it abundantly clear by publishing a book of poems called *Romances* at precisely the moment that he and Figueroa were becoming celebrities in the Cuban movement. The most consistent theme in these poems was the barrier to love across color lines. He republished the poem "Emilia" as part of the collection. In other poems too Marín made the scorn of a woman of higher status stand in for the relationship of the working-class poet to a society that cannot recognize his merits.

> And you disdain, ingrate, the sweet intentions
> Of the bard who sings to you
> And, in your unfeeling heart, my accent
> Provokes no faint echo of pity.
>
> Perhaps you think that my copper complexion
> Clouds the expression of my gaze
> And you see that my poor hair
> Has been burned by the sun of the tropics!
>
> Perhaps, little girl, in your eyes my soul is mute
> And, in your secret discernment, you cannot see

That beneath the forest of my unruly mane
Lies hidden the inspiration of the Poet!

In speeches and political writings Marín presented himself as an arrogant and indomitable spirit, but in his poetry, he fashioned himself as a "poor unhappy pilgrim," a drinker of beer, a sensitive and tormented soul, a lover of women, a bohemian. Marín the poet confesses that he has no other way, except possibly rebellion, to express his essential character as a man. "I cannot defend myself," he proclaims to a woman who has complained of his bohemian ways,

I cannot defend myself. My arrogance shouts at me,
my arrogance is a tyrant which compels me
to prefer the sharp pain of the lance
to the shameful blush of supplication.[127]

This persona must have tested the limits of both the Cuban civil rights movement and the Cuban Revolutionary Party, both of which had invested so heavily in undermining fears of black rebellion and sexuality with performances of dignified and restrained black manliness, and with the promise that civil and political rights were intended for the public sphere only. "We respect the prejudices that our neighbors might encourage in their homes, which we will never enter," proclaimed *La Igualdad* at the height of its campaign for civil rights. Meanwhile, white writers in the separatist movement sought to defuse the consistent accusation that black soldiers posed a threat to white women. Manuel Sanguily, a white journalist who eventually came to New York and will figure prominently in a later chapter, assured readers that "never did the black man even dream of possessing the white woman."[128] Of course, those who already lived in New York or read Juan Bonilla's reporting in *La Igualdad* also knew of the black men lynched in the United States based on accusations of sexual contact with white women.[129] With this as a backdrop, one of Marín's poems crashed thunderously against the boundaries constraining a poet of African descent. The poem, "Del natural," begins with the description of the naked body of a white woman—"the arm of ivory, the shoulder of alabaster, the face pale, and the bosom pressed tightly"— observed by the poet as she indulges in the private moment of her bath. The poet then enters the bathroom, pulls back a curtain, and pauses in the "ecstasy of her sinful form." The woman protests the invasion, but he quiets her with promises of love. They kiss, and "in a state of vertigo, propelled by the sylphs, into the bath she and I fall . . ."[130] Presumably he did not read this particular poem, with its provocative final ellipsis, in his celebrated performances at La Liga or at official gatherings of the Cuban Revolutionary Party. But this was a community of readers. The men who called him to the stage at these events could not have been innocent of the fact that he had published a poem that so openly addressed, in the first person, one of the most dangerous subjects in North American politics and a topic hardly comfortable for Cubans.

Marín's poetic moments of ecstasy, with all their sensibility of boastful conquest and bravado, were therefore necessarily political. Could Martí's celebrations of affection and love between white and black men, or of "our mestizo America," accommodate an alliance with writers of intermediate status who so directly addressed the themes of love and sex between themselves and white women? Did marrying a white woman, or sleeping with one, exceed the acceptable limits of upward mobility for an artisan who had transformed himself into a publisher and writer unmarked (or perhaps *usually* unmarked) by race? Was it necessary to insist that no such man had any desire for any white woman in order to defend their rights to dignified treatment and political participation? *Patria*'s review of Marín's poetry lauded his "light and elegant form," his "artistic fire and moderation," and his ability to relate "simple and personal" events through poetry, skating over any controversy in his choice of theme. The poems "here and there are too crowded with morning glories," complained the reviewer, likely using the flower to connote affectation—exaggerated or unconvincing expressions of sentiment. But overall these poems recounting the "heartaches" of the world's disregard demonstrated qualities that the reviewer defined as "the aristocracy of the soul."[131] Similarly, writers in the newspaper, including Martí, took pains to treat Figueroa's family with respect and affection. Readers outside New York might miss the subtlety of this, but readers close at hand would recognize that Martí and the other writers in *Patria* were enacting—and perhaps being forced to enact—tolerance for an ideal of social equality expressly located in the private sphere—an ideal that clashed almost unimaginably with the norms of political discourse in the United States and that profoundly tested Cuban ideas about race, yet that Figueroa, Marín, and generations of Puerto Rican writers had defended for decades.

Of course, this politics of male equality did not work equally for everyone in the migrant community. Heredia and the other women of African descent who helped build the migrant community within which male speakers and poets moved could not have failed to notice that the idea that dignified, equal manhood was being construed as access to romantic relationships with white women did little to advance their own status. When Douglass married Pitts, some African American women had objected that through his choice, he had "branded" them as inferior, or that he had "strengthened" the "malicious libel" that women of color were less refined, respectable, and desirable for bourgeois domestic life.[132] Perhaps Figueroa's choice of a mate raised similar concerns for the women of La Liga. Marín's poems, meanwhile, never named a woman with a dark complexion as an object of desire (the closest that he came was to treat a feminized Puerto Rico as *trigueña*, wheat colored). This might suggest that light-colored and white women were more beautiful than women with dark-brown skin. This idea would not have been unfamiliar to the La Liga women, who negotiated their relationships to one another and to the men in their lives in the context of a beauty culture that prized light skin and straight hair, and a beauty industry that had begun to address itself to them in the interests of selling skin-bleaching and hair-straightening products. So Heredia and her compañeras likely deplored the social prejudices that might lead some white women to reject black suitors. But they were likely aware, too, of the prejudices that might lead some black and brown men to express particular admiration for white women. Even if they did not openly criticize Figueroa's marriage, the women of La Liga probably did not view the transgressive love poems of Marín with quite the same sympathetic eye as the men who cheered and shouted for him to speak at party gatherings.[133]

Male writers and thinkers at La Liga may also have had more misgivings about these unfamiliar performances of race than they expressed publicly. Serra and the Bonillas surely noticed the strange circumstance that Figueroa, the highest-ranking African-descended member of their party, never used the phrase "the class to which I have the honor to belong," as his Cuban counterparts so often did to refer to their racial status. They probably understood the strategic value of this choice, and were surely aware of and interested in the differences between the ways that

Puerto Ricans and Cubans discussed race. But they were also familiar with the hierarchies of skin color practiced by people of African descent in both Cuba and the United States, and with the challenges that these hierarchies presented to projects to build racial pride and unity. Did they ever wonder if perhaps Figueroa did not feel that he belonged to their class or if he did not view belonging to it to be an honor? How would they measure such suspicions against his staunch support for the men of Las Dos Antillas and La Liga—black men involved in independent organizing in all but name? These impossible questions—the tension between "forgetting" that one was black in order to claim to be fully a man or asserting with pride that one was black in order to claim to be fully a man—were at the heart of the politics that they were working to invent. Martí promised a free Cuba in which race would be recognized as a fiction, and whites and blacks would "forget their color" to build a new community in shared manhood and nationality. As the Cubans discussed this promise of a raceless future in relation to their ongoing efforts to organize black political power and to secure civil rights, the two Puerto Ricans who were at once men of the class of color and simply men were probably more than just indefatigable comrades. The figures of Figueroa and Marín likely helped Martí to perform, and the men of La Liga to imagine, how a nation of men who had forgotten their race might actually work.

CRISIS

The period of intense activity and mobilization within the Cuban Revolutionary Party in New York—when Serra, Figueroa, and Marín addressed large enthusiastic crowds of workingmen and women—would soon be interrupted. Less than a year after the founding of the Club Las Dos Antillas and only weeks after Martí published his essay "My Race," expressing his belief that "Cuban is more than white, mulatto, or black. Man is more than white, mulatto, or black," the banking system in the United States collapsed, unleashing the worst economic depression in the country's history.[134] By summer 1893, cigar factories in New York began reducing production or shutting down. The members of the Club Las Dos Antillas and the Club Guerrilla de Maceo joined the armies of unemployed workers facing hunger along with the indignities of bread lines, soup kitchens, and other forms of charity. As conditions worsened, Marín, Rodríguez, Isidoro

Apodaca, Schomburg, and several white comrades called a meeting of workers in the city in order to find collective solutions to the problem of day-to-day survival. Their call sparked immediate controversy. Opponents of the Cuban Revolutionary Party gleefully reported on the proposed meeting, arguing that the working-class support on which Martí had built his movement was dissolving around him. Separatism had again failed. Perhaps under pressure from party leaders, Marín and the other men agreed to cancel the meeting, putting patriotic unity ahead of the question of their own survival. But in exchange, they announced, they had secured a promise that "if our homes are visited by affliction, those who are evicted will not be without a roof, those who are destitute will not be without shelter. The Antilles will be free and our poor in New York will be assisted by their brothers of all ranks and colors."[135] Like the project of independence, the defense of the defenseless was a collective project that unified the Cuban and Puerto Rican communities.

Patria reflected a version of this message back at workers. The United States had entered the crisis because it "has been unjust and greedy, has given more thought to protecting the fortunes of the few than to building a nation (pueblo) for the good of all." By contrast, in a free Cuba "the love of the land, and the strength of the native soil, and the abundance of the Creole heart, would remedy and console the inequalities of fortune."[136] Several months later, when workers went on strike in Key West, Martí sent a party lawyer to assist the strikers. He declared that the incidents showed that the only possible shelter for Cuban workers was a free fatherland built by their own hands. When local officials began arresting striking workers without cause and crowds of angry Anglo-American workers began stoning Cuban factories demanding that jobs in the factories be reserved for native "Americans," Martí denounced this as the work of demagogues. The Spanish government, he wrote, had found advantage in provoking the "animosity of a race that sees itself, unjustly, as superior to the other."[137] This was likely the same language that he used in his personal letters to the Club Guerrilla de Maceo during the crisis, and in his visit to a meeting of the club in November 1893.[138]

For men of Guerrilla de Maceo, and other readers of *Patria*, this now-familiar assertion of Cuban unity in the face of Anglo-American racism would also without a doubt have brought to mind the latest developments in Cuba. As the strike unfolded in Key West, news reached New York City and Florida that the colonial administration in Havana had issued a decree in favor of the civil rights of black Cubans. It soon became clear, however, that widespread resistance from café and theater owners, patrons, and even law enforcement officers would effectively nullify the civil rights decree, especially in the western provinces. This resistance included insults, threats of violence, and stones hurled at citizens who sought to integrate public establishments. As before, the Autonomista Party, though it relied heavily on the support of black and brown constituents in Oriente, declined to support the cause of civil rights. Juan Gualberto Gómez and the Directorio de Sociedades de Color responded with lawsuits and other attempts to pressure authorities to enforce the decree of equal rights.[139] According to Serra, the efforts of Gómez and the Directorio, and "the insolent and ridiculous position of their adversaries, are the topic of conversation in all of the Cuban circles in New York."[140]

This was, in other words, hardly a moment in which to draw sharp contrasts between the situation in Cuba and the rise of segregation in the United States. New Yorkers' conversations about the reaction to civil rights decrees in Cuba were well informed about the startling *similarities* between the efforts of the Directorio in Havana and the suit taken by Stewart and Fortune against the Trainor Hotel in New York. Indeed, Serra and Juan Bonilla dedicated several long articles in *La Igualdad* to highlighting these parallels. The existence of the Afro-American League in the United States (and other examples drawn from Serra's stay in Jamaica) proved the necessity of institutions like the Directorio.[141] Bonilla, Serra, and their allies understood clearly that the United States was a "plutocracy with the name of a republic."[142] They did not offer a contrast between the United States and Cuba, so much as a contrast between the United States and what Cuba might become. Serra wrote that he was in no way surprised by the resistance to civil rights in Cuba. "Separated from our land for several years . . . benefiting from the borrowed freedoms of several countries, learning from the constant motion of the earth in which we live," he had acquired "a certain degree of frankness of character." His experience observing the racial orders in other societies led him not to a blurry vision of Cuba as a racial paradise but rather to look on "certain entities" who resist the arrival of freedom in Cuba and seek to prevent the overthrow of the "clumsy reign of the oligarchy" with "inevitable revulsion."[143] For Serra and Bonilla, this was the line between the separatist movement, united in its commitment to social and racial justice, and a "ridiculous and insolent" Autonomista Party. Nevertheless, as the crisis unfolded, workers drifted away from the Cuban Revolutionary Party. The Club Las Dos Antillas, founded in the heady days of enthusiasm for Martí's workingman's party in early 1892, began to deflate as the economic depression deepened. The club lost money on a banquet intended to raise funds for the movement in December 1893. The club then ceased making any payments to the Advisory Council and held only two poorly attended meetings over the next fourteen months. The Club Guerrilla de Maceo, similarly, held only three meetings in the year and a half after Martí's visit in November 1893.[144]

The working-class clubs would begin to revive only after February 1895, when the Cuban Revolutionary Party launched a new insurgency in Cuba. But as Las Dos Antillas, Guerrilla de Maceo, and the other clubs reconstituted themselves, many of those same "entities" whose resistance to equal rights Serra found so repulsive would go into exile and would start to shift allegiances, migrating from the Autonomista Party into the separatist movement. The beginning of the armed struggle, then, would produce a new set of challenges for the pursuit of a democratic Cuba. Serra, Bonilla, Figueroa, and Marín faced these challenges by organizing within the exile community to create a new newspaper, and to invent new ways to exert influence within Cuban party politics.

▪ 6 ▪

Victory?

To forgive is not to abdicate, and the right to lay out in cordial terms the evils that need to be remedied—to avoid falling into eventual difficulties—is neither dangerous impatience nor rebelliousness. It is honesty.

—Rafael Serra, "Práctica," July 1896

Cuba will be independent . . . and we will continue making revolution, no longer against the Spaniards, but rather to rid ourselves of the vices with which we have been infected by rampant and illegitimate colonialism.

—Sotero Figueroa, "Por la revolución," July 1896

On New Year's Day in 1897, a group of Cubans, Puerto Ricans, and African Americans attended an evening of speeches and musical performances in a concert hall on the West Side of Manhattan. The theme of the evening was unity. One speaker offered a recitation of the verses of the Puerto Rican exile poet Lola Rodríguez del Tió, including, probably, her most famous poem, "Cuba and Puerto Rico Are Two Wings of the Same Bird." Figueroa gave a speech remembering the heyday of La Liga—the house of love and tenderness between men of diverse backgrounds, and the place where the Cuban revolutionary struggle had been reborn. Emilio Agramonte, who ran an Opera Academy in his elegant home on Lexington Avenue, performed a duet of Emerson's *Rondo* with Alfredo Vialet, who offered music lessons at an apartment that while only thirteen blocks away on West Thirty-Third Street, stood on the other side of the color line. Several of the Cubans played duets with African American performers. As a finale, all the musicians joined together to play a triumphal hymn titled "Cuba," a display of harmony among the various elements of the exile community and of their shared commitment to racial equality.[1] This performance of unity took on a special urgency because the ideal of a nation whose constituent parts were arranged in perfect concert was under severe strain.

The performance of unity also stood in intentional contrast to meetings held over the previous two months by a group calling itself the Sociedad de Estudios Jurídicos y Económicos, or "Study Group." At the most recent Study Group meeting, "about forty persons, distinguished by their culture and their comfortable position," gathered in the elegant parlor of a well-to-do exile family. The great Cuban philosopher Enrique José Varona, who had taken on the role of éminence grise within the exile community after Martí's death on the field of battle in Cuba, presided over the meeting. Estrada Palma, the man who had taken over as head of the Cuban Revolutionary Party, was there, as were several of the white men who had formerly participated in Martí's inner circle. With them were quite a few men who had never joined the party while Martí was alive, and several who had ardently opposed its creation. Fidel Pierra, who had made an infamous speech in 1889 warning against revolution because white Cubans did not have the resources to contain the "excesses and innovations of the blacks," was elected to lead the economics section of the Study Group. José Ignacio Rodríguez, who later described Martí as "mentally unhinged," and who criticized the party on the grounds that the separatist movement "had always before emerged from the high and wealthy classes," was selected as representative in Washington, DC. Trujillo, the editor who had led the attacks on Martí and his allies, was a member. Serra and several others (among them probably Figueroa) were invited to observe the second meeting, in Serra's words, "as a mere courtesy." But these visitors were not allowed to ask questions, even about procedure, or to propose motions.[2] The Study Group announced to the press that it was "taking steps to form a constitution for the republic" in anticipation of victory against Spain. A writer in the *Boston Globe* commented favorably on the class and racial composition of the group. "When victory is finally achieved the rulers of the island will be white men, granting a share in the fruits of victory to their colored helpers, but holding dominion of the island among themselves."[3] The Study Group held its first meetings in early November, and by the end of December, long-standing tensions within the separatist coalition in New York had broken out into open and intense political conflict.

The backdrop of this conflict is a story familiar to historians of the Cuban insurrection. A new war against Spain had been underway for nearly two years. General Antonio Maceo had led troops westward into the rich sugar districts of Santa Clara, Matanzas, and Havana, where they recruited peasants and field hands, and provisioned themselves freely from farms and plantations. As soldiers and officers witnessed the extreme exploitation that former slaves still experienced at the hands of former masters, some began to see the destruction of mills and the redistribution of land to insurgent soldiers as principal goals of the revolution rather than simply as strategies to defeat the Spanish. The military wing of the revolution became increasingly radical. The Spanish government responded to this offensive with the infamous policy of "reconcentration," forcing rural Cubans to relocate to towns and cities in order to cut off support for the insurgents. This policy provoked widespread famine and starvation. Faced with the increasingly dire conditions on the island, many planters and Autonomista Party members fled into exile, where they sought to exert a moderating influence on the civilian wing of the revolutionary movement.[4] Martí had anticipated this, encouraging his supporters to open their arms to the influx of new converts, while rejecting the "devious social vices of an impotent and ruined oligarchy" that they might bring with them.[5] But within a few months of the start of the new war, Martí had decided to refashion himself as a soldier. He departed for Cuba in April 1895 and perished in the fighting before the end of May. In his absence, the newcomers began to assert their right as the "better class" of Cubans to serve as the legitimate spokesmen for the revolution and to shape the future government of the island.

As these events unfolded, the Cuban Revolutionary Party selected Estrada Palma to replace Martí as delegate. Estrada Palma had been president of the Cuban republic in arms during the Ten Years' War. Unlike many civilian politicians of comparable stature, he had not been party to the capitulation at Zanjón and had never joined the Autonomista Party. He had relocated to Central America and then to a small town in upstate New York, where he ran a school for wealthy Latin American boys. He had also been an early supporter of Martí and the Cuban Revolutionary Party, and a polite acquaintance of the organizers of La Liga.[6] This helped make him the near-unanimous choice of the revolutionary clubs. Nevertheless, he pursued policies that were much more congenial to the newcomers than to the military leadership or the cigar makers in exile. Instead of working to provide resources for troops in Cuba, he launched a diplomatic and public relations campaign intended to elicit support in the United States for a negotiated settlement. Rather than visiting cigar factories and sociedades de color, he worked doggedly to convince politicians in Washington to recognize the belligerency of the Cuban insurgents and to persuade Wall Street investors to purchase Cuban bonds. Seeking support in Washington required maintaining a delicate balance as some politicians in the United States saw the crisis of the Spanish overseas empire as an opportunity for an expansion of US power abroad. Generally speaking, however, Estrada Palma and other wealthy exiles saw the United States as a potential ally in containing the social revolution that had unfolded in the insurgent camps, and that continued even after Maceo's death, late in 1896.[7]

In New York, Serra, Figueroa, Marín, and Juan Bonilla worked to maintain a delicate tactical balance of their own. On the one hand, they positioned themselves as the most prominent defenders of the democratic values of the movement against the machinations of newcomers and as uncompromising opponents of annexation to the United States. They warned that enemies were plotting to undermine patriotic and democratic principles. "Stay alert, *pueblo!*" Serra wrote to supporters several days after the first meeting of the Study Group, "and do not falter in this struggle, launched by your own efforts, against the foreign yoke, against all tyranny, and against all privileges." Beware, he urged, "of opportunists and profiteers" who use the "apocryphal excuse" that they seek to defend public order and the wealth of the nation in order to replace Spanish colonialism with "creole despotism."[8] Figueroa predicted that the war against Spain was only the beginning. Even after independence, he wrote, "we will continue making revolution, in order to rid ourselves of the vices with which we have been infected by rampant and illegitimate colonialism."[9] Together they worked to build and make visible to the new leadership the broad network of friends and supporters who held similar views. On the other hand, they offered themselves as Estrada Palma's lieutenants, delivering that broad network of friends in support of his leadership. As the war progressed, the poetry of their friendship with Martí faded into the terse prose of a new set of tactical alignments around Estrada Palma.

This was the double purpose of the concert on the West Side of Manhattan on New Year's Day 1897. It served to unite and mobilize the networks that Serra and his allies had built over two decades in defense of a struggle against all privileges, *and* to celebrate, in the name of democracy and patriotic unity, the loyalty of that group to the party leader. Estrada Palma attended the evening of songs and speeches, entering the room to thunderous applause. In turn, he applauded the poems of Rodríguez del Tió, the speech of Figueroa, and the performance of national harmony between white and black Cubans. He also watched, apparently without surprise or discomfort, the duets performed by Cuban and African American musicians. As the war unfolded in Cuba, and as politicians in Washington debated whether to invade Cuba and take the territory by force, Figueroa and Serra engaged in a war of position, picking their near-term battles carefully in order to situate themselves advantageously for the coming struggle to preserve democratic values within the Cuban republic and for the political competitions that would follow. Supported by the men and women who gathered in the concert hall on New Year's Day, they were about to emerge victorious in one of the few open maneuvers in this long-simmering conflict. A few days later the members of the Study Group bowed to their pressure to disband. Like the eventual defeat of Spain, the defeat of the Study Group was a victory that did not do away with deep structural inequalities in Cuban society. Yet the fact that Serra and Figueroa could still effectively maneuver within the Cuban Revolutionary Party, even after the death of Martí, sheds clear light on one of the major questions posed by this book: What lasting impact did the conflicts and alliances created within the Cuban Revolutionary Party in New York have on the evolution of Cuban politics after independence? In defeating the Study Group, Figueroa and Serra did not substantively change the policies that Estrada Palma pursued but they did begin to shape the terms of their relationship with him—a relationship that would prove extremely valuable when, five years later, he became the first elected president of Cuba. The episode also demonstrates a forgotten reality. Like so much of the political labor that they performed, Serra and his allies worked out their new relationship with Estrada Palma in full view—and with the participation—of the African American New Yorkers among whom they lived.

THE SACRED MEMORY OF THE APOSTLE

The war of position that Serra, Marín, the Bonillas, and Figueroa undertook after Martí's departure from New York had to do mostly with symbolism, and most especially with the telling of history. The bylaws of the Cuban

Revolutionary Party, originally drafted by Martí, permitted the delegate a great degree of independent action and secrecy on matters of policy. So Estrada Palma was no more required to give an account of his activities to the representatives of the revolutionary clubs than Martí had been. He did, however, have to answer to them on symbolic questions: How did the party leadership represent, through speech or action, the equilibrium among the various elements of Cuban society in the movement and the nation? As had been the case for nearly three decades, conversations about equilibrium took place against the backdrop of both Spanish propaganda and US imperialism. Representatives of the Spanish government did their best to disqualify the revolution as the work of a handful of black bandits "completely overrunning the Western Cuban districts, burning the settlements, assassinating all *pacíficos* and ill-treating helpless women."[10] The Cuban revolutionaries in the United States, Spanish representatives asserted, were nothing but charlatans who "dragged a few Cubans of color" into the struggle with "false promises" and otherwise used the movement to enrich themselves with the donations of cigar makers.[11] In an attempt to counter this propaganda, to help him present the revolution in terms that would be appealing to the public in the United States, Estrada Palma recruited well-spoken and well-dressed doctors and lawyers—including some of Martí's loyal lieutenants and some newcomers with questionable political antecedents. He prevailed on two prominent liberal journalists from Havana, Enrique José Varona and Manuel Sanguily, to come to New York and lend their prestige to the cause.[12] His refashioned inner circle gave lectures, organized rallies and speaking tours, sent letters and articles to the press, and feted politicians in Washington in order to produce a consistent message. Cuba was a cultured, freedom-loving, majority-white nation seeking to liberate itself from an oppressive European monarchy in order to pursue close commercial and political ties with its closest neighbor.[13] To be sure, there were some blacks and mulattoes in the Army of Liberation, but the struggle (and by implication, the future republic) was safely in the hands of "the most honorable of Cubans—men of the very best families."[14]

The point of these representations was to downplay the role of former slaves, black and brown commanders, and exiled factory workers in the struggle—the Cubans' "colored helpers"— not to challenge the presumption that whiteness was the sine qua non of responsible self-government.

Given what they knew about public opinion in the United States, the cigar makers might accept this as a sensible strategy, to a point. But some of Estrada Palma's most active allies in the effort were men of dubious democratic credentials to begin with. Sanguily had written, for Cuban readers, that the "revolution, in its character, its essence, and its aspirations, was the exclusive work of the whites" who had, to their great credit, called on Cubans of color to "lend eminent services."[15] Enrique Trujillo, the editor whose consistent attacks on Martí had spurred the creation of the newspaper *Patria*, took a major role in the new party activities. So did Fidel Pierra, the New York businessman who had made an openly racist speech in defense of Autonomismo only six years earlier. At the time, Serra had denounced Pierra in the pages of *La Fraternidad*, and other writers in the newspaper had begun using the term "another Pierra" as a synonym for "white racist." These newcomers did not confine their representations of a cultured white nation to the English-language press. In their writings for other Cubans, they also described a movement in which the main protagonists were enlightened planters and intellectuals. Trujillo, for instance, published a history of the independence movement in exile, in Spanish, that reduced the role of artisans and Cubans of color almost to a vanishing point. He made the defenders of popular democracy, including Martí, out to be unprincipled demagogues. In his view, after fighting honorably for reform within the Autonomista Party, the true patriots had now returned to the separatist fold, ready to take their rightful place as leaders. Trujillo's account was particularly galling, but it was only one variant of a broader pattern. The writers who surrounded Estrada Palma told the history of the movement in ways that emphasized the sacrifices of the heroic white professionals while reducing blacks and artisans to passive roles.[16]

Writers of color had contested such accounts in their various publications since at least the early 1880s. They had argued that blacks had made their own heroic sacrifices in the defense of democratic principles and the common good of the nation. Rather than passive and grateful auxiliaries, blacks had been full participants in the struggle and should be rewarded with full citizenship.[17] Martí's particular genius (with the help of Figueroa) had been to construct a careful balance in the pages of *Patria* between profiles of wealthy, white patriots and profiles of exemplary black soldiers, poets, and teachers. Now, as newcomers flooded into the party, Serra and his allies fought to preserve their place in the official history of the movement. They emphasized the dishonorable capitulation of the Autonomistas (including men like Trujillo and Pierra) at the end of the Ten Years' War. They recalled the indifference or hostility that supposed white allies had shown to the causes of abolition, national independence, and black civil rights in the intervening years. In their accounts, the capitulation and unreliability of the Autonomistas were the source of the "divisions" that had cast the independence struggle into the wilderness. The revolutionary cause had only been reborn because of the transcendent figure of Martí, and the unwavering support and sacrifice of working-class exiles and the class of color.[18]

So rather than celebrate the planters and intellectuals who had been such uncertain allies, a speaker at a gathering of the Club Las Dos Antillas declared, "A monument should be built to the artisans" because they were the ones who had started the new war. The artisans were responsible for "the principles of liberty" and "the advanced ideas." The great heroes of the struggle had "sprouted from the people." A second speaker celebrated the role of "the black race, the warrior race, virile and valiant," not just in Cuban history, but in the history of human progress, from its cradle in ancient Egypt. "¡Bravo!" the crowd replied. "And today, a black man is first among all Cubans, Maceo." "¡Bravo!" As the speaker finished, applause "rained down" in reply to these "eloquent words." After several more speakers, Arturo Schomburg, the recording secretary of the club who had been diligently taking notes on the speeches for the minutes book, called for the crowd to express its allegiance to "the sacred memory of our beloved José Martí." The crowd roared an emphatic "viva!" in response to this crucial phrase.[19] In order to gain leverage in this contest over history, artisans and their supporters invested heavily in this idea that Martí was both sacred and that he belonged especially to them. By turning him into a Christlike redeemer, they configured themselves as his disciples, present at the moment of revelation. This made them crucial figures in the sacred history of the movement.

The veneration of the sacred memory of our beloved José Martí also implied a claim to a privileged role as interpreters of Martí's teachings. Martí's writings and speeches had always been careful balancing acts, full of contradictions and extended subjunctive clauses. Even his last great essay, the "Manifesto of Montecristi," cosigned with General Máximo Gómez, lingered on the actions of generous whites whose "sincere estimation of the equal soul" of the black Cubans had helped to create the "sublime fusion" of the races. Some readers might conclude that he thought the "gratitude and good judgment" of the blacks were therefore the greatest protection against any future racial conflicts. Others might read far enough to see that he also listed "the possession of all that is real in human rights" as an important barrier against racial conflict. Similarly, some readers might conclude that he believed that the greater threat to unity came from the "provocative, aggressive, and offensive rancor of a minority of masters who have lost their privileges," while others could conclude that he worried more about the "censurable haste with which a minority, still invisible, of freedmen might someday aspire" to "social regard that can only come, and surely will come, if they prove themselves, first, in matters of virtue and talent."[20] In their own accounts, the veterans of La Liga resolved such tensions by recalling an instinctively democratic and unpretentious Martí who wanted neither flattery nor blind adoration from his black allies but rather the honesty and love of "complete men." They drew instructive contrasts for a new generation of "swollen and proud" politicians "who wish to be loved, but [had] still not come to understand why the pueblo had so much love for el Maestro."[21] New converts were welcome under the banner of national unity. But reunion was only possible if the newcomers recognized and accepted the true origins of the revolution, which were "essentially and profoundly of the people."[22] In the first months after Martí's death, this view had, if anything, a privileged space in the party newspaper, *Patria*, which was now published and administered by Figueroa.

But then, in fall 1895, Estrada Palma succeeded in bringing Varona to New York, and in convincing the illustrious philosopher, journalist, and former Autonomista representative in the Cortes to declare his allegiance to the insurgency. Estrada Palma put him on the party payroll in exchange for "services." He then commissioned Varona to draft a pamphlet outlining the case for independence. Party coffers subsidized the pamphlet's printing (at Figueroa's workshop), distribution, and translation. Varona described the revolution as a campaign led by creole politicians who rejected their unfair exclusion from a role in the government of Cuba. He advocated civil liberties, economic growth, and good government, and railed against a regime of corruption, political manipulation, and mismanagement. The abolition of all privileges, however, could not have been further from his account. The destruction of the sugar economy was unthinkable. Even such relatively flexible terms as "equality," "equilibrium," or "democracy" played no part in his view of the revolution.[23]

Estrada Palma also turned over to Varona the job of editing the newspaper *Patria*. With a full-time editor, *Patria* now appeared twice a week, but it took on a decidedly new tone. Varona demoted Figueroa from his role as administrator of the newspaper and pushed him to the sidelines on editorial matters (he stayed on as publisher).[24] As a result, the democratic wing of the movement was suddenly without two of its most reliable outlets. *La Igualdad* had closed its doors when authorities in Havana had arrested Juan Gualberto Gómez and sent him to a penal colony in Africa earlier in the year. Serra, Figueroa, and Bonilla responded by creating their own newspaper the following summer in order to defend the sacred teachings of Martí. They called it *Doctrina de Martí* (Martí's doctrine), adding the subtitle, "The Republic with All and for the Good of All." Under the umbrella offered by the veneration of Martí, they again made the point that the ideals of the separatist movement were their own ideals. It was Martí, Serra maintained, who had taught the principle that the "most unshakeable foundation of harmony" was not the gratitude or passive loyalty of black Cubans but rather "the practice of true democracy."[25] For his own part, he added, "to forgive is not to abdicate, and the right to lay out in cordial terms the evils that need to be remedied—to avoid falling into eventual difficulties—is neither dangerous impatience nor rebelliousness. It is honesty."[26]

Yet even as Serra mobilized a broad following around the unwavering call for social justice, he carefully avoided any criticism of Estrada Palma, whom he counted as a friend and ally. Before the start of the war, Serra and Estrada Palma had exchanged several cordial letters, and Estrada Palma had written a complimentary review of Serra's book in *Patria*.[27] Serra was probably part of the network of prominent figures in the party who used their influence in the clubs to ensure Estrada Palma's selection as delegate.[28] But the origins of their unique political relationship seem to lie in a letter that Serra wrote to Estrada Palma in the immediate wake of the election. Serra had been unsettled, he explained, in the run-up to the election. He knew that only a man of "talent" could represent the fatherland in this position, but believed that it was also necessary to choose a man of "great nobility of heart." He was therefore relieved that the émigrés had been "awake" enough to select Estrada Palma and not one of the other candidates who had expressed interest in the post. Since the election, though, he had received a flood of communications from friends far and wide expressing doubts about the new leadership and future direction of the party. He was sure, he wrote, that if Estrada Palma had been inattentive to some constituents, it was because of an "excess of work." He knew that the delegate would recognize the need to take the matter seriously for reasons of "political precaution."[29]

In this he was not wrong. Even as Estrada Palma made a series of profoundly undemocratic moves, he took the political precaution to respond to the needs of some key black and brown constituents. Juan Latapier, for instance, was a contributor to *La Igualdad* and one of the first African-descended Cubans to study law at the University of Havana. His studies had been interrupted by the war, and he was living in Key West, working as a lector in the cigar factories, when he was struck by a terrible case of laryngitis and left unable to support himself. Estrada Palma appointed him as a bookkeeper for the national lottery, with a small stipend from the party.[30] Similarly, Estrada Palma found a way to use party funds to support the family of Juan Gualberto Gómez, including his wife and his aging parents, Serafina Ferrer and Fermín Gómez, the couple who had taken in laundry, and had grown and sold vegetables to buy his freedom and their own. They had also arrived, destitute, in Key West when Gómez was sentenced to prison in Ceuta. The sociedades de color in Florida had organized a collection to support the family, but Estrada Palma also approved a request from one of the local organizations that he controlled in Tampa to divert an additional small quantity to the family on a weekly basis.[31]

But if Estrada Palma knew enough to disburse this sort of favors, he nevertheless needed help in managing his relationship to the wide base of the party. Serra concluded his letter with the most important point. "I have no greater value," he wrote, than "to do justice to your virtue, which is still unknown to the great part of the popular masses, for reasons that are only natural. And you, my dear Palma, will be known very soon by my friends, who are very many and very useful."[32] By the following summer, *Doctrina de Martí* became a platform for living up to this promise, and for Estrada Palma to return the favor, through public support for the newspaper and a subvention for its publication. The first issue of the paper featured a letter on its front page in which Estrada Palma ratified the central argument of the newspaper: that "the teachings of the noble Apostle and sublime martyr" should be the governing doctrine of the movement, and that Martí's doctrine dictated that "we must enter into the new society forthrightly, through the wide door of justice, with equal rights for all and with privileges for none." He acknowledged that Martí was an "instinctive democrat." Still, he emphasized his predecessor's warnings against censurable haste. He wrote, "Let us also be tolerant and benevolent, seeking the perfection to which we aspire, but trusting more in the influence of reason, employed with discrete moderation, than in fiery impatience, which is always loaded with dangers for the community to which we belong."[33] In exchange for his support, Serra provided Estrada Palma—who did not keep up Martí's exhausting schedule of travel and meetings with working-class constituents—a platform from which to communicate to his wide network of friends.

MANY FRIENDS, AND USEFUL ONES

Who were these friends? *Doctrina de Martí* reached the same network of black and brown readers and allies in the sociedades de color in Key West, Tampa, Kingston, Port-au-Prince, Panama, Costa Rica, and Veracruz as had *La Igualdad* and *La Fraternidad*. It was almost certainly read aloud in cigar factories in each of the exile communities. It was probably smuggled into Havana as well.[34] Some issues reached the insurgent camps in the Cuban countryside. General Agustín Cebreco, on whose staff Serra had served in the failed 1885 expedition, received the paper and sent occasional letters from the front. The physician Fermín Valdés Domínguez also sent dispatches.[35] A childhood friend of Martí and his comrade during their student days in Madrid, Valdés Domínguez now served as chief of staff for General Máximo Gómez. He was an outspoken antiracist and one of those who came to see attacks on property as vital to the project of the revolution.[36] Still, the friends over whom Serra had the most influence, and who most actively supported the newspaper, were the black and brown migrants who for almost three decades had built institutions and networks to contend with the idiosyncratic contours of New York's color line. Members of this community, organized within two fraternal lodges, an educational society, several mutual aid societies, and two political clubs, now became the advertisers and subscribers who supported the newspaper, and eventually the membership of a formal "Committee to Aid *Doctrina de Martí.*" These were the friends who attended the 1897 New Year's Day concert, which was originally planned as a fund-raiser for the newspaper.

The newspaper itself offers many glimpses of this community. For instance, the paper was available on Sullivan Street at the barbershop of Sixto Pozo, who was a founding member of Sol de Cuba, La Liga, and the Club Guerrilla de Maceo. Salomé Rencurrel appeared on a list of donors to the paper. He had been the Bonillas' neighbor in Key West in 1870, and was later a resident of the Sandovals' apartment at 89 Thompson Street and a leader of the Logia San Manuel. Marcelino Piedra also donated to the paper. He had shipped out to Kingston with Serra at the start of the failed expedition in 1885. He later helped to create the Cuban Republican Association and was one of the men who had gone to the courthouse with Serra to naturalize as US citizens on October 10, 1888. By the late 1890s, he was also an officer in the Club Guerrilla de Maceo. Carolina Peñalver also made a significant contribution of cash to the newspaper and lent Serra a photograph for publication. She and her husband had sent their son Pastor to attend secondary school in New York twenty years before. She then made the same journey with her other children while she was eight months pregnant. She worked as a seamstress, so had income to donate using her own name, although it was her husband's surname. Olayo Miranda and Pedro Calderín, officers in the Club Guerrilla de Maceo, the Committee to Support *La Igualdad,* and La Liga, were president and vice president of the Committee to Aid *Doctrina de Martí.* These are just a few examples.[37]

Few in this community still lived in Greenwich Village. Serra opened his editorial offices in a two-story building on West Thirty-Third Street in the heart of the Tenderloin. This area was already growing a reputation as a center of African American musical and cultural production, but also suffered from city policies that pushed illicit activities out of surrounding neighborhoods and into the same areas that were open to black settlement.[38] Heredia and Serra lived with their daughter Consuelo in this building, which was also near to the homes of wealthy Cubans, including de Quesada, across Sixth Avenue to the east and across Eighth Avenue to the west. The Club Guerrilla de Maceo now met nearby on West Twenty-Fourth Street, and Juan Bonilla presided over the Logia San Manuel in an apartment on West Thirty-Second (see map 5). The Serras' apartment was the bustling center of the community served by the paper. The violinist Vialet (who played the duet with Agramonte at the New Year's celebration in 1897 and later married Harriet Reason, the "mistress of the house" at 74 West Third Street) lived in the apartment and offered music lessons there. Evarista Corrales, a seamstress, also lived with the Serras, along with her son.[39] The flat also received constant visits from journalists, readers, and politicians. Estrada Palma paid a call. And when Juan Gualberto Gómez was finally released from prison, the great party to welcome him to New York took place there too.[40]

One advertisement that appeared regularly in *Doctrina de Martí* provides particular insight into the shape of the community that grew up around the newspaper. Heredia, a "midwife certified at the Havana Birthing Clinic," advertised her practice, also located in the family apartment on West Thirty-Third Street. Visitors to the apartment later remembered that Heredia was her husband's "collaborator," sitting with Consuelo bundling issues of *Doctrina de Martí* while Serra braved the "harsh winter nights" to bring the packets to the post office. Consuelo also "labored" with her father, helping him to translate texts from English into Spanish. Yet the advertisements for Heredia's practice suggest that even as the many residents of the building engaged in politics, and as others played music, exchanged cigars, or sewed, the home was a space for activity around childbirth and maternal health too—matters that were at least as important to the building of community. The close quarters in which all this work took place is visible in a short notice in *Doctrina de Martí* announcing the birth of a healthy boy to a couple identified as "our esteemed friends,"Ana Luisa Valdes and Francisco Zayas. The baby was born in the Serras' home, where Valdes and Zayas were also living at the time. Heredia therefore almost certainly organized the lying-in and delivery. At some point, however, she or one of the men in the house called in a physician named Enrique Agramonte (a resident of one of the fancier buildings nearby). He likely performed one of a relatively few interventions available to doctors at the time (the ministration of chloroform or the application of forceps) under the watchful eye of the experienced midwife, who almost certainly knew much more about obstetrics than he did.[41] After the birth, Serra and the doctor, who was the son of one of the great heroes of the first Cuban war of independence, engaged in a playful argument over what name to give the child. The editor favored the name Juan Gualberto. The physician favored the name Maceo. While the men shared this easy social intimacy (most likely accompanied by fine Cuban cigars), Heredia, perhaps along with Consuelo and other women, would have attended to the postpartum needs of the new mother and cared for the newborn child.

The other prominent Cuban midwife in New York, Josefa Blanco, lived on Third Avenue near Ninety-Ninth Street with her husband, Isidoro Apodaca, at the center of a second cluster of Cuban and increasingly Puerto Rican settlement (see map 6). Blanco not only ran her own household but she also played an important role in the lives of the other families within the larger enclave of friends who lived in the surrounding blocks. She delivered the babies of the Puerto Rican women of color, Pilar Cazuela and Dominga Curet, for instance, as well as of several Cuban women and at least one African American woman married to a Cuban cigar maker. She was probably also the one who sent for a doctor to sign a death certificate when Curet's three-year-old daughter died. And it must have been Blanco who rushed to the apartment on East Eighty-Fourth Street that her daughter Dionisia and her son-in-law Juan Bonilla shared when Dionisia went into labor in 1897. It was likely Blanco who was attending Dionisia when she began to hemorrhage (though Josefa Dorticos and Isabel Acosta likely rushed over too). So perhaps it was Blanco who first realized that nothing could be done to save Dionisia or the child, though a doctor had to be called to sign the death certificate.[42] The brief notice in *Doctrina de Martí* gives only a hint at the deep wave of sorrow that this event must have sent through the densely intertwined households along Upper Third Avenue and on the West Side. Serra commented that the funeral was the largest gathering of Cubans that he could remember.[43] It also barely hints at the paid and unpaid work of community building that women did—nursing babies, caring for sick family members, and facing the joys, pain, and dangers of childbirth—in the same confined apartments where the men in their families undertook the political work of participating in the Cuban Revolutionary Party.[44]

Women may therefore have been physically present for much of the political organizing that took place in these apartments, even if they were not typically recorded in meeting minutes or imagined to be participants in the politics. This may help explain how, in one instance, "Señora Doña Silvestre Pivaló" appeared in the minutes of the Club Las Dos Antillas making a donation of a rifle and cartridges. Pilar Cazuela de Pivaló was not a member of the club nor did she figure on the list of men attending the meeting. Yet the secretary of the club saw no need to explain how she came to be there.[45] It is clear, furthermore, that Cuban and Puerto Rican women of color, and even some men, understood gender equality, including the right of women to participate in politics, to be one of the principles of what Serra called the "left wing" of the separatist movement. By the time that he founded *Doctrina de Martí*, Serra went well beyond the typical messages directed at women of color: admonitions to proper domestic comportment and decency. Some men, he noted, wanted to "legalize unjust privileges of sex just the same as they want to establish unjust privileges of race." But such "theories" were clearly "clumsy, egotistical, and ridiculous."[46] Serra, by contrast, intended to "teach" his female readers the principles of female equality and empowerment. Roger, Martínez, Cazuela, Blanco, and Heredia may not have agreed that they needed instruction on this topic from male comrades (especially the ones with whom they shared their beds or to whom they had given birth). But they surely appreciated the argument that inequalities of sex, like inequalities of race, being social rather than natural, were a form of injustice.

One group of women wrote to Serra that they supported the newspaper because of its contention that "the abolition of privileges ought to be radical." Likely influenced by anarchist thought about the family, they understood this proposition to be applicable not just to privileges of class, race, or even sex. "Because we understand," they wrote, "that if women struggle to have our rights and guarantees, we should not, after acquiring them, forget ourselves, and exercise despotism over our children only because they are weaker, but should rather dedicate ourselves to educating them for freedom."[47] But whether or not they saw themselves as Serra's dutiful students, as radical egalitarians in the mold of anarchists Emma Goldman and Lucy Parsons, or as dignified colored club women on the model of Ida B. Wells, it is clear that the Cuban and Puerto Rican women who lived in the segregated apartment buildings of the Tenderloin and East Harlem saw themselves as political actors. In December 1896, Blanco, Heredia, Cazuela, and Curet created their own political club. It is not clear how frequently they met or what activities they undertook. Nevertheless, when the members of the Club José Maceo attended the New Year's Day concert in 1897, they did so as political subjects, as members of the Cuban Revolutionary Party.[48]

THE COLOR LINE

The cramped apartments where this network of friends undertook their political and domestic labors as well as everyday activities such as sleeping, eating, friendship, and intimacy continued to be located squarely within relatively few apartment buildings open to black New Yorkers. Cubans and Puerto Ricans also continued to participate in a set of relationships with their African American neighbors that went well beyond enforced residential proximity. When Serra expressed regrets, in the pages of *Doctrina de Martí,* for missing the wedding ceremony of Magín González (a member of Sol de Cuba lodge) and Mary Ellen Watson (an African American woman), he did not say what most of his readers probably knew: that this kind of match was a regular feature of their community.[49] When Julio Justiniani died, Serra commented in the pages of *Doctrina de Martí* that hardly a week went by that he was not called on to go to a funeral of a "countryman" or a "friend." He did not say where the bulk of these funerals took place, telling readers only that Justiniani's fraternal brothers gathered to bid him farewell at St. Mark's Church on West Forty-Eighth Street. A lodge elder spoke in Spanish, and the minister of the church, Reverend Ernest Lyons, delivered a eulogy in English.[50] Serra did not mention what, again, most readers in New York already knew. St. Mark's AME Church was a black congregation. Reverend Lyons was an immigrant from British Honduras and a leading figure in the city's Colored Republican Annex.[51]

Lyons, in fact, appeared in the pages of *Doctrina de Martí* multiple times. For instance, he was mentioned in September 1896 when the newspaper announced a "noisy party" organized by a group calling itself the Friends of Antonio Maceo to benefit soldiers wounded in battle. The "gathering of Americans and Cubans in support of Cuba" was more or less the same Cuban American picnic that Germán Sandoval had organized for nearly two decades, bringing together the Cuban class of color with African Americans to raise funds for a variety of causes. Sandoval served as the president of the organizing committee. Albert Mando, an African American composer, donated the services of his dance orchestra; presumably they played some mix of the Cuban danzón and the early ragtime sounds for which the nightspots of the Tenderloin were known. Perhaps the African American songwriter William Tyers (who lived nearby on

Manhattan's West Side) was among those who attended. This was about the time that he composed his first major hit, a syncopated "Cuban dance" named for the line of Spanish defenses that Maceo crossed in his invasion of Western Cuba, "La Trocha." Within a few years, with US troops in control of Cuba and Puerto Rico, this number would become a hit, played by African American dance bands across the country.[52]

Within a few months, Serra's supporters would begin mobilizing this same group of musicians, speakers, and dancers to participate in fundraising events for *Doctrina de Martí*. But the exchanges that took place at New York's Cuban American picnics and benefit concerts continued to go far beyond questions of musical style and dance. Sometimes Reverend Lyon addressed the crowd. Sometimes T. Thomas Fortune spoke. In one instance, Alexander Walters, the bishop of the African Methodist Episcopal Church and a leading force behind the attempt to create the Afro-American League, also spoke. In another, T. McCants Stewart, the civil rights lawyer and, by then, a Democratic member of the Brooklyn Board of Education, gave an address.[53]

Nor is it likely that these were the only places where Cubans and African Americans shared political ideas. Serra noted, in the pages of *Doctrina de Martí*, that he was friends with an African American poet named R. Plummer. Plummer, other sources indicate, was the foreman at the Cosmopolitan Barbershop, located on the same city block as the Serras' home, directly across from the Sixth Avenue elevated railroad station. Next to African American newspapers, Fortune commented in 1883, black barbershops were "the great dispensaries of news." Fortune lamented, with tongue in cheek, that it was not possible to patronize one of these establishments "without being compelled to sit with a face half lather until his artist concluded some point in an argument, or returned from a visit to the window, whither he had flown to feast his eyes upon some lady acquaintance who had passed." All complaints aside, Fortune, like any good newspaperman, depended on barbershops (including both the Cosmopolitan on Sixth Avenue and the Thomas Barber Shop on Upper Third Avenue) to distribute his paper, and frequented them to pick up news, opinion, and gossip. Serra probably did the same. Just as they continued to live and socialize in close quarters with African Americans, the network of male activists who led the Club Las Dos Antillas, the Club Guerrilla de Maceo, the two lodges, and now the efforts to support *Doctrina de Martí* likely all frequented black barbershops, and took part in the arguments and political commentary that unfolded in those businesses. It is not clear whether hair dressing or other elements of personal grooming provided a similar set of interactions between the women of the Club José Maceo and African American women in their neighborhoods.[54]

Conversations with African Americans, in apartment buildings, in lodges, at family gatherings, at weddings and funerals, at picnics and dances, and in barbershops, were the local context within which Serra and his allies produced their strategies of political engagement, their war of position. The Cubans and Puerto Ricans surely heard the opinions of African American preachers, newspapermen, and politicians as the United States descended into the "nadir of American race relations." They heard the reactions of black New Yorkers in fall 1895 when Booker T. Washington made his famous Atlanta compromise speech, announcing that in exchange for support in the project of industrial education and moral uplift, African Americans would not pressure national Republicans for civil rights and would not challenge racial segregation. They learned, in summer 1896, that the Supreme Court had ruled against Homer Plessy's challenge to segregated railcars and heard continued accounts of lynching in the South. As they engaged in a battle over the history of their own movement, they witnessed the dramatic shift in the way that white northerners recounted the history of the Civil War. White New Yorkers no longer saw the War between the States as a heroic crusade for justice, but rather as a tragic confrontation, pitting men of honor against one another. Many had been in New York when two Confederate officers were selected to carry the coffin of President Grant (the great Union general and abolitionist) to his final resting place. The Cubans and Puerto Ricans observed as this shifting view of history—hand in hand with the evolution of race science—helped justify a call to reunion between white northerners and southerners, and erased the project of interracial democracy. They surely knew of the protest, led by Wells and Douglass, when African Americans were excluded from the pavilions representing US history at the Columbian Exposition in Chicago in 1893.[55]

Both Cubans and African Americans therefore measured the opportunities and risks presented by the revolution in Cuba—including the question of whether or how to support Estrada Palma—against this backdrop.[56] That party bosses or national leaders would be selected from among the educated and the powerful, that they might be awkward or inattentive in their appeals to working-class constituents, and that they might be less supportive of black civil rights when in office than when on the campaign trail was no surprise. This familiar political predicament cast Estrada Palma and the Cuban Revolutionary Party in a comparatively positive light, even if he was clearly no Martí. The same backdrop cast Martí in an *especially* positive light, even if he was not the immaculate saint that Serra and others made him out to be. Estrada Palma followed a game plan that Martí had spelled out before his death, winning over the support of Cuban planters and politicians, and appealing to the public in Latin America and the United States, while preserving the support of the cigar workers in New York, Jamaica, and Florida, even if he was less attentive to this last element of the strategy than his predecessor. So he supported *Doctrina de Martí*. He and his allies preserved, or permitted the preservation of, the symbolic gestures of recognition and inclusion that were deeply embedded in party culture. The Advisory Councils still operated independently. The club presidents still sat in a place of honor at party functions. Even Pierra—the infamous racist whose performance of genteel civilization was so effective in the speeches that he made to white North Americans—worked to build and preserve ties with black constituents. He contributed money and articles to *Doctrina de Martí*, and invited Serra to attend some of his speeches for conservative white audiences. Pierra also invited the black and brown men in the revolutionary clubs to create booths of their own design to be included in the major Cuban American Fair that he organized at Madison Square Garden. The contrast with the exclusion of African Americans from the Columbian Exposition could not have been clearer.[57]

Perhaps most notable of all, Estrada Palma, Pierra, and other prominent white exiles regularly attended public events organized by black and brown constituents in New York. The delegate himself made an appearance at the Cuban American picnic in September 1896. Even as he performed whiteness and civilization for one segment of the public in the United States, he joined Sandoval and the Friends of Maceo in a performance of racial unity without flattery or humiliation for another segment of that public, African Americans.[58] Not surprisingly, African American politicians, journalists, and citizens took away a largely positive impression from their encounters with Cubans. Shortly after the

United States invaded Cuba, Booker T. Washington posed the question, "Why is it that the [N]egro in Cuba has surpassed us in settling his race problem?" The answer, he argued, supported his own strategy of compromise: "The Negro in Cuba has made the white man's interest his own." A writer in the *Washington Bee* disagreed. "As to the course of the [N]egro in Cuba, it is only necessary to state that his environment is quite different from our own. He is a recognized coordinate factor in the island and has not been discriminated against because of his color. His right to exercise untrammeled participation in public affairs has never been questioned." "The Negro" was the "leader of the Cuban forces, not their follower," he contended, and therefore the Cuban example suggested none of the "obsequiousness" recommended by Washington.[59] The *Colored American* took this position as well. The Cuban had "not been trained to the submission and obedience of his American brothers," and the Cubans' resistance to segregation and degradation might "stir the latent manhood" of African Americans fortunate enough to serve in the occupation of Cuba.[60] Indeed, when Maceo was killed, Reverend Lyons hosted an assembly at the St. Mark's Lyceum, promising to recruit one thousand African American soldiers should the United States enter the war. When the United States did invade, many African Americans volunteered for service, expressing sympathy for the Cubans of color and with the hope that patriotic military service might improve their own claims to full citizenship in the United States.[61] Others, including Serra's personal friend, the Reverend Granville Hunt, named their sons Maceo after the fallen Cuban general.[62]

At the same time, Estrada Palma, an aging politician who had grown up in Cuba during the period of slavery and had spent more than a decade educating the children of wealthy Latin Americans in a small town upstate, became practiced in the kind of respectful interpersonal interactions with a diverse public that would prove fundamental in the field of Cuban politics in the years after the war.

TWO WINGS OF THE SAME BIRD

The question of whether to support Estrada Palma was more complicated for Figueroa, Marín, and the other Puerto Ricans who had joined the Cuban Revolutionary Party. As the war in Cuba progressed, the Puerto

Rican artisans who had created the Club Borinquen and the Club Las Dos Antillas faced competing pressures. Their Cuban comrades, who lived in the same buildings, worked in the same factories, and participated in the same clubs and lodges, declared themselves disciples of Martí and supporters of the new delegate. But Estrada Palma was an unreliable friend to Puerto Rico. He was reluctant to expend party funds to expand the conflict to the smaller island. As a result, he grew increasingly estranged from the handful of highly educated and wealthy Puerto Ricans in the city.[63] This was the background for a meeting of the Club Las Dos Antillas in March 1896. First, the men voted (as did the members of all the clubs in New York, Key West, and Tampa) to confirm their support for Estrada Palma. Then Marín took the floor. In the meeting minutes, the club secretary noted that he was as "full of fire and eloquence as always" as he expressed the particular frustrations of the moment. He told the assembled members of the club that they were "soldiers without glory, infertile, and without the satisfaction of being a soldier who fights for unfortunate Cuba and my disgraced Puerto Rico." Yet, he said, the moment of redemption was at hand. Juan Ruis Rivera, a Puerto Rican-born general in the Cuban forces, had recently arrived in New York, and was in negotiations with the Cuban and Puerto Rican leadership about the possibility of leading an expedition to Puerto Rico.[64]

Marín told the crowd that he had met with Ruis Rivera and hinted that he would join the expedition. But it soon became apparent that a rebellion in Puerto Rico was unlikely. Ruis Rivera would not launch an invasion unless forces on the island rose up first. Potential allies on the island sent word that they would happily join the fight, but only after an expedition arrived from abroad. For Puerto Rican New Yorkers eager for battle, it became increasingly clear that it was better to throw in their lot with the revolution underway in Cuba rather than wait for the situation to change in Puerto Rico. Puerto Rico and Cuba were two wings of the same bird, but that bird, for now, was the Cuban insurgency. Marín's younger brother Wenceslao volunteered for service in Cuba as did several of his cousins from Ponce. In June 1896, news arrived that Wenceslao had been killed in the fighting. "I cannot call myself his brother," Marín wrote in *Patria*, until "I too fall immolated."[65] Then, only weeks before his friends launched the newspaper *Doctrina de Martí*, Marín left on an expedition to Cuba. Among the dispatches that he sent for publication in the newspaper was a poem in which he explained his decision to join the revolution. He could not go to Puerto Rico, but

Ah, with what satisfaction
Beneath the banner of Cuba
Will I quench my desire,
Fighting in the magnificent
Legions of Maceo!

And in his final stanza, he linked his own manly sacrifice to the sacred memory of Martí:

Aboard the Mambí ship
Longing to achieve
What was, upon a sacred altar,
Sworn to us by José Martí.[66]

Marín served as war correspondent for the paper until his death from fever in November 1897. Modesto Tirado, also by then an officer in the Army of Liberation, retrieved his last effects, which consisted of his military commission, a notebook, a few letters, drafts of poems, pamphlets, newspapers, clippings, and a copy of Serra's book, *Political Essays*.[67]

Figueroa remained in New York, where he continued to pursue the possibility of an expedition to Puerto Rico for several more years, to no avail.[68] But at the same time, he allied himself closely with Serra in the battle to ensure that workers, people of color, and Puerto Ricans were recognized as a "coordinate factor" of the revolutionary movement. He was demoted from the editorial committee at *Patria* and lost his position as secretary of the Advisory Council. Citing his enormous workload at the printing house, he declined the post of editor in chief of *Doctrina de Martí*. He nevertheless published frequently in the newspaper. His major contribution was a series of articles dedicated to dismantling Trujillo's history of the revolutionary movement in exile. The book, he wrote, was little more than a compilation of all the accusations, insinuations, and "bile" that Trujillo had long hurled at Martí and the Cuban Revolutionary Party in his newspapers, now compounded by an intentional and dishonest elision of the participation of the popular classes in the history of the revolution.

To publish such material in newspapers was one thing, Figueroa objected, but to publish it "in a book that would like to present itself as *historical*" was to go beyond the pale.[69] More significantly, Figueroa worked to prevent a fracture between Cubans and Puerto Ricans in New York, and joined Serra in the practice of party politics. In order to achieve the society that Martí had promised, he did not join the legions of Maceo but rather threw his support behind Estrada Palma.

UNTRAMMELED PARTICIPATION IN PUBLIC AFFAIRS

It can be hard, from a distance of more than a century (and with the knowledge of the profoundly flawed politician that Estrada Palma became as president of Cuba), to see past the deep compromises that the decision to support the delegate required. Yes, he attended their rallies, and sent funds and approving letters to their newspaper. Yes, he provided much-needed resources to a handful of allies: the voiceless lector Juan Latapier, and the family of Juan Gualberto Gómez. Yes, he joined them in gatherings with leading African American figures of the day. Yes, he was willing to endorse, at least rhetorically, the contention that a republic with all and for all was a sacred principle of Cuban patriotism. But at the same time, he appointed his own deputies to oversee the elected Advisory Councils in each city. When the Provisional Government canceled the sugar harvest in 1896, authorizing the destruction of mills that continued grinding cane, Estrada Palma bypassed the Party Advisory Councils to convene an unofficial "consultation committee" composed of planters and intellectuals. This committee decided not to announce the policy in the party newspaper *Patria*, reasoning, in the words of Varona, a member of the committee, that such a policy was "inexplicable" according to the "norms of civilized countries." Meanwhile, Estrada Palma collected large contributions from planters in exchange for case-by-case permission to proceed with the harvest. He disregarded military commanders' urgent requests to stop focusing on diplomacy and to shift his efforts to providing supplies to Maceo's troops in Western Cuba. He also continued to negotiate bank loans on Wall Street, with the understanding that the United States would establish a protectorate over an independent Cuba to ensure repayment. The Provisional Government did not look kindly on his independence. It subjected him to an investigation and asked him to account for certain ir-regularities. With his legitimacy in question, he offered his resignation.[70]

Was this not exactly the kind of "creole despotism" and creeping annex-ationism that Serra and Figueroa had warned about? Was it not strange that they would help such a man present himself to their friends and sup-porters as a defender of democratic principles? Yet as they prepared for a future conflict over the nature of the Cuban republic, capturing symbolic terrain was no small matter. The widespread belief that a nation with all and for all was a sacred patriotic principle was open to broad interpreta-tion, to be sure. Nevertheless, it was a significant victory that would have a dramatic effect on Cuban politics in the coming decades. Furthermore, although Serra and Figueroa argued for public education and some degree of land reform, their view of a socially just society was not tied to a spe-cific repertoire of redistributive policies. To them, social justice depended mainly on honest and able administration, the abolition of formal legal distinctions of race and class, the disqualification of public displays of ra-cial and class derision, and a political system that through the mechanism of popular suffrage and mass parties, was responsive to the people rather than entrenched interests or monopolies.[71]

The point of "untrammeled participation in public affairs," then, was not to secure progressive taxation or what would later be called affirma-tive action, or to exert unilateral control over either party leadership or political platform. It was instead to prepare for the coming battles over the shape of the republic by defending the principle of inclusion as a na-tional value while ensuring the right of popular suffrage. Finally and per-haps most crucially, it was about creating an expectation of a fair share of influence within the party structures that would manage the business of democratic politics. Here the context in which they had spent much of their adult lives is important. As a longtime Republican political activ-ist, Serra was familiar with the challenges of supporting imperfect candi-dates and the need to describe them while campaigning as better friends to people of color than they actually were. He and his supporters were also familiar with the way that party politics worked to integrate various fac-tions, not by creating *policies* according to the desires of each voter, but by distributing *resources* among the leaders of distinct factions in proportion to their ability to mobilize supporters. Indeed, at the very moment when Estrada Palma took over the Cuban Revolutionary Party, a candidate from

Serra's Republican Party, supported by reform Democrats as well, finally won control of city hall. This, among other things, propelled a young police commissioner named Theodore Roosevelt to national prominence. Roosevelt would soon play a major role in the fate of the Cuban republic.[72]

But the Republican victory did not significantly improve the fortunes of the leading black Republicans in the city. During summer 1896, Reverend Lyons (who hosted Cuban funerals at his church, and spoke at Cuban dances and rallies) and Reverend Hunt (whom Serra described as a friend, and who later named his son Maceo McKinley Hunt) organized protests against the exclusion of African Americans from municipal jobs.[73] Fortune and Stewart, who both also spoke at rallies to support *Doctrina de Martí*, took a stronger position still. They argued that neither national political party consistently defended the rights of African Americans. The loyalty of black voters to the Republican Party, furthermore, had allowed the party to ignore black politicians when it came time to distribute jobs. Black voters, they proposed, ought to become political independents, supporting local candidates who reciprocated.[74] Politics within major national parties—not just the Cuban Revolutionary Party—required a delicate balance. It was important for black leaders not to undermine their leverage either by appearing too faithful or (especially given widespread prejudices about the capacities of black voters) to disqualify themselves by appearing altogether faithless.[75] Given that Lyons, Hunt, Fortune, and Stewart were the same men whom they invited to speak at their political rallies, it seems impossible that Serra, Bonilla, and Figueroa were ignorant of this debate. Nor would it have been difficult for them to see the similarities between these discussions among black New Yorkers and the debates over black political participation that had unfolded in Cuba.

To understand the ways that the Cuban exiles would have viewed these similarities, it is necessary to briefly return to the moment of controversy over the creation of the Directorio de Sociedades de Color several years earlier. Critics of the Directorio hurled all sorts of accusations, but the incident that provoked the single-greatest outcry was a maneuver by allies of the Directorio seeking greater influence within the Autonomista Party in Santiago de Cuba. The restriction of suffrage to those who paid a minimum tax still excluded most Cubans of color from the right to vote, especially in elections for representatives in the Spanish Cortes in Madrid. But in municipal contests, the required taxes were low enough to enfranchise a substantial group of men of color, particularly in Eastern Cuba. Like the Republicans in the United States, by the early 1890s the Autonomistas in Oriente represented themselves as the party of abolition and argued that they deserved the absolute loyalty of black voters. The Directorio de Sociedades de Color and the newspaper *La Igualdad* pointed out that despite their claim of friendship, the Autonomistas had never been reliable supporters of black political or civil rights.[76] Yet controversy erupted when Manuel Bergues Pruna, journalist from Santiago who was typically identified as mulatto, protested the exclusion of men of color from appointments to party posts and as candidates.[77]

During the political campaign in early 1893, Bergues Pruna had called on readers of his paper, *La Democracia*, to abstain from voting until the Autonomista Party changed its policy. This stance provoked predictable accusations from predictable sources. In New York, Trujillo accused Bergues Pruna of auctioning off the opinions of the men of color to the "highest bidder."[78] In Cuba, Morúa continued his attacks on the Directorio and on Serra. Sanguily wrote that it was "inconceivable" to him that Cubans of color "mindful only of caste interests" would "show scorn for the invaluable and magnificent sacrifice of two generations of white people" who were the "redeemers of the slave during the war and his defenders in peace."[79] The secretary of the Autonomista Party in Santiago, however, a white journalist named Eduardo Yero, broke ranks and announced his support for Bergues Pruna. Yero and Juan Gualberto Gómez then helped the sparring factions to work out a compromise. In exchange for bringing his supporters back to the party, Bergues Pruna, who had completed his secondary education, received the opportunity to compete for an appointment as public prosecutor in the city of Santiago. He became the first man of color to hold that post.[80]

Returning to the events of summer 1896, Serra's network of supporters understood the challenge of responding to the new leadership of the Cuban Revolutionary Party not only in relationship to the struggles of black Republicans in New York but also in relation to the events in Santiago three years earlier. They had participated in the debates over voter abstention in Santiago as writers and agents for the newspaper *La Igualdad*; indeed, Serra had argued, in the midst of this controversy, the example of Fortune's Afro-American League in the United States proved the necessity of an organization like the Directorio.[81] Since then, many of the participants in the conflicts within the Autonomista Party in Santiago had passed through or settled in New York.[82] The circle of men around Estrada Palma, for instance, included some of those who had most bitterly attacked Bergues Pruna for his call to abstention, men like Sanguily and Trujillo. But Bergues Pruna had also come to New York, where he settled in an apartment building on Third Avenue and joined the Club Las Dos Antillas, serving as the club's auxiliary secretary.[83] Yero had come too (though he lived among white New Yorkers) and had found a place in Estrada Palma's inner circle. He became Estrada Palma's personal secretary early in 1896 and accompanied the delegate to the Cuban American picnic in September of that year. The New Yorkers had not only the memory of the successful play within the Autonomista Party to work with (or to regale friends with at the barbershop); their party now included the key players.[84]

This backdrop suggests that Serra and Figueroa knew that effective party politics required neither absolute support of party leaders nor in-flexible commitment to principle. Participation in public life was never lit-erally "untrammeled." It required striking a balance between loyalty and pressure. Sometimes a letter, reporting rumblings among constituents, along with a promise to set any concerns to rest, was necessary to remind the leadership of the value of one's "many friends, and useful ones." But sometimes the moment called for a bolder political maneuver to force the interests of a political patron back in line with those of a group of forgot-ten supporters or to help him fend off unwanted pressure from an oppos-ing camp. It is not clear whether, in fall 1896, it was Yero who decided that the moment was ripe for such a move, if the idea came from Serra and Figueroa, or if the political mastermind was Estrada Palma himself.

THE STUDY GROUP

Whatever the case, the opportunity came in November 1896, when a group of exiles, led by Varona, convened the first meeting of the Study Group. The gathering included many of the wealthy and educated figures in the exile community, such as Estrada Palma, Pierra, and Yero, as well as a variety of medical doctors, dentists, lawyers, manufacturers, and planters, some of whom had never joined the Cuban Revolutionary Party. It included none of the artisan intellectuals who had helped to build the movement alongside Martí. Speaking to the press, members of the group declared their intention to create a draft constitution for the future government of Cuba. North American journalists noted approvingly that the men desired Cuba "to be wholly a white man's republic, and while not wishing to deny their colored fellow workers a part in the victory that is to be achieved they do not intend that there shall be negro domination of the island."[85] The Study Group represented a return to the tradition of a movement whose spokesmen consisted of a self-appointed committee of notables with loosely defined ties to the republic in arms. This principle of "the best men" coming together to take power back from otherwise hopelessly corrupt party institutions—institutions that depended on the manipulation of working-class voters—can also be read against the backdrop of New York City politics. The same principle guided the emerging municipal reform movement in New York as well, aiding in the rise of Roosevelt.

To their credit, members of the Study Group recognized that any laws or structures that they proposed would need ratification by a constitutional convention once the war was over. Some even asserted their support for popular suffrage and the principle that "we will not have an aristocracy in Cuba." Serra, writing in *Doctrina de Martí*, recognized these democratic gestures. Yet he also noted the "private" membership of the Study Group.[86] Perhaps aware of how this all looked, Pierra invited Serra and several others to attend the second meeting of the organization in the capacity of observers. Even after attending, Serra wrote that he did not yet have any firm basis for judgment as to the merits of "such an unexpected organization." If in addition to "their talents and their interests" these "distinguished compatriots" proved to have sufficient "love of our country" and "democratic procedures," their efforts would be welcome.[87] This, of course, was a big if. Still, Serra remained extremely restrained in his public criticism until the end of December, when something happened to make Yero and party treasurer Benjamín Guerra announce their resignations from the Study Group. At this point, Serra sharpened and shifted his line of attack. The Study Group was a "note played out of tune, an exclusive note in the concert that has been wisely prepared for the resolution of the Cuban problem." Even setting aside "certain democratic deficiencies," it was unacceptable that the Study Group had failed to recognize and accept the principles and bylaws of the Cuban Revolutionary Party, or to contribute funds to the revolution through participation in the party. Having helped to make sure that the "popular elements" demonstrated perfect discipline, Serra could not countenance, he wrote, any group, no matter the goodwill and virtues of its members, that did not accept fully the principle that the party was the only genuine and legal representative of the separatist movement in exile.[88]

But what had happened to open up the conflict between Varona and his supporters and Guerra and Yero? It seems that a member named Héctor de Saavedra (a man known for his propensity for public insult) took things too far, challenging Estrada Palma at a public meeting of the Study Group. Personal attacks were typical within the field of Cuban politics. After all, opponents had publicly accused Martí of wearing a skirt. Morúa had called Serra a "rodent" and "a crazed issuer of challenges, a defamer of his own virtuous wife, and an idiotic flirt." Yero and Sanguily insulted one another so frequently in this period that their representatives eventually met to negotiate and sign a peace treaty. Personal animosity and the defense of honor thus blended with political disagreements and battles over personal influence, often in ways that are difficult to disentangle. For Saavedra's part, it seems that he had been rebuffed in his bid for a formal position in the party. Perhaps believing that the investigation that the Provisional Government had recently conducted into Estrada Palma's performance as plenipotentiary minister made him especially vulnerable to pressure or a leadership challenge, other members of the Study Group tolerated Saavedra's figurative slap in Estrada Palma's face. This suggests an already-emerging rift between some in the Study Group and the delegate—a rift that Yero and Serra quickly worked to widen and exploit. In their accounts, what had transpired was not an individual affront to the delegate by a single member but instead a generalized attack on the delegate and the party by the Study Group as a whole.[89]

The response of the Study Group, when Yero and Serra raised their objection, was also telling. Varona might have distanced himself from Saavedra, declared allegiance to the party, and made the minimal necessary gestures of inclusiveness without making significant changes to the group's membership or goals. Instead, he used the pages of *Patria* to defend the right of the members to form a private association outside the party that would serve a different purpose. Democracy required respect for minority viewpoints, he argued. He denounced critics for "the spirit of Jacobinism, which is to say, the spirit of intolerance and intransigence." Meanwhile, the members of the Study Group provided more fuel to the fire. They distributed a manifesto to the press in the United States, laying out the complaints and aspirations of the Cuban people. The pamphlet was signed by Varona, president of the Study Group, not Estrada Palma, the elected representative of the party and the appointed representative of the Provisional Government of Cuba. The Study Group also called a mass meeting to protest the diplomatic policies of the United States, abrogating to itself the right to convoke the national community, and to invite the delegate and the Cuban clubs and societies to participate. These acts confirmed Serra's warnings: the Study Group was willfully and without justification setting itself up as an authority, able to speak on behalf of the Cuban cause and unconcerned about democratic procedure. The Study Group was subverting the legitimate authority of the party, and thereby insulting both the delegate and the clubs that had elected him. By the second week of January, de Quesada and other party officials had resigned their membership. Several of the remaining members proposed that the Study Group resolve the conflict by voting to accept the principles and bylaws of the party. The majority, however, voted to dissolve the Study Group. This provided still more evidence that Varona and his allies were enemies of the revolution. They would rather disband than accept the legitimacy of the Cuban Revolutionary Party.[90]

In the next issue of *Doctrina de Martí*, Serra took the gloves off. This was no longer a matter of waiting and seeing, or of missteps that might be corrected. The Study Group was a clear manifestation of the creole despotism against which he had been warning and thus a grave threat to democracy. We might accept, he wrote, *"to a degree"* that the members of the Study Group were distinguished by their learning and culture— something about which they "constantly boast." The "general interests of the country," however, should not be determined by "intellectual supremacy" but rather by the "consent of the majority of the *pueblo*, which is capable of freely expressing its will." We are not "intransigent," he noted, but instead defenders of "unity that will be useful and dignified for all." Jacobinism, he sustained, is the "natural and logical" response to those who "fight to preserve" for themselves the "same irritating privileges" instituted by the Spanish monarchy.[91] Writing for the first time in *Doctrina de Martí*, Yero made the same argument. He denounced the presence in the Study Group of "men who are, at base, anti-revolutionary, who cherish the idea of planting their conservative spirit" and the aristocratic habits of a fallen regime into "the laws, institutions, and customs" of the republic.[92] The rejection of the Study Group was therefore consistent with the idea that new converts should be welcomed only if they accepted the democratic principles of the movement and the legitimacy of the party, and not if they were unwilling to shed the vices that they had acquired over generations of colonialism and slavery.

"There is a tremendous internal struggle here," Saavedra complained in a letter to an ally. The Study Group "had to disband out of patriotism, so as not to provide fodder to the chattering of a certain 'democratic black' element here that calls us the 'intellectuals.'" According to Saavedra, Yero had attacked Varona because he wanted to become editor of *Patria*, and Estrada Palma was "bullied by two blacks, Serra and Figueroa, and various cigar makers, with Yero in the lead, who dominate Estrada Palma through terror and seek to establish the doctrine that they, those of the rabble, are the only ones with the right to direct things in Cuba. With imagine what future end!"[93] Yet "bullying" and "terror" seem to have had little to do with this. Quite the opposite. Yero, Serra, and Figueroa carefully arranged their attacks on the Study Group as a *defense* of the delegate against external challengers. Things took a sour turn for Saavedra and Varona because the delegate took Yero and Serra up on their offer of support. Thus, only days after Serra first attacked the Study Group in print, Estrada Palma attended the New Year's Day benefit concert planned by Calderín, Miranda, and the other members of the Committee to Aid *Doctrina de Martí*. This seems to have been planned, weeks earlier, as an opportunity to gather with African American allies and to listen to speeches by prominent African American politicians. But in the context of the conflicts over the Study Group, it became a political rally. Both Estrada Palma and party treasurer Guerra attended and received thunderous applause from the public, and—as important—Serra reported on this moment of adulation to his wide network of readers.[94] At the very moment that writers in *Doctrina de Martí* denounced the authoritarianism and exclusivity of the Study Group, they presented their own events as demonstrations of a national concert performed without exclusive notes. Rather than criticizing Estrada Palma for his initial participation in the Study Group (or the earlier consultation committee), they presented the delegate, the clubs, and the inseparable principles of unity and democracy as if all were perfectly aligned, equally offended by the insults of the Study Group.

Even after the Study Group voted to dissolve, the maneuver was not complete. In *Doctrina de Martí*, Yero warned that the same individuals who had failed to establish a rival authority to the party were now seeking to wrest control over it. Wealthy exiles in New York were creating new clubs in order to control a majority of seats on the Advisory Council. This would give them the procedural high ground, even as they acted in ways that undermined the democratic goals of the revolution. Yero's warning became a rallying cry for a new burst of party building by supporters of *Doctrina de Martí*. During the third week in January, one group of these supporters met at the home of Silvestre Pivaló and Pilar Cazuela on Third Avenue to create a club "in order, by electing a president, to reinforce the local Advisory Council." They called the new organization the Club Manuel Bergues Pruna, honoring the hero of the earlier confrontation within the ranks of the Autonomista Party (recently killed in action in Cuba) and nodding in the direction of Yero, who had been an ally to Bergues Pruna and was now theirs. In total, Serra and Figueroa rallied their supporters to create four new clubs, defending the council and the delegate from the "machinations of a certain element, recently arrived."[95] Heredia and Blanco created the Club José Maceo during this burst of organizing. Inocencia Martínez relaunched the dormant Club Mercedes Varona. It is not clear, however, whether either of the groups led by women claimed a seat on the council. In any event, by the meeting on January 20, 1897, Serra, Figueroa, and Yero had the Advisory Council safely under their control. At that meeting, the council took a vote of confidence in Estrada Palma. The Advisory Councils in Tampa and Key West soon seconded this vote. Shortly thereafter, the Provisional Government of Cuba abandoned its investigation and rejected Estrada Palma's resignation, confirming his posting as plenipotentiary minister.[96]

The maneuver had been largely successful. It was a triumph for Estrada Palma. Whether or not the challenges from the Study Group or the Provisional Government had really put Estrada Palma's position at risk, it was clear that with the help of a few well-placed intermediaries, the party remained a formidable base of support. It was also a great triumph for Yero, who had proven himself particularly effective in the role of intermediary. A week after the vote of confidence, the New York Advisory Council met again, voting to request that Estrada Palma remove Varona from his post as editor of *Patria*. This was a source of conversation in the clubs as

Estrada dragged his feet for several months before turning the newspaper (and presumably the salary) over to Yero. Under the new editor, there was still plenty of room in *Patria* for Varona and other men whose wealth and erudition made them privileged participants in the game of political spoils and influence. But those "intellectuals" had to accommodate themselves to sharing those pages with men who knew how to wield the power of party politics in a context of broad popular suffrage.[97] The conflict with the Study Group was also a clear victory for Serra, consolidating his status as the leading spokesman for the democratic faction of the movement and especially for the class of color. Readers far and wide sent letters of congratulations on the victory against the Study Group, which he republished in *Doctrina de Martí*. In Tampa, conversations about the January issues of the newspaper among the customers and sitters at the barbershop of Manuel Granados led to the formation of a local Committee to Aid *Doctrina de Martí*. Soon a similar committee had been formed in Key West.[98]

A bold move against a rival faction created ripples of enthusiasm throughout the widely distributed public sphere that Serra had helped to create, but it did not remove the need to carefully cultivate and manage the loyalties of supporters. At the time of the conflict over the Study Group, two factions were locked in a bitter dispute over leadership in the most important institutions for people of color in Key West. In the aftermath of the maneuver, one of these groups—including Miguel Gualba, whose baby Heredia had helped to deliver in Havana in 1888, and Carlos Borrego, one of the authors of the "Protest of Cubans of Color" in Key West in 1881—had signed and sent a letter of support for *Doctrina* without inviting their rivals to join. Serra wrote to the men whose names were missing—a group that included Enrique Medín Arango, the son of Plácido's widow and an old friend of Serra's from Matanzas, and Juan Latapier, the former law student who became a lector and then a bookkeeper for the national lottery—that he could not possibly publish this partial list. He implored them to convene a new meeting, expressing unanimous support for him. He adopted the posture of a political suitor (reminiscent of the letters that Martí had written to him years before). Pen and paper were an insufficient medium to express his feelings toward them, he wrote. He longed to speak with them in person. He begged their pardon if he had not been able to pay them sufficient attention, attributing the oversight to the situation of "scarcity in which we live and the immense labors that drain my body and my soul." But, he assured them, "I love you as flesh of my flesh." He hoped that they would not imagine that he sought to take over leadership "without waiting for it to be conferred on me through the spontaneous will of my brothers." Yet he implored them, in the name of Martí and Gómez, to put aside "this past foolishness" in order to preserve the moral high ground. If "our own elements" could not manage to set aside such differences in the name of patriotic harmony, "with what right shall we demand unity from the others?"[99]

The great victory for the principles of democracy and unity also required a great degree of compromise. In exchange for the support of the Advisory Councils, Estrada Palma changed his policies only slightly, if at all. Serra and Figueroa remained conspicuously silent when Estrada Palma signed a contract with a group of investors on Wall Street to issue a loan for the purposes of purchasing Cuba from Spain. Serra argued that workers should stay involved in the party. It was important, he conceded, to demand the rights and dignity of labor, and to contest the machinations of capital. But the argument—made by anarchists—that workers should abstain from politics was incorrect. Politics, he explained, meant "distributing equitably among the residents of a country that which nature and justice have provided for the good of all." Politics therefore "should not be a matter of indifference for the workers, who have so much to hope for and demand of their political representatives, who are not their bosses but rather their servants."[100] Then Estrada Palma supported a proposal to extend the right to vote in elections for new representatives to the Provisional Government to exiles, but to limit this right to men who made a minimum contribution to the party. In a private letter to an ally in Tampa, Yero called this poll tax an "iniquity," a "mystification of liberalism," and the "pure Spanish system" that we "thundered against in Cuba." He promised to "rebel" against these "schemes." Rather than rebel, though, the Advisory Councils in New York, Florida, and Jamaica (still controlled by the "democratic black element" in alliance with white workers and democratic politicians like Yero) voted to abstain from the elections. In explaining the decision to abstain, Serra was eminently politic. Don Tomás had hoped to extend suffrage to the migrant communities out of a spirit of unity, he wrote, but he had inadvertently risked the creation of "divisions."[101] The effect of this abstention was mainly symbolic, as the Provisional Government was extremely weak, and largely unable to impose its will over either its plenipotentiary minister in the United States or the commanders of the Army of Liberation. Yet the symbolism of abstention was no small matter. The rank and file voted not to yield, even temporarily, on the principle of universal suffrage. Even if it meant ceding the opportunity to participate in one contest, they would not allow some to be enfranchised at the expense of others. At the same time, they preserved the power of the Advisory Councils, retaining for themselves the decision over when and how they would vote.

THE IMPERIAL MOMENT

The decision to work within the highly imperfect realm of party politics and to intervene on behalf of Estrada Palma was thrown into new relief with the assassination of the Conservative prime minister of Spain in August 1897. By the end of the year, resurgent Liberals in Madrid, under substantial pressure from the McKinley administration to find a peaceful settlement to the war, had granted fairly broad powers to locally elected provincial assemblies in Cuba and Puerto Rico, and universal manhood suffrage for all Puerto Ricans and Cubans. In Puerto Rico, where, despite deep anticolonial resentments, the interests of professionals, landowners, and peasants had never aligned sufficiently to produce a sustained uprising against Spain, the Autonomistas declared victory. They immediately threw themselves into the project of mass party politics, with two liberal factions each recruiting rural voters and urban artisans into new coalitions. Both groups—one led by the man who had married Pachín Marín's cousin and inherited Ramón Marín's printing presses, and the other led by a black medical doctor from an artisan family in Bayamón—claimed to be the inheritors of Baldorioty's radically democratic brand of Autonomismo. This effectively put an end to any hope that the war would spread to Puerto Rico. In response, several wealthy Puerto Rican exiles began lobbying to ensure that the United States would include Puerto Rico in whatever plan was developed for intervening in Cuba.[102] None of this was at all pleasing to Sotero Figueroa.

In Cuba, the Spanish plan to grant autonomy did not work quite so smoothly. In the countryside, the insurgents took the reforms as still more evidence that they were within sight of victory. Although their ranks were ragged and hungry, they did not waver in their insistence on full independence. In the cities, the most important supporters of Spanish rule, including property holders and merchants, Conservative politicians, and Spanish troops, felt betrayed and demoralized by the reforms. Fearful that the concessions signaled an inevitable insurgent victory, and a threat to their economic and social position, some shifted their allegiances, becoming open proponents of annexation to the United States. Others joined the separatists, producing yet another wave of newcomers hoping to moderate the independence movement and position themselves advantageously in the event of an insurgent victory. Still others rioted in the streets of Cuban cities or refused to fight in defense of an Autonomista government. Yet if the last-minute reforms did little to salvage the hopes of Spanish colonialism in Cuba, they were a remarkable turning point in the struggle for civil and political rights. Even as Serra and his allies stepped up their denunciations of the Autonomista Party as an institution of creole despotism, they celebrated a victory. Now that universal manhood suffrage had been instituted in the overseas provinces, there could be no going back. An independent Cuban republic, they asserted, possibly for the benefit of some in their own movement, could not possibly be *less democratic* than the Spanish monarchy.[103]

It was soon abundantly clear, in any event, that the threat to Cuban sovereignty posed by the United States was far more serious than the risk that Spanish reforms would succeed in undermining the revolution. On the one hand, newspaper accounts of Spanish authorities' widespread brutality against civilians had helped to build broad public support in the United States for the Cuban cause, understood—thanks to countless letters to the editor, speeches, and rallies organized by Estrada Palma and his companions—to be a struggle by prosperous white patriots against a despotic monarchy, analogous to the American Revolution. Drawing on this groundswell, congressmen in both major parties regularly called on the White House to intervene. At the same time, a growing contingent of unabashed imperialists, including Undersecretary of War Theodore Roosevelt, understood overseas expansion to be an especially urgent project, necessary to control naval and shipping lanes, to provide new outlets for agricultural products and manufactures, to invigorate Anglo-American manhood, to fulfill Anglo-American racial destiny, and to assert the place of the United States among the major world powers. They regarded the crisis of the Spanish administration as an opportunity to acquire Cuba and the Philippines for the United States at a relatively low cost.[104]

For his part, President William McKinley, like many of his wealthy backers, doubted that an independent Cuba would adequately protect US interests. He pressured Spain to grant reforms that might bring the rebellion under control, and when that failed, offered to purchase Cuba. By the early part of 1898, he decided to go to war. Capitalizing on public sympathy for the Cubans, he justified the invasion in humanitarian terms, not as an imperialist venture, but as the defining expression of the generous and democratic American national character. Yet his administration remained resolutely opposed to any move that might leave Cuba in the hands of the insurgents. As a result, the United States officially entered Cuba as a neutral party seeking the pacification of the island and its return to civilized government. Congress tied McKinley's hands by attaching authorization for war to a promise not to absorb the island. But the invading forces accepted no obligation to consider the desires of the Provisional Government, the Army of Liberation, or indeed any representative of the Cuban people. The United States claimed full authority to dictate the terms of Spanish surrender and to determine the political system that would follow, in Cuba, Puerto Rico, and the Philippines.[105]

For the first time in history, the US government took on the task of constructing a government in a foreign territory with the ostensible goal of preparing the population for eventual self-rule. The challenge was to ensure an outcome favorable to US investors and strategic interests without reneging on the promise to withdraw, or seeming to violate the democratic or humanitarian values that McKinley had expressed when launching the invasion. As Secretary of War Elihu Root put it, "It is better to have the favors of a lady with her consent, after judicious courtship, than to ravish her."[106] Estrada Palma and de Quesada became the linchpins of the rapidly changing political situation. They dissolved the Cuban Revolutionary Party and presented themselves as willing collaborators of the invasion, helping to find and recommend the "best men" for positions in the government. Soon the most conservative of the New York émigrés—the very men against whom Figueroa and Serra had held the line—emerged as the most prominent civilian administrators aligned with the military government. Varona became secretary of finance and then secretary of public instruction. Nearly every prominent member of the Study Group also received university posts or other positions in the new government. Estrada Palma and de Quesada also encouraged their contacts in Washington to compromise and to bring separatists into the fold. Officers in the Army of Liberation and some civilians from the separatist camp received important appointments to provincial and municipal posts. Serra, for instance, received an appointment to the Santiago City Council (a body with little administrative autonomy under the military occupation). He seems not to have taken up the post, preferring to remain in New York. In Cuba, the occupation and its native collaborators promoted a raft of transformations: hygiene campaigns, educational reforms, infrastructure projects, and modern consumer goods. They presented these changes as modernization, a deep cleansing of the structures of the decrepit colony.[107]

As these events unfolded, Figueroa made regular visits to Estrada Palma and de Quesada in their offices on New Street to keep abreast of the political situation and to communicate messages from allies in Cuba. He also made appeals to them and to friends on the island for assistance in securing a government appointment and in transporting his print workshop, the lead types that had been "sanctified" by their role in publishing the "luminous ideas of *el Maestro*," to Havana. Though his appeals for an official post were unsuccessful, after months of delay he found the necessary resources for the move, departing for Cuba to help create a political party around General Máximo Gómez, who had recently resigned his commission to enter civilian life. Figueroa was elected secretary of the newly formed National Party of Cuba and became the editor of its short-lived newspaper.[108] He began the work of building a new coalition to compete in a round of municipal elections, which the occupying government planned for early spring 1900.

The political structures that Cubans started to create in advance of these elections were typically organized in support of individual leaders rather than broad political platforms, and often made tactical allies of politicians with deeply divergent policy agendas. Former officers of the insurgency began to transform the command structure of the Liberation Army into disciplined, regionally based political organizations.[109] These new political structures, especially in Eastern Cuba, relied on high-ranking officers of African descent like Generals Quintín Banderas and Cebreco. Around the country, in rural districts and small provincial towns, lower-ranking black and brown officers played a key role in recruiting and mobilizing support among the rank and file on behalf of local political bosses. And in Havana, a handful of civilian figures of African descent with national stature helped each of the emerging political factions appeal to the class of color through the publication of newspapers, the creation of new veterans' organizations, and ties with the sociedades de color, while also seeking to exert pressure on the new political organizations to adopt democratic and antiracist principles. Figueroa was part of this effort. Along with a multiracial group of veterans of the Cuban Revolutionary Party, he traveled the country attending patriotic gatherings and rallies, and working to build popular support for the National Party and to "assure the conquests of the Redemptive Revolution." He also helped to create several committees and organizations: one for returning émigré revolutionaries called Workers of the Emigration, one to collect money in Key West to place an engraved marker at the house where Martí had been born, and one to collect funds for a monument to Maceo.[110]

By this time, the leadership of the occupying forces had convinced themselves that the former insurgents, with their anti-American rhetoric and democratic appeals, were more of a hindrance than a help. Believing that "American" sacrifice and industry had selflessly rescued helpless Cubans from oppression, representatives of the United States resented the distrust with which many Cuban nationalists regarded them. US officials stacked the commission established to draw up the rules for the municipal contests with men regarded as friendly to the occupation: Pierra, Varona, Sanguily, and other members of the Study Group as well as leading Autonomistas. This group agreed with the North Americans that suffrage should be restricted in order to limit the power of the populist factions and guarantee the influence of the "best men." Reversing the expansion of suffrage enacted in the last months of Spanish rule, the commission determined that voters had to be literate. If they could not read and write, they had to hold property of at least $250. These restrictions were a major reversal of the principle of universal manhood suffrage, long a cornerstone of the separatist program, and more recently, a principle supported by the Autonomistas and adopted by the Spanish administration. The limits on suffrage provoked widespread expressions of outrage, including in the African American press in the United States. Morúa, the only man of color on the commission, resigned in protest. In a concession to popular sentiment, the commission decided to exclude veterans of the Army of Liberation from the property and literacy requirements.[111]

From New York, Serra offered the opinion that not only voting rights but all the civil rights victories of the previous decade were in jeopardy because the "familiar vices inherited from the old regime" had made common cause with the "new vices, the imported injustices that the *yankee philanthropists* have brought on the tips of their bayonets."[112] Deploying this message and rallying voters across racial lines, the nationalist political organizations, led by former officers of the insurgency, handily defeated the group backed by the occupiers in both elections. Figueroa's National Party won control over city governments in Havana and most of Western Cuba. The Republican Party, supported by Juan Gualberto Gómez, won most of the municipalities in Oriente. Each of these parties also helped to elect a few black and mulatto candidates as mayors and city councilmen.[113]

Governor-General Leonard Wood imposed the same restriction on suffrage for the elections to a Constituent Assembly, scheduled for later in the year. He encouraged Cubans to send their "best men," men capable of drafting an effective legal document, to the convention. Wood threatened to reject any constitution that did not "provide for a stable government," suggesting that he would use his own authority to ensure that Cuba did not become "a second Haiti."[114] To his chagrin, the two nationalist parties, represented by men that Wood considered "rascals," "adventurers," and "radicals," trounced the party of "the more intelligent and farseeing Cuban planters."[115] Juan Gualberto Gómez and Morúa were seated as delegates, and Cebreco and Yero were named as alternates. Overall, the convention was dominated by white politicians whose parties had organized voters across racial lines, who appealed to voters on patriotic grounds, and who at least rhetorically presented themselves as defenders of the democratic ideals of the separatist movement.[116]

Serra observed and participated in these campaigns, and from a unique vantage point. As local voter registration boards created electoral lists, and as friends and foes campaigned for seats at the convention, a group of policemen and a mob of white citizens perpetrated the worst race riot in New York City since the Civil War. Angered by the death of a white police officer during an altercation with an African American man, crowds indiscriminately attacked and brutally beat black men and women for several days in the Tenderloin, the neighborhood where Serra, Heredia, and their daughter Consuelo still lived. In early September, as the campaign for seats in the Constituent Assembly in Cuba heated up, Fortune and other

African American activists called a mass meeting at St. Mark's Church to convene a Citizens' Protection League and press for an investigation of police involvement in the riot.[117] None of Serra's writings mention this wave of racial terror. By the end of the year, however, the family had relocated to an apartment in a small cluster of buildings that rented to black people on East Seventy-Fifth Street, out of reach of the simmering violence on the West Side. There, the Serras were neighbors of many longtime comrades: Gerónimo and Isabel Bonilla, Marcelino and Hannah Piedra, and Germán Sandoval and his second wife, Floretta (see map 6).

From his new apartment, Serra took part in the campaign to defend the project of popular democracy and offered a critical view of the leadership of all the emerging political factions. In early January 1901, he wrote to the Havana newspaper *El Pueblo Libre* that none of the principal factions had made racial equality a central political project. They "declare that the problem of the races in Cuba is already resolved," he observed, giving as evidence the veneration of the "glorious memory of Martí and Maceo." But "black Cubans" would be "poor unfortunates" if the only thing that they achieved "as a just recompense for their sacrifices" was the satisfaction of commemorating "our glorious martyrs" and singing the national anthem. Because at the same time that they celebrated Martí, Cuban politicians had already begun to break the "pact" formed under the umbrella of patriotism. In particular, he noted, politicians of various stripes proposed whitening the population of the island through subsidized immigration from Europe, others supported annexation to the United States, and some fretted about the widespread influence of black voters in Oriente. "No, my brothers, we deserve justice, and we ought not to continue cheering on a humiliating and ridiculous form of patriotism." He called on the class of color to organize itself to exert political pressure more effectively. This was not, as some Cubans continued to argue, a form of "racism." Although everyone spoke constantly of unity, in fact all the sectors of society were busy organizing to compete in national politics. Why, he asked, should blacks be the only citizens prevented from asserting themselves through independent organizations?[118] But Serra did not call on black Cubans to remove themselves from the emerging political competition. He continued, as he would for the rest of his life, to favor what he termed "eclecticism": a balance between clear-eyed critique and pragmatic accommodation, between independent organizing and party loyalty.[119]

This strategy became significantly more important only a few days after the publication of Serra's essay when the representatives to the Constituent Assembly voted twenty-five to three, against the pleading of the US government, to restore universal manhood suffrage in Cuba with no property or literacy requirements. In part, this outcome was a measure of the success that radicals within the movement had achieved in establishing the idea of a nation with all and for all as a sacred national-ist principle—what Serra called the "pact" of affection forged under the umbrella of patriotism. Yet it was also a mark of the success of black and brown politicians in positioning themselves within multiracial political networks: the maneuvers in Santiago in 1893 and New York in 1896, and the mobilization that had begun in the towns and cities of Cuba under the US occupation. Most of the delegates were white men who had sought and received the support of black and brown constituents. Most of the delegates had little trouble imagining a future republic in which mak-ing appeals to voters of color and denouncing the racism of opponents remained one of the ways that white politicians engaged in political com-petition with one another, even white politicians who did not support any policies promoting racial equality.[120]

The vote to restore universal manhood suffrage in Cuba produced a cri-sis for the representatives of the United States in Cuba. They recognized that such an inclusive electorate was unlikely to elect a government favor-able to the United States. Shortly after the vote on suffrage, the occupiers demanded that the Constituent Assembly accept the establishment of a US protectorate as a condition for withdrawing troops. A furious new round of political debates unfolded, with Gómez and others speaking out forcefully against these humiliating conditions, and others arguing that compromise was unavoidable and that the most important thing was to get the Americans to withdraw. Eventually the assembly passed the Platt Amendment, preventing the Cuban government from pursuing foreign policy independent of the United States, granting the United States a mil-itary base on the island, and affirming that the United States had a right to intervene in Cuban affairs in defense of US interests. It was still not clear, however, that the US government would accept the results of the first national elections if Cuban voters elected a candidate viewed as too radi-cal or anti-American. Far from the fray of Cuban politics, Estrada Palma again benefited from his position in the center of the political spectrum.

He was known as a nationalist—a reputation earned though his participation in both the wars of independence. But as a supporter of close ties
with the United States, he also had the trust of the military occupiers, who
stacked the electoral commission with his supporters. At the last minute,
under pressure to compromise and ensure the departure of US forces, the
candidate of the Republican Party withdrew from the race. In December
1901, running as a unity candidate favored by all the parties and by the
occupying forces, Estrada Palma won without campaigning or even returning to Cuba.[121]

This left Serra in an enviable position. Despite his sharp criticisms of
the Cuban political class as a whole, Serra had preserved his ties with the
man who was now president elect.[122] Several weeks after the presidential
election, Serra sent Estrada Palma a letter of congratulations that echoed
the one that he had sent seven years earlier in the immediate wake of his
first election as party delegate. He pronounced himself a "loyal friend,
who will not abandon you nor betray you nor abuse your generous protection." He told Estrada Palma that he knew him to be the rightful heir to
Martí and the right choice to transform Cuba, bringing justice and unity
to a population divided by generations of colonial rule. For this reason,
"the large portion of the class of color that favors me with its confidence
has turned its back on those false apostles" in order to throw their support behind Estrada Palma.[123] "I would wish to get closer to you still," he
proposed in a second letter several weeks later. Since the election, Serra
had been astonished, he wrote, by the arrival of a "world of letters" expressing faith in the "paternity" of Estrada Palma and confidence in "the
assistance that they suppose I might lend to you, given the sentiments
of justice and Concord that I have demonstrated in all of my public ex-
positions." He warned of the growing influence exerted by Morúa, who
had been elected to the Senate. This was not because Morúa had much
support from the class of color, he assured, but rather because he had
the protection of a leading white political figure. The popular elements
only followed Morúa because "no other man of color has the protection
of legitimate authorities."[124] The incoming president, for instance, had not
promoted any leading figure from among the veterans of the civil rights
and separatist struggles. But, he suggested, that was a problem that could
easily be remedied.

Endings

I.

On April 17, 1902, President Elect Tomás Estrada Palma gathered his retinue at the Munro Hotel on Fourteenth Street in Manhattan. In the company of reporters, the group boarded a steamer bound for Cuba, where on disembarking, they commenced a large and deliberately paced "civic parade." Landing in the east of the island, they visited the battle site at San Juan Hill for a ceremony to lower the US flag and raise the Cuban standard. Then the group made its way by train, over the course of nearly a month, from town to town and city to city, westward to Havana. At each stop, local organizing committees took charge of the arrangements, constructing triumphal arches and laying out banquets. Large crowds greeted the new head of state as bands played patriotic and popular songs. Setting aside all the bitter divisions that had emerged during the war and its aftermath, the nation engaged in an elaborate celebration of the transfer of sovereignty and a careful performance of a republic by all and for all. In each town Estrada Palma met with military leaders, with the members of the former Provisional Government, with former Spanish officials and clubs, and with artisans' clubs. The new president, who had not set foot in Cuba for seventeen years, mingled, shook hands "American style," and conscientiously spoke with everyday citizens about the issues that concerned them. This performance of unity, however, also laid the groundwork for the bitter electoral battles that would soon recommence. Those with the capacity to raise funds, organize banquets, and mobilize crowds in the towns and cities on the island gained access to the man who would occupy the Presidential Palace, and to the group of men with whom he chose to surround himself.[1]

This vignette is a fitting, if not altogether heroic, ending point to our story. Three "gentlemen of color" joined the party at the Munro Hotel and appeared with Estrada Palma at each stop along the way. One of these gentlemen was Rafael Serra. Born in Havana in 1858, the child of a free moreno couple, and the nephew of a seamstress and elementary school teacher of "extremely humble birth," Serra learned the basics of reading, writing, geography, and arithmetic as a child. Then while working in a cigar factory, by "his own efforts" he became a writer and teacher. He married the granddaughter of Lucumí elders from the city of Matanzas, but he developed a reputation as an austere and dignified moralist who rejected Afro-Cuban culture in favor of racial uplift. He fled into exile around the time of the Guerra Chiquita and several years later joined an unsuccessful military expedition led by Antonio Maceo in order to "strum his lyre on the field of battle." He became a "bard" of the revolution, then a Republican politician, then a close ally of Martí, and finally the standard-bearer for the radical faction of the separatist movement in its conflict with newcomers after Martí's death. Another of the gentlemen was Juan Bonilla. Born in Key West, Bonilla was a member of one of the first black Cuban families to settle in Florida during the Ten Years' War. He grew up in the southern United States during the period of Reconstruction, speaking both English and Spanish. His father and older brother both naturalized shortly after the law was changed to allow men of African descent to become citizens. They became two of the first Cubans of color to exercise the right to suffrage within an interracial democracy. Juan moved to New York as a teenager, becoming a leader in the Odd Fellows lodge, a writer in both Cuban and African American newspapers, and a staunch supporter of Serra and Martí. He married the daughter of a Cuban midwife, but she died while giving birth to his child. He now traveled with Estrada Palma on a return to a country that he had never visited. The third gentleman was Manuel de Jesús González, a cigar maker from Oriente. González has not appeared as frequently in these pages as Bonilla and Serra, but he was their close friend and ally, the third of Martí's most famous "disciples." González was the author of the most extensive accounts of the activities at La Liga, including the episode in which Martí was caught off guard, one night at the apartment on West Third Street, by a question about the impossibility of sincere friendship between men of different social status.

The three New Yorkers told their stories to crowds in Eastern Cuba. Even as they helped Estrada Palma assume the democratic mantle of the revolution, they used the opportunity to introduce themselves to local political leaders, military veterans, and journalists, and to reconnect with old comrades from exile who had served in the Army of Liberation. When the procession arrived in Havana, it made contact with most of the black and brown politicians in the city, some from the ranks of the Army of Liberation, others returning from Florida, Jamaica, or Haiti, and others who had lived in or passed through New York. Among them was their long-time comrade Sotero Figueroa. The son of an unmarried pardo couple, Figueroa attended the charitable elementary school of Maestro Rafael Cordero in San Juan, and then learned the trade of typesetter in the printing house of the Liberal and abolitionist José Julián Acosta. He married a seamstress who was the "natural" daughter of a small-town politician, and made himself into a writer, journalist, and politician in Ponce. When he moved to New York, he found a place within the Hispanic American literary establishment, and became a close ally of both Martí and Serra in the Cuban Revolutionary Party. In Havana, Serra, Bonilla, and González also renewed their ties with Juan Gualberto Gómez, the son of an enslaved couple on a Matanzas plantation whose parents had purchased his freedom, educated him, and sent him to France, where he became a journalist, civil rights activist, and in 1900, a delegate to the Constituent Assembly.[2]

With the economy increasingly dominated by foreign capital, politics would become the primary realm of economic opportunity for Cubans during the first Republic of Cuba (1902–33). Even members of the former landowning class joined the scramble for public office. By the same token, because Cuban sovereignty was severely constrained by the oversight of the US government, Cuban politics would be largely confined to battles over who would control the distribution of patronage rather than contests among competing policy agendas. Black politics would be no exception. Serra and others would continue to articulate devastating critiques of Cuban racism. But much as they had done as members of the Republican, Autonomista, and Cuban Revolutionary Parties, they would also work to ensure their access to the same system of political favors that all Cuban political constituencies sought to control.[3]

Given their long relationship with Estrada Palma, the men returning from New York were comparatively well positioned in this competition, but even this advantage required further negotiation. By summer, Serra wrote to the president that having received no assistance in his efforts to find a way to earn a decent living, he felt "deeply injured by [you,] my illustrious friend." He assured his old ally that he did not harbor any exaggerated aspirations for a high intellectual or administrative post. But the question of a government job, he urged, was more than a painful personal matter between the two friends. It was a political problem. In Santiago and in New York, he warned, constituents were whispering about the break between Estrada Palma and Serra. Enemies were making use of these rumors. As a result, Serra argued, all that had been won in demonstration of "your noble democratic sentiment" by inviting Serra, Bonilla, and González to join him on the civic march across the island two months earlier, "you have begun losing."[4] The letter seems to have worked. That summer, Serra received a job in the Post Office. Bonilla took a job in the Department of Public Instruction. González took a job in the Customs House.[5] Figueroa received a position in the Department of Governance, and after making his own case that this was not sufficient recompense for his loyal service, was promoted to a post in the Government Printing Office.[6]

With his livelihood secure, Serra worked to build his popularity in Eastern Cuba into a political organization. With the help of allies returned from New York, he made appeals to cigar makers, carpenters, and other labor unions in the city of Santiago as well as the sociedades de color. His friends and comrades also traveled the countryside around Santiago, where black and brown voters constituted majorities in many districts, recounting Serra's triumphs during his decades in exile, and publicizing his relationship with Martí, his battles with the Study Group, and his affection for President Estrada Palma. In print, Serra developed these same themes. He also advocated access to public jobs for people of color, expanded public education, the protection of minors from abuse, the protection of the rights of Cuban workers, the rights of tenants, and criminal justice reform. Cuban politicians, he said, believe that the poor "have no common sense, have no heart, have no taste, have no pressing and legitimate needs to satisfy, nor interests to protect." This is why every Cuban politician "praises us, kisses us, and hugs us as elections approach," only to abandon us in "our damp and dreary slums" once in office.[7] Yet he too was a Cuban politician. In local politics, he affiliated with the National Party of Oriente, aligning his supporters behind a white lawyer in Santiago named Antonio Bravo Correoso. In national politics, he was consistent in his support for Estrada Palma's Moderate Party.[8] In 1904, he secured a nomination from the Moderates in Oriente for a seat in the House of Representatives, then defeated his old ally Juan Gualberto Gómez, who stood as a candidate for an opposing party.[9] That same year he founded a new newspaper, *El Nuevo Criollo*, in which he continued to combine his own philosophy of equal citizenship and racial uplift with support (and increasingly excuses) for Estrada Palma, up until the moment in 1906 when the Moderate Party's attempt to secure reelection through electoral fraud provoked an uprising by the Liberal opposition, a constitutional crisis, and a second US occupation.[10]

In 1899, Serra had warned that the transformations wrought by the war did not guarantee a path toward a republic for all. They merely meant, he argued, that white Cubans, if pressed by a disciplined and well-organized class of color, were somewhat more likely to "soften" the harshness of their prejudices "than the other white people" in the many other societies recovering from slavery.[11] In 1907, with US forces in control for a second time, the moment was ripe for a new round of organizing to exert this kind of pressure. In Central and Western Cuba, most of this organizing took place within the two principal factions of the Liberal Party, one backed by Gómez and the other by Morúa. Few politicians of color joined forces with a civil engineer and military officer named Evaristo Estenoz when he created the Independent Association of Color (Agrupación Independiente de Color) to apply pressure to the parties for more appointments specifically for men of color. Serra did express sympathy for Estenoz, and he supported a broader call for a national convention of the class of color, a gathering of old allies who were now arrayed against one another in opposing political camps, to "define our aspirations and to struggle without rest in order to satisfy them."[12] He helped in this moment to resurrect the Directorio de Sociedades de Color for this purpose. But as Estenoz and his allies created their own party and fielded candidates for the 1908 elections, Serra (along with Cebreco and other black and mulatto leaders from Oriente) worked instead to link the unions, clubs, and veterans' groups within which he had influence to a new political coalition, the Conservative Party.[13]

In 1908, the Liberals won the presidency, and the following year the United States again withdrew from Cuba. The Liberal victory set off a chilling chain of events. In advance of partial elections in 1910, Estenoz and his group, now called the Independent Party of Color, organized electoral committees and recruited candidates in an attempt to exact concessions from the Liberals. Rather than negotiating, the Liberals arrested

Estenoz, and outlawed all political parties whose members belonged to only one race and that pursued "racist goals." Two years after that, in advance of presidential elections, the Independientes started an uprising, not unlike the one that the Liberals had staged in 1906, intended to force the government to negotiate or face another US intervention. President José Miguel Gómez accused the Independientes of starting a "race war" and ordered a bloody repression in the name of patriotic unity. Scholars have correctly seen this episode as evidence of the severe restraints that the political regime in Cuba placed on black and mulatto political participation under the justification that Cuba was a society that did not recognize racial difference. But the spiraling confrontations between the Independientes and the Liberals were only part of the story of race and politics in Cuba in this period. The extensive mobilization of voters of African descent within the two major parties during the campaign of 1908 helped to elect fourteen black and mulatto candidates, Serra and Cebreco among them, to seats in Congress that year—more than triple the totals from three years earlier. According to one of Serra's allies, nearly half the seats on Provincial Councils and 40 percent of seats on Municipal Councils went to black and mulatto candidates in that election.[14]

For better or for worse, this was the victory that the participants in three wars of independence had won: a Cuba in which the concentration of land in the hands of foreign sugar companies effectively excluded most of the rural population from any share in national prosperity; a Cuba in which a government project to attract white immigrants undercut Cuban workers, white, black, and mulatto; a Cuba in which labor struggles continued to unite workers across color lines; a Cuba in which men of color had the right to vote, but the political system was dominated by clientelism and patronage; and a Cuba in which all successful political figures declared themselves the true defenders of the ideals of Martí, including some who used Martí's memory to justify racial terror and the repression of black political organizations. This was the Cuba that generations of African American visitors would laud as an example of democracy in action, and would also frequently puzzle over or seek to expose as something less than promised, the "world's zig-zaggiest color line."[15]

In this book I have tried to demonstrate that this victory, with all its promises, all its compromises, and all its limitations, was crafted by a generation of politicians and intellectuals who intervened in the Cuban struggle and shaped the politics of the Republic of Cuba from their unique vantage point as black and brown migrants in the greater Caribbean, and settlers in the tenements of Gilded Age New York.[16] These migrants not only helped to craft the ideals that would become the guiding myths of Republican politics; they participated in the struggles to win universal manhood suffrage, and those who returned to Cuba after the war played crucial roles in each of the major political formations on the island. The radial lines of resurgent nationalism that had their points of origin in humble cradles in San Juan, Matanzas, Key West, and Havana, had been "irresistibly drawn" to the public square in the print shops of Puerto Rico and the artisan clubs of Cuba and Key West, and had converged heroically around Martí in New York once again intersected within the world of Cuban politics under the US protectorate, a world in which few, if any, heroes remained uncompromised.[17]

II.

Or maybe a more fitting end to the story is summer 1905, when, his body already starting to fail him, Serra, a forty-seven-year-old employee of the Cuban Postal Service, editor, and member of the Cuban House of Representatives, walked down the gangplank of the *SS Vigilancia* in New York City. Port authorities no longer permitted travelers like Serra to descend from the boat directly onto New York City piers and then set off toward the nearby Cuban cigar factories, restaurants, and publishing houses, as he had done in previous decades. Since 1892, the US government required all newly arriving passengers to undergo inspection at the new facility on Ellis Island. In 1905, the middle-aged politician experienced the evolving immigration regime firsthand, as line inspectors examined him and recorded a series of details, deemed by Congress to be important to his status as a visitor to the United States: What was his "race or people"? Had he ever been in an almshouse? Was he a polygamist, a contract laborer, an anarchist, or "deformed or crippled?" This inspection likely highlighted a contrast that he was used to—between the regime of official examination and classification that was emerging in the United States, and the efforts by civil rights activists in Cuba to eliminate the use of color and racial terms from all public documents so as to be Cubans without qualifiers. It was also a reminder of the interesting slippage between race and nationality that still operated in the United States, especially with respect to Latin Americans. Serra may have appreciated that the inspector recorded his race as "Cuban."[18]

The passage through Ellis Island marked a return home for a man who had spent much of his adult life in New York. He used the trip to New York to reunite with his wife, Gertrudis Heredia, the oldest daughter of the oldest daughter of Lucumí elders in Matanzas and one of the first Cuban women of African descent to complete the midwife certification program at the University of Havana. She had remained in New York with their daughter, Consuelo, when Serra returned to Havana in 1902. Consuelo had since graduated with a degree in English from New York Teacher's College and had a job teaching at the school run by Saint Benedict the Moor, the "colored" Roman Catholic Church that was now located on Manhattan's West Side.[19] In the blocks around the family apartment on West Fifty-Ninth Street, Serra must have seen the continued and growing impact of the steady influx of African Americans that would reshape the city over the next several decades into a black metropolis. What had been a patchwork color line within disproportionately black neighborhoods was giving way to much-larger and much more concentrated black neighborhoods, in which it might be easy to overlook or forget the few hundred Spanish-speaking revolutionaries who had played such an active role in African American community life at the end of the nineteenth century. Likewise, if he paid a visit to Sixto Pozo's barbershop, still operating on Sullivan Street, Serra would have seen almost no trace of the earlier era of African American settlement in Greenwich Village. "Little Africa" had been giving way to "Little Italy" for more than a decade. The former Bethel AME Church building, next door to the barbershop, now housed an Italian congregation. The row house at 74 West Third Street, the home of Charles and Hattie Reason where Juan and Gerónimo Bonilla had rented rooms, the central point of the sphere through which all the tangent lines of resurgent patriotism had intersected, had been knocked down in 1903. In its place stood one of the new, much-larger tenements that were going up for white residents all around the neighborhood.[20]

Yet the community within which Serra had made his political career, and had helped Martí to make his, had not vanished. Germán Sandoval and Gerónimo Bonilla still lived with their families on East Seventy-Fifth Street, where they remained active in the Grand United Order of the Odd

Fellows. Isidoro Apodaca and Josefa Blanco still lived in their apartment on Third Avenue. Pilar Cazuela and Silvestre Pivaló had moved across the river to the Bronx. Pastor Peñalver, who had travelled as a boy from Havana to New York to attend the public high school for colored students, remained in the city, still playing the intersection of Cuban and African American musical traditions. It would not be long before orchestra leaders in New York's jazz scene began seeking out other black and brown musicians from Puerto Rico and Cuba.[21] In politics, as in music, African Americans and Cubans continued to engage in what historian Frank Guridy has called "rich cross-national relationships," during the First Republic and beyond.[22] Juan Gualberto Gómez sent his son to study at Tuskeegee Institute, and when Rafael Serra returned to Cuba from his visit to New York, he carried a collection of clippings from the African American press, photographs of the African American military units that had fought in Cuba, reports of patronage positions given by the Roosevelt administration to African American supporters, and accounts of the school at Tuskeegee. He translated and published these in his Havana newspaper and in a collection of essays produced as he shifted his allegiance from the Moderate Party to the Conservative Party.[23]

In New York, for those who knew how to look, the legacies of the nineteenth-century community that Serra had led were still visible. The Maceo Hotel, one of the finest serving African Americans in the city and a gathering place for religious leaders, intellectuals, and politicians, attested to the memory of the Cuban independence struggle in the city. In 1905, it stood only about ten blocks from the San Juan Hill apartment where Lieutenant Colonel Tomás Maceo (the younger brother of Antonio and José) lived. He had been in the city for about five years, working as a cigar maker.[24] Of course, many New Yorkers did not know to look for these traces. Still, the new relationships between African Americans and Cubans of African descent that unfolded during the twentieth century rested on the foundations laid by the generation of migrants whose stories this book has told.

III.

Maybe, then, it is best to end the story at the elegant Maceo Hotel, where in fall 1905, shortly after Serra departed from New York, the young

Puerto Rican intellectual Arturo Schomburg organized a birthday party for an aging African American journalist named John Edward Bruce. Schomburg was twenty years younger than Sotero Figueroa, but he had grown up in much the same world. He was the student of a self-taught black elementary school teacher in San Juan. He became an apprentice in a liberal print shop (literally a few steps from the shop where Figueroa had first learned to set type). He took night classes taught by Figueroa's former mentor, Acosta, at an artisan club. He came to New York in 1891, settling with his mother (a woman originally from Saint Croix and who may have been a midwife) in the building on West Sixty-Second Street where Juan Bonilla and Dionisia Apodaca then lived. He found a job as an elevator operator and took over as secretary of the Club Las Dos Antillas. In that capacity, he reported on club activities to the newspaper *Patria* throughout the 1890s and kept the meticulous minutes of club meetings that have appeared so frequently in the footnotes of this book. After the war, he remained in New York, where he began to fill the void left by the departure of Marín, Bonilla, Figueroa, and Serra. He made an audacious leap into the debates of the public square, publishing no fewer than eleven letters to the editor in the *New York Times* between September 1901 and the end of 1903 on topics relating to US imperial expansion, lynching, and black politics. He started to assert himself too within the Sol de Cuba lodge, eventually becoming its leader. And he continued to build the alliance with African American politicians, journalists, and preachers, especially the group whom he invited to the Maceo Hotel to celebrate his friend Bruce. One former comrade from the Club Las Dos Antillas attended. From Havana, the Honorable Rafael Serra sent his regrets.[25]

The partnership between Bruce and Schomburg would blossom over the next few years into a shared project of historical research, collection, and compilation. They coedited an "Anthology of Negro Poets," and together collected more than 150 books by 1911, when they created the Negro Society for Historical Research. The society was to be an international network of intellectuals who would dedicate themselves to collecting and sharing documents, images, manuscripts, or publications by people of African descent, and making them available to "members of the race who are interested in knowing what Negroes who wrote books fifty or a hundred years ago had to say and how they said it." By the time that they founded the society in 1911, Serra had passed away, but their first book list prominently featured his *Political Essays* along with the poems of Plácido and Pachín Marín. Schomburg's private collection included the minutes book of the Club Las Dos Antillas. Bruce and Schomburg's network of foreign correspondents included Evaristo Estenoz, the leader of the Independent Party of Color in Cuba. Like many of his contemporaries in the United States, Bruce saw the struggle against racism through the lens of racial destiny—a destiny inseparable from biology. He argued that the "Negros" were "indissolubly linked together for weal or for woe, wherever under the sun of heaven one of our race and blood is found."[26] Schomburg seems not to have fully adopted Bruce's biological view of racial unity, but the two men found common ground in the idea that racial unity could be built through cultural work, especially through the production of shared historical memory.[27] Schomburg explained that Negroes should follow the example of the Jews, who remained connected to one another even as they lived scattered among various nations that despised them. He did not use the word, but he outlined a project that later scholars would describe as the African "diaspora." He called this project "racial integrity." It would be accomplished not through racial hygiene or eugenics but rather through historical research. "We need a collection or list of books written by our men and women," Schomburg asserted in 1913. "We need the historian and philosopher to give us, with trenchant pen, the story of our forefathers and let our soul and body, with phosphorescent light, brighten the chasm that separates us."[28] Schomburg became that historian, amassing an extraordinary collection of documents and books in his home in Brooklyn, and rising to prominence within the emerging African American intellectual elite of Harlem.

Of all the lines that intersected at La Liga, Schomburg's trajectory may be the one that most clearly links these stories to the history of race and ethnicity in New York in the century that would follow—a history in which Puerto Ricans would figure much more prominently than Cubans. In the aftermath of the war, the US government decided not to withdraw troops from Puerto Rico. Instead, Congress unilaterally declared the smaller island to be an "unincorporated territory" of the United States. In summer 1902, as Estrada Palma took power in Havana, the Roosevelt administration decided further that Puerto Ricans, though governed by the United States, would be treated as aliens within the increasingly rigid immigration system. Schomburg wrote a letter to the *Times*, protesting the decision.[29] Only days before his article appeared, a line inspector on Ellis Island detained a Puerto Rican woman named Isabela González after discovering that she was pregnant. According to the logic of the immigration authorities, an unwed mother arriving from the colony was morally suspect, an alien who was excludable on the grounds that she was "likely to become a public charge." González was the niece of Domingo Collazo, a Puerto Rican typographer who had been a member of the Club Las Dos Antillas, and had helped to produce and administer *Doctrina de Martí*.[30]

Collazo and a group of Puerto Rican politicians with whom he was allied helped González to bring her case to court to test the applicability of immigration law to Puerto Ricans. They did not contest the idea that she was likely to be a public charge but rather the notion that she was an alien in the first place. If the United States was going to hold the territory of Puerto Rico, they reasoned, it must recognize people born in Puerto Rico as US citizens and must govern the island in accordance with the US Constitution. In 1904, the Supreme Court disagreed, making one of a series of rulings that permitted Congress to establish a permanent colony in Puerto Rico, and thereby to restrict Puerto Ricans' access to both self-government and equal protection under the law. Congress and the courts continued to deny equal protection and full voting rights to Puerto Ricans even after granting them citizenship in 1917 and home rule in 1952. Indeed, Congress continues to deny Puerto Ricans these rights (and to deny the Puerto Rican government the right to declare bankruptcy) even today. Yet on one narrow question, the Supreme Court found in favor of González. For the purposes of regulating immigration, Puerto Ricans could not be considered aliens.[31]

The impact of this decision and the experiment in formal colonialism that it helped to justify would not have been visible yet in New York City when Serra visited in 1905, or several months later when Schomburg organized the party for Bruce. Yet US officials were already at work on projects to transfer large numbers of Puerto Rican workers to other US territories. When migration from Europe plummeted during World War I, and after the war, when Congress erected increasingly restrictive measures to prevent the entry of Italians and Jews, Puerto Ricans became a crucial source of labor for the War Department and for civilian employers in New York. After World War II, as colonial rule created great disruptions in the Puerto Rican economy and commercial airlines started offering cheap direct flights from San Juan to New York, northward migration exploded. Thus at about the same time that New York became the largest black city in the United States, it became the largest Puerto Rican city on the mainland and a major Latino metropolis.[32] Already by the time of Schomburg's death in 1938, scholars and politicians had begun to puzzle over the relationship between New York's two largest racial minorities, and the apparent divide between them. By the end of the twentieth century, Schomburg's own story had captured the imagination of scholars grappling with the long relationship between Puerto Ricans and African Americans in the city. To some he appeared as an anomaly—a Puerto Rican whose choice to identify openly as "Negro," and to participate in African American social and intellectual life, was the exception that proved the rule that Puerto Ricans and African Americans organized their racial identities and politics in ways that were mutually incompatible. To others his migration served as a way to explore the porous boundaries between these communities, and to reimagine both the frictions and potential intersections in their experiences of race. To others he served to emphasize the importance of migrants living in the mainland to the history of Puerto Rican letters. And to still others, he became a touchstone figure in a project to make visible the complex experience of Afro-Latinos amid the standard narratives of African American and Puerto Rican history, and within mainstream histories of New York City.[33]

But however one chooses to remember Schomburg, the stories related in this book show how deeply situated his intellectual projects were in the experiences of the migrants, settlers, and exiles among whom he first settled. His friendship with Bruce would not have surprised anyone who had participated in the Club Las Dos Antillas or the Sol de Cuba lodge, but neither would his differences with Bruce over the biological basis of race. The presence of a well-spoken and erudite Spanish speaker at elite African American gatherings would not have surprised any of the African Americans who had participated in Republican Party politics or in the creation of the Afro-American League over the preceding decades. Most of all, though, Schomburg's *historical* project and his decision to work with Bruce to pursue it were both deeply embedded within practices that had long been common among the network of revolutionaries who had settled in New York in earlier years. Schomburg had read the many biographical sketches produced by intellectuals in the movement, starting with

Figueroa's accounts of Campeche and Cordero, which appeared in print when he was a fifteen-year-old apprentice in San Juan. He had taken part in the battles over history that had emerged after the death of Martí. Indeed, he had been the recording secretary on the evening when speakers at the Club Las Dos Antillas discussed the contributions of "el negro" to world civilization. He had witnessed the boom in publishing among exiles of color at the end of the war, which included Serra's *Ensayos políticos*, Domínguez's *Figuras y figuritas*, and the volume *Rectificaciones*, written by Risquet in Key West and published by Figueroa shortly after he moved to Cuba. Knowing that the archives and libraries established by Cubans of color in the new republic were likely to diminish their contributions, or erase them from national memory altogether, these authors left a printed trail of clues in plain sight. Their books detailed the history of the Cuban civil rights struggle and the efforts of exiles in the national cause primarily through brief sketches and photographs of notable Cuban men and women of color.[34]

Picking up this trail in New York, Bruce and Schomburg began to imagine a project to collect the similarly scattered clues that intellectuals of African descent had inserted into the narrow confines of various national bibliographies and libraries across the Americas and Africa. They hoped to compile these records into a different kind of archive that would express the unity of black people across national borders. This idea was in some ways novel, but it reflected a pattern that had long developed within the Cuban migrant community. For years, Bonilla and Serra had acted as translators, sending reports of the activities, struggles, and triumphs of African Americans for the edification of Cuban readers. Risquet had taken this project a step further, publishing, in his book on Cubans of color, a list of notable persons of color from Puerto Rico and from "other countries," including the United States, France, Venezuela, and even Russia. Not only did the experience of "migrating while black" help create the conditions for imagining racial unity across national lines but the same networks necessary to support migration—and that supported the intellectual work of civil rights activism and radical nationalism—also supported the intellectual work of forging the ideas and practices of a black diaspora. Schomburg's genius was to imagine that this network of international travelers and correspondents could be transformed into the overseas membership of the Negro Society for Historical Research.

They could be prevailed on to share books, documents, and biographical sketches for the purposes of his collection. The collection, in turn, could build feelings of racial pride and solidarity, and further the project of racial advancement across the globe.

The modest row house on West Third Street where, on a frigid night in January 1890, a group of Cubans and Puerto Ricans of the class of color gathered to create La Liga, the institution that would help them remake themselves into intellectuals and revolutionaries, the building in which they helped to shape the course of Cuban history, has long since vanished. The much-larger building that replaced it in 1903 still stands today. It is just across the street from the southern limit of the NYU campus. The storefront at 74 West Third where La Liga was headquartered now houses a pub serving artisanal barrel-aged ale; there is a Dunkin' Donuts next door. There is no plaque or monument, nor any hint of the remarkable lives that crossed paths there more than a hundred years ago. There is no marker to help contemporary New Yorkers learn about the politics of racial harmony that the people who frequented that building helped to construct. There is certainly no opportunity for residents of the neighborhood or visitors to learn that this idea of racial harmony, so often imagined to have emerged on the battlefields of Cuba or to have sprung fully formed from the brilliant mind of José Martí, was also—to a large degree—produced out of an encounter between a group of extraordinary black and brown migrants and the city of New York. Nor would the thousands who pass by the corner each day guess that the gatherings held at that location provide an indispensable starting point for understanding the evolving borderlands between African American and Latino communities, cultures, and politics in New York. A thirty-minute subway ride uptown, however, visitors can find an impressive monument to the lives and work of these migrants. In 1926, Schomburg sold his collection of books and documents to the New York Public Library. Those materials became the basis for what is now the Schomburg Center for Research in Black Culture. The Schomburg Center has remained one of the most important institutions in the field of African American Studies and especially African Diaspora studies over the past century. It is a fitting legacy to the New York stories that began in "humble cradles" in Havana, Matanzas, San Juan, and Arecibo so long ago, and it is a reminder of the profound but now nearly silent way that these stories continue to shape our world.

ACKNOWLEDGMENTS

I wish to offer my deepest gratitude to the colleagues who read this book in manuscript form, and who provided crucial comments, insights, and encouragement: Jeremy Adelman, Paulina Alberto, Alberto Arce, Nicholas Bagley, Samuel Erman, John Mack Faragher, Ada Ferrer, Alejandro de la Fuente, Michele Hoffnung, Matthew Lassiter, Danielle LaVaque-Manty, and Rebecca Scott.

I also benefited from comments on presentations or chapters from María del Carmen Baerga, Andrew Cohen, Astrid Cubano, Arcadio Díaz-Quiñones, John French, Lea Geler, Julie Greene, Miriam Jiménez-Román, Eileen Suárez Findlay, and Lorrin Thomas, for which I am deeply thankful. Juan Flores and Christopher Schmidt-Nowara, both fondly remembered and sorely missed, were sources of inspiration and brilliant guidance. Thanks go out as well to a larger group of colleagues that participated in workshops or presentations at the Grupo de Estudios Afro-Latinoamericanos in Buenos Aires, Yale University, the University of California at Los Angeles, the University of Maryland, the University of Chicago, Northwestern University, Syracuse University, Duke University, and Rutgers University.

The project would simply not have been possible without the assistance, generosity, and keen insights of María de los Angeles Meriño Fuentes and Aisnara Perera Díaz. I am deeply indebted also to many other generous colleagues who helped me to locate research materials, while also sharing ideas and materials of their own: Adriana Chira, Marie Cruz-Soto, Lillian Guerra, Antonio Hernández Matos, Marial Iglesias Utset, John Logan, Carla Peterson, Matthew Smith, and Asiel Sepúlveda. I would especially like to thank Enrique López Mesa and Félix Ojeda Reyes for their groundbreaking work, and for their generosity in sharing materials from afar.

I am grateful to the compañeros who organized and hosted joint symposia at the University of Michigan and the University of Puerto Rico in 2008 and 2009, respectively, and who otherwise welcomed me into the intellectual life of the University of Puerto Rico: María del Carmen Baerga, Isabel Córdova, Marie Cruz-Soto, Astrid Cubano, Samuel Erman, Juan Hernández, Maritza Maymi, Carlos Pabón, Manuel Rodríguez, Lanny Thompson, and Lenny Ureña, and especially Carmen Suárez. Equal thanks go to the organizers and participants of the 2011 research practicum at the Centro Juan Marinello in Havana: the staff members of the Marinello, the Fundación Antonio Núñez Jiménez, and the Archivo Nacional de Cuba as well as Natalie Zemon Davis, Ada Ferrer, Alejandro de la Fuente, Reinaldo Funes-Monzote, Orlando García Martínez, Jean Hébrard, Oilda Hevia Lanier, Marial Iglesias Utset, Jean-Frederíc Schaub, Rebecca Scott, Ibrahima Thioub, and Michael Zeuske.

I offer thanks as well to the student researchers who assisted with various aspects of the project over the years: Simren Atal, Ashleigh Begres, Meghan Berry, Simone González-Nagy, Chiara Kalogjera-Sackellares, Jacob Sigman, Alexandrea Sommers, and Yuting Sun. Data librarians Justin Jocque, Alexa Pierce, and Nicole Scholtz helped me to compile and process the census, GIS, and network analyses, and cartographer Adrian Kitzinger turned this work into beautiful maps. Thanks too to my colleagues in the Mapping Migrant Stories Project, Sigrid Cordell and Joshua Miller, and to June Howard, for helping us to assemble and fund the project.

The ten years that I spent working on this book were full of life-changing and life-sustaining events: the loss of my father, the unwavering love of my mother and stepfather, the support of my stepmother and *suegros*, the pleasure of growing into middle age with my siblings and siblings-in-law, the joy of time spent with my nephews and niece, the making of new friends, and the comfort of old friends. But two things marked this period of my life more than anything else: the arrival of two curious, funny, and kind new people, Lalo and Pía, and the miracle of sharing their lives and mine with Paulina. It is to her that I dedicate this book.

A NOTE ON SOURCES

A colleague who read an early draft of this manuscript noted, generously, that I had managed to piece together a narrative history based on sources that were "thin as gruel." It is true that assembling source material for this project was a challenge. Still, compared with the individual lives traced by Natalie Zemon Davis in *The Return of Martin Guerre*, Tiya Miles in *Ties That Bind*, or Rebecca Scott and Jean Hébrard in *Freedom Papers*, the principal figures in *Racial Migrations* appear in an extraordinarily rich range of sources. This is, in large measure, a result of their efforts to publish their own thoughts and stories in the newspapers, pamphlets, poems, and biographical essays. Their close relationships with Martí and Estrada Palma meant, too, that some of their correspondence was preserved. And the fact that they lived in the United States at the end of the nineteenth century meant that various agencies of the increasingly developed administrative state recorded and preserved details about their movements and activities, producing ship manifests, naturalization petitions, censuses, marriage and birth certificates, passport applications, and other similar documents. So the challenge lay not simply in the relative paucity of sources but rather in finding and developing the right method to locate and manage the sources that did exist, and especially in making use of tools available in the "digital age."

The first of these tools is text searching, a technique about which some scholars have raised reasonable concerns, but that twenty-first-century historians are pretty much all using, whether we admit it or not. I searched a lot. As I read the published works, archival sources, and key newspaper collections in their entirety, I collected names and addresses, focusing especially on the membership lists of key clubs and lodges. I was then able to search these names across a range of digital platforms, Google Books, Hathi Trust, Worldcat, and digital newspaper archives, to pick up additional traces. For instance, a specialized search on Worldcat on the name of a publisher mentioned in *Doctrina de Martí* turned up a manifesto signed by 120 émigrés of color in New York in 1899 that I had never seen cited before. I could then search each of those names, and so on. The full-text databases of African American periodicals were especially helpful in tracing connections across linguistic divides. This is how I found Serra, the Bonillas, and the other Cubans in the *New York Age*. And it is how I located details about Charles and Hattie Reason, the Bonillas' landlords, who lived upstairs in the house at 74 West Third Street.

Second, I made extensive and possibly obsessive use of two genealogy websites—FamilySearch.org and Ancestry.com—searching for the names of the individuals I had compiled on my various membership lists in the census collections, naturalization records, passport applications, ship manifests, and city directories. This allowed me to trace all the people who lived in the home of the Sandoval family on Thompson Street, and to recognize among them many of the founding members of the Logia San Manuel. Because I had searched for Germán Sandoval's naturalization record, I knew the name Cándido Olivo, who was his witness. I was therefore able to recognize Olivo as a fellow passenger when I found the manifest for the ship that brought the young Pastor Peñalver to the city. On a whim, I looked up the home of Philip White and Elizabeth Guignon on the 1880 census. I nearly fell over when I discovered Carlos and Sarah Crespo living there. This kind of searching also allowed me to collect information on occupation, address, birth, age, household composition, and racial ascription for many individuals who otherwise appeared only on a list of members of a club or a lodge.

Finally, with generous support from the University of Michigan, I experimented with new kinds of computing tools to make sense of the abundance of data available on genealogy websites and elsewhere as social history. The maps in this book illustrate patterns of residential segregation at the level of individual buildings, and the distribution of Cubans and Puerto Ricans across those color lines. I downloaded census data from the North Atlantic Population Project. Using digitized manuscript censuses on FamilySearch.org, I cross-referenced these data files against 1880 census returns and "scraped" additional data out of the 1900 census returns. I combined these data with GIS coordinates for New York City addresses, generously shared by John Logan's team at Brown University. Once I had collected and compiled these data, I layered the information onto insurance maps of New York City from the period. Likewise, by collecting and analyzing all the 2,056 records relating to persons of Spanish nationality in the index of naturalizations in New York City between 1872 and 1888, and processing them with a digital network visualization tool, I was able to identify clear patterns of political activity among Cuban exiles. Just a few people served as witnesses on the naturalizations of hundreds of Cubans in the weeks immediately preceding elections, suggesting the emergence of political coalitions. Because I could cross-reference these records against other sources, I could locate the members of the Sol de Cuba and San Manuel lodges, and La Liga, in these networks. I plan to publish a longer discussion of digital methods in an essay currently under revision.

NOTES

PROLOGUE

1. The description of the apartment comes from González, "Una clase en la Liga." The founding document of La Liga is reprinted in Serra, *Ensayos políticos, sociales y económicos*, 145–52. The text of Serra's speech is reprinted in Serra, *Ensayos políticos*, 43–60. On Serra, the key biographical sources are Despradel, *Rafael Serra*; González Veranes, *La personalidad de Rafael Serra*; Deschamps Chapeaux, *Rafael Serra*. González Veranes was Serra's son-in-law. More recent works that discuss Serra's activities in New York or in early republican Cuba include Bronfman, *Measures of Equality*; Guerra, *The Myth of José Martí*; Pappademos, *Black Political Activism*; Mirabal, *Suspect Freedoms*; Fusté, "Translating Negroes into Negros."

2. On the concept of Afro-Latinas/os, see Dzidzienyo and Oboler, *Neither Enemies nor Friends*; Jiménez Román and Flores, *Afro-Latin@s in the United States*; Rivera-Rideau, Jones, and Paschel, *Afro-Latin@s in Movement*.

3. On the emergence of Martí as a sacred nationalist hero claimed by politicians across the ideological spectrum, see Iglesias Utset, "José Martí: mito, legitimación y símbolo"; Guerra, *The Myth of José Martí*. For the extent to which Cuban scholars of widely divergent political perspectives continue to debate the meaning of Martí's legacy, see Ripoll, "The Falsification of José Martí in Cuba"; Estrade, *Martí en su siglo y en el nuestro*.

4. For the detail of the two portraits near the door of the flat, see González, "Una clase en la Liga." On the three wars of independence and the end of slavery, see Ferrer, *Insurgent Cuba*; Scott, *Slave Emancipation in Cuba*. For the divisions within the exile community in this period, Poyo, *With All, and for the Good of All*; Pérez, *Sugar, Cigars, and Revolution*.

5. Key biographies and interpretations of Figueroa and Marín include Esteves, *Estudio biográfico del poeta arecibeño*; Toledo, *Sotero Figueroa*; Ojeda Reyes, *Peregrinos de la libertad*; Hoffnung-Garskof, "To Abolish the Law of Castes."

6. Martí, *Obras completas*, 4:279; "Mi raza," *Patria*, April 16, 1893.

7. Wade, "Images of Latin American Mestizaje and the Politics of Comparison"; de la Fuente, "Myths of Racial Democracy"; Alberto and Hoffnung-Garskof, "'Racial Democracy' and Racial Inclusion."

8. Despradel, *Rafael Serra*, 4.

9. Rebecca Scott and Jean Hébrard call the method of following migrants across distinct social contexts "microhistory set in motion." Scott and Hébrard, *Freedom Papers*; Scott, "Microhistory Set in Motion."

10. For a particularly eloquent version of the argument that disjunctures between the ways that Afro-Latinos articulate their racial identities and the expectations of broader US societies are the result of friction between varying systems of racial knowledge (rather than insufficient racial consciousness), see Torres-Saillant, "The Tribulations of Blackness." See also Duany, "Reconstructing Racial Identity"; Itzigsohn, Giorguli, and Vázquez, "Immigrant Incorporation and Racial Identity": Ramos-Zayas, *Street Therapists*; Carlo-Becerra, "Which Is 'White' and Which 'Colored'?"

11. Here I am in the company of quite a few scholars who have investigated the "something else" that stories of movement and interaction, and broader transnational framing, add to comparative studies of race. Scott, *Degrees of Freedom*, 4; Putnam, *Radical Moves*; Hoffnung-Garskof, *A Tale of Two Cities*. Micol Seigel in *Uneven Encounters* provides another important model, though she presents the transnational approach as a rebuttal rather than a complement to comparative studies.

12. Deschamps Chapeaux, *Rafael Serra*, 148.

13. On the ways that Americans and Cubans of African descent engaged with one another in the twentieth century, see Guridy, *Forging Diaspora*. On the broader question of how to define African diasporas, and an emphasis on the evolution of diasporic solidarities, see Patterson and Kelley, "Unfinished Migrations"; Palmer, "Defining and Studying the Modern African Diaspora." On the consequences for coalition building between Afro-Latinos and African Americans, see Flores, "Que Assimilated, Brother, Yo Soy Asimilao"; Thomas, "Resisting the Racial Binary?"; Lee, *Building a Latino Civil Rights Movement*.

14. The choice to write narrative history is not unusual, by any means. My own explorations with the form began in a course I took with James Goodman in 1992. Goodman explains his approach to storytelling and the controversies over narrative that emerged in the 1990s in his "For the Love of Stories." More recently I have been fortunate to have been close enough to eavesdrop on (and sometimes take part in) the conversations of my two colleagues, Tiya Miles and Paulina Alberto, as they taught a graduate seminar on history and narrative, and developed their own narrative projects.

15. Two important models for my approach are Davis, *The Return of Martin Guerre*; Miles, *Ties That Bind*. LaKisha Simmons, citing Paula Fass, calls this method "disciplined imagination." Simmons, *Crescent City Girls*, 10–11.

CHAPTER 1: BEGINNINGS

1. Despradel, *Rafael Serra*, 4.

2. Domínguez, *Figuras y figuritas*, xiv. This scarcity of detail is reproduced in the biographical sketch by Pedro González Veranes—a lecture delivered at the prestigious black social club, the "Club Atenas," in 1942. González Veranes, *La personalidad de Rafael Serra*, 12–13.

3. The most interesting expression of this comes in a biography of the composer Juan Morel Campos, a man of partial African ancestry, written by his brother, the typographer and journalist Ramón Morel Campos. Ramón wrote that his brother was frequently described as humble, in reference to his unassuming personality. But, the biographer noted, sometimes "this 'humble' is interpreted another way,"

leading readers to imagine a subject "born outside the city limits, in the domains of a plantation or colony and beneath the merciless whip of some overseer, etc., etc."

4. "La Liga Antillana," *Patria*, January 28, 1893.

5. Toledo, *Sotero Figueroa*.

6. "Acta de bautismo, María Gertrudis Heredia," February 16, 1856, Matanzas, Parroquia de San Carlos, Libro 23 de bautismos de pardos y morenos, Hoja 246 vuelto, número 1072. Personal collection of Aisnara Perera Díaz and Maria de los Ángeles Meriño Fuentes.

7. "Certificación literal de partida de bautismo de José Rafael Simón Agapito Serra," April 3, 1858, Havana, Parroquia Nuestra Señora de Monserrate, Libro 4 de bautismos de pardos y morenos, folio 226, vuelto, no. 858

8. Martínez Alier, *Marriage, Class, and Colour*, 11–14.

9. Martínez, Nirenberg, and Hering Torres, *Race and Blood in the Iberian World*; "Decreto derogando cuantas disposiciones."

10. "Acta de Bautismo de José Julián Martí Pérez," January 28, 1853, Havana, Iglesia de Santo Ángel Custodio, Libro 18 de bautismos de blancos, folio 61 vuelto. Reprinted in Roig de Leuchsenring, *Martí en España*, 6.

11. For the bishop's decree, see "Santa visita de la Catedral y Parroquia de Puerto Rico," July 1852, Parroquia de Nuestra Señora de los Remedios, Libro 27 de bautismos de pardos y morenos, folio 238, PRCCR. This decision seems to have been taken as part of a campaign to create a higher standard of professionalism and improve the moral behavior of local priests, and to discourage the common-law relationships that dominated on the island. See Esteve, *Pastoral*; Chirinos, "Los límites del poder disciplinario."

12. "Acta de bautismo, Francisca Figueroa Fernández," January 22, 1848, Libro 27 de bautismos de pardos y morenos, folio 9; "Acta de bautismo, Jesús María Figueroa Fernández," October 15, 1851, Libro 27 de bautismos de pardos y morenos, folio 198; "Acta de bautismo, Sotero Figueroa Fernández," June 28, 1853, Libro 18 de bautismos, folio 65. All three are from San Juan, Parroquia de Nuestra Señora de los Remedios, PRCCR.

13. Barcia Zequeira, *Los ilustres apellidos*; López Valdés and Alegría, *Pardos y morenos*; Deschamps Chapeaux, *El negro en la economía*; Sartorius, "My Vassals."

14. Kinsbruner, *Not of Pure Blood*, 30–32.

15. Ferrer, *Freedom's Mirror*; Fradera, *Colonias para después de un imperio*.

16. US War Department, *Report on the Census of Porto Rico*, 33; US War Department, *Report on the Census of Cuba*, 710–12. For the concentration of exports in Western Cuba, see Pérez de la Riva, *El barracón*, 175–76. On the geography of slaveholding, see Bergad, Iglesias García, and Barcia Zequeira, *The Cuban Slave Market*, 32; Scarano, *Sugar and Slavery in Puerto Rico*.

17. Ferrer, *Freedom's Mirror*, especially 38–43; Reid-Vazquez, *The Year of the Lash*, 26–41; Sartorius, *Ever Faithful*, 40–46.

18. Enrique Medín Arango, who became a labor activist, orator, and factory reader, was the son of Secundino Arango and María Gil Morales. Risquet, *Rectificaciones*, 145–46. On the events of 1844, see Finch, *Rethinking Slave Rebellion*; Reid-Vazquez, *The Year of the Lash*; Paquette, *Sugar Is Made with Blood*; Pletch, "Isle of Exceptions."

19. Sacramental books in Cuba were finally desegregated between 1899 and 1904. Logan, "Each Sheep with Its Mate."

20. Abbad y Lassiera and Acosta y Calbo, *Historia geográfica*.

21. Baerga, *Negociaciones de sangre*, 101–32.

22. "Bando contra la raza africana, 31 Mayo 1848," in *Boletín histórico de Puerto Rico* (San Juan: Editorial LEA, 2004), 1–2:122–26; Baralt, *Esclavos rebeldes*, 127–34; Díaz Soler, *Historia de la esclavitud negra en Puerto Rico*.

23. This, for instance, is consistent with the description offered in Tapia y Rivera, *Mis memorias*, 148.

24. Acta de bautismo, Francisca Figueroa Fernández," January 22, 1848, Libro 27 de bautismos de pardos y morenos, folio 9; "Acta de bautismo, Jesús María Figueroa Fernández," October 15, 1851, folio 198, Libro 27 de bautismos de pardos y morenos, folio 238; "Acta de bautismo, Sotero Figueroa Fernández," June 28, 1853, Libro 18 de bautismos, folio 65. All three are from San Juan, Parroquia de Nuestra Señora de los Remedios, PRCCR.

25. Baerga, *Negociaciones de sangre*; Twinam, *Purchasing Whiteness*; Chira, "Uneasy Intimacies." It is interesting to compare this situation to ethnographic work that highlights the "linguistic inconsistency in racial classification" in late twentieth-century Puerto Rico. Godreau, "Slippery Semantics." Clarence Gravlee's "Ethnic Classification in Southeastern Puerto Rico: The Cultural Model of 'Color'" finds a high degree of semantic consistency in contemporary Puerto Rico using Marvin Harris's classic instruments. Harris, "Referential Ambiguity in the Calculus of Brazilian Racial Identity."

26. *Resumen del censo de poblacion de la isla de Cuba a fin del año de 1841*. For 1861 census in Cuba, see Sagra, *Cuba en 1860*, 21. For an interpretation of the Puerto Rican census of 1846, see Abbad y Lassiera and Acosta y Calbo, *Historia geográfica*, 302. For 1860 estimates from Puerto Rico, see Bona, *Cuba, Santo Domingo y Puerto-Rico*, 84. An interesting commentary on this process is offered by authors of the report on the Puerto Rican census of 1899. They posed the question of whether the "line of separation between whites and mestizos" had been drawn by census enumerators with sufficient care. Sanger, Gannett, and Willcox, *Informe sobre el censo de Puerto Rico, 1899*, 89.

27. For the 1841 and 1861 census, officials evidently collected data on the numbers of pardos and morenos but did not include a tabulation of these results in their published results. Subsequent Cuban censuses seem not to have even collected these data. Instituto Geográfico y Estadístico, *Censo de la poblacion de España*, xxxii–xxxiii.

28. Helg, *Our Rightful Share*, 3, 40.

29. Roig de Leuchsenring, *Martí en España*, 8–9.

30. Grandío Moráguez, "The African Origins"; Hall, *Slavery and African Ethnicities*, 132–43.

31. Smallwood, *Saltwater Slavery*; Van Norman, "The Process of Cultural Change."

32. Miller, *Voice of the Leopard*.

33. Rafael Serra, "Soneto," *El Pueblo*, June 13, 1880.

34. Rafael Serra, "En defensa propia II," *La Igualdad*, March 30, 1893.

35. Rafael Serra, "Nadie lo sabe," *La Igualdad*, March 8, 1894.

36. Lucena Salmoral, "El derecho de coartación"; de la Fuente, "Slaves and the Creation"; Bergad, Iglesias García, and Barcia Zequeira, *The Cuban Slave Market*, 122–42; Perera Díaz and Meriño Fuentes, *Para librarse de lazos*.

37. Baptismal record reproduced in Cabrera, *La juventud de Juan Gualberto Gómez*, 21–22; Horrego Estuch, *Juan Gualberto Gómez*, 4–5.

38. Lucena Salmoral, "El derecho de coartación"; de la Fuente, "Slaves and the Creation"; Bergad, Iglesias García, and Barcia Zequeira, *The Cuban Slave Market*, 122–42.

39. This detail comes from the death certificate of Figueroa's sister, "Civil Registration of the Death of Francisca Figueroa y Fernández" (San Juan: Departamento de Sanidad de Puerto Rico, April 24, 1935), PRCR.

40. Lovejoy, "Old Oyo Influences"; Law, "Ethnicity and the Slave Trade."

41. I am deeply indebted to Aisnara Perera Díaz and María de los Ángeles Meriño Fuentes for sharing with me their database of baptisms collected at the cathedral in Matanzas, from which all this information is drawn. See similar cases from Oriente in Chira, "Uneasy Intimacies."

42. Moliner Castañeda, *Los cabildos afrocubanos en Matanzas*. This author identifies Campos as the *capataz* of the cabildo Fernando VII, at 157 Calle Daoíz, from 1840 to 1866. Moliner also notes that oral tradition suggests the cabildo was Oyo and that in 1864 the cabildo hosted forty-five dances. Marta Silvia Escalona provides the detail of the Feast of the Rosary in Escalona, *Los cabildos de africanos*, 165–66.

43. Valdés Domínguez, "Ofrenda de hermano."

44. On the interactions between cabildos and constables (*celadores*), see Moliner Castañeda, *Los cabildos afrocubanos en Matanzas*, 35–36. On the role of male and female leadership in cabildos, see Barcia Zequeira, *Los ilustres apellidos*, 84–112. On Lucumí spiritual practices in Matanzas, see Brown, *Santería Enthroned*.

45. Martínez-Fernández, *Protestantism*, 30–34.

46. Ann Twinam argues that prejudices and discrimination based on color increased in the late eighteenth century, especially in the Caribbean. Twinam, *Public Lives, Private Secrets*, 196, 208–15.

47. "Acta de bautismo, Manuela Aguayo Pulido," October 26, 1855, Toa Baja, Parroquia del Apostol, Libro 10 de bautismos, folio 100, PRCCR.

48. "Acta de bautismo, María Eustaquia Cabrera," November 13, 1830, San Juan, Parroquia de Nuestra Señora de los Remedios, Libro 22 de bautismos de pardos, folio 174, identifies Ezequiela's mother, Juana Gregoria Cabrera, as parda. This is either Ezequiela's own baptismal record (and her name was copied wrong) or it is that of a sibling. Later children born to Juana Gregoria Cabrera and "Don" Andrés Pulido were inscribed as natural children in the libro de blancos. See, for instance, "Acta de bautismo, Manuela Pulido y Cabrera," January 12, 1835, San Juan, Parroquia de Nuestra Señora de los Remedios, Libro 14 de bautismos de blancos, folio 27, PRCCR.

49. "Acta de matrimonio, Manuel Aguayo y Matilde Hernández," April 2, 1856, Toa Baja, Parroquia del Apostol, Libro de matrimonios (1815–63), folio 138; "Acta de bautismo, Josefa Aguayo Hernández," April 11, 1859, Toa Baja, Parroquia del Apostol, Libro 11 de bautismos, folio 6, PRCCR.

50. For evidence of this younger sibling, see "Acta de matrimonio, José Rudolfo Pulido y Josefa Felicita Miró," July 25, 1887, San Juan, Parroquia Nuestra Señora de los Remedios, Libro 12 de matrimonios, folio 77. For the baptism of Manuela and Sotero's child, see "Acta de bautismo, Francisco Figueroa Aguayo," June 6, 1880, San Juan, Parroquia Nuestra Señora de los Remedios, Libro 26 de bautismos, folio

294, PRCCR. On the broader intersection between illegitimacy, female honor, and race, see Baerga, *Negociaciones de sangre*; Twinam, *Public Lives, Private Secrets*; Martínez Alier, *Marriage, Class, and Colour*.

51. Barcia Zequeira, *Los ilustres apellidos*, 327–72.

52. Rodríguez San Pedro, *Legislación ultramarina*, 45–104.

53. Picó, *Educación y sociedad en el Puerto Rico*.

54. For a detailed description of this system, see Davis, *Report of the Military Governor*, 120–22; Dumás Chancel, *Guía del profesorado*.

55. See the tables collected by Cayetano Coll y Toste and republished in Special Commissioner for the United States to Puerto Rico, *Report on Puerto Rico*, 200.

56. The 1860 census in Puerto Rico recorded fifteen teachers who were persons of color. US War Department, *Report on the Census of Porto Rico*, 34. We can identify, for instance, Eleuterio Derkes, the son of a shoemaker from Curaçao who was educated in Guayama by a local priest before becoming a primary school teacher. Ramos-Perea, *Literatura puertorriqueña negra*, 19–40. For the cases, for example, of Ramón Marín and Pancasio Sancerrit, see Hoffnung-Garskof, "To Abolish the Law of Castes." On Benigno López-Castro, for instance, see Risquet, *Rectificaciones*, 162.

57. Cited in Figueroa, *Ensayo biográfico*, 182–83.

58. Ibid., 147.

59. Álvarez Curbelo, *Un país del porvenir*.

60. Hostos, *Ciudad murada*; Matos Rodríguez, "Spatial and Demographic Change"; Kinsbruner, *Not of Pure Blood*; Suárez Findlay, *Imposing Decency*; Martínez Vergne, *Shaping the Discourse*.

61. Coll y Toste, *Historia de la instrucción pública*; Acosta y Calbo, "Discurso pronunciado."

62. Picó, *Educación y sociedad en el Puerto Rico*.

63. Tapia y Rivera, *El bardo de Guamaní*, 6.

64. Pezuela, *Diccionario geográfico*, 3:8.

65. Risquet, *Rectificaciones*, 137–41; Barcia Zequeira, *Los ilustres apellidos*, 341.

66. Bachiller y Morales, *Apuntes para la historia de las letras*, 7–9; Risquet, *Rectificaciones*, 104–5, 100–115.

67. Valdés Domínguez, "Ofrenda de hermano"; López, *José Martí*, 29–36.

68. This includes all girls ages one to fifteen; school age would have been seven to twelve. Pezuela, *Diccionario geográfico*, 4:25, 28.

69. More than half of white women in Matanzas reported that they were occupied with domestic tasks in their own homes. Fewer that 10 percent of free women of color could make the same claim. Ibid., 4:25–28.

70. Deschamps Chapeaux, *Rafael Serra*, 23; González Veranes, *La personalidad de Rafael Serra*.

71. Pezuela, *Diccionario geográfico*, 3:14–18; Chancel, *Guía del profesorado*.

72. Horrego Estuch, *Juan Gualberto Gómez*, 4.

73. Barcia Zequeira, *Los ilustres apellidos*, 367; Risquet, *Rectificaciones*, 147.

74. Of more than three thousand students who received free education, fewer than seventy-five were identified as nonwhite.

75. Reid-Vazquez, *The Year of the Lash*, 108–9.

76. Reid-Vazquez, "Tensions of Race, Gender, and Midwifery in Colonial Cuba."

77. "Expediente para la expedición del título de comadrona a la morena María Gertrudis Heredia," May 24, 1890, Fondo Instrucción Pública, legajo 570, número 34 762, ANC; *Legislación de instrucción pública*; "Profilaxia de la fiebre puerperal."

78. "Acta de bautismo, María Justa Rufina de la Merced," July 26, 1881, Havana, Parroquia de Nuestra Señora de Monserrate, Libro número 9 de bautismos de pardos y morenos, folio 200, no. 593. On naming and racial markers, see Zeuske, "Hidden Markers, Open Secrets."

79. Céspedes, *La prostitución*, 171; Giralt, *El amor y la prostitución*; Lagardere, *Blancos y negros*; "Odiosa injusticia," *La Fraternidad*, August 21, 1888; "La raza negra cubana ante la ciencia, la experiencia, la justicia y la conciencia," *La Fraternidad*, October 10, 1888.

80. Sippial, *Prostitution*, 88–89; Fraunhar, "Marquillas Cigarreras Cubanas."

81. Céspedes, *La prostitución*, 177.

82. "Expediente promovido por Da. Estefanía Barrera de Meireles solicitando simultanear el segundo con el tercer año de práctica de comadrona," October 31, 1883, Fondo Instrucción Pública, legajo 457, número 27 280, ANC. Interestingly, Barrera de Meireles later advertised in the newspaper *La Igualdad*, suggesting that she did have a longer relationship with the writers and editors of the class of color.

83. "Mosaico," *La Fraternidad*, March 12, 1889.

84. González Font, *Tratadito de tipografía*.

85. Coronel, *Un peregrino*, 27.

86. González Font, *Tratadito de tipografía*, 44–47. This text, despite its emphasis on precision, included a list of errata. Ibid., 104.

87. Coronel, *Un peregrino*, 29.

88. See Acosta's introduction to Figueroa, *Ensayo biográfico*, 17. On this phenomenon in Europe, see Darnton, *The Great Cat Massacre*.

89. See biographies for Aguayo, González, and Sancerrit in Figueroa, *Ensayo biográfico*. See also "Acta de bautismo, Pascacio Sancerrit," March 3, 1833, San Juan, Parroquia de Nuestra Señora de los Remedios, Libro 22 de bautismos de pardos, folio 355, PRCCR.

90. Figueroa, *Ensayo biográfico*, 207–14.

91. Cabrera Salcedo, *De la pluma a la imprenta*.

92. For instance, teachers Eleuterio Derkes and Eleuterio Lugo, and typographers Jorge Alonso Fernández, José Ramos Brans, Alonso Pizarro, and Ramón Morel Campos. Ramos-Perea, *Literatura puertorriqueña negra*, 77–127; Risquet, *Rectificaciones*, 161–65.

93. On the cigar industry and the white-only typographers' union, see Casanovas, *Bread or Bullets*, 24–32, 180–82. See also Stubbs, *Tobacco on the Periphery*.

94. Araceli Tinajero provides an excellent overview of this work process in *El Lector*, 14–19.

95. Rivero Muñiz, "La lectura en las tabaquerías"; Tinajero, *El Lector*; Tinajero, "El Siglo."

96. See, for instance, the cartoons by Victor Patricio Landaluz published in *Don Junípero* in 1866, reprinted in Casanovas, *Bread or Bullets*, 86–87.

97. A reproduction of this press coverage is included in Rivero Muñiz, "La lectura en las tabaquerías."

98. Casanova *Bread or Bullets*, 34–36; Rivero Muñiz, "La lectura en las tabaquerías," 216.

99. *Información sobre reformas*; Schmidt-Nowara, *Empire and Antislavery*, 106–125; Álvarez Curbelo, *Un país del porvenir*, 123–39; Figueroa, *Sugar, Slavery, and Freedom*, 109–11.

100. Morales, *Misceláneas*, 199.

101. *Información sobre reformas*, 181.

102. Ibid., 252, 175. Pozos Dulces was somewhat of an exception. See ibid., 133.

103. Casanovas, *Bread or Bullets*, 35–38. On whites-only hiring at the Partagas factory and in labor organizations, see Daniel, "Rolling for the Revolution," 53, 85.

104. Tapia y Rivera, *La cuarterona*.

105. Brunson, "'Writing' Black Womanhood."

CHAPTER 2: THE PUBLIC SQUARE

1. Serra, *Ensayos políticos*, 22.

2. See the founding document of La Liga, reprinted in Serra, *Ensayos políticos, sociales y económicos*, 145.

3. Manuel de Jesús González, "El Maestro," *Patria*, July 2, 1895; "En casa," *Patria*, May 14, 1892.

4. González, "Una clase en la Liga," 183.

5. Each of these citations is from ibid., 182.

6. Most of these questions are from ibid., 183-4. The question about the Senate in a republic is from "Noche hermosa en 'La Liga,'" *Patria*, November 4, 1893.

7. "Tres notas," *Patria*, March 14, 1892. This is an account of the second branch of La Liga, created in Tampa in 1892. The exact quote is "quejas viriles."

8. "Noche hermosa en 'La Liga,'" *Patria*, November 4, 1893.

9. González, "Una carta del Maestro."

10. Sotero Figueroa and Ramón de Armas, "El Club 'Los Independientes' a José Martí," *Patria*, July 20, 1895.

11. Manuel de Jesús González, "El Maestro," *Patria*, July 2, 1895.

12. Juan Bonilla, "La política yankee," *Patria*, November 13, 1893.

13. Stubbs, "Social and Political Motherhood of Cuba"; Brown, "Negotiating and Transforming the Public Sphere"; Glymph, "Rose's War."

14. Bergad, "Toward Puerto Rico's Grito de Lares"; Jiménez de Wagenheim, *El grito de Lares*; Pérez Moris and Cueto y González Quijano, *Historia de la insurrección de Lares*.

15. Pérez, *Cuba: Between Reform and Revolution*, 90–93; Ferrer, *Insurgent Cuba*, 15–22.

16. Mata, *Conspirações da raça de cor*; Chira, "Uneasy Intimacies."

17. Ferrer, *Insurgent Cuba*, 56–60; Portuondo Zúñiga, "El padre de Antonio Maceo"; Ferrer Cuevas, *José Maceo*; Padrón Valdés, *El general Flor Crombet*.

18. Rebecca Scott notes that civilian leaders who favored annexation also shifted toward abolitionism after the passage of the Thirteenth Amendment in the United States, and that the leadership from Puerto Príncipe helped to pressure representatives from Manzanillo and Bayamo on the question of slavery. Scott, *Slave Emancipation in Cuba*, 45–62; Ferrer, *Insurgent Cuba*, 44–69; Pérez, *Cuba: Between Reform and Revolution*, 92–96.

19. García Muñoz, "La documentación electoral"; Cabrera Salcedo, *De la pluma a la imprenta*. For an excellent discussion of the main variants of liberalism in Spain in this period, see Schmidt-Nowara, *Empire and Antislavery*, 73–99. For more on this political history in Spain, see Navarro, "De la esperanza a la frustración"; Serrano García, *España, 1868–1874*.

20. Ramos-Perea, *Literatura puertorriqueña negra*, 12–39.

21. "Suplemento, Censo Electoral para Diputados a Cortes Constituyentes," *Gazeta de Puerto-Rico*, January 20, 1869; García Muñoz, "La documentación electoral."

22. Cited in Díaz Soler, *Historia de la esclavitud negra en Puerto Rico*, 299, 304–5.

23. "Decreto derogando cuantas disposiciones."

24. "Circular número 20," *Gazeta de Puerto-Rico*, March 18, 1871.

25. Figueroa, *Ensayo biográfico*, 171–76.

26. Pérez Moris and Cueto y González Quijano, *Historia de la insurrección de Lares*, 83.

27. Figueroa and Morel Campos, *Don Mamerto*, 20.

28. "Cuban Affairs: The Troubles at Porto Rico," *New York Times*, August 11, 1871.

29. Pérez Moris and Cueto y González Quijano, *Historia de la insurrección de Lares*, 311–12; Brincau, *Bosquejo histórico de la institución de Voluntarios en Puerto Rico*, 29–33.

30. "Cuban Affairs: The Troubles at Porto Rico," *New York Times*, August 11, 1871.

31. Sotero Figueroa, F. Gonzalo Marín, and Antonio Vélez Alvarado, "La dominación y la independencia," *Patria*, July 16, 1892.

32. Cruz Monclova, *Historia de Puerto Rico (1868–1885)*, 874, 921.

33. In 1877, "Don Facundo Peña" (a man of African descent) was president of the Casino de Artesanos in San Juan. Juan Loredo, Simplicio Angulo, Pío Bacener, and José Landor, also men of color, were officers in this institution. José Chavarría y Jiménez, a typographer of African descent employed by the Conservative printer José Pérez Moris, was an officer of the Círculo de Recreo de Amigos. For the list of officers of these associations, see Pérez Moris, *Guía general de la isla*, 118. Both Bacener and Chavarría y Jiménez are identified as Puerto Ricans "of color" in Risquet, *Rectificaciones*, 164–65. Peña, Angulo, Loredo, and Landor are each identified as nonwhite in subsequent civil registry documents or US censuses.

34. Peris Menchieta, *De Madrid a Panamá*, 76.

35. On the invitation of Eleuterio Derkes to the Gabinete de Lectura in Ponce, see Ramos-Perea, *Literatura puertorriqueña negra*, 288–92. On Figueroa's election to the post of secretary, see "El 22 de marzo de 1873," *Patria*, April 1, 1893.

36. "El 22 de marzo de 1873," *Patria*, April 1, 1893.

37. Quotations are from Figueroa, *Ensayo biográfico*, 258; Cruz Monclova, *Historia de Puerto Rico (1868–1885)*, 472–74. In the city of Ponce, the number of eligible voters in elections for representatives in the Cortes dropped from 3,433 in 1873, to 1,624 in 1875, to a mere 278 in 1881—79 of whom qualified as capacidades. "Censo electoral para Diputado á Cortes, distrito de Ponce," 1873, S-604-2, AHMP; "Censo electoral formado, distrito de Ponce," 1875, S-604-6, AHMP; "Listas electorales," 1881, 6-606-(5,11), AHMP.

38. Figueroa, *Ensayo biográfico*, 261; Coll y Toste, *Puertorriqueños ilustres*, 92–93.

39. Secretaría, Gobierno General de Puerto Rico, "Carta Sobre Publicación de 'El Eco de Ponce,'" June 9, 1880, Correspondencia del Ayuntamiento de Ponce, G-8-4-1, AHMP.

40. Baerga, *Negociaciones de sangre*, 189–203; Twinam, "The Etiology of Racial Passing."

41. For Manuela's father's political career, see *Gazeta de Puerto Rico*, February 23, 1856, May 14, 1857, October 16, 1860, July 19, 1870, August 9, 1879, November 11, 1879, and July 1, 1890.

42. Gallart Folch, *Mis memorias*, 40. This party was also sometimes called the Spanish Party or the Unconditionally Spanish Party.

43. Ciudad de Ponce, "Listas electorales," 1881, 6-606-(5,11), AHMP.

44. Quintero Rivera, *Patricios y plebeyos*, 23–98; Schmidt-Nowara, *Empire and Antislavery*, 165–66.

45. Rodríguez-Silva, *Silencing Race*, 91–102; Suárez Findlay, *Imposing Decency*.

46. Quintero Rivera, *Workers' Struggle in Puerto Rico*; Dávila Santiago, *Teatro obrero*, 37–47; Ramos-Perea, *Literatura puertorriqueña negra*, 86–109.

47. *El Eco de Ponce*, July 19, 1880.

48. Ibid.

49. Cruz Monclova, *Historia de Puerto Rico (1868–1885)*, 551; Coll y Toste, *Puertorriqueños ilustres*, 157–58. For Ramón Marín, see also letters dated October 14, 1881, July 28, 1885, and August 7, 1885. Correspondencia del Ayuntamiento de Ponce, G-10-2 (14), G-12-16 (6), G-12-17 (11), G-18-3 (4). AHMP.

50. *El eco de Ponce*, July 19, 1880.

51. Figueroa, *Ensayo biográfico*, 174.

52. *El Eco de Ponce*, July 19, 1880.

53. Lane, *Blackface Cuba*. The first Cuban bufo troop visited Puerto Rico in 1879 and may have been the company that Figueroa saw perform in Ponce in 1880. See Leal, *La selva oscura*, 48, 295; Rivero, *Tuning out Blackness*, 22–65. For a criticism of the depiction of people of color in bufos, see *El Buscapié*, May 20, 1887, reprinted in Ramos-Perea, *Literatura puertorriqueña negra*, 429.

54. Figueroa and Morel Campos, *Don Mamerto*, 6, 10, 11.

55. Marín, *Las fiestas populares de Ponce*, 101–5, 111–13.

56. Tapia y Rivera, *Mis memorias*, 128.

57. Brau, *Disquisiciones sociológicas*, 206; Quintero Rivera, "The Somatology of Manners."

58. Toledo, *Sotero Figueroa*, 25–26. The correspondence of the Ayuntamiento of Ponce reveals that *El Eco de Ponce* was still in publication on August 20 of 1880, G-8-18 (7), AHMP, and that *La Avispa* began publication on April 5, 1881, G-9-24 (2), AHMP.

59. Toledo, *Sotero Figueroa*, 25–26.

60. "Noticias," *La Iberia*, February 24, 1897.

61. *Internal Revenue Record and Customs Journal*, 69; Pérez, *On Becoming Cuban*, 3–31, 49–50.

62. Bureau of Statistics, *Statistical Abstract of the United States*, 359; González-Ripoll Navarro, "La emigración cubana de Cayo Hueso."

63. "Classified Advertisements," *New York Age*, February 27, 1892.

64. For the Bonillas, see 1870 Census, NARA M593, roll 132, page 361B, image 211663. For the number of Cubans in Monroe County, see see 1870 data from Minnesota Population Center, *National Historical Geographic Information System*.

Racial ascriptions for Cubans in Key West are from the index of the 1870 US Federal Census on Ancestry.com.

65. 1870 Census, NARA M593, roll 132, page 342B, image 692.

66. On the founding of the San Carlos and worker-nationalist alliances, see Casanovas, "El movimiento obrero." See also Poyo, *With All, and for the Good of All*, 71–73.

67. Poyo, "Cuban Revolutionaries and Monroe County Reconstruction."

68. Xi, *The Trial of Democracy*, 68–78.

69. A third petitioner that day was José Perdomo, who was later one of the authors of Borrego et al., "Protesta de los cubanos de color de Key West." See the Declarations of Intention for Citizenship of Francisco Bonilla, Salomé Rencurrel, and José Perdomo, United States District Court for the Southern District of Florida, Key West, October 1, 1870, Florida Naturalization Records, NAA, 21.

70. Browne, *Key West*, 134.

71. Castellanos, *Motivos de Cayo Hueso*, 159, 343.

72. Shofner, "Cuban Revolutionaries and the 1876 Election Dispute"; Poyo, "Cuban Revolutionaries and Monroe County Reconstruction"; Ortiz, *Emancipation Betrayed*.

73. Aguilera, *Epistolario*, 143.

74. Ferrer, *Insurgent Cuba*, 38.

75. Petition for Naturalization of Gerónimo Bonilla, United States District Court for the Southern District of Florida, Key West, October 2, 1875, Florida Naturalization Records, NAA, 21. On this document, Gerónimo swore that he was twenty-one years old, although other sources suggest that he was only seventeen at the time. This implies that his motive for naturalization was voting.

76. Shofner, "Cuban Revolutionaries and the 1876 Election Dispute"; Poyo, "Cuban Revolutionaries and Monroe County Reconstruction"; Ortiz, *Emancipation Betrayed*.

77. L. W. Livingston, "Freest Town in the South," *New York Age*, December 11, 1888. Livingston is mentioned in Jonatás [Emilio Planas], "De Cayo Hueso," *La Fraternidad*. January 22, 1889; Risquet, *Rectificaciones*, 168; Gutiérrez, *Páginas para la historia*, 11. On the longer history of African American politics in Key West, see Rivers and Brown, "African Americans in South Florida."

78. For schooling options, see *El Republicano*, March 26 and April 3, 1870, September 3, 1870; Maloney, *A Sketch*, 39–41.

79. "The Key West Cigars," *New York Times*, October 27, 1889.

80. Brooks, *The Official History*, 134; Maloney, *A Sketch*, 38; Brown, *Florida's Black Public Officials*.

81. See US Passport Applications for Carlos Borrego (June 28, 1878), José Florencio Villavicensio (December 31, 1878), and Guillermo Sorondo (December 9, 1878), NARA, M1372, rolls 224-01 and 226-01. These were important leaders among cigar workers of color in Key West, as seen by their election to draft a statement of protest in 1881. "Acta del meeting general de los emigrados de la clase de color"; Borrego et al., "Protesta de los cubanos de color de Key West."

82. Deschamps Chapeaux, *Rafael Serra*, 24–25.

83. Tinajero, *El Lector*, 61–77; Fernández and Shofner, "Martyrs All"; Valdés Domínguez, *Tragedy in Havana*; Roig de Leuchsenring, *Martí en España*; Paz, *Martí en España, España en Martí*.

84. Trujllo y Monagas, *Los criminales de Cuba y d. José Trujillo*, 162.
85. Mercadal, "Ciudadanos o súbditos"; Tarragó, "La lucha en las Cortes de España por el sufragio universal en Cuba."
86. On the broader panorama of the political parties, see Pérez, *Cuba: Between Reform and Revolution*, 105–8; Roldán de Montaud, *La Restauración en Cuba*, 122–64. Juan Gualberto Gómez offered an excellent description of the evolution of these parties between 1878 and 1884, by which point he had come to support the Autonomistas. Gómez, *La cuestión de Cuba en 1884*. At the end of the century, Serra and other exiles published a particularly interesting account of the failings of the Autonomista Party over the preceding decades. See *Contestación a dos desdichados autonomistas de la raza de color*.
87. Schmidt-Nowara, "From Slaves to Spaniards."
88. Casanovas, *Bread or Bullets*, 129–34.
89. In 1900, Martínez wrote to Serra addressing him as "old compañero from the workshop, and from assiduous labor in the creation of the first organization of artisans in Cuba." Letter from Martínez to Serra, Havana, March 30, 1900, reprinted in Despradel, *Rafael Serra*, 16–17. On the participation of Cubans of color in political life in this moment, see Sartorius, *Ever Faithful*, 131–78.
90. For an account of this civil rights struggle, see Risquet, *Rectificaciones*, 97–106. For a description of the creation of both casinos and sociedades, see Sartorius, *Ever Faithful*, 132–53; Barcia Zequeira, "Casinos españoles ¿de color?"
91. Horrego Estuch, *Juan Gualberto Gómez*, 18–24. On the exile experience in Mexico, see Muller, *Cuban Émigrés and Independence in the Nineteenth Century Gulf World*.
92. González Veranes, *La personalidad de Rafael Serra*, 13; Deschamps Chapeaux, *Rafael Serra*, 26–28; Figarola y Caneda, *Guía oficial de la Exposición de Matanzas*, 159.
93. For ties between Bernardo Costales Sotolongo (a founder of La Armonía) and Azcárate and Martí, see de Armas and Costales y Sotolongo, *El museo*. For the list of founding members of La Armonía, see Deschamps Chapeaux, *Rafael Serra*, 28. Many of these men appear as educators or journalists in Figarola y Caneda, *Guía oficial de la Exposición de Matanzas*. David Sartorius notes that "unless new publications—black newspapers in particular—had clear ties to the two political parties or official state institutions, few of them had extended runs." Sartorius, *Ever Faithful*, 149.
94. Montoro, *Discursos políticos*, 24, 27. Both quotes are from a speech to the Autonomista Party in 1882.
95. This quote, in the English translation, appears in Schmidt-Nowara, "From Slaves to Spaniards," 185. For more details on the apprenticeship, see Scott, *Slave Emancipation in Cuba*, 127–200.
96. Moliner Castañeda, *Los cabildos afrocubanos en Matanzas*, 91. La Armonía was located at Calle Daóiz 187½. In 1878, there were five cabildos between 114 and 217 Calle Daóiz, including the Lucumí cabildo San Carlos at 187, the property immediately adjacent. Two additional cabildos, including Fernando VII, were on Daóiz, but the street address was not recorded. This suggests the possiblity that La Armonía was actually located in the same house as the cabildo Fernando VII, but I have not been able to confirm this suspicion.

97. "Cinco monografías sobre La Asociación Unión Fraternal, presentadas a un concurso por la misma," 1918, Fondo Adquisiciones, caja 75, número 4317, pieza 2, ANC.

98. Jonatás [Emilio Planas], "De Cayo Hueso."

99. Helg, *Our Rightful Share*, 132.

100. Ferrer, *Insurgent Cuba*, 70–89. For the prohibition of entry for "individuos de color ó de raza negra africana," see García Morales, *Guía de gobierno y policía de la isla de Cuba*, 64. For a rejection of the rebellion by a Liberal politician, see Trujillo, *Apuntes para una historia*, 6–7.

101. Joaquín Granados, "Un saludo y un reproche a Rafael Serra," *Patria*, May 28, 1892.

102. Reprinted by Serra in "Nos quedamos solos," *El Pueblo*, July 11, 1880. For an excellent analysis of the rhetoric of loyalty and civilization as expressed by Cuban journalists of African descent in this period, see Sartorius, *Ever Faithful*.

103. Schmidt-Nowara, *Empire and Antislavery*, 74–88; Horrego Estuch, *Juan Gualberto Gómez*, 9.

104. "Nos quedamos solos," *El Pueblo*, July 11, 1880.

105. See, for instance, Serra, *Ecos del alma*. This work is discussed in detail in chapter 4.

106. "Miscelánea," *El Pueblo*, March 14, 1880.

107. Rafael Serra, "En defensa propia II," *La Igualdad*, March 30, 1893.

108. Martín Morúa Delgado, "Avisos," *El Pueblo*, July 25, 1880

109. *El Pueblo* announced itself as the "organ of the class of color" on its masthead. According to Pedro Deschamps Chapeux, the approvals granted to Juan Gualberto Gómez and Manuel García Alburquerque to publish the first newspapers for the class of color in Havana identified the men as *moreno ingenuo* and *pardo ingenuo*. Compare this with the authorization granted to Figueroa, identifying him as "Don Sotero Figueroa, vecino de esta capital." Deschamps Chapeux, *El negro en el periodismo*, 31, 53–54.

110. Martín Morúa Delgado, "Las sociedades," *El Pueblo*, July 18, 1880; Martín Morúa Delgado, "Estamos Acordes," *El Pueblo*, July 18, 1880; Rafael Serra, "Quisieramos callar," *El Pueblo*, August 1880.

111. Lane, *Blackface Cuba*, 60–105. Jill Lane notes that bufos also deployed these satirical figures in order to critique Spanish colonialism and mock the pretensions of the creole elite. Blackface characters were therefore often seen through a sympathetic nationalist lens. Nevertheless, they remained insulting caricatures of black intellectual pretension.

112. Perfecto Ponce de León, "Discurso," *El Pueblo*, June 13, 1880.

113. Rafael Serra, "Quisieramos callar," *El Pueblo*, August 1880.

114. Rafael Serra, "En defensa propia II," *La Igualdad*, March 30, 1893. By this point, Serra and Morúa were sworn enemies.

115. Miguel Failde and Raimundo Valenzuela, "Complacidos," *La Fraternidad*, July 31, 1888.

116. "Misceláneas," *El Pueblo*, March 21, 1880.

117. Castellanos, *Motivos de Cayo Hueso*, 118.

118. This was a small world; a member of Failde's family attended Serra's school. "Alumnos aventajados del Colejio 'La Armonia,'" *El Pueblo*, June 13, 1880.

Another relative placed a wedding announcement. "Gacetillas," *El Pueblo*, March 14, 1880. Failde also offered subscriptions to the newspaper in his tailor shop. "Puntos de suscrición," *El Pueblo*, March 21, 1880.

119. "Misceláneas," *El Pueblo*, March 21, 1880; Martín Morúa Delgado, "Una junta," *El Pueblo*, August 15, 1880.

120. Rafael Serra, "Quisieramos callar," *El Pueblo*, August 1880.

121. Martín Morúa Delgado, "Las sociedades," *El Pueblo*, July 18, 1880.

122. Rafael Serra, "La moral," *El Pueblo*, March 21, 1880.

123. Rafael Serra, "Nos quedamos solos," *El Pueblo*, July 11, 1880. On the Maestro Inspector, see Serra, *Ensayos políticos, sociales y económicos*, 152.

124. José Martí, "Rafael Serra: para un libro," *Patria*, March 26, 1892; "Ensayos políticos," *Patria*, April 16, 1892; González Veranes, *La personalidad de Rafael Serra*, 14–15. For the broader trend of mixed-race schools run by sociedades de color, see Casanovas, *Bread or Bullets*, 132–33.

125. "En defensa propia II," *La Igualdad*, March 30, 1893. On the Little War, see Pérez and Sarracino, *La Guerra Chiquita, una experiencia necesaria*; Ferrer, *Insurgent Cuba*, 70–92; Foner, *Antonio Maceo*, 95–106.

126. Borrego et al., "Protesta de los cubanos de color de Key West" and "Acta del meeting general de los emigrados de la clase de color."

127. Serra, *Lamentos de un desterrado: ensayo poético, canto 1o*, 8.

128. Serra, *Lamentos de un desterrado: ensayo poético, canto 2o*.

129. Domínguez, *Figuras y figuritas*, 15.

CHAPTER 3: COMMUNITY

1. This section is drawn from multiple accounts of Monday activities at La Liga, especially "Los lunes en La Liga," *Patria*, March 26, 1892; "Lunes en la Liga," *Patria*, April 23, 1892.

2. Serra, *Ensayos políticos, sociales y económicos*, 145.

3. Ibid., 145–51.

4. From a speech at La Liga, reprinted in Serra, *Ensayos políticos*, 20.

5. Martí, *Obras completas*, 20:406.

6. "En casa," *Patria*, May 21, 1892.

7. "Los lunes en La Liga," *Patria*, March 26, 1892.

8. Martí, *Obras completas*, 26:248–49.

9. Serra, *Ensayos políticos, sociales y económicos*, 147.

10. This is not mere supposition. A report in the *New York Freeman* noted that the police had done "their best to kill a Cuban," adding "one officer defied the crowd which had surrounded him while the other beat and hammered the Cuban's head with a club. It is high time that the police of this city were disciplined in humanity instead of brutality. Colored men are being clubbed on the slightest provocation." "Local Gossip," *New York Freeman*, July 31, 1886. For a discussion of African American experiences of discrimination in nineteenth-century New York, see Peterson, *Black Gotham*, 191–206. For an important case from later in the century, see T. Thomas Fortune, "A Brutal Police Outrage," *New York Age*, June 7, 1890. On "mental mapping" of racial geographies and the movement of women and girls through urban space, see Simmons, *Crescent City Girls*.

11. For a discussion of the problems of using racial enumeration on US census returns in this way, see Hoffnung-Garskof, "The World of Arturo Schomburg."

12. Francisco Gonzalo Marín, "Nueva York por dentro," in Kanellos, *En otra voz*, 198–201.

13. Geli appears twice on ship manifests, traveling as the servant of the Brooks family. May 13, 1874, NARA 36, M237, roll 389, line 26, number 454; June 15, 1876, NARA 36, M237, roll 404, line 32, list number 520. She was still living in their home in 1880. 1880 Census, NARA T9, roll 880, Enumeration District 292, 330D. On the Brooks family, see Carlson, "The First of Earlier Revolutions."

14. For the entry of Coroneau as the servant of Julia and Lilia de Mensigniac, see the manifest for *SS Morning Star* on May 23, 1870, NARA 36, M237, roll 328, line 7, list number 423. See also the entry for Julia de Mensigniac and other residents of her boarding house at 120 East Twenty-Fourth Street in 1880 Census, NARA T9, roll 880, Enumeration District 277, 75C; "Certificate of Marriage, Magin Coroneau and Lorenza Geli," December 10, 1878, MACNY.

15. The 1870 US Federal Census reported 1,824 Cuban-born persons in New York State, of whom 135 were "colored." Minnesota Population Center, *National Historical Geographic Information System*.

16. Pérez, *On Becoming Cuban*, 32–43; Abad, "Las emigraciones cubanas en la Guerra de los Diez Años. Apuntes," 8; Pérez, *Sugar, Cigars, and Revolution*, 124–84.

17. Indexes available on Ancestry.com allow me to identify 183 Cubans living in New York City in 1870 who were identified on the census as black or mulatto. Consulting the manuscript census for each of those persons, I have been able to determine that 83 of them (44 percent) lived as servants or children of servants in households headed by persons enumerated as white.

18. See, for instance, the passport application of Félix Govín, a lawyer, businessman, and major figure in separatist politics in New York and the Florida Republican campaigns of the 1870s (December 13, 1883), which specifies that "when husband, wife, minor children, and servants travel together, a single passport for the whole will suffice." NARA, M1372, roll 260–01.

19. On the activities of this group, see Casasús, *La emigración cubana*, 69–147. Hilario Cisneros, for example, a wealthy lawyer and member of the Cuban Junta in the city, was the head of a large household, including two black domestic servants (one Cuban and one French) and three Irish domestic servants. 1870 Census, NARA M593, roll 996, Ward 16, District 13, 556B. In another illustration, Félix Govín also had a large household in New York employing several Irish maidservants and a black Cuban coachman. 1880 Census, NARA T9, roll 881, Enumeration District 297, 426C. And the family of Gonzálo de Quesada employed two black Cubans in their home in New York. One of these servants, Cristina Quesada, used the family's last name. This suggests that at some point before coming to New York, she or her parents were enslaved by the Quesada family. 1880 Census, NARA T9, roll 888, Enumeration District 437, 514D; 1870 Census, NARA M593, roll 993, Ward 15, District 4, 494B. See also Pérez, *Sugar, Cigars, and Revolution*, 165–8.

20. Application to become a citizen of the United States of Magin Carauneau, May 28, 1877, Superior Court of the City of New York, NANYC, RG 21/85; Last Will and Testament of Magin Corrouneau, November 6, 1909, "New York Probate Records, 1629–1971," 897:6–8.

21. In 1870, for example, Joaquín Toscano, a man born in China, and Dolores Toscano, a Cuban woman of African descent, were married to one another and working as servants in the household of a wealthy Cuban family (also named Toscano). 1870 Census, NARA M593, roll 1045, Ward 19, District 27, 509A. A decade later, the couple lived with their children in their own apartment. Joaquín worked as a porter, and Dolores kept house. 1880 Census, NARA T9, roll 875, Enumeration District 193, 383A. The Toscanos' daughter, Valentina, was later a member of the women's groups at La Liga. "Liga Antillana," *Patria*, September 17, 1892. To cite another example, Cristina Quesada and Faustino Socarrás, both servants in the childhood home of Gonzalo de Quesada, married and settled into their own home in 1880. Certificate of Marriage of Faustin Socarrias and Christina Quesada, July 2, 1881, MACNY.

22. When Coroneau applied for a passport, he indicated his intention to travel with a servant. Passport application of Magin Carauneau, March 2, 1881, NARA, M1372, roll 260-01. This may have provided the travel document that his sister needed in order travel with him when he returned to New York. Manifest for *SS Santiago*, April 19, 1881, NARA 36, M237, roll 435, line 40, list number 422. When he applied for US citizenship, a man who lived and worked in the Brooks household (where Lorenza worked) served as his witness. Application to Become a Citizen of the United States, "Magin Carauneau," May 28, 1877, Superior Court of the City of New York, NANYC, RG 21/85. When the couple married, a dressmaker named Magdalena Hernández was their witness. Even Cubans of African descent who arrived in service to wealthy white families depended on this sort of horizontal social network to manage the challenges of settling in the city. Of the ninety-eight Cubans of color who lived outside domestic service arrangements in New York in 1870, sixteen were married to other Cubans of color. Another thirty-one were single but lived together or in the immediate vicinity of other, unrelated Cubans of color NARA, M1372, roll 260–01.

23. Although Marcus appears on US censuses as born in Cuba, an 1872 naturalization petition lists him as a subject of the king of Portugal, as does a record of his arrival from Panama in 1888. It is possible that there were two men named Lafayette Marcus in New York, or that his national identity or trajectory before arriving in New York was more complicated than it appears. In the 1872 *New York City Directory*, Marcus was a "waiter" living at 138 Thompson Street. In 1875, *Goulding's Manual of New York and General Statistical Guide* listed him as a seaman living at 21 Minetta Lane. The next year, the *City Directory* again listed him as a waiter, at 21 Minetta Lane. In 1877 he was again a seaman, still at 21 Minetta Lane. In 1886, he was a caterer living at 16 Cornelia Street. See US City Directories, 1822–1995. For a description of the accommodations on these ships, Collins, *Guide to Nassau, Cuba, and Mexico*; Scott, *Journal of the New York and Cuba Mail Steamship Company*. It is also interesting to note that John Benjamin, a black man born in Cuba, appears as "cook on a steamer" in the 1880 Census (NYC), NARA T9, roll 877, Enumeration District 234, 560C.

24. 1870 Census, NARA M593, roll 102, Ward 8, District 18, 370B. The suspicion that they may have been kin is based on the fact that all the women in the household were, like Fredericka, born in Connecticut.

25. See shipping company advertisements and timetables in Disturnell, *New York as It Was*; Casanovas, *Bread or Bullets*, 125.

26. Riis, *How the Other Half Lives*, 148–53 (quote on 149).

27. Logan, Zhang, and Chunyu, "Emergent Ghettos."

28. Of 2,159 Cubans identified as white and living in Manhattan on the 1880 census, 1,788 lived in 621 all-white buildings, and 268 more lived in 69 buildings where the only persons counted as black were also listed as servants. Only 26 Cubans counted as white (1.2 percent) lived in buildings in which any person counted as nonwhite lived independently (buildings in which at least one household head or spouse of a household head was counted as black or mulatto). Even this may be an overcount, as several of those who appear as white Cubans living in mixed buildings in 1880 appear as nonwhite in other documents. By contrast, of the 320 Cubans who were counted as black or mulatto, 273 (85.3 percent) lived in 111 buildings where non-Cubans enumerated as black or mulatto also lived. Only 13 Cubans who were counted as black or mulatto, and who were not servants, lived in buildings with no non-Cuban persons counted as black or mulatto (a total of only four buildings). I tabulated these results using the machine-readable census files available through Minnesota Population Center, *National Historical Geographic Information System*, and cross-referenced with manuscript censuses on Ancestry.com.

29. Deschamps Chapeaux, *Rafael Serra*, 147.

30. See entries at that address between 1874 and 1886 for Ramón Fernández, Domingo Hernández (cigar maker), Margaret (widow of Joseph Rodrigue), Anselmo Olivarez (cigar maker), Francis Berdai (cigar maker), Abraham Seino (cigar maker), Helman Sanders, Pantaleón Pons, Salomé Rencurrel, Francis Bonell, and Antonio García (cigar maker) in US City Directories, 1822–1995. See also Application for Admission as a Citizen of Geronimo Bonilla, October 22, 1884, NANYC, RG 21/85.

31. 1880 Census, NARA T9, roll 872, Enumeration District 118, 232B. For Charles Tilman (barber), see 1876 New York City Directory, US City Directories, 1822–1995. For Charles Tilman (musician), see 1877 New York City Directory, US City Directories, 1822–1995.

32. Logan, Zhang, and Chunyu, "Emergent Ghettos."

33. For the two cases cited above, see "A Savage Negro," *New York Times*, January 17, 1876; "A Cuban Negro's Crime," *New York Times*, August 3, 1883. See also "The Cuban Murderer," *New York Times*, June 22, 1884; "His Scar Betrayed Him: A Boy Who Saw the Murder of Antonio Soloa," *New York Times*, November 21, 1885; "New York's Jack the Ripper: Proves to Be a Cuban Negro Who Lived with Mary Martin," *St. Louis Post-Dispatch*, April 4, 1895; "Both Loved Same Girl," *Morning Telegraph*, October 10, 1898.

34. Riis, *How the Other Half Lives*, 156.

35. Crane, "Minetta Lane, New York," 155.

36. Deschamps Chapeaux, *Rafael Serra*, 148.

37. For the Crespos, see 1880 Census (Brooklyn), NARA T9, roll 841, Enumeration District 25, 589B. See also listings in New York City directories from 1876 to 1881 in US City Directories, 1822–1995. On White and Guignon, see Peterson, *Black Gotham*, 310–44; Gatewood, *Aristocrats of Color*, 105–6.

38. Gatewood, *Aristocrats of Color*, 105–6; Charles A. and Hattie Reason, 1880 Census, NARA T9, roll 874, Enumeration District 159, Page 468D; "A 'Son of New York,'" *New York Age*, August 20, 1887; "Mrs. Maria E. Pratt," *New York Age*, February 27, 1892. By the time of the 1900 US Federal Census, Hattie Reason was widowed and operating a rooming house at 80 West Third Street that was home to seven Cuban cigar makers, all men of color. One of these men may have been Rencurrel (Salomon Ranko). 1900 Census, NARA T623, Enumeration District 51, 8B. Also, 80 West Third Street was the address of a mutual aid society, the Sociedad Los Treinta, run by men of color. See *Doctrina de Martí*, July 25, 1896. We can first place the Bonillas at 74 West Third Street when Gerónimo was a witness for Serra's petition for naturalization, October 20, 1888, Superior Court, New York County, NANYC, RG 21/85.

39. Certificate of Marriage, Alfred Vialet and Harriet Reason, September 11, 1899, MACNY. For a story about Martí chatting with the Reasons and giving candy to one of their children, see Plochet and Plochet Lardoeyt, *El capitán Plochet recuerda a José Martí*, 19.

40. "Newark Notes," *New York Globe*, August 18, 1883; "New York City News," *New York Age*, May 11, 1889; Serra, *Ensayos políticos, sociales y económicos*, 148.

41. See, for instance, a report on the gathering called by Peter Ray (who was a member of St. Philip's and the uncle of Elizabeth Guignon) in "The Cuban Negroes," *New York Times*, December 14, 1872. See also a report of an event organized by the New York Anti-Slavery Society that included an address by Henry Highland Garnett and a speech in Spanish by Lorenzo Portela, a mulatto cigar maker, in "The Freedom of Cuba: Enthusiastic Meeting in Cooper Institute," *New York Times*, October 25, 1877. See also Mirabal, *Suspect Freedoms*, 70–5, 87–91; Boutelle, "Manifest Diaspora."

42. Foner, *Antonio Maceo*, 88; 1878 New York City Directory, US City Directories, 1822–1995.

43. "The Colored Schools," *New York Age*, February 17, 1883; "The Governor Signs the New York City School Bill," *New York Age*, May 10, 1884; *Annual Report of the Board of Education*, 1885, 52–53.

44. "La música no reconoce colores," *La Fraternidad*, November 10, 1888. This biographical sketch suggests that he continued his studies at the City College of New York after graduating. Pastor's younger brother Francisco was later a star pupil at the school, even after ward schools had been opened to black children. Francisco was one of the few who attended the City College of New York after graduating. "Grammar School No. 80," *New York Age*, June 25, 1887.

45. *Annual Report of the Board of Education*, 1876, 31–32, 148–49.

46. Manifest for *SS Crescent City* on November 8, 1876, NARA 36, M237, roll 406, line 8, list number 1054. The best evidence as to Olivo's racial identity comes from his passport applications (June 10, 1875, and July 30, 1877), on which his hair is described as "woolly" and his complexion is described as "colored (negro)." NARA, M1372, rolls 209, 218.

47. The founders included Philip White and Patrick Reason, brother of the educator Charles L. Reason and uncle of the engraver Charles A. Reason (yes, this was a small world!). Brooks, *The Official History*, 12–14, 51, 142. Sandoval and Rencurrel are identified as the "soul" of the Logia San Manuel in Serra, *Ensayos políticos, sociales y económicos*, 148.

48. Summers, *Manliness and Its Discontents*; Muraskin, *Middle-Class Blacks*.

49. See 1880 Census, NARA T9, roll 884, Enumeration District 351, 210B (Abraham and Emma Seino); 1880 Census, NARA T9, roll 877, Enumeration District 223, 384A (Amalio and Wilhelmina Roche); 1880 Census, NARA T9, roll 889, Enumeration District 471, 590A (Ramón and Sarah Romay); 1880 Census, NARA T9, roll 848, Enumeration District 128, 490B (Ramón and Delilda Angulo).

50. Petition for a warrant for a new lodge to be named Sol de Cuba, submitted to "the M.W. Grand Master of the H.F. of F.A.M. for the state of New York" in New York, June 26, 1880, by P. M. Lafayette Marcus, Manuel Coronado, Abraham Seino, Sixto Pozo, John Johnson, Andrew N. Postro, and Abony Brown. On this document, Marcus appears as P. M., meaning that he was a "Past Master" of the Mt. Olive Lodge. "Report of the Sol de Cuba Lodge No. 38 F. and A. M. to the Grand Lodge of the State of New York," June 5, 1901 (including membership list); "The History of Prince Hall Lodge No. 38"; Harry Albro Williamson Papers, SSRBC.

51. "G.U.O. of O.F.," *People's Advocate*, March 27, 1880.

52. "Masonic," *New York Globe*, January 12, 1884.

53. "Masonry," *New York Freeman*. October 3, 1885.

54. "Multiple Classified Advertisements," *New York Age*, July 25, 1885. Other members of the organizing committee were José Alonzo, Ruperto (Roberto) Bravo, Domingo Álvarez, Amalio Roche, and Ramón Romay.

55. See, for instance, "Five Nights' Celebration at Bethel," *New York Globe*, October 6, 1883; "Local Gossip," *New York Freeman*, January 31, 1885.

56. Roberts, *The Latin Tinge*, 38–50; Washburne, "The Clave of Jazz."

57. *The Trow City Directory of New York City*, 64 lists "Federico Knudsen & Co. (Germain Sandoval, Salomé Rencurrel, and Pantaleón Pons)." J. P. Roig regularly advertised a shop at this address in the newspaper *Patria* in the 1890s. Evan Matthew Daniel also identifies Roig, Garcia, Llano, and Co. at this address in 1883 as well as F. Kunder (which may be a misspelling of F. Knudsen). Daniel, "Rolling for the Revolution," 281.

58. Schneider, "The New York Cigarmakers Strike of 1877."

59. "New York City Cigarmakers," *Weekly Graphic*, October 28, 1887.

60. Daniel, "Rolling for the Revolution," 146–49, 281.

61. The cigar industry average for "handwork" was $10.76 in weekly wages in 1884. Ibid., 266. The workers at Knudsen's Factory earned a wage of $12 a week according to the 1880 US Census Non-Population Schedule, NYSL, roll 88, 73, line 35.

62. For instance, Rafael Delgado, who appears in 1900 Census, NARA T623, roll 1124, 6A, and in advertisements in Serra's paper, such as *Doctrina de Martí*, August 22 1896. Tiburcio Aguilar is mentioned as a "Cuban Negro cigar manufacturer" in "Seeking Information," *New York Freeman*, April 30, 1887.

63. "El Coronel José C. López," *Doctrina de Martí*, August 31, 1897.

64. "His Scar Betrayed Him: A Boy Who Saw the Murder of Antonio Soloa," *New York Times*, November 21, 1885.

65. For a remarkable view of this waterfront, including the Ward and Morrow piers, see Porter, *Panorama Water Front and Brooklyn Bridge from East River*, especially 1:51–2:15.

66. See listings for Antono Llerena and Co. Cigars, Davy and McCabe Druggists, Louis Salomon, Wholesale Paints, W. Graney House Painting, and Jeremiah Kennedy Liquors, all at 105 Maiden Lane, New York City Directory, 1875–1877, US City Directories, 1822–1995.

67. "Will You Dine Here, Senor? Among the Gourmet Cigareros Down in Maiden Lane," *New York Times*, February 25, 1894.

68. Antonio Soloa (also known as Chang Ong), a Chinese man who had lived for many years in Cuba, owned one such establishment. "His Scar Betrayed Him: A Boy Who Saw the Murder of Antonio Soloa," *New York Times*, November 21, 1885. Two participants in the social networks established by Sandoval, José Chacón and Pedro Calderín, also ran eating houses, though these were located in Greenwich Village. Petition for the Naturalization of José Chacón, December 4, 1875, filed before the Common Pleas Court of New York City, NANYC, RG 21/85; New York City Directory 1877, US City Directories, 1822–1995. Chacón later advertised in Serra's newspaper, *Doctrina de Martí*, July 25 1896. Chacón's passport applications (October 4, 1879, and April 8, 1885) do not identify him as "colored" or "negro," as some did, but describe his nose as "flat," his hair as "curled," and his complexion as "dark." NARA, M1372, rolls 231, 271. Calderín was a close ally of Serra in the early 1890s and served as president of La Liga. See Serra, *Ensayos políticos, sociales y económicos*, 157. Listings for his restaurant on Sullivan Street appear multiple times in *Patria*.

69. "Will You Dine Here, Senor? Among the Gourmet Cigareros Down in Maiden Lane," *New York Times*, February 25, 1894.

70. The best evidence of this involvement in labor organizing is the case of Margarito Gutiérrez, the principal author of the statement of protest issued by the Cuban émigrés of color in Key West in January 1881 and, at the end of this story, a candidate for the Independent Party of Color in Cuba in 1908. He relocated to New York in the early 1880s, where he also immediately "had occasion to demonstrate his abilities as an organizer," helping to resolve a dispute between Cuban and Spanish cigar makers, and laying the groundwork for an 1883 strike, when Cubans and Spaniards joined forces and walked out of most of the shops around Maiden and Pearl. In 1884, Gutiérrez was elected as a delegate for Cuban workers at a mass meeting of cigar workers (including Spaniards, Germans, Bohemians, and Chinese) to protest a new treaty that would reduce tariffs on imported Cuban cigars. He was then elected to the committee on propaganda and translation. Domínguez, *Figuras y figuritas*, 44–45; Daniel, "Rolling for the Revolution," 21–22, 258–61, 279–86; Casanovas, *Bread or Bullets*, 113, 146–77; J. S. Moore, "Cigarmakers and the Treaty," *New York Times*, December 17, 1884.

71. This is evident, for instance, in the lists of Cuban businesses and professionals published in *Patria* in the early 1890s.

72. Poyo, *With All, and for the Good of All*, 83; Abad, "Las emigraciones cubanas en la Guerra de los Diez Años. Apuntes"; Franco, *Antonio Maceo*, 100–101, 161–214; Ferrer, *Insurgent Cuba*, 59–60.

73. Poyo, *With All, and for the Good of All*, 35–51; Pérez, *Sugar, Cigars and Revolution*, 185–247.

74. "Aguilera's Burial," *New York Herald*, February 27, 1877.

75. "Carta y clave de Mr. Du-Defair, referente a la Liga Antillana," December 10, 1880, Archivo de Camilo García de Polavieja, legajo 8, ramo 1, número 68,

Archivo General de Indias. Thanks to Adriana Chira for sharing her transcription of this document.

76. Logia Luz de Caballero, "Libro de actas," vol. 1, acta 24, September 3, 1873, Historical Society of Pennsylvania (HSP); Gran Logia Caballeros de la Luz, "Libro de actas," acta 22, February 11, 1878, HSP (letter from fifteen Caballeros de la Luz members living in New York City, requesting a letter of foundation for a lodge, notifying that they found a spot for their meetings, Military Hall, 193 Bowery); Gran Logia Caballeros de la Luz, "Libro de actas," acta 23, April 11, 1878, HSP.

77. Orden Caballeros de la Luz, *Liturgia*, 26–27, HSP.

78. Logia Luz de Caballero, "Libro de actas," vol. 1, acta 67, June 26, 1874, HSP.

79. Logia Luz de Caballero, "Libro de actas," vol. 1, acta 219. September 21, 1877, HSP.

80. For the use of the term *mesalina*, see Logia Luz de Caballero, "Libro de actas," vol. 2, acta 293, March 21, 187, HSP. For the objection to fraternity and equality, see Logia Luz de Caballero, "Libro de actas," vol. 2, acta 291, March 7, 1879. HSP.

81. Ferrer, *Insurgent Cuba*, 23.

82. See, for instance, the extended discussion of the exchange between Martí and the men of La Liga over who should exit a room first. González, "Una clase en la Liga."

83. Quigley, *Second Founding*, 140–60. Even after he conceded the presidential election, Tilden supported a plan in the New York State Assembly to disenfranchise urban workers. The 1877 assembly elections amounted to a referendum on this proposal.

84. Margarito Gutiérrez, the author of the protest statement of the émigrés of color in Key West in 1881 and the most prominent black Cuban labor activist in New York in the early 1880s (and later, a candidate for office for the Independent Party of Color), also went to naturalize with Yorca almost immediately after arriving in the city. Oath of Margarito Gutiérrez, August 29, 1881, District Court of the Southern District of New York, NANYC, RG 21/85.

85. In 1876, Yorca was also the witness for Ramón Angulo, Raymundo Virloche, Ruperto Bravo, and Mariano Estrada, all of whom were or would become members of the two lodges.

86. Many appear in *List of Registered Voters in the City of New York, for the Year 1880.*

87. One of the best accounts of Election Day in New York in these years comes from none other than José Martí, "Letter to the editor," *La Nación* (Buenos Aires), January 7, 1885, in Martí, *Obras completas*, 10:101–7.

88. Quigley, *Second Founding*, 71–90; Field, *The Politics of Race in New York*, 188–218; Czitrom, *New York Exposed*, 76–101.

89. The nonpopulation censuses of the city in the 1880s and 1890s confirm this pattern. Cuban cigar factories reported almost no female workers. NYSL. According to the 1880 population census, more than six hundred Cuban women lived in New York, but only eight (six white and two nonwhite) were cigar makers. For Magdalena and other residents of 89 Thompson Street, see 1880 Census, NARA T9, roll 872, Enumeration District 118, 232B.

90. On this concept, see Gardner, *Qualities of a Citizen*, esp. 13–14.

91. Simmons, *Crescent City Girls*, 7–9, 58–59, 68–78.

92. "Will You Dine Here, Senor? Among the Gourmet Cigareros Down in Maiden Lane," *New York Times*, February 25, 1894.

93. "Passenger List of the Steamship *City of Washington*," June 4, 1879, NARA 36, M237, roll 418, list number 560.

94. "Passenger List of the *SS Saratoga*," September 25, 1879, NARA 36, M237, roll 420, list number 1090.

95. Birth Certificate for Lucas Peñalver, October 18, 1879, MACNY.

96. This is actually somewhat difficult to reconstruct. But see Fraser, *African American Midwifery*; Hernández Sainz and Martel Martínez, "La práctica social de las comadronas"; Jimeno Herld, "De Cienfuegos," *La Fraternidad*, January 31, 1889. For the relationship between *recibidoras* (unlicensed midwives), *comadronas (licensed midwives)*, and doctors in Cuba, see various entries in *Anales de la Academia de Ciencias Médicas*, 1895; Valdés, *Memoria oficial*, 292–94.

97. Birth Certificate for Lucas Peñalver, October 18, 1879, MACNY; Todd, *Julio José Henna, 1848–1924*.

98. Consider also the case of Margarita, a young woman from Matanzas who lived temporarily with the Sandovals at 89 Thompson Street after the death of her first husband. New York City Directory, 1876, US City Directories, 1822–1995. In October 1876, as Yorca was busy rounding up cigar makers and marching them to swear loyalty to the US Constitution at the Federal Courthouse, Margarita gave birth to a child in an apartment that she shared with a cigar maker named Felipe Olave, a future member of the Sol de Cuba lodge. The birth certificate for the baby reports that the child was born with the help of a white Cuban doctor named José E. Ramos. Birth Certificate for Felipe Guadalupe Olabe, October 12, 1876, MACNY. Ramos would return to Havana after the war, joining the faculty of medicine at the university and becoming a member of the Academy of Medical Sciences. *Anales de la Academia de Ciencias Médicas*, 1893, 12–13. This is just one of many similar instances. Other doctors who appear on birth certificates of babies born to émigrés of color include the Cubans Enrique Agramonte, J. A. Álvarez, E. J. Sarlabous, and a Chilean named J. Hermida. Álvarez also appears on several death certificates of children in this community.

99. Crowell, "The Midwives of New York"; Leavitt, *Brought to Bed*; Dye, "Modern Obstetrics and Working-Class Women."

100. Cowling, *Conceiving Freedom*, esp. 151–73. We can glimpse something of the kinds of the expressions of community that might have passed between Henna and the Peñalver family in a later episode, "Gacetillas," *Doctrina de Marti*, July 15, 1897; Birth Certificate for Francisco G. Zayas, July 12, 1897, MACNY.

101. See entry for G. Heredia, "Passenger List for *SS Newport*," September 3, 1883, NARA 36, M237, roll 469, line 18, list number 1128. According to the 1900 Census, NARA T623, Enumeration District 0677,5A, the couple's daughter, Consuelo Serra, was born in July 1884, which could be explained if Heredia arrived in New York in September 1883 and remained for several months. The 1905 New York State Census Assembly District 17, Election District 20, 27, NYSA, suggests that Consuelo was born in 1886. This would be possible if Heredia stayed with Serra in New York until he went to Kingston in June 1885. The certified copy of the couple's marriage record that appears in Heredia's university file, however, is dated January 1884. If we presume that she was the person who requested this copy, she would either have had to conceive Consuelo before January 1884, suggesting a birth date in 1884, or would have had to travel abroad a second time in order to conceive Consuelo, perhaps in Jamaica, which could yield a birth date in 1886. "Expediente para la expedición del título de comadrona a la

morena María Gertrudis Heredia" (1890), Fondo Instrucción Pública, legajo 570, no. 34, 762, ANC.

102. Rafael Serra, "En defensa propia II," *La Igualdad*, March 30, 1893.

103. This report appears in "The Cuban Revolutionists," *New York Times*, August 20, 1883. Even more visible in these events than Serra was Morúa, the man who had been Serra's mentor in Matanzas, but with whom he had quarreled in Key West. Morúa allied himself with several of the leading military veterans from the Ten Years' War and worked as a journalist at the main nationalist newspapers in New York. Morúa, "Ideas sobre la política del último movimiento" (originally published in *El Separatista*, New York, March 5–June 25, 1887)," in *Vida pública de Martín Morúa Delgado*, 62–72; Trujillo, *Apuntes históricos*, 8–10; Tinajero, *El Lector*, 64.

104. Serra reports being summoned to the Griffou in a letter from Crombet. Rafael Serra, "En defensa propia II," *La Igualdad*, March 30, 1893. Padrón Valdés, *El general Flor Crombet*, includes a description of an exchange between a cigar worker and Crombet that suggests that the generals held meetings with workers and volunteers in their hotel. Hernández, "El periodo revolucionario de 1879 a 1895," 32, reproduces the letter from Ramón Rubiera de Armas to Hernández with the names of a group of men embarked to Jamaica, including Serra and Marcelino Piedra (a future member of Sol de Cuba and La Liga). The hotel appears on the 1880 Census, NARA T9, roll 874, Enumeration District 174, 52B.

105. Hernández, "El período revolucionario de 1879 a 1895."

106. Ramírez, "El vínculo de Martí con el Plan Gómez-Maceo"; Hernández, "El periodo revolucionario de 1879 a 1895," 26–30. On the underwear episode, see Lomas, *Translating Empire*, 242–43; Quesada y Miranda, *Así fue Martí*, 26–27; Plochet and Plochet Lardoeyt, *El capitán Plochet recuera a José Martí*, 16. The original quotation is, "No solamente no puedo usar sayas, sino que soy tan hombre que no quepo en los calzones."

107. Hernández, "El período revolucionario de 1879 a 1895," 30–34.

108. Ferrer Cuevas, *José Maceo*, 41.

109. Sotero Figueroa, "Calle la pasión y hable la sinceridad III," *Doctrina de Martí*, November 10, 1896. Figueroa objected to this accusation, and to a similar insinuation by Enrique Trujillo. Trujillo, *Apuntes históricos*, 18–20.

110. Holt, *Children of Fire*, 177–81.

111. For their residence at this address, see Application for Admission of Gerónimo Bonilla, October 22, 1884, NANYC, RG 21/85. At the time, Juan was a young teenager and likely to be living with his older brother. For their previous relationship with Rencurrel, see 1870 Census, NARA M593, roll 132, 361B. For their role in the San Manuel, see "Local Gossip," *New York Age*, January 21, 1888; *Doctrina de Martí*, August 31, 1897. For Sol de Cuba, see "Masonic Elections," *New York Age*, December 24, 1887; Certificate of Marriage for John Bonilla and Dionisia Apodaca, November 18, 1889, MACNY. Dionisia's birth mother was named Paula. Certificate of Death, Mrs. Apodaca Bonilla, April 9, 1897, MACNY. But she had been raised by her father's second wife, Josefa Blanco, also known as Pepilla. See "Dionisia Apodaca de Bonilla," *Doctrina de Martí*, April 15, 1897; Certificate of Marriage for Geronimo Bonilla and Isabel de Acosta, August 8, 1889, MACNY.

CHAPTER 4: CONVERGENCE

1. Declarations of Rafael Serra, Gregorio Graupera Portillo, Dionicio Borrón, and Severino Cortés, October 10, 1888, Superior Court of the County of New York, NANYC, RG 21/85. There may have been two more men with them as well. See the declaration of Pablo Beato, a member of Sol de Cuba lodge, on the same day. Beato's witness, Marcelino Piedra, was also an officer in Sol de Cuba, had been a member, along with Serra, of the 1885 expedition, and was also an officer in the political club led Bonilla and Serra, described below. "De Nueva York," *La Fraternidad*, October 10, 1888.

2. "De New York," *La Fraternidad*, November 20, 1888; Eneerg, "Political Pointers," *New York Age*, September 8, 1888; Eneerg, "Political Pointers," *New York Age*, August 25, 1888; "Correspondencia, Nueva York," *La Fraternidad*, July 9, 1888. "Eneerg" was clearly a pseudonym, possibly for William C. Greene (whose last name backward would be Eneerg), a member of St. Philip's Church and a Republican activist. For information on Greene, see Eneerg, "Political Pointers," *New York Age*, October 13, 1888; "St. Philip's Sunday School," *New York Age*, June 20, 1891. On black Republican organizing in New York, see Peterson, *Black Gotham*, 363–73. On similar political clubs in other parts of the urban North, see Bergeson-Lockwood, *Race over Party*.

3. For the full explanation of this program, see his "Letter to General Máximo Gómez, 16 de diciembre, 1887," in Martí, *Obras completas*, 1:216–22. For the quote about kneading the dough of the republic, see the text of Martí's speech at the Masonic Temple, October 10, 1887, in Martí, *Obras completas*, 4:220.

4. This letter is reproduced in Martí, *Obras completas*, 1:226. On the anniversary celebration in 1888, see Trujillo, *Apuntes históricos*, 34.

5. Martí, "Rafael Serra: para un libro," *Patria*, March 26, 1892.

6. Pérez, *To Die in Cuba*, 75–76. Serra wrote that the men who followed Maceo to Kingston knew they would suffer hunger, foul weather, rugged landscapes, prison, and even death, yet "as if made of iron," they "valiantly awaited the moment of sacrifice." Serra, *Ecos del alma*, 5.

7. Deschamps Chapeaux, *Rafael Serra*, 42.

8. In particular, Serra was critical of his former mentor, Morúa, whom he accused of this kind of "self love" and "vanity" in seeking to attach himself to the highest-ranking officers. Rafael Serra, "En defensa propia III," *La Igualdad*, April 1, 1893.

9. Deschamps Chapeaux, *Rafael Serra*, 43.

10. The quote is from Morúa Delgado, "Ideas sobre la política del último movimiento" *El Separatista*, March 5–June 25, 1887, reprinted in Morúa, *Vida pública de Martín Morúa Delgado*, 101–5. For the importance and meanings of poets who "strummed their lyres" on the field of battle and the explicit link to the Greek poet Pindar, see José Martí, "Heredia," *El Economista Americano*, July 1888, reprinted in Martí, *Obras completas*, 5:133–39. For examples of the phrase "strum his lyre" in nationalist poetry, see "La estación del norte" and "Niágara," in Heredia, *Poesías de José María Heredia*, 53, 104; Olmedo, *La Victoria de Junín*.

11. Despradel, *Rafael Serra*, 42. In English this quote is often translated "same race."

12. Serra, *Ecos del alma*, 4, 5.

13. Ibid., 13, 18.

14. Ibid., 8, 19–20.
15. Ibid., 11.
16. Ibid., 6, 8, 10–11.
17. Franco, *Antonio Maceo*, 245–90; Cordero Michel, "La prisión de Máximo Gómez." On Maceo and Gómez in New Orleans, see Scott, *Degrees of Freedom*, 76.
18. Hernández, "El período revolucionario de 1879 a 1895," 40–41; Morúa, *Vida pública de Martín Morúa Delgado*, 103–5; Franco, *Antonio Maceo*, 288–91.
19. Poyo, *With All, and for the Good of All*, 70–94.
20. Senior, *Dying to Better Themselves*, 63–81.
21. "Special," *Daily Gleaner*, March 9, 1885. When a group of Cubans tried, unsuccessfully, to hijack the steamship *San Jacinto* in Colón harbor in 1884, hoping to force the captain to take them and their cache of weapons to Cuba, they briefly turned the ship's passengers, "most of whom were Jamaicans," into hostages. Morúa, *Vida pública de Martín Morúa Delgado*, 78–80.
22. These small producers included Antonio Maceo's wife (with whom Serra apparently became friends), his mother, and the families of several of his brothers. See Franco, *Antonio Maceo*, 268. On the exile community in Haiti, the racial politics of colonial reform, and the *Florence* affair, see Smith, *Liberty, Fraternity, Exile*, 185–89, 229. On contacts between Maceo's supporters and Haitian exiles, see Zacaïr, "Haiti on His Mind."
23. Martín Morúa Delgado, "Remenicencia," *Cuba y América* 6, no. 5 (January 12, 1902): 62, 67.
24. For Morúa's account of the company's misadventures in Panama, see Morúa, *Vida pública de Martín Morúa Delgado*, 107–12 (quote on 109); Peris Menchieta, *De Madrid a Panamá*, 132–49; Nelson, *Five Years at Panama*, 7, 136–42.
25. Hernández, "El período revolucionario de 1879 a 1895," 43–44.
26. Ibid., 46; Morúa, *Vida pública de Martín Morúa Delgado*, 119–20.
27. Padrón Valdés, *El general Flor Crombet*, 133–53; Foner, *Antonio Maceo*, 128–32. On February 25, 1887, Crombet (then in Bohio, Panama) addressed a letter to Serra in Bas Obispo, reprinted in Despradel, *Rafael Serra*, 39–40.
28. They may well be visible, too, in Serra's "Ideas and pensamientos," published in Kingston in 1886, and cited in Trelles, "Bibliografía de autores de la raza de color de Cuba." I have not been able to locate a copy of this work.
29. Deschamps Chapeaux, *Rafael Serra*, 43.
30. Casanovas, *Bread or Bullets*, 168–69; Poyo, *With All, and for the Good of All*, 74–94.
31. Avrich, *The Haymarket Tragedy*.
32. Daniel, "Rolling for the Revolution," 253; Casanovas, *Bread or Bullets*, 178–202.
33. "Local Gossip," *New York Freeman*, August 21, 1886; "Grammar School No. 80," *New York Age*, June 25, 1887; "Local Gossip," *New York Freeman*, August 6, 1887.
34. "The West Indian Abroad," *New York Globe*, February 2, 1884. By this he probably meant, at least in part, that African American leaders should develop their ties with prominent men of color on the islands as a way of preparing themselves to serve as diplomatic representatives to Santo Domingo or Haiti, the highest political appointments available to black men at the time. Derrick seems to have seen the Cubans living near his church as a resource for building his own ties to leading mulatto military leaders in Cuba and Santo Domingo, and his outreach to counterparts in the Caribbean. We know, for instance, that he recruited Margarito

Gutiérrez to help translate his correspondence with the mulatto Dominican general Gregorio Luperón. "Personal and General Notes," *Daily Picayune*, May 10, 1887; Domínguez, *Figuras y figuritas*, 43.

35. "Funerals at Bethel Church," *New York Freeman*, December 25, 1886.

36. Julian Ralph, "New York Notes," *Milwaukee Sentinel*, November 21, 1886.

37. "Local Gossip," *New York Freeman*, December 25, 1886.

38. "Local Gossip," *New York Freeman*, February 12, 1887; "Grand Army Notes," *New York Freeman*, February 19, 1887.

39. "Odd Fellows' Celebration, Forty-Fifth Anniversary of the Order," *New York Age*, March 10, 1888; "Masonic Elections," *New York Age*, December 24, 1887; "Local Gossip," *New York Age*, January 21, 1888.

40. Horrego Estuch, *Juan Gualberto Gómez*, 8–19.

41. Ibid., 29–37; Risquet, *Rectificaciones*, 106–9. Details of a 1885 case brought by José Beltran against a café owner in Pinar del Río appear in *Gaceta de la Habana*, November 19, 1887.

42. The director of the newspaper, Santiago Pérez, was the president of the Directorio, originally founded in 1885. A "directory"or listing with the names and addresses of the leaders of each club was a regular feature of the paper.

43. Deschamps Chapeaux, *El negro en el periodismo*, 52–62.

44. The logistics of fund-raising and distribution were by no means easy, and reports in the newspaper show considerable frustration with readers who pledged donations but did not produce the money. It was not their business, the editors announced, to "put anyone in evidence," but soon they would make the list of donors public and recommended that all who had pledged send their money "to prevent any injuries." "Para la imprenta," *La Fraternidad*, August 1, 1888. Private correspondence between Serra and Gómez shows that having collected funds and sold subscriptions, the committee in New York found itself frustrated with how irregularly the newspaper actually reached it for distribution. See letter from Juan Gualberto Gómez to Rafael Serra, January 18, 1891, reprinted in Despradel, *Rafael Serra*, 32–36.

45. "Correspondencia," *La Fraternidad*, September 20, 1888; *La Fraternidad*, October 30, 1888. For another instance, see "Mosaico," *La Fraternidad*, January 22, 1889.

46. "De New York," *La Fraternidad*, November 20, 1888.

47. "Mosaico," *La Fraternidad*, March 12, 1889.

48. "Correspondencia," *La Fraternidad*, September 20, 1888. It is also clear in some of Serra's dispatches that he was following the ongoing debate between *La Fraternidad* and the Autonomistas over the legacy of the Ten Years' War, and the implications for black citizenship and political loyalty. See, for instance, his remarks on the polemic between *La Fraternidad* and a rival newspaper named *La Lealtad* in "De Nueva York," *La Fraternidad*, October 10, 1888; "Nunca es tarde," *La Fraternidad*, October 20, 1888. Whether this kind of rebuke was intended primarily for Cubans who might read the newspaper in New York and who knew Pierra, or for those living on the island and elsewhere, it seems that the opinion of this extended reading public was not wholly inconsequential to white intellectuals. Perhaps to make amends, Trujillo sent word to *La Fraternidad* that when he published Pierra's arguments in pamphlet form, he would donate the proceeds to schools for children of color in Cuba.

49. "Correspondencia, Nueva York," *La Fraternidad*, August 10, 1888.

50. "De New York," *La Fraternidad*, February 22, 1889.

51. Rafael Serra, "Herrar o quitar el banco," *La Fraternidad*, March 12, 1889.

52. "Correspondencia, Nueva York," *La Fraternidad*, August 10, 1888.

53. "Correspondencia, Nueva York," *La Fraternidad*, March 30, 1888; "De New York," *La Fraternidad*, November 20, 1888; "Frederick Douglass," *La Fraternidad*, February 22, 1889; "Correspondencia, Nueva York," *La Fraternidad*, July 9, 1888. Much of this reporting seems to be drawn from the *New York Age*, such as the coverage of Stewart's legal strategy. See "In the Lion's Den," *New York Age*, June 23, 1888. Serra's writing about Chinese exclusion may be drawn from "A Chinese Lawyer: Hong Yen Chang and a Colored Student Admitted to the Bar," *New York Times*, May 18, 1888.

54. Eneerg, "Political Pointers," *New York Age*, September 29, 1888; Eneerg, "Political Pointers," *New York Age*, September 8, 1888; Eneerg, "Political Pointers," September 29, 1888..

55. "Se acerca el momento I," *La Fraternidad*, November 30, 1888; "Se acerca el momento II," *La Fraternidad*, December 30, 1888; "Se acerca el momento III," *La Fraternidad*, January 22, 1889; "Se acerca el momento IV," *La Fraternidad*, February 11, 1889. For debates over electoral law in Spain and in the overseas provinces, see Andrés, *La reforma electoral en nuestras Antillas*; Tarragó, "La lucha en las Cortes de España por el sufragio universal en Cuba"; Mercadal, "Ciudadanos o súbditos." The rules for local elections cited by *La Fraternidad* can be consulted in Guerrero, *Leyes electoral, municipal y provincial de 20 de agosto de 1870*, 2–4.

56. "De New York," November 20, 1888.

57. Serra, *Ensayos políticos*, 53.

58. Ibid., 18, 19, 22. This kind of argument would have been familiar to readers of *La Fraternidad*, which served as an unofficial organ of the sociedades de color on the island. More often than not, discussions of the sociedades in the paper reflected bitter disillusionment with the conduct of the class of color, especially the "feverish agitation for all that has to do with dancing, which dominates the young people of color," and other evidence of the deplorable moral state of the class of color. Writers emphasized the desperate need to "improve our customs, to elevate our concept of true dignity, create, in one word, the home, the sacred and true home of the modern man, surrounded by consideration and respect, at whose threshold, as if before an impregnable granite wall, any infamous treachery shatters, and in whose august precincts the poisonous vapor of concupiscence and dishonor can never penetrate." This fundamental task of uplift would be possible, the writers in *La Fraternidad* argued, if the government would only live up to its obligation to provide schools, and if the sociedades, rather than focusing exclusively on recreation, would take on the task of instruction, the "object for which they were created." B. F., "¡Alerta! ¡Alerta!," *La Fraternidad*, November 10, 1888; Miguel Failde and Raimundo Valenzuela, "Complacidos," *La Fraternidad*, July 31, 1888; Cosme Castaño, "Correspondencia, de Regla," *La Fraternidad*, October 10, 1888; Gimeno Herld, "De Cienfuegos," *La Fraternidad*, November 20, 1888; "El hogar," *La Fraternidad*, September 10, 1888; "Inexplicable conducta," *La Fraternidad*, November 10, 1888; "Mal camino," *La Fraternidad*, August 1, 1888; "Pan y baile," *La Fraternidad*, December 10, 1888.

59. T. Thomas Fortune, "The Afro-American League," *New York Freeman*, June 4, 1887; Thornbrough, "The National Afro-American League"; Alexander, *An Army of Lions.*

60. José Martí, "Lectura en Steck Hall, January 24, 1880," in *Obras completas*, 4:201–4.

61. Martí's birthday dinner at Delmonico's in 1895, hosted by wealthy Cuban expatriates, is the stuff of legend. But the logs kept by private detectives hired to track his movements in 1880 show several meals at the restaurant. Estrade, *Martí en su siglo y en el nuestro*, 65–66.

62. Casasús, *La emigración cubana*, 200; Pérez, *Cuba between Empires*, 15. The figure who more closely aligned with this kind of popular nationalism in New York (the counterpart to Juan María Reyes in Key West) was Ramón Rubiera de Armas, a journalist and factory reader who had been a key supporter of the Maceo-Gómez expedition. See "Has Become Very Devout," *New York Times*, July 8, 1886.

63. See Martí's account of Labor Day in New York, published in *La Nación*, September 5, 1884, in Martí, *Obras completas*, 10:77–92.

64. "La revolución del trabajo," in Martí, *Obras completas*, 10:393–99.

65. Ibid., 10:313–17. Perhaps the only thing that might have predicted his later partnership with Serra was Martí's firm support for universal manhood suffrage. He saw the solution to this problem in education, not disenfranchisement.

66. Ibid., 10:411–17, 445–59; Conway, "The Limits of Analogy."

67. Martí, *Obras completas*, 11:96.

68. Ibarra, "Martí and Socialism"; Conway, "The Limits of Analogy"; Martí, *Obras completas*, 11:237, 262–64, 436–37.

69. Serra, *Ensayos políticos*, 34–35.

70. Ibid., 40.

71. Ibid., 41–42.

72. José Martí, "Mi amigo Serra," March 1889, in *Obras completas*, 20:345–46.

73. Ibid.

74. José Martí, "Mi amigo querido" (Juan Bonilla), November 21, 1889, in *Obras completas*, 20:359.

75. Manuel de Jesús González, "El Maestro," *Patria*, July 2, 1895.

76. José Martí, "Mi amigo Serra," July 1889, in *Obras completas*, 20:350–51.

77. José Martí, "Mi señor Serra," August 1890, in *Obras completas*, 20:370.

78. José Martí, "Mi querido Juan," June 12, 1890, in *Obras completas*, 20:368–69.

79. José Martí, "Mi amigo Serra," July 1889, in *Obras completas*, 20:350–51.

80. José Martí, "Amigo mío," August 15, 1889, in *Obras completas*, 20:351–52.

81. Serra, *Ensayos políticos*, 53, 32–33.

82. José Martí, "A Manuel de Jesús González," May 17, 1890, in *Obras completas*, 20:366–67; José Martí, "Mi querido amigo Juan," 1890, in *Obras completas*, 20:365.

83. González, "Una carta del Maestro."

84. José Martí, "Mi muy querido Serra," September 1890, in *Obras completas*, 20:372.

85. González, "Una carta del Maestro."

86. José Martí, "Mi querido González," September 1890, in *Obras completas*, 20:374.

87. On the differences between manliness and masculinity in the US culture of this period, see Bederman, *Manliness and Civilization*; Helg, "Black Men, Racial Steroetyping."

88. José Martí, "Mi muy querido Serra," September 1890, in *Obras completas,* 20:372–73. On this question, see also an essay submitted to Martí at one of the Thursday classes and published in *Patria,* asking whether La Liga would shift into a more combative mode when the war began: "It makes perfect sense, because there is no hatred here, that La Liga has been called the house of kindness and the house of love. But since changing circumstances tend to turn things around, since life is a flux and reflux of things that come and go, has not the day arrived when La Liga will be a refuge for wounded men, and a flagpole on which to raise our banner?" "Otra vez en 'La Liga,'" *Patria,* November 21, 1893.

89. José Martí, "Mi querido González," September 1890, in *Obras completas,* 20:374.

90. José Martí, "Mi muy querido Serra," September 1890, in *Obras completas,* 20:372–73.

91. The lectores who led the two revolutionary clubs were Ramón Rivero and Nestor Carbonell. Carbonell wrote for *El Porvenir.* Bruno Roig, a small businessman who had raised funds for the press for *La Fraternidad,* paid for Martí's transportation expenses. Emilio Planas, a former correspondent for *La Fraternidad,* and Joaquin Granados, who had worked with Serra to found La Armonía in Matanzas in 1878, were both also involved. See Rivero Muñiz, "Los cubanos en Tampa"; Poyo, *With All, and for the Good of All,* 87.

92. Poyo, *With All, and for the Good of All,* 97–99; Rivero Muñiz, "Los cubanos en Tampa," 48–58; Mañach, *Martí, el apóstol,* 216.

93. José Martí, "Discurso en el Liceo Cubano, Tampa," November 26, 1891, in *Obras completas,* 4:269–79.

94. As, for instance, in José Martí, "Discurso en el Masonic Temple," October 10, 1888, in *Obras completas,* 4:231–32.

95. José Martí, "Discurso en el Liceo Cubano, Tampa," November 26, 1891, in *Obras completas,* 4:276–77, 279.

96. Rivero Muñiz, "Los cubanos en Tampa," 58.

97. Ibid., 58–62.

98. Martí also made a point of lodging with a black couple, Paulina and Ruperto Pedroso, on his visits to Tampa. See Greenbaum, "Afro-Cubans in Tampa," 53–54.

99. Ronning, *José Martí and the Emigré Colony,* 40–65; Peláez, *Primera jornada de José Martí en Cayo Hueso;* Estrade, *Martí en su siglo y en el nuestro,* 71–88; Abad, *De la guerra grande al Partido Revolucionario Cubano,* 194–209.

100. Martí, *Obras completas,* 1:279–80.

101. These men included Carlos Borrego and Guillermo Sorondo.

102. Peláez, *Primera jornada de José Martí en Cayo Hueso;* Ronning, *José Martí and the Emigré Colony.*

103. Martí, *Obras completas,* 1:281–84.

104. The frustrations of Martí's opponents are expressed clearly in Trujillo, *Apuntes históricos,* 95–104. Figueroa refuted Trujillo's account in "Calle la pasión y hable la sinceridad I," *Doctrina de Martí,* October 2, 1896; Ronning, *José Martí and the Emigré Colony,* 65–82.

105. Serra, *Ensayos políticos,* 29.

106. Rodríguez, *Estudio histórico sobre el origen,* 280–82.

107. "El periódico Patria," *Doctrina de Martí,* January 15, 1897. On Cuban Revolutionary Party activity in Veracruz, see Muller, *Cuban Émigrés and Independence in*

the Nineteenth Century Gulf World. On similar activity in New Orleans, see Scott, *Degrees of Freedom.*

108. Martí, *Obras completas,* 2:72.
109. Serra, *Ensayos políticos,* 12.
110. Rafael Serra, "Gonzalo de Quesada y Aróstegui," *Patria,* March 11, 1895.

CHAPTER 5: CROSSING

1. Club Las Dos Antillas, "Libro de Actas," April 3, 1892.
2. Club Las Dos Antillas, "Libro de Actas," April 3, 1892. The publisher Antonio Vélez Alvarado attended the first meeting. The manufacturer Manuel Barranco and the doctor Buenaventura H. Portuondo (both also supporters of La Liga) appear on the club membership lists too, though they did not attend this first meeting.
3. Club Las Dos Antillas, "Libro de Actas," April 9 and July 24, 1892. See also "Los clubs," *Patria,* April 10, 1892. To explain my conclusion that this was a club with important ties to La Liga, the president of Las Dos Antillas, as noted earlier, was Rodríguez, a Puerto Rican cigar maker who was also vice president of La Liga. Other important figures in the club were Silvestre Pivaló, a veteran of the Ten Years' War and a member of the Committee to Support *La Igualdad,* and Isidoro Apodaca, a member of La Liga and father-in-law of Juan Bonilla. The wives of these two men, Pilar Pivaló and Josefa Blanco de Apodaca, were leaders in the women's group, La Liga Antillana. "La Liga Antillana," *Patria,* January 28, 1893. The founding secretary of Las Dos Antillas, also as mentioned earlier, was Benech, a man frequently mentioned in descriptions of activities at La Liga. See, for instance, "Los lunes en La Liga," *Patria,* March 26, 1892.
4. Club Guerrilla de Antonio Maceo, "Libro de Actas," August 29, 1892, Fondo Partido Revolucionario Cubano, legajo 44 B 1, ANC. The members of the new club included officers in La Liga, several participants in the 1885 expedition, and most of the former leadership of the Cuban Republican Club.
5. Hevia Lanier, *El directorio central;* Risquet, *Rectificaciones,* 112–36; Deschamps Chapeaux, *El negro en el periodismo,* 75–80.
6. Manuel de Jesús González, "Al Sr. Juan Gualberto Gómez," March 26, 1891, Fondo Adquisiciones, caja 23, número 1862, ANC; Juan Bonilla, "Al Sr. Juan Gualberto Gómez," September 28, 1890, Fondo Adquisiciones, caja 13, número 575, ANC.
7. Juan Bonilla, "Asamblea de sociedades de color," *Patria,* September 10, 1892.
8. The clearest evidence of this comes from Tampa, where a group of men met at the local branch of La Liga to form a sociedad de color and join the Directorio. "Desde Ibor City," *La Igualdad,* May 4, 1893. In New York, members of La Liga, the Logia Sol de Cuba, and the Logia San Manuel also formed new sociedades in this period. It is not possible to confirm their adhesion to the Directorio, but the names that they adopted, La Igualdad, La Fraternidad, La Equidad, and Los Treinta, all suggest a link to Gómez. "Presidentes de sociedades cubanas y puertorriqueñas," *Patria,* March 19, 1892; "En casa," *Patria,* June 25, 1892.
9. Bonilla identifies Pivaló and Miranda as members of the committee in "A Sr. Enrique Cos," January 25, 1891, Fondo Adquisiciones, caja 45, número 3579, ANC.

"Advertencia," *La Igualdad*, February 4, 1893, identifies Calderín as the agent for the newspaper. Calderín was also the president of Sociedad de Socorros Mutuos Los Treinta, which may have been a sociedad de color, aligned with the Directorio. "Presidentes de sociedades cubanas y puertorriqueñas," *Patria*, March 19, 1892; "Presidentes," *Patria*, June 25, 1895.

10. Junta del Directorio de Sociedades de Color, "Acta," May 14, 1892, Fondo Adquisiciones, caja 75, número 4310, ANC; Hevia Lanier, *El directorio central*, 43–64; Deschamps Chapeaux, *El negro en el periodismo*, 75–80, 86–88; "Cuestión mal planteada," *La Igualdad*, February 16, 1893; "Labor patriótico," *La Igualdad*, March 21, 1893; "Directores y dirigidos," *La Igualdad*, April 21, 1893; "Nuevo procurador," *La Igualdad*, September 22, 1893.

11. Rafael Serra, "Al Sr. Francisco Giralt," *La Igualdad*, March 7, 1893.

12. Rafael Serra, "En defensa propia," *La Igualdad*, March 28, 1893; Rafael Serra, "En defensa propia II," *La Igualdad*, March 30, 1893; Rafael Serra, "En defensa propia III," *La Igualdad*, April 1, 1893; José Margarito Gutiérrez, "Una carta," *La Igualdad*, April 6, 1893; "Aplazado o suprimido," *La Igualdad*, April 29, 1893.

13. José Martí, "Mi raza," *Patria*, April 16, 1893, republished in *La Igualdad*, April 27, 1893.

14. Ibid. On Martí's participation in the committee to support *La Fraternidad*, see Rafael Serra, "A Sr. Enrique Cos," June 9, 1891, Fondo Adquisiciones, caja 45, número 3579, ANC. He does not figure in the reconstituted committee to support *La Igualdad*. Juan Bonilla, "A Sr. Enrique Cos," January 25, 1891, Fondo Adquisiciones, caja 45, número 3579, ANC. For a note to the Bonillas written in October 1892, reporting that he had accidentally left "on the table" a manifesto and a protest sent by Gómez, and pleading with them to send it to Martí, see Martí, *Obras completas*, 2:166.

15. "La Igualdad," *Patria*, April 16, 1892.

16. "Los lunes en La Liga," *Patria*, March 26, 1892.

17. In addition to members of Martí's inner circle, the membership of the club also included some cigar makers whom US census officials identified as white, such as club vice president Leopoldo Acosta. 1900 Census, NARA T623 (New York City), Enumeration District 0909, roll 1121, 11A. This may signal an unusual willingness among some white Cubans and especially Puerto Ricans to support black leaders, and may reflect the unusually durable ties that some exiles had built across racial lines. Or it may reflect the unpredictable contingencies of racial classification on censuses for men of intermediate racial status.

18. See, for instance, "Cuerpos de consejo," *Patria*, July 23, 1892. At the time, Joaquín Granados, also a man of color, was the secretary of the Advisory Council in Tampa. Granados, formerly a comrade of Serra in the Sociedad La Armonía in Matanzas, was also the president of La Liga in Tampa. Later, the black labor leader Guillermo Sorondo would serve as the president of the council in Ocala. Simón Poveda Ferrer, a journalist and "industrialist" of African descent from Santiago, who had first sparred and then reconciled with Bergues Pruna and Gómez in the conflicts over the abstentions in 1893, became secretary of the council in Port-au-Prince. Juan Prego, a barber who may have been a man of color, was secretary of the council in Kingston. It seems that the community of readers and writers that migrants of color had constructed helped propel them to positions

in the movement that required a high degree of facility with pen and paper. "Cuestión mal planteada," *La Igualdad*, February 16, 1893; "Saludo y despedida," *La Igualdad*, June 3, 1893; "En La Liga," *Patria*, July 1, 1893. In Veracruz, the African-descended tailor and journalist Nicolás Valverde, a close ally of Gómez and Serra, was an officer of one of the revolutionary clubs led by white professionals, though deep divisions eventually emerged between Valverde and party leaders in 1896 and 1897. Valverde y Bascó, *Páginas de mi vida en la emigración*; Muller, *Cuban Émigrés and Independence*, 61–73.

19. "La sesión del Club 'Borinquen,'" *Patria*, March 14, 1892; Trujillo, *Apuntes históricos*. On their mentorship role, see Club Las Dos Antillas, "Actas,' April 2 and April 9, 1892. On Marín's celebrity, see Francisco Gonzalo Marín, "Mi hermano ha muerto," *Patria*, June 13, 1896.

20. Quintero Rivera, *Patricios y plebeyos*, 41; US War Department, *Report on the Census of Porto Rico*, 153; *El Pueblo*, July 3, 1883; O'Neill, "National Register of Historic Places."

21. See, for instance, the newspaper *El Popular*, produced at the Establecimiento Tipográfico el Vapor in the late 1880s. For comparison, see Caimari, "News from around the World."

22. Between 1878 and 1890, the right to vote for the Cortes in Iberian Spain was limited to men over the age of twenty-five who paid at least 25 pesetas in taxes on rural property, or 50 pesetas in taxes on urban or industrial property. In the overseas provinces, however, electors also had to be legally free (in Cuba) and had to pay at least 125 pesetas in tax on either urban or rural property. Governors-general also had extensive control over the drawing up of electoral lists and the naming of candidates as well as the drawing of district lines, all of which they deployed to ensure Conservative electoral victories. See *Ley electoral de 28 de diciembre de 1878 para diputados a Cortes*. For estimates of the proportion of the population eligible to vote, see Andrés, *La reforma electoral en nuestras Antillas*. On the politics of suffrage in the colonies and Madrid, see Mercadal, "Ciudadanos o súbditos." For the electoral census in Ponce, see Ciudad de Ponce, "Listas electorales," 1881, 6-606-(5,11), AHMP.

23. On the shared worldview of Conservatives and Liberals, see Picó, *Al filo del poder*, 43. See also Quintero Rivera, *Patricios y plebeyos*; Suárez Findlay, *Imposing Decency*; Rodríguez-Silva, *Silencing Race*.

24. Campos, *Guía local*.

25. Taller Benéfico de Artesanos, *Reglamento*. By 1890, the mulatto typographer Ramón Morel Campos was the secretary of the Taller Benéfico. See his letters in the Correspondencia del Ayuntamiento de Ponce, C-15-4, C-15-8, C-15-9, AHMP.

26. Two Aguayos (whose kinship to Manuela I have not been able to confirm) were authors and leading citizens in Ponce, and important members of Figueroa's professional circle. Manuel Mayoral Barnes indicates that Don Ricardo and Don Antonio Aguayo were gentleman who enjoyed prestige: "fueron caballeros que gozaron de gran predicamento en esta." Mayoral Barnes, *Ponce*, 97. Ricardo was especially prominent in the nascent tobacco industry. Abad, *La exposición agrícola*, 9, 12, 31–32, 66, 75. Their brother Nicolás was a "coeditor" of the newspaper *El Derecho*, along with Baldorioty, Acosta, and Morales. Pedreira, *El periodismo*, 374.

27. "Padrón de Almas y Riqueza. Bo. Rosario. Lista de individuos que poseen bienes," 1847, Fondo Municipal de Arecibo, caja 68, AGPR.

28. Hoffnung-Garskof, "To Abolish the Law of Castes." Marín was counted as white on the "Censo, barrio la Cantera," 1875, S-551-5, AHMP. Interestingly, this document attributes his surname to his mother, suggesting that the census takers had some notion that Vicente had not formally recognized him. This was a bit of sleight of hand, however, as Rosa's surname was typically reported as Solá.

29. Cruz Monclova, *Historia de Puerto Rico (1868–1885)*, 551.

30. Rodríguez-Silva, *Silencing Race*, 59–128.

31. Antonio Salvador Pedreira identifies Figueroa as the director of *El Eco de Ponce* for several months in 1880 and *La Avispa* for several months in 1881, as "editor and collaborator" in the Ponce newspaper *La Civilización*, as a "collaborator" in Marín's paper *El Pueblo* (1881–87), and as collaborator, editor, and director of *El Popular* (1887–89). Pedreira, *El periodismo*, 354, 364, 382, 432, 440.

32. Secretaría, Gobierno General de Puerto Rico, "Carta Sobre Publicación de 'El Eco de Ponce,'" June 9, 1880, Correspondencia del Ayuntamiento de Ponce, G-8-4-1, AHMP; "Civil Registration of the Death of Manuela Aguayo y Pulido," June 3, 1886, PRCR.

33. "Así se hace," *La Igualdad*, January 18, 1894; Lane, *Blackface Cuba*, 133–41.

34. Jay Kinsbruner argues that in San Juan, the honorifics were used "so indiscriminately by census enumerators that they serve as an unreliable guide to race." His formulation perhaps overstates the degree to which this use was *indiscriminate* rather than part of a general system of social demarcation. Kinsbruner, *Not of Pure Blood*, 53. Astrid Cubano Iguina shows that official records were more scrupulous about the attribution of don and doña in Arecibo, with no change until the legal extension of the terms to nonwhites in 1893. Cubano Iguina, *Rituals of Violence*, 41. Adriana Chira demonstrates that the use of don was more flexible in Oriente than in Western Cuba. Chira, "Uneasy Intimacies."

35. Partido Liberal Reformista, *Plan de Ponce*.

36. See entry for Marín family 1910 Census NARA T624 (Arecibo), Enumeration District 184, 4B.

37. Francisco Gonzalo Marín, "Wenceslao Tomás Marín. Mi hermano ha muerto," *Patria*, June 13, 1896; Cubano Iguina, *Rituals of Violence*, 82–104. For a particularly telling anecdote relating to these questions, see Suárez Findlay, *Imposing Decency*, 39.

38. Marín, *Mi obolo*.

39. On passing, see Hobbs, *A Chosen Exile*; Twinam, "The Etiology of Racial Passing." On Marín's play, see Hoffnung-Garskof, "To Abolish the Law of Castes." On public and private secrets, see Twinam, *Public Lives, Private Secrets*.

40. Sotero Figueroa et al., "Al pueblo puertorriqueño," *Patria*, March 14, 1892.

41. Cruz Monclova, *Historia del año 1887*, 221.

42. Sotero Figueroa et al., "Al pueblo puertorriqueño," *Patria*, March 14, 1892. A cigar maker from Ponce named Rosendo Rodríguez appears as a contestant in a cigar-rolling competition held as part of the Tobacco Agricultural and Industrial Fair in the city in 1883. Abad, *La exposición agrícola*, 65. Rosendo Rodríguez y Rivera seems to have been born in San Juan around 1856. "Civil Registration of the Death of Rosendo Rodríguez y Rivera," November 18, 1913, PRCR.

43. Partido Liberal Reformista, *Plan de Ponce*. Men who were not eligible to vote were still allowed to become members of party committees, but party rules required a majority to be men with the right to suffrage.

44. Picó, *1898 la guerra después de la guerra*.

45. Cited in Cruz Monclova, *Historia del año 1887*, 222. Several sources indicate Marín's involvement in these activities. A witness, "el paisano Don Julián Figueroa," returned to the authorities to add detail to his statement because he "recalled that one of those who took part in the meeting the night that he took his oath was named Don Francisco Marín, a. Pachín." Audiencia Territorial Criminal, "Componte," 1887, Pieza 6, 48–49, AGPR. Cayetano Coll y Toste also recalled Marín's enthusiasm for the boycott. Coll y Toste, "Francisco Gonzalo Marín."

46. Originally published in "La Unidad Nacional," cited in Cruz Monclova, *Historia del año 1887*, 245.

47. Cruz Monclova, *Historia del año 1887*, 252–63.

48. For Honoré's written account, which communicates these sensibilities, see Audiencia Territorial Criminal, "Componte," caja 107, pieza 8, AGPR. For an estimate that 197 pardo and moreno artisans were arrested, of whom 130 were tortured, see *La Revista de Puerto Rico*, June 18, 1890, cited in Rodríguez-Silva, *Silencing Race*, 124–25. This seems to reflect the racialization of the category artisan by the author in *La Revista de Puerto Rico* rather than any explicit project to target only men of color for arrest. The judicial records of the *compontes* (the tortures) typically describe witnesses in racially inflected class terms, such as "jornalero" and "paisano," and only rarely in color terms such as "moreno." These records also treat many artisans and even "paisanos" with the honorific don, including some individuals who the writer in *La revista de Puerto Rico* would likely have identified as pardos. In other words, this wave of repression, though clearly laden with racial meaning for many who witnessed it, did not have the explicit and intentional racializing intent of the Escalera repression in Cuba in 1844 or the repression of the Guerra Chiquita in 1879–80. On the use of color terminology in Puerto Rican criminal records more generally, see Cubano Iguina, *Rituals of Violence*, 41. On the illegality of torture during interrogation under Spanish law, see Pletch, "Isle of Exceptions."

49. In the case of the slap delivered to Francisco Cepeda, the officer subsequently apologized for his behavior, recognizing that it was dishonorable to give such affront to a gentleman while he, surrounded by armed guards, was unable to respond. He offered to meet Cepeda and give him satisfaction once the investigation was behind them. Cruz Monclova, *Historia del año 1887*, 288–90. Eduardo Neumann Gandía remembered the indignation expressed at the treatment of Cepeda, which consisted almost entirely of an insult to his honor as a gentleman. He noted, however, that the prisoners who were transferred to the Morro Prison in San Juan were treated with "perfect chivalry" (*perfecta caballerosidad*). Neumann Gandía, *Verdadera y auténtica historia*, 233–36.

50. Cruz Monclova, *Historia del año 1887*, 282–97.

51. Audiencia Territorial Criminal, "Componte," caja 107, pieza 8, AGPR.

52. Coronel, *Un peregrino*, 147–48.

53. García, "Los que conocieron a Martí."

54. Gobierno Político Superior de Puerto Rico, "Application for Passport of Silvestre Pivaló," March 22, 1888, Puerto Rico, Pasaportes, 1795–1889, FRC; "Civil Registration of the Birth of Pilar Pivaló y Cazuela," September 17, 1888, PRCR. For a reference to Pilar Pivaló in later years, see Vega, *Memorias*, 111.

55. Cubano Iguina, *Rituals of Violence*, 82.

56. Ramón Emeterio Betances to Ramón Marín, June 5, 1888, in Bonafoux y Quintero, *Betances*, 128–32.

57. Sociedad del Parque Abolición, *Libres*; Schmidt-Nowara, *Empire and Antislavery*, 165–67; Rodríguez-Silva, *Silencing Race*, 112–22.

58. Brau, *Rafael Cordero*.

59. For essays on Cordero, José Campeche, and Segundo Ruis Belvis, see Figueroa, *Ensayo biográfico*. Figueroa also mentions Wendell Phillips in his essay on Cordero, suggesting that he may have been familiar with Phillips's biography of Toussaint-Louverture, translated by the Puerto Rican abolitionist and separatist Betances in 1852. On Betances and Haiti, see Chaar-Pérez, "A Revolution of Love"; Arroyo, *Writing Secrecy*, 93–99.

60. On these attacks and the countercompontes, see Cruz Monclova, *Historia de Puerto Rico (1885–1898)*, 188, 204–5. On the role of Américo Marín in the countercompontes, see Neumann Gandía, *Verdadera y auténtica historia*, 186–87. On the attack on Pachín, see Luis Muñoz Rivera, "La caida de 'El Postillón,'" originally published in *La Democracia*, reprinted in Coronel, *Un viaje por cuenta del estado*, 48–52.

61. Coronel, *Un peregrino*, 74–102; Quintana, "La expulsión de Venezuela de Francisco Gonzalo Marín."

62. Luis Muñoz-Rivera, cited in Delgado Pasapera, *Puerto Rico*, 413–14. Here he was talking about the boycott movement in particular.

63. Rodríguez-Silva, *Silencing Race*, 125.

64. "Discípulos contra maestros," *Boletín mercantil*, June 21, 1890. This article was a response to conflict between a different artisan newspaper, *El Obrero*, and the Autonomist newspaper *Revista de Puerto Rico*.

65. "Providencias judiciales," *Gaceta de Puerto Rico*, September 15, 1891.

66. Hochschild and Powell, "Racial Reorganization."

67. Friss, "Blacks, Jews, and Civil Rights Law in New York." On the Trainor Hotel incident, see "Justice: Suit against Hotel-Keeper Trainor Won," *New York Age*, November 14, 1891; Juan Bonilla, "Carta al Sr. Juan Gualberto Gómez," *La Igualdad*, April 14, 1894. On tensions over color among African American writers and the use of the term "white Negro" to describe Fortune, see Crowder, *John Edward Bruce*, 187; Moses, *Alexander Crummell*, 256. On the more famous case of Homer Plessy, also a man whose appearance did not immediately signal African ancestry, see Scott, "Public Rights, Social Equality."

68. "Manifiesto del Directorio del Partido Autonomista portorriqueño," December, 19, 1891, reproduced in *La autonomía colonial en España: discursos*, 304–14.

69. Sotero Figueroa et al., "Al pueblo puertorriqueño," *Patria*, March 14, 1892.

70. "Discursos pronunciados en la confirmación de la proclamación del Partido Revolucionario Cubano, Hardman Hall, 17 de April 1892," *Patria*, April 23, 1892.

71. Francisco Gonzalo Marín, "La bofetada," *Patria*, March 26, 1892.

72. Sotero Figueroa et al., "Al pueblo puertorriqueño," *Patria*, March 14, 1892. It seems likely that they were referring to the treatment of sovereign indigenous communities in the West, and that this idea of conflict and disappearance was largely formed through the coverage of Buffalo Bill's Wild West Show, which had performed in New York each year from 1886 to 1888, and was on a much-discussed European tour spring 1892. Warren, *Buffalo Bill's America*, 344–56. Martí had written a long *crónica* describing the show, which clearly influenced his thinking about Anglo-Saxon and Latin American civilizations. José Martí, "Magnífico espectáculo," in *Obras completas*, 11:31–43.

73. "Passenger List of the *SS Knickerbocker*," July 8, 1889, roll 535, list number 902, NARA 36, M237; "Despedida," *El Popular*, March 5, 1889; "Movimiento de pasageros," *El Popular*, June 29, 1889.

74. Martí, *Obras completas*, 10:82–86; *The Sun's Guide to New York*, esp. 240–41; Wallace, "A Height Deemed Appalling."

75. Chamberlain and Schulman, *La Revista Ilustrada*; Kanellos, "Hispanic American Intellectuals." Trujillo published on a press belonging to "El Sr. Probst" at 36 Vesey Street. Sotero Figueroa, "Calle la pasión y hable la sinceridad II," *Doctrina de Martí*, October 10, 1896. Modesto Tirado, who used 36 Vesey Street as his address as well, seems to have done the actual typography. "Presidentes," *Patria*, June 25, 1895; "Ensayos políticos," *Patria*, April 16, 1892. Vélez Alvarado made use of presses on Park Row, owned by Louis Weiss. Roca, "La Emulsión de Scott en la cultura hispanoamericana," 500. For the relationship between Vélez Alvarado and Pachín Marín, see "Palabra generosa," *Patria*, April 10, 1892. The first issues of *Patria* were printed by the Italian tradesmen Francesco Frugone, Agustino Balleto, and Giuseppe Gardella with oversight from Figueroa in a workshop on Park Row. See advertisement for Frugone, Balletto, y Gardella in *Patria*, April 10, 1892; "Los viernes en Patria," *Patria*, September 10, 1892. P. J. Díaz, the Puerto Rican typographer who composed Serra's newspaper, *Doctrina de Martí*, had access to a workshop at 115 Park Row, possibly the same one operated at that address by Alfred J. Howes, who published dozens of Spanish-language books, including Serra's 1899 *Ensayos politicos*. "Gacetillas," *Doctrina de Martí*, August 8, 1896.

76. Armas, *La América ilustrada*, 16; Kanellos, "Hispanic American Intellectuals."

77. Chamberlain and Schulman, *La Revista Ilustrada*, 1–13.

78. Martí, *La edad de oro*; Agramonte, *Las doctrinas educativas y políticas de Martí*; Belnap and Fernández, *José Martí's "Our America."*

79. José Martí, "Al secretario de la Sociedad Literaria Hispano-Americana" October 30, 1891, *Obras completas*, 20:392–93.

80. "Will You Dine Here, Senor? Among the Gourmet Cigareros Down in Maiden Lane," *New York Times*, February 25, 1894.

81. Martí, *Obras completas*, 21:399. Also cited in Lomas, "El negro es tan capaz."

82. José Martí, "Discurso pronunciado en la velada artístico-literaria de la Sociedad Literaria Hispanoamericana, el 19 de diciembre de 1889, a la que asistieron los delegados a la Conferencia Internacional Americana," in *Obras completas*, 6:139–40. See also José Martí, "Letter to the Editor, on the Character of the Cuban People," *New York Evening Post*, March 25, 1889.

83. Trujillo, *Album de "El Porvenir,"* 113; Chamberlain and Schulman, *La Revista Ilustrada*, 200; Sotero Figueroa, "Calle la pasión y hable la sinceridad VI," *Doctrina de Martí*, February 15, 1897.

84. José Martí, "Sotero Figueroa," *Doctrina de Martí*, March 2, 1897.

85. This essay was also published in *El Partido Liberal* in Mexico City. That version is the one reproduced in Martí, *Obras completas*, 6:15–23.

86. Francisco Gonzalo Marín, "Nueva York por dentro," in Kanellos, *En otra voz*, 181–201.

87. José Martí, "Nuestra América," in *Obras completas*, 6:22.

88. Martí, *Obras completas*, 6:18. This view was deeply influenced by Ernest Renan's speech "What Is a Nation?" (1882), a rejection of German notions that shared race was the fundamental basis for nationhood. Novoa, "José Martí and Evolution"; Rojas and Fiol-Matta, "The Moral Frontier."

89. José Martí, "Discurso pronunciado en la velada artístico-literaria de la Sociedad Literaria Hispanoamericana, el 19 de diciembre de 1889, a la que asistieron los delegados a la Conferencia Internacional Americana," in *Obras completas*, 6:140.

90. Martí, *Obras completas*, 6:17.

91. José Martí to José Ignacio Rodríguez, January 10, 1890, in Martí, *Obras completas*, 20:366.

92. "The 'Evening Telegraph' de Filadelfia," *Patria*, August 13, 1892.

93. "Ensayos políticos," *Patria*, April 16, 1892.

94. José Martí to Sotero Figueroa, December 12, 1890, in Martí, *Obras completas*, 20:376–77.

95. Figueroa, Sotero, "Calle la pasión y hable la sinceridad, VII," *Doctrina de Martí*, March 2, 1897. Martí and his allies seem to have attempted something similar with the resolutely elite Hispanic American Benevolent Society, a charity organization. In early 1893, *Patria* noted that Gerónimo Bonilla had become the first black Cuban to apply for membership in the society, and celebrated the inclusion of rich and poor as well as black and white at a society fund-raiser. "En casa," *Patria*, February 14, 1893. The cost of membership (sixty cents each month, paid in advance), however, probably reduced the pressure to democratize the organization during the deep recession of 1894. "Sociedad de Beneficiencia Hispano-Americana," *Patria*, October 24, 1894.

96. "El periódico Patria," *Doctrina de Martí*, January 15, 1897.

97. Their address was 178 Park Row. *Phillips' Business Directory*, 735.

98. "Los viernes en Patria," *Patria*, September 10, 1892.

99. Ibid. It is notable that Serra and Figueroa sought to preserve the memory of this early, radically democratic period in the production of *Patria* in the period after Martí's death. See particularly "El periódico Patria," *Doctrina de Martí*, January 15, 1897.

100. "Cuba y Puerto Rico. Vengo a darte patria," *Patria*, March 14, 1893.

101. "La Imprenta de Figueroa," *Patria*, September 8, 1894.

102. Ibid.

103. José Martí, "Sotero Figueroa," *Doctrina de Martí*, March 2, 1897. Interestingly, the reverse was true when Marín first appeared in *La Igualdad*. He sent salutations to Gómez primarily in the name of the brotherhood of journalists, but also

"in echo of my race and my people." But the editors (perhaps cautious about inferring the meaning of *mi raza*) referred to him only as "the brilliant Puerto Rican
journalist." Francisco Gonzalo Marín, "De Nueva-York a Cuba," *La Igualdad*,
June 18, 1893.

104. Sotero Figueroa, "Declaraciones," *Patria*, June 30, 1894. Martí seemed to be suggesting that Figueroa was in charge of editorial content rather than just production when he wrote, "In your hands, *Patria* is safe." José Martí to Sotero Figueroa,
Cape Haitien, June 9, 1893, in Martí, *Obras completas*, 2:353–54.

105. "10 de octubre," *Patria*, October 15, 1892.

106. Ibid.; "El meeting de Hardman Hall," *Patria*, May 8, 1893; "Lunes en la Liga,"
Patria, April 23, 1892; "Noche hermosa en 'La Liga,'" *Patria*, November 4, 1893;
"Club Rifleros de la Habana No. 2. La fiesta campestre," *Patria*, August 27, 1892.

107. "El Postillón," *Patria*, October 22, 1892.

108. See, for instance, the testimony of the Cuban liberal, Pozos Dulces, as part of the
Commission on Colonial Reforms in Madrid in 1866, in which he celebrates the
propensity of the "Latin race" to amalgamate and civilize, and predicts a slow
process of whitening in Cuba through immigration and intermixture. *Información
sobre reformas*, 223; Stepan, *The Hour of Eugenics*; Novoa, "José Martí and Evolution." For a clearer instance of this, see the commentary on an article in the
Revista de Puerto Rico that saw the "invigoration of the Caucasian race through
immigration and through crossings" as a sign of the harmony that reigned on the
island, and of the capacity of Puerto Ricans for autonomous government. Sotero
Figueroa, Francisco Gonzalo Marín, and Antonio V. Alvarado, "La dominación y
la independencia III," *Patria*, September 24, 1892.

109. Godreau, "Slippery Semantics."

110. Hodes, *White Women, Black Men*; Pascoe, *What Comes Naturally*; Hochschild and
Powell, "Racial Reorganization."

111. Mitchell, *Righteous Propagation*, 197–212.

112. Grimké, "The Second Marriage of Frederick Douglass"; Blissit, "The Amalgamation of the Personal and the Political."

113. See, for instance, two studies from the 1940s: Rogler, "The Morality of Race Mixing in Puerto Rico"; Colomban Rosario and Carrión, *El negro*.

114. "Civil Registration of the Marriage between Sotero Figueroa Fernández and
Inocencia Martínez Santaella," June 28, 1889, PRCR.

115. Figueroa, *Ensayo biográfico*, 23.

116. Marín, *Romances*, 101–16.

117. Ibid., 106.

118. "Justice: Suit against Hotel-Keeper Trainor Won," *New York Age*, November 14,
1891.

119. Vega, *Memorias*, 109.

120. Certificate and Record of Birth, Julia Figueroa, July 15, 1891, MACNY. The attending doctor here was Joseph L. de Victoria.

121. Certificate and Record of Death, Julia Figueroa, September 5, 1893, MACNY.
The doctor who recorded this death was J. A. Álvarez. His wife was a member of
the Club Mercedes Varona. Inocencia was the president of this club. "Los clubs,"
Patria, April 10, 1892.

122. For instance, Damaso Callard, Marecelino Piedra, Abraham Seino, and Rosendo Rodríguez.

123. Logan, Zhang, and Chunyu, "Emergent Ghettos."

124. This is a point discussed at length in the following chapter.

125. Certificate of Marriage, Cayetano Alfonso and Elisa Baer, February 16, 1899, MACNY; Certificate and Record of Birth, Adel Conde, August 22, 1893, MACNY.

126. "Married a Negro Instead of a Cuban," *New York Times*, September 28, 1888. Similarly, William Ellis, a wealthy African American man from Texas who lived in New York at the time, refashioned himself as Guillermo Eliseo, a Cuban revolutionary. Jacoby, *The Strange Career of William Ellis*, 121–41. The African American writer James Weldon Johnson recalled an instance when having accidentally been identified as Cuban by white riders on a train, was treated to cordial sociability and conversation, rather than segregation and violence. Johnson, *Along This Way*, 87–89.

127. Marín, *Romances*, 16, 45.

128. *La Igualdad*, cited in Helg, *Our Rightful Share*, 39; Sanguily cited in Ferrer, *Insurgent Cuba*, 121.

129. See, for instance, Juan Bonilla, "Sombras y luces," *La Igualdad*, September 28, 1893.

130. Marín, *Romances*, 40.

131. "El poeta Marín," *Patria*, April 23, 1892.

132. "Mr. Douglass' Marriage," *New York Globe*, February 9, 1884.

133. Blissit, "The Amalgamation of the Personal and the Political"; Rooks, *Hair Raising*; Lindsey, "Black No More."

134. Carlson, "The Panic of 1893"; Waugh, "Give This Man Work!"; Painter, *Standing at Armageddon*, 110–40.

135. Gabriel P. López et al., "A los cubanos y puertorriqueños residentes en New York," *Patria*, August 19, 1893.

136. "La crisis y el Partido Revolucionario Cubano," *Patria*, August 19, 1893. See also "Pobreza y patria," *Patria*, August 19, 1893.

137. "El conflicto en Cayo," *Patria*, January 6, 1894. See also "Los sucesos del Cayo," *Patria*, March 31, 1894; "Opinión imparcial," *Patria*, January 6, 1894.

138. Club Guerrilla de Maceo, "Libro de Actas," August 8, 1893; Club Guerrilla de Maceo, "Libro de Actas," November 4, 1893; Club Guerrilla de Maceo, "Libro de Actas," March 30, 1894.

139. Hevia Lanier, *El directorio central*, 57–60; Helg, *Our Rightful Share*, 42–47.

140. Rafael Serra, "Mi querido Juan," *La Igualdad*, February 21, 1894

141. Rafael Serra, "Al Sr. Francisco Giralt," *La Igualdad*, March 7, 1893; Juan Bonilla, "Carta al Sr. Juan Gualberto Gómez," *La Igualdad*, April 14, 1894; Juan Bonilla, "Cartas americanas," *La Igualdad*, October 14, 1894; "Justice: Suit against Hotel-Keeper Trainor Won," *New York Age*, November 14, 1891.

142. Juan Bonilla, "Una carta," *Patria*, November 12, 1892.

143. Rafael Serra, "Sin desengaño," *La Igualdad*, April 5, 1894.

144. Club Las Dos Antillas, "Libro de Actas," especially entries for December 1893–July 1895: Club Guerrilla de Maceo, "Libro de Actas," February 2, 1894, March 30, 1894, June 7, 1894.

CHAPTER 6: VICTORY?

1. "Gacetillas," *Doctrina de Martí*, December 30, 1896; "Gracias a todos," *Doctrina de Martí*, January 15, 1897.
2. "Sociedad de Estudios Jurídicos y Económicos," *Doctrina de Martí*, November 30, 1896; "La Sociedad Jurídica y 'La Doctrina de Martí,'" *Doctrina de Martí*, January 15, 1897; Hidalgo Paz, *Cuba, 1895–1898*, 123–24; Rodríguez, *Estudio histórico sobre el origen*, 280–82.
3. "Spain Losing Grip," *Boston Daily Globe*, November 9, 1896. The meeting was at the home of Emilio del Junco at 141 W. Fourteenth Street. See New York City Directory, 1898, US City Directories, 1822–1995.
4. Ferrer, *Insurgent Cuba*, 141–47; Pérez, *Cuba between Empires*, 119–34.
5. "José Martí to Gonzalo de Quesada and Benjamín Guerra, February 26, 1895," reprinted in Martí, *Obras completas*, 4:73–74.
6. "Un padre de la patria," *Patria*, April 10, 1892; "El colegio de Tomás Estrada Palma en Central Valley," *Patria*, July 2, 1892. See, for instance, "Sobre los *Ensayos políticos*," *Patria*, May 28, 1892.
7. On long-standing ideas that the acquisition of Cuba was necessary and inevitable, see Pérez, *Cuba in the American Imagination*. On the rise of imperialism and anti-imperialism, see Kinzer, *The True Flag*. On the attitude of the McKinley administration, Louis Pérez sees early evidence that some in the government favored annexation. Pérez, *Cuba between Empires*, 110–17. John Offner suggests that both William McKinley and his predecessor Grover Cleveland mainly hoped for a speedy resolution to the conflict, preferring a negotiated settlement and continued Spanish government to independence or intervention by a European power. Offner, *An Unwanted War*.
8. Rafael Serra, "Alerta pueblo," *Doctrina de Martí*, November 10, 1896.
9. Sotero Figueroa, "Por la revolución," *Doctrina de Martí*, July 25, 1896.
10. "Knife and Torch: Maceo's Negro Bands Overrunning Western Cuba," *Los Angeles Times*, September 23, 1896.
11. Enrique Dupuy de Lome, "The Spanish Minister in the Cuban Insurrection," *Harper's Weekly*, August 31, 1895; "Comunicado interesante," *La Vanguardia*, June 13, 1895.
12. Provisional president Salvador Cisneros Betancourt and General Máximo Gómez both encouraged Estrada Palma (despite his misgivings) to recruit Sanguily to the cause. Cisneros also suggested turning over the direction of *Patria* to Martí's great rival, Trujillo. Recruiting Varona was Estrada Palma's own initiative. See Partido Revolucionario Cubano, *La revolución del 95*, 1:246–47, 269, 347–51.
13. Guerra, *The Myth of José Martí*, 62–88; Hidalgo Paz, *Cuba, 1895–1898*, 5–82.
14. "Senor de Lome Refuted: Cubans in This City Indignant about His Statements. Views of Editor Enrique Trujillo. The Revolutionists Are Patriots and Not Adventurers They Say—the Best Cuban Blood Engaged in the Contest," *New York Times*, August 28, 1895.
15. Ferrer, *Insurgent Cuba*, 120–27.
16. Trujillo, *Apuntes históricos*.
17. Ferrer, *Insurgent Cuba*, 125–27.

18. "Pobres y ricos," *Patria*, August 17, 1895; "Nuestro partido," *Patria*, September 14, 1895.

19. Club Las Dos Antillas, "Libro de Actas," October 6, 1895.

20. José Martí and Máximo Gómez, "Manifiesto de Montecristi," March 25, 1895, in Martí, *Obras completas*, 4:93–104.

21. González, "Una carta del Maestro." See also Sotero Figueroa, "Inmortal," *Patria*, June 25, 1895; Gerónimo Bonilla, "José Martí," *Patria*, July 2, 1895; Manuel de Jesús González, "El Maestro," *Patria*, July 2, 1895; Juan Bonilla, "Martí," *Patria*, July 8, 1895; "Discurso del Señor Serra," *Patria*, October 23, 1895; Rafael Serra, "Condolencias," *Patria*, June 25, 1895.

22. "Pobres y ricos," *Patria*, August 17, 1895

23. Varona, *Cuba contra España*. On negotiations over Varona's salary preceding his move to New York, see Partido Revolucionario Cubano, *La revolución del 95*, 1:347–51.

24. "Administración de 'Patria,'" *Patria*, August 10, 1895; "De administración," *Patria*, October 9, 1895; Enrique José Varona, "Administración," *Patria*, December 18, 1895; Toledo, *Sotero Figueroa*, 69–70.

25. Rafael Serra, "Nuestra labor," *Doctrina de Martí*, July 25, 1896.

26. Rafael Serra, "Práctica," *Doctrina de Martí*, July 25, 1896.

27. Despradel, *Rafael Serra*, 22–23, 38–39; Deschamps Chapeaux, *Rafael Serra*, 147–48; "Sobre los Ensayos políticos," *Patria*, May 28, 1892.

28. The visit of New York Advisory Council president Juan Fraga to the Club Guerrilla de Maceo, to address the members immediately before their unanimous vote for Estrada Palma, suggests that this kind of political mobilization was behind his election. See Club Guerrilla de Maceo, "Libro de Actas," July 8, 1895.

29. Rafael Serra, "Al Sr. Delegado del P.R.C.," July 23, 1895, Fondo Partido Revolucionario Cubano, caja 21, número 3235, ANC.

30. Partido Revolucionario Cubano, *La revolución del 95*, 2:172–73.

31. Ibid., 1:214–15.

32. Rafael Serra, "Al Sr. Delegado del P.R.C.," July 23, 1895, Fondo Partido Revolucionario Cubano, número 21-3235, ANC.

33. "Abrumadora deferencia," *Doctrina de Martí*, July 25, 1896. For an account of which newspapers in the United States received subventions from Estrada Palma, see Héctor de Saavedra, "A Domingo Figarola y Caneda," February 9, 1897, Fondo Academia de la Historia Cubana, caja 167, signatura 557, ANC.

34. On the mechanisms for smuggling printed material "through Ibern, whose brother had a loyal friend in the post office in Havana," see Martí, *Obras completas*, 4:113. Serra was in contact with Ibern, who advertised in *Doctrina de Martí*.

35. Augustín Cebreco, "Carta de Cuba Libre," *Doctrina de Martí*, June 30, 1897; Augustín Cebreco, "De Cuba Libre," *Doctrina de Martí*, October 10, 1896; Fermín Valdés Domínguez, "24 de febrero," *Doctrina de Martí*, April 20, 1898.

36. Helg, *Our Rightful Share*, 60; Pérez, *Cuba between Empires*, 133–35.

37. For more detail on each of these stories, see chapter 3 of this book.

38. Gilbert, *The Product of Our Souls*, 99–135.

39. 1900 Census, NARA T623 (Manhattan), roll 1111, Enumeration District 677, 5A. Her maiden name, Granados, suggests that she may have been related to the Serras' comrade from Matanzas (now one of the leaders of La Liga in Tampa),

Joaquín Granados. "State of New York Birth Return, [Albert] Corrales," August 13, 1882, MACNY. For Vialet, see the advertisements in *Doctrina de Martí*, August 8, 1896.

40. "En casa," *Patria*, April 8, 1895; "Gacetillas," *Doctrina de Martí*, August 8, 1896; "Gacetillas," *Doctrina de Martí*, September 2, 1896; "Gacetillas," *Doctrina de Martí*, June 30, 1897; "Gacetillas," *Doctrina de Martí*, April 20, 1897; advertising in *Doctrina de Martí*, July 15, 1897. For the Logia San Manuel, see *Doctrina de Martí* April 15, 1897. Meetings of the Club Guerrilla de Maceo moved to West Twenty-Fourth Street in 1895, and to 132 West Thirty-Third Street, just across the street from the Serras' home, by the end of the war. Club Guerrilla de Maceo, "Libro de Actas."

41. "Gacetillas," *Doctrina de Martí*, July 15, 1897; "Certificate and Record of Birth, Francisco G. Zayas," July 12, 1897, MACNY. On the role of physicians in childbirth, see Leavitt, *Brought to Bed*; Dye, "Modern Obstetrics and Working-Class Women." The accounts of Heredia and working alongside Serra come from Asociación Nacional de los Emigrados Revolucionarios, "Expediente personal de Consuelo Serra de G. Veranes," February 10, 1936, Fondo Donativos y Remisiones, caja 589, número 136, ANC.

42. See, for instance, Certificate and Record of Birth for Maria Isidora Gomero, April 4, 1893, MACNY; Certificate and Record of Birth for Juan Gualberto Pivaló, July 12, 1893, MACNY; Certificate and Record of Birth for Isidoro Muriel, April 4, 1897, MACNY; Certificates and Record of Birth for Miguel Olave, April 10, 1899, MACNY; Certificate and Record of Birth for Atney Antonio González, September 26, 1899, MACNY. See also Certificate and Record of Death for Francisca Murel, December 10, 1895, MACNY; Certificate and Record of Death for Mrs. Apodaca Bonilla, April 9, 1897, MACNY.

43. "Dionisia Apodaca de Bonilla," *Doctrina de Martí*, April 15, 1897.

44. For indications that meetings took place in the homes of Francisco Acosta, Francisco Araujo, and Rosendo Rodríguez as well as discussions of the inconveniences of holding meetings in private apartments and the unwelcome expense of renting public meeting halls, see Club Las Dos Antillas, "Libro de Actas," especially August 29, 1895. For meetings held at the homes of Silvestre and Pilar Pivaló and Isidoro and Josefa Apodaca, see "Club Bergues Pruna," *Doctrina de Martí*, February 15, 1897. Meetings of the Club Guerrilla de Maceo took place near the Serra residence, on the West Side of Manhattan. Of course, sometimes the men in these households tended to domestic tasks too. When Pilar became ill, her husband, Silvestre, found himself unable to keep up with his duties as treasurer of the Club Las Dos Antillas. This was seemingly either because he took on the work of caring for Pilar or took over the household work that she normally did, or both. Club Las Dos Antillas, "Libro de Actas," August 27; Club Las Dos Antillas, "Libro de Actas," August 29; Club Las Dos Antillas, "Libro de Actas," September 3; Club Las Dos Antillas, "Libro de Actas," September 28, 1895.

45. Club Las Dos Antillas, "Libro de Actas," July 26, 1896.

46. "A nuestras damas," *Doctrina de Martí*, October 10, 1896. See also Rafael Serra, "Buen viaje," *El Nuevo Criollo*, July 29, 1905. For contrast see the exhortations to "elevate the family" in the magazine for the women of the class of color, *Minerva*,

published by Miguel Gualba and Enrique Cos in the late 1880s, for which Deschamps Chapeaux, *El negro en el periodismo*, 85–86; Montejo Arrecha, "Minerva"; Barcia Zequeira, "Mujeres en torno a Minerva." On Martí's encounter with the anarchist feminist Lucy Parsons, Lomas, "El negro es tan capaz."

47. Inocencia Araujo, Antonia Fernández, and Julia Guerra, "De nuestras heroinas del destierro," *Doctrina de Martí*, May 6, 1898. A group of women in Port-au-Prince, having heard of a new lodge called the Order of Martí, wrote, "May ladies on their own, or gentleman and ladies together, create a Lodge?" "Gacetillas," *Doctrina de Martí*, July 15, 1897.

48. "Gacetillas," *Doctrina de Martí*, January 15, 1897. Other women associated with La Liga (Petrona Calderín and Juana Rosario) seem to have created the political club Céspedes-Martí in March of the previous year. Partido Revolucionario Cubano, *La revolución del 95*, 2:383.

49. "Gacetillas," *Doctrina de Martí*, November 10, 1896. See also the following notices of marriages: "Señor H. Rowlett y la señorita Julia Díaz," in "Gacetillas," September 2, 1896; "Señor G. J. Sneads y Srita. América A. Fernández," in "Gacetillas," *Doctrina de Martí*, October 31, 1897. Two other examples can be seen in Certificate of Marriage of Arturo Schomburg and Elizabeth Hatcher, August 19, 1896 and Certificate and Record of Birth for Working [Joaquín] Gorozabe, April 12, 1898. MACNY. This was the son of Joaquín Gorozabe, President of the Club Guerrilla de Maceo, and Maylena Bogart. The Gorozabe and the Schomburg families lived near to one another in San Juan Hill.

50. "Gacetillas," *Doctrina de Martí*, December 15, 1896.

51. "Men of the Month," *Crisis*, November 1918; *The World Almanac and Book of Facts*, 439.

52. "Gran noche de verano," *Doctrina de Martí*, September 16, 1896; "Musical Notes," *Washington Bee*, December 10, 1898. Tyers lived on West Sixty-Sixth Street at the time of the 1900 Census, NARA T623 (Manhattan), Enumeration District 1102, roll 458, 8.

53. "Gran noche de verano," *Doctrina de Martí*, September 16, 1896; "Gacetillas," *Doctrina de Martí*, December 30, 1896. On these figures, see Alexander, *An Army of Lions*.

54. On Plummer, see "Gacetillas," July 15, 1897. On the Cosmopolitan Barbershop, see "Multiple Classified Advertisements," *New York Age*, October 23, 1886. For Fortune's quotation, see "The Globe Man about Town," *New York Globe*, March 17, 1883; "Where the Age Can Be Had," *New York Age*, November 19, 1892; Mills, *Cutting along the Color Line*.

55. Logan, *The Betrayal of the Negro*; Blight, *Race and Reunion*; Wells-Barnett et al., *The Reason Why the Colored American Is Not in the World's Columbian Exposition*; Holt, *Children of Fire*, 185–237.

56. A glimpse of this is visible in the fictional account of a conversation between a Cuban man of color and an African American lodger in Johnson, *Autobiography*, 69–72.

57. On Martí's strategy as explained in early 1895, see the letters to Guerra, Quesada, and Estrada Palma in Martí, *Obras completas*, 4:73–150. For the assertion that Pierra (among other white Cubans) was a supporter of the newspaper, see

"Para que se sepa," *Doctrina de Martí*, July 15, 1897. For the invitation to participate in the Cuban American Fair, see Las Dos Antillas, "Libro de Actas," April 22, 1896. For more on this event, see Guerra, *The Myth of José Martí*, 77.

58. "Gran noche de verano," *Doctrina de Martí*, September 16, 1896.

59. Both citations are from "The Last Ditch," *Washington Bee*, April 15, 1899.

60. E. E. Cooper, editor of *Colored American*, cited in Gatewood, "Black Americans and the Quest for Empire," 549.

61. "En Honor de Maceo," *Doctrina de Martí*, December 30, 1896; Scott, *Degrees of Freedom*, 162–75; Gatewood, *Smoked Yankees*; Charleston, "The Fruits of Citizenship."

62. "Gacetillas," *Doctrina de Martí*, October 31, 1897. On this phenomenon more broadly, see Gaines, *Uplifting the Race*, 56. The indexes for the 1900 and 1910 census, on Ancestry.com, include hundreds of African American boys named Maceo.

63. Delgado Pasapera, *Puerto Rico*, 480–94.

64. Las Dos Antillas, "Libro de Actas," March 18, 1896.

65. Francisco Gonzalo Marín, "Wenceslao Tomás Marín. Mi hermano ha muerto," *Patria*, June 13, 1896.

66. Francisco Gonzalo Marín, "Mi madre," *Doctrina de Martí*, August 22, 1896. On Marín's departure, see Francisco Gonzalo Marín, "De New York a Cuba Libre: impresiones de viaje," *Doctrina de Martí*, September 16, 1896.

67. Esteves, *Estudio biográfico*, 26. For his work as a correspondent, see especially the fascinating Francisco Gonzalo Marín, "Cuba Libre: de nuestro corresponsal en campaña," *Doctrina de Martí*, December 15, 1896.

68. Delgado Pasapera, *Puerto Rico*, 496–580.

69. Sotero Figueroa, "Calle la pasión y hable la sinceridad I," *Doctrina de Martí*, October 2, 1896.

70. Hidalgo Paz, *Cuba, 1895–1898*, 13–26, 104–22.

71. On the question of land reform, see Juan Bonilla, "Una carta," *Patria*, November 12, 1892. Otherwise, see the essays "Educación y dinero" and "Paciencia y labor," both reprinted in Serra, *Ensayos políticos, sociales y económicos*.

72. Czitrom, *New York Exposed*.

73. "Colored Republicans Treated Badly: They Demand Recognition," *New York Times*, July 31, 1896.

74. Stewart, *The Afro-American in Politics*.

75. For an exploration of the political culture of "faithfulness" in colonial Cuba and its importance for understanding racial politics, see Sartorius, *Ever Faithful*.

76. Ferrer, *Insurgent Cuba*, 133–35.

77. Bergues Pruna may already have crossed paths with Serra before this. In 1885, he had been in Panama, where he had worked to raise funds in support of Maceo's stalled expedition. Forment, *Crónicas de Santiago*, 38.

78. "Contestación satisfactoria," *La Igualdad*, February 9, 1893; "Con toda claridad," *La Igualdad*, February 11, 1893; "Impresiones electorales," *La Igualdad*, February 14, 1893; "Labor patriótico," *La Igualdad*, March 21, 1893; "Cuestión mal planteada," *La Igualdad*, February 16, 1893.

79. Cited in Ferrer, *Insurgent Cuba*, 134–35.

80. "Nuestro triunfo," *La Igualdad*, April 18, 1893; "Nuevo procurador," *La Igualdad*, September 22, 1893.

81. "El Radical," *La Igualdad*, February 9, 1893.

82. In June 1893, the New Yorkers had read Gómez's article introducing Simeon Poveda Ferrer and Benito Magdariaga, two men of color from Santiago who had opposed the abstention, but had since reconciled with Bergues Pruna and the Directorio. Juan Gualberto Gómez, "Saludo y despedida," *La Igualdad*, June 3, 1893. A week later, the two men were in New York for a party at La Liga. Poveda continued on to Chicago, published an account of the Columbian Exposition and his travels in the United States, and then settled in Port-au-Prince, becoming the secretary of the Advisory Council of the Cuban Revolutionary Party. Magdariaga stayed in New York, becoming an officer in the Club Guerrilla de Maceo and a member of the Club Las Dos Antillas. "En La Liga," *Patria*, July 1, 1893; Club Las Dos Antillas, "Libro de Actas," August 27, 1895. Both Poveda and Magdariaga appear as "merchants" on "Passenger List of the *SS Panama*," June 5, 1893, roll 610, line 6, NARA 36, M237. Magdariaga also signed *Contestación a dos desdichados autonomistas de la raza de color*.

83. "Passenger List of the *SS Santiago*," March 9, 1895, roll 637, line 268, NARA 36, M237; Club Las Dos Antillas, "Libro de Actas," June 11, 1895.

84. "A Izaguirre en Managua," *La revolución del 95* 3 (1933): 269–70; "Gran noche de verano," *Doctrina de Martí*, September 16, 1896.

85. "Spain Losing Grip," *Boston Daily Globe*, November 9, 1896.

86. "El Señor B. J. Guerra y el 'Journal,'" *Doctrina de Martí*, December 30, 1896; "Claridad," *Doctrina de Martí*, November 30, 1896.

87. "Sociedad de Estudios Jurídicos y Económicos," *Doctrina de Martí*, November 30, 1896.

88. "La Sociedad de Estudios Jurídicos y el Partido Revolucionario Cubano," *Doctrina de Martí*, December 30, 1896.

89. Guerra, *The Myth of José Martí*, 68–69; "Copia del acta levantada con motivo de una cuestión personal entre los Sres. Manuel Sanguily y Eduardo Yero," July 9, 1897, Fondo Academia de la Historia Cubana, número 66, caja 61, ANC. Transcription available in LGP, dLOC.

90. "La Sociedad Jurídica y 'La Doctrina de Martí,'" *Doctrina de Martí*, January 15, 1897; Eduardo Yero, "Vientos de fronda," *Doctrina de Martí*, January 15, 1897; Sotero Figueroa, "El señor Varona y el periódico Patria," *Doctrina de Martí*, January 30, 1897. I have not found the manifesto titled "El Mensaje y la opinión cubana: Manifiesto que dirije la Sociedad de Estudios Jurídicos al pueblo americano," but it is referenced in Yero's article and several bibliographies. The contents can be inferred from "Laid Bare in a Cuban Manifesto," *Chicago Daily Tribune*, January 16, 1897.

91. "La Sociedad Jurídica y 'La Doctrina de Martí,'" *Doctrina de Martí*, January 15, 1897.

92. Eduardo Yero, "Vientos de fronda," *Doctrina de Martí*, January 15, 1897.

93. Héctor de Saavedra, "A Domingo Figarola y Caneda," February 9, 1897.

94. "Gacetillas," December 30, 1896; "Gracias a todos," *Doctrina de Martí*, January 15, 1897.

95. Eduardo Yero, "Vientos de fronda," *Doctrina de Martí*, January 15, 1897; "Club Bergues Pruna," *Doctrina de Martí*, February 15, 1897; "Gacetillas," *Doctrina de Martí*, January 30, 1897; "Gacetillas," *Doctrina de Martí*, December 30, 1896.

Similar leadership conflicts erupted within the Partido Revolucionario Cubano organization in Key West, Port-au-Prince, and Veracruz, though the dynamics of alliance and fracture were distinct in each location. Partido Revolucionario Cubano, *La revolución del 95*, 3:277–81; Partido Revolucionario Cubano, *La revolución del 95*, 5:299–301; Valverde y Bascó, *Páginas de mi vida en la emigración*; Muller, *Cuban Émigrés and Independence in the Nineteenth Century Gulf World*.

96. Hidalgo Paz, *Cuba, 1895–1898*, 140–41.

97. Llaverías y Martínez, *Los periódicos de Martí*, 88–96; Deschamps Chapeaux, *Rafael Serra*, 133; "Gacetillas," *Doctrina de Martí*, August 31, 1898; Club Guerrilla de Maceo, "Libro de Actas," July 18, 1897 and August 26, 1897; Dámaso Callard, "Al Ciudadano Tomás Estrada Palma," August 28, 1897, Fondo Partido Revolucionario Cubano, caja 98, número 14 511, ANC.

98. "El decoro popular en acción," *Doctrina de Martí*, February 15, 1897; "Cayo en su puesto," *Doctrina de Martí*, March 31, 1897; "Gracias," *Doctrina de Martí*, November 30, 1897.

99. Rafael Serra, "A los Señores Medín Arango. Leon Quesada, Enrique Cos, y Latapier," October 25, 1897, Fondo Adquisiciones, caja 59, número 4102, ANC; José Leon Quesada et al., "A R. Serra," November 2, 1897, Fondo Adquisiciones, caja 58, número 4049, ANC.

100. Rafael Serra, "Errores populares," *Doctrina de Martí*, March 31, 1897.

101. Eduardo Yero, "A Ramón Rivero," June 19, 1897, Fondo Academia de la Historia Cubana, número 41, caja 61, ANC, transcription available in LGP, dLOC; "Los hechos, el sufragio, las elecciones, los emigrados," *Doctrina de Martí*, June 30, 1897; Guerra, *The Myth of José Martí*, 72–74. At about the same time, the members of the Club Guerrilla de Maceo, frustrated in their attempts to get members to pay dues, discussed the possibility of reserving voting rights for those who were in financial good standing. Pedro Calderín argued against the proposal, which was discussed and rejected. Club Guerrilla de Maceo, "Libro de Actas," March 28, 1897.

102. Cubano Iguina, "Political Culture"; Negron Portillo, *Las turbas repúblicanas*; Cruz Monclova, *Historia de Puerto Rico (1885–1898)*, 200–210.

103. Dos manifiestos," *Doctrina de Martí*, February 15, 1898; "¿A dónde irémos?," *Doctrina de Martí*, July 9, 1899, reprinted in Serra, *Ensayos Políticos, sociales y económicos*; Pérez, *Cuba between Empires*, 144–67; *Contestación a dos desdichados autonomistas de la raza de color*.

104. On the position of McKinley, see Offner, *An Unwanted War*; Pérez, *Cuba between Empires*, 180–90. On the ideology of the imperialists, see Gerstle, *American Crucible*, 14–65; Kramer, "Empires, Exceptions, and Anglo-Saxons." For two accounts of anti-imperialist arguments about race, labor, and tariffs, see Love, *Race over Empire*; Merleaux, *Sugar and Civilization*, 28–38.

105. Pérez, *Cuba between Empires*, 200–206.

106. Ibid., 279.

107. For Pierra's perspective on this, see, for instance, "Cuba Nationalist Party," *New York Times*, September 9, 1898. See also Pérez, *Cuba and the United States*, 114–18; Wood, *Civil Report, 1899–1900*; Iglesias Utset, *Las metáforas del cambio*. For Serra's appointment, see Meriño Fuentes, *Gobierno municipal y partidos políticos en*

Santiago de Cuba (1898–1912), 32–36. There is no evidence that he returned to Cuba until 1902.

108. See Figueroa's letters to Juan Gualberto Gómez from 1889 and 1900. Fondo Adquisiciones, caja 21, número 1386, ANC; "Proposición de ley concediendo pensión a Sotero Figueroa," June 22, 1921, Fondo Adquisiciones, caja 77, número 4340(3), ANC.

109. Scott, *Degrees of Freedom*, 178–88, 202–9; Zeuske, "Clientelas regionales, alianzas interraciales."

110. "Proposición de ley concediendo pensión a Sotero Figueroa," June 22, 1921, Fondo Adquisiciones, caja 77, número 4340(3), ANC; Toledo, *Sotero Figueroa*, 97–99; Orum, "Politics of Color," 54–74.

111. On the composition of the committee, see Wood, *Civil Report, 1899–1900*, 92. The commission also included several prominent white members of the military faction, including Juan Ruis Rivera and Eusebio Hernández. On pressure from the occupying forces to restrict suffrage, see Orum, "Politics of Color," 67–70; de la Fuente, "Myths of Racial Democracy," 1999. For criticism in the African American press, see "Our Governor General," *Washington Bee*, January 13, 1900.

112. Rafael Serra, "Suplemento: Carta abierta [al] Coronel José C. López y Teniente Coronel Julián V. Sierra . . . ," *Doctrina de Martí*, April 1900.

113. Orum, "Politics of Color," 75–76. The Puerto Rican typographer Modesto Tirado won the race for mayor in Manzanillo after organizing a Veterans' Association and promising to set aside key municipal posts for men of color.

114. "Gen. Wood to the Cubans," *New York Times*, August 27, 1900.

115. For Wood's opinion that the delegates were rascals, adventurers, and radicals, see Pérez, *Cuba between Empires*, 318. For the lament that the more "farseeing planters" had been defeated, see Robert P. Porter, "United States and Cuba," *New York Times*, February 11, 1901.

116. *Diario de sesiones de la Convención Constituyente de la isla de Cuba*; de la Fuente, "Myths of Racial Democracy," 1999.

117. Johnson, *Black Manhattan*, 127–29; Osofsky, "Race Riot, 1900."

118. "Carta abierta al Sr. Juan Sardiñas y Villa," January 26, 1901. Originally printed in *El Pueblo Libre*, reprinted as a pamphlet, and included in Serra, *Para blancos y negros*, 84–98.

119. For this term, see his 1903 essay "De raiz," reprinted in Serra, *Para blancos y negros*, 45.

120. Scott, *Degrees of Freedom*, 203–7; de la Fuente, "Myths of Racial Democracy,";

121. Pérez, *Cuba between Empires*, 316–26, 368–73.

122. In 1899, he published the third of his volumes titled *Ensayos políticos*, an ambitious documentary project that chronicled the exile community in New York, and highlighted the accomplishments of a generation of activists and politicians of color as they sought to insert themselves in Cuban politics. He dedicated the volume to Estrada Palma. Serra, *Ensayos políticos, sociales y económicos*. Serra initially appealed to Máximo Gómez for help in paying for the publication the book, relying on both de Quesada and Juan Gualberto Gómez as intermediaries. Rafael Serra, "A Juan Gualberto Gómez," February 10, 1899, Fondo Adquisiciones, caja

45, número 3579, ANC. The dedication may be a clue that the funds eventually came from the delegate.

123. Rafael Serra, "Al Sr. Tomás Estrada Palma," January 19, 1902, Fondo Tomás Estrada Palma, ANC, transcription available in LGP, dLOC.

124. Rafael Serra, "Al Sr. Tomás Estrada Palma," February 13, 1902, Fondo Tomás Estrada Palma, ANC, transcription available in LGP, dLOC.

ENDINGS

1. "Palma Begins Trip to Land He'll Rule," *New York Press*, April 17, 1902; Pérez-Stable, "Estrada Palma's Civic March."

2. Orum, "Politics of Color," 93–101. Colonel José C. López, who had been one of the founders of the Club Guerrilla de Maceo and vice president of La Liga in New York, and General Generoso Campos Marquetti, who had spent part of the war in New York, were key members of the group that reconnected in Havana in 1902. So were Miguel Gualba and Juan Felipe Risquet, who returned to Cuba from Key West, where they had been in the opposing camps that fought bitterly at the end of the war. Also present were Simeón and Antonio Poveda Ferrer, who had been opponents of Bergues Pruna in Santiago in 1893, had made peace with Gómez and Serra the following summer, and finally relocated to Port-au-Prince where they became important figures in the Cuban Revolutionary Party. For communications from Poveda and López, even before the return to Cuba, see Rafael Serra, "Al Sr. Tomás Estrada Palma," February 13, 1902, Fondo Tomás Estrada Palma, ANC, transcription available in LGP, dLOC.

3. Pappademos, *Black Political Activism*; Fernández Robaina, *El negro en Cuba*. Juan Gualberto Gómez and Generoso Campos Marquetti met with Estrada Palma to complain of discrimination in appointments to the police and the mail service. Serra later claimed that Estrada Palma was unaware of these problems and quickly moved to remedy the situation. Serra, *Para blancos y negros*, 82.

4. Rafael Serra, "Al Sr. Tomás Estrada Palma," July 26, 1902, Fondo Tomás Estrada Palma, ANC, transcription available in LGP, dLOC.

5. Rafael Serra, "El problema," *El Nuevo Criollo*, October 29, 1904; Rafael Serra, "A 'La Antorcha' de Trinidad," *El Nuevo Criollo*, November 5, 1904.

6. Toledo, *Sotero Figueroa*, 100–101.

7. Rafael Serra, "De raíz," *Redención*, July 30, 1903, reprinted in Serra, *Para blancos y negros*, 43–45.

8. An account of his campaigning in Santiago indicates that he was accompanied in his visits to local clubs and meetings by Justo Castillo and Hermenegildo Galán, both of whom had been members of the Club Guerrilla de Maceo in New York. "No hay tal cosa señor," *El Nuevo Criollo*, October 15, 1904. The account of Galán's political speeches outside Santiago and the claim that *El Nuevo Criollo* was popular in the countryside comes from a letter from Pedro Ivonet (also a Moderate Party loyalist in these years) to Estrada Palma. Cited in Cárdenas, "Pedro Ivonnet: pasión y muerte de un protestante del 12." Former New York cigar maker and La Liga vice president Colonel José C. López was also part of this political formation as were Antonio Poveda y Ferrer, Juan Felipe Risquet,

and Agustín Cebreco. On the evolution of the National Party of Oriente and the Moderate Coalition in Santiago, see Meriño Fuentes, *Gobierno municipal y partidos políticos en Santiago de Cuba (1898–1912)*.

9. Orum, "Politics of Color," 101–4; Pappademos, *Black Political Activism*, 60.
10. On the dissatisfaction of the electoral agents loyal to Serra in Santiago in 1906, after a purge of men of color from the police force and punitive raids on the sociedades de color, see Serra, *Para blancos y negros*, 204–5. On the rebellion in 1906, see Zeuske, "Clientelas regionales, alianzas interraciales"; Ibarra, *Cuba, 1898–1921*; de la Fuente, *A Nation for All*, 99–171.
11. Rafael Serra, "Educación y dinero," in *Ensayos políticos, sociales y económicos*, 172.
12. Rafael Serra, "Resumen," *Para blancos y negros*, 215.
13. On the emergence of the Conservative Party in Santiago, see Meriño Fuentes, *Gobierno municipal y partidos políticos en Santiago de Cuba (1898–1912)*, 71–85. For the longer history of black and mulatto participation in the Conservative Party, see Pappademos, *Black Political Activism*.
14. While it is clearly necessary to introduce the Partido Independiente de Color to adequately depict the context of Cuban politics in 1908, and while it seems impossible to ignore the violent repression that followed, a detailed analysis of those extremely complex events is beyond the scope of this book. For a variety of perspectives, see Pérez, "Politics, Peasants, and People of Color"; Fernández Robaina, *El negro en Cuba*; Helg, *Our Rightful Share*, 162–284; de la Fuente, *A Nation for All*, 66–91; Scott, *Degrees of Freedom*, 225–52. See also the essays by Alejandra Bronfman and Jorge Ibarra Cuesta in Martínez Heredia, Scott, and García Martínez, *Espacios, silencios y los sentidos de la libertad*, 270–94.
15. Hellwig, "The African-American Press and United States Involvement in Cuba"; Gatewood, "Black Americans and the Quest for Empire"; "No Color Line Down in Cuba, Logan Finds," *Afro-American*, September 9, 1933; Mercer Cook, "Cuba Has the World's Queerest Color Line," *Baltimore Afro-American*, July 19, 1941.
16. For an account of the ways that migration shaped the political imagination of a later group of migrants who followed similar trajectories, see Putnam, *Radical Moves*. In this later case, Lara Putnam concludes, West Indians developed a keen awareness of the socially constructed nature of race because they moved in and out of various regimes of racial classification. This gave rise to a politics of racial internationalism. In the earlier case of Cuban and Puerto Rican migrants, racial internationalism was only part of their political response to migration, and this same set of insights also deeply informed their investments in race-blind nationalism.
17. The presence of former émigrés from New York, Haiti, Jamaica, and Florida in the Moderate coalition is clear in *El Nuevo Criollo*. Most prominent in those pages were the Moderados, López, Cebreco, Poveda, and Risquet. But Josefa Dorticos, José Fernández Mesa, Policarpo Mira, Emilio Planas, Tirado, and Magdariaga all received mention in the pages of *El Nuevo Criollo*, some as agents or supporters, some as political figures, and some as authors. Germán Sandoval appeared as a visitor from New York, participating in an Odd Fellows gathering organized by Juan Bonilla and Luis Vialet, leaders of the affiliated lodges in Havana. Rafael Serra, "Los Odd Fellows de Cuba," *El Nuevo Criollo*, April 13, 1905. Gerónimo

Bonilla sent at least one correspondence from New York. Gerónimo Bonilla, "Pilar Bravo," *El Nuevo Criollo*, February 1, 1906. Vialet, Margarito Gutiérrez, Mira, Tiburcio Aguirre, and Planas (aka Jonatás) all appeared regularly in the newspaper *Previsión*, the organ of the Independent Party of Color. Vialet and Gutiérrez were Independent Party of Color candidates in 1908. Morúa, Juan Gualberto Gómez, Generoso Campos Marquetti, and Juan Tranquilino Latapier were all in the Liberal Party, though Morúa and Gómez were in competing factions of it.

18. "Passenger List of the Steamship *Vigiliancia*," July 29, 1905, NARA 36, M237, roll 604, 113. On shifting immigration procedure, see Lee, "Immigrants and Immigration Law." On the campaign to erase racial nomenclature from all official documents in Cuba, see "Labor de unión y respeto," in Gutiérrez, *Páginas para la historia*, 41–50.

19. Rafael Serra, "Buen viaje," *El Nuevo Criollo*, July 29, 1905; Miguel Gualba, "Consuelo Serra," *El Nuevo Criollo*, June 18, 1905; "Takes Course While on 'Little Vacation': Dr. Consuelo Serra de G. Veranes of Cuba Is Founder of School and Professor," *New York Amsterdam News*, July 25, 1936.

20. NYC Department of Buildings, "Actions: Premises 234 Thompson Street," accessed April 1, 2014, http://bisweb.nyc.gov/; McFarland, *Inside Greenwich Village*, 24–36; Johnson, *Black Manhattan*, 58–73, 127–29, 145–53.

21. For these residences, see New York State Census, 1905, NYSA. On the continued musical exchanges, see Washburne, "The Clave of Jazz"; Glasser, *My Music Is My Flag*.

22. Guridy, *Forging Diaspora*, 5; Mirabal, *Suspect Freedoms*; Benson, *Antiracism in Cuba*.

23. Serra, *Para blancos y negros*.

24. New York State Census, 1905, Assembly District 19, Election District 3, 48, NYSA.

25. For the event in 1905, see Guarionex [Arturo Schomburg], "Bruce Grit Honored," *Guardian*, October 7, 1905. On Schomburg's biography, see Sinnette, *Arthur Alfonso Schomburg*; Hoffnung-Garskof, "The Migrations of Arturo Schomburg." For the detail about his teacher, Benigno López Castro, see Risquet, *Rectificaciones*, 162. For the letters to the editor, see, for instance, Arthur A. Schomburg, "The Negro and His Rights," *New York Times*, May 24, 1903; Arthur A. Schomburg, "Questions by a Porto Rican," *New York Times*, August 9, 1902; Arthur A. Schomburg, "The Roosevelt Doctrine," *New York Times*, November 22, 1903.

26. Guarionex [Arturo Schomburg], "Bruce Grit Honored," *Guardian*, October 7, 1905.

27. On Schomburg's racial thought, see Arroyo, *Writing Secrecy*.

28. Schomburg, *Racial Integrity*, 19.

29. Arthur A. Schomburg, "Questions by a Porto Rican," *New York Times*, August 9, 1902.

30. Club Las Dos Antillas, "Libro de Actas," Domingo Collazo, "Deber cumplido," *Doctrina de Martí*, July 25, 1896.

31. Erman, "Meanings of Citizenship in the U.S. Empire."

32. Thomas, *Puerto Rican Citizen*; Duany, *The Puerto Rican Nation on the Move*; Sánchez Korrol, *From Colonia to Community*.

33. James, *Holding Aloft the Banner of Ethiopia*; Hoffnung-Garskof, "The Migrations of Arturo Schomburg"; Torres-Saillant, "One and Divisible"; Lee, *Building a Latino Civil Rights Movement*; Sánchez González, *Boricua Literature*; Laurent Perrault, "Invoking Arturo"; Valdés, *Diasporic Blackness*; Jones, "Afro-Latinos."

34. For an interesting analysis of this historical work see Mirabal, *Suspect Freedoms*, 135–8. A poignant example of this impulse to assert a presence in the archives can be seen in the final meeting of the Club Guerrilla de Maceo in January 1899. The officers voted to donate their papers and several artifacts to the party leadership to be included in a future national museum. The minutes book, membership lists, and accounts books currently reside in ANC. See Club Guerrilla de Maceo, "Libro de Actas," January 15, 1899.

BIBLIOGRAPHY

ARCHIVES CONSULTED

Archivo General de Puerto Rico (AGP)

Archivo Histórico Municipal de Ponce (AHMP)

Archivo Nacional de Cuba (ANC)

Centro de Investigación Histórica, University of Puerto Rico, Río Piedras (CIH)

Historical Society of Pennsylvania (HSP)

Lillian Guerra Papers, Digital Library of the Caribbean, University of Florida Libraries (LGP, dLOC).

Municipal Archives of the City of New York (MACNY)

Schomburg Center for Research in Black Culture (SSRBC)

Utah Genealogical Society Family Research Center, Saline, MI (FRC)

COLLECTIONS CONSULTED ON ANCESTRY.COM

Florida, Naturalization Records, 1847–1995
  National Archives in Atlanta, Record Group 21 (NAA, 21)

New York, Index to Petitions for Naturalization Filed in New York City, 1792–1989
  Soundex Index, National Archives of New York City (NANYC Soundex)

New York, State and Federal Naturalization Records, 1794–1940
  National Archives of New York City Record Groups 21 and 85 (NANYC, RG 21/85)

New York State Census, 1905 Population Schedules
  New York State Archives (NYSA)

Passenger Lists of Vessels Arriving in New York City, 1820–97
  National Archives and Records Administration Record Group 36, M237 (NARA 36, M237)

US City Directories, 1822–1995

US Federal Census Collection
  1870 Federal Population Census (NARA M593)
  1880 Federal Population Census (NARA T9)
  1900 Federal Population Census (NARA T623)
  1910 Federal Population Census (NARA T624)
  Federal Non-Population Schedules for New York, New York State Library (NYSL)

US Passport Applications, 1795–1925
  National Archives and Records Administration Film M1372 (NARA, M1372)

COLLECTIONS CONSULTED ON FAMILYSEARCH.COM

New York Probate Records, 1629–1971
Puerto Rico, Catholic Church Records, 1645–1969 (PRCCR)
Puerto Rico, Civil Registration, 1805–2001 (PRCR)

NEWSPAPER COLLECTIONS

(Consulted in their entirety)

Doctrina de Martí (New York), 1896–98
El Eco de Ponce (Ponce), 1880
El Nuevo Criollo (Havana), 1904–6
El Pueblo (Matanzas), 1880
El Popular (Ponce), 1889
La Fraternidad (Havana), 1888–89
La Igualdad (Havana), 1893–94
Patria (New York), 1892–96
Previsión (Havana), 1908–9

(Consulted with the aid of online search tools)

Gaceta de Puerto Rico
New York Age / Freedman / Globe
New York Times

PRIMARY SOURCES

Abad, José Ramón. *La exposición agrícola e industrial de tabaco realizada en Ponce, P.R.* Ponce: Tipografía el Vapor, 1884.

Abbad y Lassiera, Iñigo, and José Julián Acosta y Calbo. *Historia geográfica, civil y natural de la Isla de San Juan Bautista de Puerto Rico.* Puerto Rico: Imprenta de Acosta, 1866.

Acosta y Calbo, José Julián. "Discurso pronunciado en la inauguración del Instituto Civil de Segunda Enseñanza de Puerto Rico." *Boletín histórico de Puerto Rico*, no. 9 (1968): 378–82.

"Acta del meeting general de los emigrados de la clase de color cubanos, Key West." January 5, 1881. Fondo Adquisiciones, caja 71, número 4253, ANC.

Aguilera, Francisco Vicente. *Epistolario.* Havana: Editorial de Ciencias Sociales, 1974.

Anales de la Academia de Ciencias Médicas, Físicas y Naturales de la Habana. Vol. 30. Havana: Imprenta de A. Álvarez y Compañía, 1893.

Anales de la Academia de Ciencias Médicas, Físicas y Naturales de la Habana. Vol. 32. Havana: El Figaro, 1895.

Andrés, S. *La reforma electoral en nuestras Antillas.* Madrid: Imprenta de la "Revista de España," 1889.

Annual Report of the Board of Education of the City and County of New York. New York: Hall of the Board of Education, 1876, 1885.

Armas, Juan Ignacio de. *La América ilustrada.* Vols. 1–2. New York: Imprenta de "La América Ilustrada," 1872.

Armas, Juan Ignacio de, and Bernardo Costales y Sotolongo, eds. *El museo: semanario ilustrado de literatura, artes, ciencias y conocimientos generales.* Havana: Imprenta "Avisador Comercial," 1882.

La autonomía colonial en España: discursos. Madrid: Los Sucesores de Cuesta, 1892.

Bachiller y Morales, Antonio. *Apuntes para la historia de las letras y de la instrucción pública de la isla de Cuba.* Havana: P. Massana, 1859.

Blas Guerrero, Andrés de. *Leyes electoral, municipal y provincial de 20 de agosto de 1870: anotadas y concordadas con arreglo a las reformas introducidas en las mismas por la ley de 16 de diciembre de 1876.* Madrid: Oficina Tipográfica del Hospicio, 1877.

Bona, Felix de. *Cuba, Santo Domingo y Puerto-Rico: Historia y estado actual de Santo Domingo.* Madrid: M. Galiano, 1861.

Borrego, Carlos, Manuel Gutiérrez, José Herrera, Gullermo Sorondo, José de Jesús Perdomo, and José Margarito Gutiérrez. "Protesta de los cubanos de color de Key West." January 5, 1881, Fondo Adquisiciones, caja 71, número 4253, ANC.

Brau, Salvador. *Disquisiciones sociológicas, y otros ensayos.* Edited by Eugenio Fernández Méndez. Río Piedras: Universidad de Puerto Rico, 1956.

———. *Rafael Cordero: elogio póstumo.* Puerto Rico: Tipografía de Arturo Córdova, 1891.

Brincau, Rafael Rosado. *Bosquejo histórico de la institución de Voluntarios en Puerto Rico.* Puerto Rico: Imprenta de la Capitán General, 1888.

Brooks, Charles H. *The Official History and Manual of the Grand United Order of Odd Fellows in America.* Philadelphia: Odd Fellows' Journal Print, 1902.

Browne, Jefferson Beale. *Key West: The Old and the New.* Saint Augustine: Record Company, 1912.

Bureau of Statistics. *Statistical Abstract of the United States.* Vol. 20. Washington, DC: Government Printing Office, 1898.

Campos, Ramón Morel. *Guía local y de comercio de la ciudad de Ponce.* Ponce: Imprenta "El Telégrafo," 1895.

Casasús, Juan José Expósito. *La emigración cubana y la independencia de la patria.* Havana: Editorial Lex, 1953.

Castellanos, Gerardo. *Motivos de Cayo Hueso (contribución a la historia de las emigraciones revolucionarias cubanas en Estados Unidos).* Havana: Ucar, García y Cía., 1935.

Céspedes, Benjamín. *La prostitución en la ciudad de la Habana.* Havana: O'Reilly, 1888.

Club Guerilla de Maceo. "Libro de Actas." Fondo Partido Revolucionario Cubano, legajo 44, B1, ANC.

Club Las Dos Antillas. "Libro de Actas." Micro R-2251, Schomburg Center for Research on Black Culture.

Collins, Edmund. *Guide to Nassau, Cuba, and Mexico.* New York: James E. Ward and Co., 1888.

Contestación a dos desdichados autonomistas de la raza de color formulada por la colonia de Nueva York. New York: Imprenta de A. W. Howes, 1898.

Coronel, Juan. *Un peregrino.* Bogotá: Múnera Editores, 2008. First published 1895.

———. *Un viaje por cuenta del estado.* Ponce: Tipografía El Vapor, 1891.

Crane, Stephen. "Minetta Lane, New York." In *Last Words*, 154–66. London: Digby, Long, and Co., 1902. First published 1896.

Davis, George W. *Report of the Military Governor of Porto Rico on Civil Affairs.* Washington, DC: Government Printing Office, 1902.

"Decreto derogando cuantas disposiciones y prácticas hacen necesaria la llamada información de limpieza de sangre en ultramar, Madrid, Marzo 20 de 1870." *Boletín histórico de Puerto Rico* 9, 384–86. San Juan: Editorial LEA, 2004.

Despradel, Lorenzo. *Rafael Serra: álbum político*. Havana: Imprenta El Score, 1906.

Diario de sesiones de la Convención Constituyente de la isla de Cuba. Havana, 1900.

Disturnell, John. *New York as It Was and as It Is*. New York: D. Van Nostrand, 1876.

Domínguez, Teófilo. *Figuras y figuritas: ensayos biográficos*. Tampa: Imprenta Lafayette Street 105, 1899.

Dumás Chancel, Mariano. *Guía del profesorado cubano para 1868: anuario de pedagogía y estadística de la enseñanza*. Matanzas: Imprenta El Ferro-Carril, 1868.

Esteve, Gil. *Pastoral que el Escmo. Sr. Dr. D. Gil Esteve, Obispo de Puerto-Rico, dirige a sus diocesanos al despedirse de ellos*. Barcelona: Imprenta de Pons, 1854.

Esteves, José de Jesús. *Estudio biográfico del poeta arecibeño F. Gonzalo Marín*. Manatí: Manatí Print Co., 1913.

Figarola y Caneda, Domingo. *Guía oficial de la Exposición de Matanzas*. Matanzas: Imprenta La Nacional, 1881.

Figueroa, Sotero. *Ensayo biográfico de los que más han contribuido al progreso de Puerto-Rico*. Ponce: Establecimiento Tipográfico el Vapor, 1888.

Figueroa, Sotero, and Juan Morel Campos. *Don Mamerto, zarzuela en un acto*. Ponce: Establecimiento Tipográfico el Vapor, 1886.

Gallart Folch, José. *Mis memorias*. Barcelona: Elite Gráf, 1971.

García Morales, Francisco. *Guía de gobierno y policía de la isla de Cuba*. Havana: La Propaganda Literaria, 1881.

Giralt, Pedro. *El amor y la prostitución, replica a un libro del Dr. Céspedes*. Havana: Ruíz y Hermano, 1889.

Gómez, Juan Gualberto. *La cuestión de Cuba en 1884: historia y soluciones de los partidos cubanos*. Madrid: Imprenta de A. J. Alaria, 1885.

González Font, Carlos. *Tratadito de tipografía*. San Juan: Tipografía "El Comercio" de J. Anfosso, 1887.

Gutiérrez, José Margarito. *Páginas para la historia, recuerdos de un viaje*. Havana: Tipografía "Los Niños Huérfanos," 1900.

Heredia, José María. *Poesías de José María Heredia*. New York: Librería de Behr y Kahl, 1825.

Hernández, Eusebio. "El período revolucionario de 1879 a 1895." *Revista de la Facultad de Letras y Ciencias* 19, no. 1 (July 1914): 1–58.

"The History of Prince Hall Lodge No. 38." In *Souvenir Program—75th Anniversary*. New York: Prince Hall Lodge No. 38, F. and A. M., 1956.

Información sobre reformas en Cuba y Puerto Rico celebrada en Madrid en 1866 y 67. New York: Imprenta de Hallet y Breen, 1877.

Instituto Geográfico y Estadístico. *Censo de la población de España según el empadronamiento hecho en 31 de diciembre de 1887*. Madrid: Imprenta de la Dirección General del Instituto Geográfico y Estadístico, 1891.

Internal Revenue Record and Customs Journal. Vol. 11. New York: P. Vr. Van Wyck, 1869.

Lagardere, Rodolfo de. *Blancos y negros. Refutación al libro "La Prostitución" del Dr. Céspedes*. Havana: Imprenta "La Universal," 1889.

Legislación de instrucción pública de la isla de Cuba. Havana: Imprenta del Gobierno y Capitanía General, 1881.

Ley electoral de 28 de diciembre de 1878 para diputados a Cortes. San Juan: Tipografía de Acosta, 1879.

List of Registered Voters in the City of New York, for the Year 1880. New York: M. B. Brown, 1881.

Maloney, Walter C. *A Sketch of the History of Key West.* Newark, NJ: Advertiser Printing House, 1876.

Marín, Francisco Gonzalo. *Mi obolo.* Ponce: Establecimiento Tipográfico el Vapor, 1887.

———. *Romances.* New York: Modesto A. Tirado, 1892.

Marín, Ramón. *Las fiestas populares de Ponce.* San Juan: Editorial de la Universidad de Puerto Rico, 1994.

Martí, José. *La edad de oro.* Barcelona: Linkgua digital, 2017.

———. *Obras completas.* 26 Vols. Havana: Editorial Ciencias Sociales, 1991.

Mayoral Barnes, Manuel. *Ponce y su historial geopolítico-económico y cultural.* Ponce, 1946.

Montoro, Rafael. *Discursos políticos y parlamentarios.* Philadelphia: Levytype Impresores y Grabadores, 1894.

Morales, José Pablo. *Misceláneas.* San Juan: Sucesión de José J. Acosta, 1895.

Morúa Delgado, Martín. *Vida pública de Martín Morúa Delgado.* Edited by Rufino Pérez Landa and María Rosell Pérez. Havana: Carlos Romero, 1957.

Nelson, Wolfred. *Five Years at Panama: The Trans-Isthmian Canal.* New York: Belford Company Publishers, 1889.

Olmedo, José Joaquin de. *La victoria de Junín: canto a Bolívar.* London: Imprenta Española de M. Calero, 1826.

Orden Caballeros de la Luz. *Liturgia.* New York: Imprenta E. Pérez, 1879.

Partido Liberal Reformista. *Plan de Ponce para la reorganización del Partido Liberal de la provincia, y Acta de la Asamblea Constituyente del Partido Autonomista Puertorriqueño.* San Juan: Instituto de Cultura Puertorriqueña, 1991. First published 1887.

Partido Revolucionario Cubano. *La revolución del 95, según la correspondencia de la Delegación cubana en Nueva York.* Edited by León Primelles. 5 Vols. Havana: Editorial Habanera, 1932.

Peláez, Angel. *Primera jornada de José Martí en Cayo Hueso.* New York: Impr. "América" de S. Figueroa, 1896.

Pérez Moris, José. *Guía general de la isla de Puerto-Rico, con el almanaque correspondiente al año de 1879.* San Juan: Establecimiento Tipográfico del Boletín, 1879.

Pérez Moris, José, and Luis Cueto y González Quijano. *Historia de la insurrección de Lares: precedida de una reseña de los trabajos separatistas que se vienen haciendo en la isla de Puerto-Rico.* Barcelona: Establecimiento Tipográfico Narciso Ramírez y Compañía, 1872.

Peris Menchieta, F. *De Madrid a Panamá: Vigo, Tug, Tenerife, Puerto Rico, Cuba.* Madrid: Antonio de San Martín, 1886.

Pezuela, Jacobo de la. *Diccionario geográfico, estadístico, histórico, de la isla de Cuba.* Vol. 3. Madrid: Imprenta del Establecimiento de Mellado, 1863.

Pezuela, Jacobo de la. *Diccionario geográfico, estadístico, histórico, de la isla de Cuba.* Vol. 4. Madrid: Imprenta del Banco Industrial y Mercantil, 1866.

Phillips' Business Directory of New York City. Vol. 19. New York: W. Phillips and Co., 1889.

"Profilaxia de la fiebre puerperal. Reglamento para las comadronas, aprobado por la Real Academia de Ciencias de Habana." *Crónica Médica* 8, no. 93 (September 30, 1891): 247–51.

Resumen del censo de población de la isla de Cuba a fin del año de 1841. Havana: Imprenta del Gobierno, 1842.

Riis, Jacob. *How the Other Half Lives.* New York: Charles Scribner and Sons, 1895. First published 1890.

Risquet, Juan Felipe. *Rectificaciones: la cuestión político-social en la isla de Cuba.* Havana: Tipografía "América," 1900.

Rodríguez, José Ignacio. *Estudio histórico sobre el origen, desenvolvimiento y manifestaciones prácticas de la idea de la anexión de la isla de Cuba a los Estados Unidos de América.* Havana: Imprenta La Propaganda Literaria, 1900.

Rodríguez San Pedro, Joaquín. *Legislación ultramarina.* Madrid: Establecimiento Tipográfico de José Fernández Cancela, 1865.

Sagra, Ramón de la. *Cuba en 1860.* Paris: L. Hachette y Ca., 1862.

Sanger, Joseph Prentiss, Henry Gannett, and Walter Francis Willcox. *Informe sobre el censo de Puerto Rico, 1899.* Translated by Frank Joannini. Washington, DC: Imprenta del gobierno, 1900.

Schomburg, Arthur A. *Racial Integrity: A Plea for the Establishment of a Chair of Negro History in Our Schools and Colleges, Etc.* Negro Society for Historical Research as Occasional Paper 3. Baltimore: Black Classic Press, 1979. First published 1913.

Scott, Alfred. *Journal of the New York and Cuba Mail Steamship Company.* New York: New York and Cuba Mail Steamboat Company, 1883.

Serra, Rafael. *Ecos del alma, ensayo literario.* Kingston: Mortimer C. DeSouza, 1885.

———. *Ensayos políticos.* New York: Imprenta de "El Porvenir," 1892.

———. *Ensayos Políticos. Segunda serie.* New York: P. J. Díaz, 1896.

———. *Ensayos políticos, sociales y económicos.* New York: Imprenta de A. W. Howes, 1899.

———. *Lamentos de un desterrado: ensayo poético, canto 1o.* Key West: Imprenta "El Obrero," 1881.

———. *Lamentos de un desterrado: ensayo poético, canto 2o.* Key West: Imprenta "El Obrero," 1882.

———. *Para blancos y negros, ensayos políticos, sociales y económicos.* Havana: Imprenta El Score, 1907.

Sociedad del Parque Abolición. *Libres.* Ponce: Tipografía La Democracia, 1896. Special Commissioner for the United States to Puerto Rico. *Report on Puerto Rico.* Washington, DC: Government Printing Office, 1899.

Stewart, T. McCants. *The Afro-American in Politics.* Brooklyn: Brooklyn Citizen Print, 1891.

The Sun's Guide to New York. Jersey City: R. Wayne Wilson and Company, 1892.

Taller Benéfico de Artesanos. *Reglamento para el gobierno del Taller Benéfico de Artesanos de la ciudad de Ponce.* Ponce: Establecimiento Tipográfico El Vapor, 1888.

Tapia y Rivera, Alejandro. *El bardo de Guamaní: ensayos literarios.* Havana: Imprenta del Tiempo, 1862.

———. *La cuarterona, drama original en tres actos.* Madrid: Establecimiento Tipográfico de T. Fortanet, 1867.

———. *Mis memorias o Puerto Rico como lo encontré y como lo dejo.* Río Piedras: Editorial Edil, 1973. First published 1928.

The Trow City Directory of New York City. New York: Trow, 1878.

Trujillo, Enrique. *Album de "El Porvenir."* Vol. 2. New York: Imprenta de "El Porvenir," 1891.

————. *Apuntes históricos: propaganda y movimientos revolucionarios cubanos en los Estados Unidos desde enero de 1880 hasta febrero de 1895*. New York: El Porvenir, 1896.

————. *Apuntes para una historia*. New York, 1881.

Trujillo y Monagas, José. *Los criminales de Cuba y d. José Trujillo: narración de los servicios prestados en el cuerpo de policía de la Habana*. Barcelona: Establecimiento Tipográfico de F. Giró, 1882.

US War Department. *Report on the Census of Cuba*. Washington, DC: Government Printing Office, 1900.

————. *Report on the Census of Porto Rico*. Washington, DC: Government Printing Office, 1900.

Valdés, Juan B. *Memoria oficial: Séptima Conferencia Nacional de Beneficencia y Corrección de la Isla de Cuba, celebrada en Cárdenas del 18 al 20 de abril de 1908*. Havana: Librería "La Moderna Poesía," 1908.

Valdés Domínguez, Fermín. "Ofrenda de hermano." *Opus Habana* 7, no. 1 (November 30, 2003): 8–11. First published 1908.

————. *El 27 de noviembre de 1871*. Havana: Imprenta La Correspondencia de Cuba, 1887.

Valverde y Bascó, Nicolás. *Páginas de mi vida en la emigración*. Cienfuegos: Imprenta de B. Valero, 1900.

Varona, Enrique José. *Cuba contra España: manifiesto del Partido Revolucionario Cubano a los pueblos hispano-americanos*. New York: S. Figueroa, 1895.

Vega, Bernardo. *Memorias de Bernardo Vega, contribución a la historia de la comunidad puertorriqueña en Nueva York*. Edited by César Andreu Iglesias. Río Piedras: Ediciones Huracán, 1977.

Wells-Barnett, Ida B., Frederick Douglass, Irvine Garland Penn, and Ferdinand L. Barnett. *The Reason Why the Colored American Is Not in the World's Columbian Exposition*. Edited by Robert W. Rydell. Champaign: University of Illinois Press, 1999. First published 1893.

Wood, Leonard. *Civil Report, 1899–1900*. 1900.

The World Almanac and Book of Facts. New York: Press Publishing Company, 1894.

SECONDARY SOURCES

Abad, Diana. *De la guerra grande al Partido Revolucionario Cubano*. Havana: Editorial de Ciencias Sociales, 1995.

————. "Las emigraciones cubanas en la Guerra de los Diez Años. Apuntes." *Santiago* 53 (1984): 143–84.

Agramonte, Roberto D. *Las doctrinas educativas y políticas de Martí*. Río Piedras: Editorial de la Universidad de Puerto Rico, 1991.

Alberto, Paulina L., and Jesse Hoffnung-Garskof. "'Racial Democracy' and Racial Inclusion: Hemispheric Histories." In *Afro-Latin America: An Introduction*, edited by George Reid Andrews and Alejandro de la Fuente, 264–316. Cambridge: Cambridge University Press, 2018.

Alexander, Shawn Leigh. *An Army of Lions: The Civil Rights Struggle before the NAACP*. Philadelphia: University of Pennsylvania Press, 2012.

Álvarez Curbelo, Silvia. *Un país del porvenir: el afán de la modernidad en Puerto Rico, siglo XIX*. San Juan: Ediciones Callejón, 2001.

Aronja Siaca, Ernesto. *Juan Morel Campos: biografía*. Ponce: Tipografía Morel Campos, 1937.

Arroyo, Jossianna. *Writing Secrecy in Caribbean Freemasonry*. New York: Palgrave Macmillan, 2013.

Avrich, Paul. *The Haymarket Tragedy*. Princeton, NJ: Princeton University Press, 1984.

Baerga, María del Carmen. *Negociaciones de sangre: dinámicas racializantes en el Puerto Rico decimonónico*. San Juan: Iberoamericana-Vervuert-Ediciones Callejón, 2015.

Baralt, Guillermo A. *Esclavos rebeldes: conspiraciones y sublevaciones de esclavos en Puerto Rico (1795–1873)*. Río Piedras: Ediciones Huracán, 1982.

Barcia Zequeira, María del Carmen. "Casinos españoles ¿de color?" *Sémata: Ciencias Sociais e Humanidades*, no. 24 (2012): 351–74.

———. *Los ilustres apellidos: negros en La Habana colonial*. Havana: Ediciones Boloña, 2009.

———. "Mujeres en torno a Minerva." In *Afrocubanas: historia, pensamiento y prácticas culturales*, edited by Daysi Rubiera Castillo and Inés María Martiatu Terry, 77–92. Havana: Editorial de Ciencias Sociales, 2011.

Bederman, Gail. *Manliness and Civilization: A Cultural History of Gender and Race in the United States, 1880–1917*. Chicago: University of Chicago Press, 2008.

Belnap, Jeffrey Grant, and Raúl A. Fernández. *José Martí's "Our America": From National to Hemispheric Cultural Studies*. Durham, NC: Duke University Press, 1998.

Benson, Devyn Spence. *Antiracism in Cuba: The Unfinished Revolution*. Chapel Hill: University of North Carolina Press, 2016.

Bergad, Laird W. "Toward Puerto Rico's Grito de Lares: Coffee, Social Stratification, and Class Conflicts, 1828–1868." *Hispanic American Historical Review* 60, no. 4 (November 1980): 617–42.

Bergad, Laird W., Fe Iglesias García, and María del Carmen Barcia Zequeira. *The Cuban Slave Market, 1790–1880*. Cambridge: Cambridge University Press, 1995.

Bergeson-Lockwood, Millington W. *Race over Party: Black Politics and Partisanship in Late Nineteenth-Century Boston*. Chapel Hill: University of North Carolina Press, 2018.

Blight, David W. *Race and Reunion: The Civil War in American Memory*. Cambridge, MA: Harvard University Press, 2002.

Blissit, Jessica L. "The Amalgamation of the Personal and the Political: Frederick Douglass and the Debate over Interracial Marriage." Master's thesis, Ohio University, 2013.

Bonafoux y Quintero, Luis. *Betances: biografía del doctor Betances*. San Juan: Instituto de Cultura Puertorriqueña, 1987. First published 1901.

Boutelle, R. J. "Manifest Diaspora: Black Transamerican Politics and Autoarchiving in *Slavery in Cuba*." *MELUS* 40, no. 3 (September 2015): 110–33.

Bronfman, Alejandra. *Measures of Equality: Social Science, Citizenship, and Race in Cuba, 1902–1940*. Chapel Hill: University of North Carolina Press, 2005.

Brown, Canter. *Florida's Black Public Officials, 1867–1924*. Tuscaloosa: University of Alabama Press, 1998.

Brown, David H. *Santería Enthroned: Art, Ritual, and Innovation in an Afro-Cuban Religion*. Chicago: University of Chicago Press, 2003.

Brown, Elsa Barkley. "Negotiating and Transforming the Public Sphere: African American Political Life in the Transition from Slavery to Freedom." *Public Culture* 7, no. 1 (September 21, 1994): 107–46.

Brunson, Takkara. "'Writing' Black Womanhood in the Early Cuban Republic, 1904–16." *Gender and History* 28, no. 2 (August 2016): 480–500.

Cabrera, José Manuel Pérez. *La juventud de Juan Gualberto Gómez: discurso.* Havana: Academia de la Historia de Cuba, 1945.

Cabrera Salcedo, Lizette. *De la pluma a la imprenta: la cultura impresa en Puerto Rico, 1806–1906.* San Juan: Museo de Historia, Antropología y Arte, Universidad de Puerto Rico, 2008.

Caimari, Lila. "News from around the World: The Newspapers of Buenos Aires in the Age of the Submarine Cable, 1866–1900." *Hispanic American Historical Review* 96, no. 4 (2016): 607–40.

Cárdenas, Raúl Ramos. "Pedro Ivonnet: pasión y muerte de un protestante del 12." Unpublished manuscript. 2012. http://www.afrocubaweb.com/ivonet-pasion.pdf.

Carlo-Becerra, Peter L. "Which Is 'White' and Which 'Colored'?": Notes on Race and/or Color among Puerto Ricans in Interwar New York City." PhD diss., State University of New York at Binghamton, 2012.

Carlson, David C. "In the First of Earlier Revolutions: Postemancipation Social Control and State Formation in Guantánamo Cuba, 1868–1902." PhD diss., University of North Carolina, 2007.

Carlson, Mark. "The Panic of 1893." In *Routledge Handbook of Major Events in Economic History*, edited by Randall E. Parker and Robert Whaples, 40–49. London: Routledge, 2012.

Casanovas, Joan. *Bread or Bullets: Urban Labor and Spanish Colonialism in Cuba, 1850–1898.* Pittsburgh: University of Pittsburgh Press, 1998.

———. "El movimiento obrero cubano durante la Guerra de los Diez Años (1868–1878)." *Anuario de Estudios Americanos* 55, no. 1 (1998): 243–66.

Chaar-Pérez, Kahlil. "'A Revolution of Love': Ramón Emeterio Betances, Anténor Firmin, and Affective Communities in the Caribbean." *Global South* 7, no. 2 (2013): 11–36.

Chamberlain, Vernon A., and Ivan A. Schulman, eds. *La Revista Ilustrada de Nueva York: History, Anthology, and Index of Literary Selections.* Columbia: University of Missouri Press, 1976.

Charleston, Sherri Ann. "The Fruits of Citizenship: African Americans, Military Service, and the Cause of Cuba Libre, 1868–1920." PhD diss., University of Michigan, 2009.

Chira, Adriana. "Uneasy Intimacies: Race, Family, and Property in Santiago de Cuba, 1803–1868." PhD diss., University of Michigan, 2016.

Chirinos, César Augusto Salcedo. "Los límites del poder disciplinario: el Seminario Conciliar y la formación del clero en Puerto Rico (1805–1857)." *Caribbean Studies* 41, no. 2 (2013): 3–30.

Coll y Toste, Cayetano. "Francisco Gonzalo Marín." *Boletín Histórico de Puerto Rico* 12 (1926): 219–25.

———. *Historia de la instrucción pública en Puerto Rico hasta el año de 1898.* San Juan: Real Academia de la Historia, 1910.

———. *Puertorriqueños ilustres, segunda selección*. Río Piedras: Editorial Cultural, 1978.

Colomban Rosario, José, and Justina Carrión. *El negro: Haití, Estados Unidos, Puerto Rico*. San Juan: Negociado de Materiales, Imprenta, y Transporte, 1940.

Conway, Christopher. "The Limits of Analogy: José Martí and the Haymarket Martyrs." *A Contracorriente* 2, no. 1 (2004): 33–56.

Cordero Michel, Emilio. "La prisión de Máximo Gómez en Santo Domingo, 1886." In *Máximo Gómez: a cien años de su fallecimiento*, edited by Emilio Cordero Michel, 379–401. Santo Domingo: Archivo General de la Nación, 2005.

Cowling, Camillia. *Conceiving Freedom: Women of Color, Gender, and the Abolition of Slavery in Havana and Rio de Janeiro*. Chapel Hill: University of North Carolina Press, 2013.

Crowder, Ralph. *John Edward Bruce: Politician, Journalist, and Self-Trained Historian of the African Diaspora*. New York: NYU Press, 2004.

Crowell, F. Elizabeth. "The Midwives of New York." *Charities and the Commons* 17 (1907): 667–77.

Cruz Monclova, Lidio. *Historia de Puerto Rico (1868–1885)*. Vol. 2. Río Piedras: Editorial de la Universidad de Puerto Rico, 1957.

———. *Historia de Puerto Rico (1885–1898)*. Vol. 3. Río Piedras: Editorial de la Universidad de Puerto Rico, 1962.

———. *Historia del año 1887*. Río Piedras: Editorial de la Universidad de Puerto Rico, 1958.

Cubano Iguina, Astrid. "Political Culture and Male Mass-Party Formation in Late-Nineteenth-Century Puerto Rico." *Hispanic American Historical Review* 78, no. 4 (November 1998): 631–62.

———. *Rituals of Violence in Nineteenth-Century Puerto Rico: Individual Conflict, Gender, and the Law*. Gainesville: University Press of Florida, 2006.

Czitrom, Daniel. *New York Exposed: The Gilded Age Police Scandal That Launched the Progressive Era*. Oxford: Oxford University Press, 2016.

Daniel, Evan Matthew. "Rolling for the Revolution: A Transnational History of Cuban Cigar Makers in Havana, Florida, and New York City, 1853–1895." PhD diss., New School University, 2010.

Darnton, Robert. *The Great Cat Massacre: And Other Episodes in French Cultural History*. New York: Basic Books, 2010.

Dávila Santiago, Ruben. *Teatro obrero en Puerto Rico*. Río Piedras: Editorial Edil, 1985.

Davis, Natalie Zemon. *The Return of Martin Guerre*. Cambridge, MA: Harvard University Press, 1984.

de la Fuente, Alejandro. "Myths of Racial Democracy: Cuba, 1900–1912." *Latin American Research Review* 34, no. 3 (January 1, 1999): 39–73.

———. *A Nation for All: Race, Inequality, and Politics in Twentieth-Century Cuba*. Chapel Hill: University of North Carolina Press, 2001.

———. "Slaves and the Creation of Legal Rights in Cuba: Coartación and Papel." *Hispanic American Historical Review* 87, no. 4 (November 1, 2007): 659–92.

Delgado Pasapera, Germán. *Puerto Rico: sus luchas emancipadoras*. Río Piedras: Editorial Cultural, 1984.

Deschamps Chapeaux, Pedro. *El negro en el periodismo cubano en el siglo XIX*. Havana: Ediciones R[evolución], 1963.

———. *El negro en la economía habanera del siglo XIX*. Havana: Unión de Escritores y Artistas de Cuba, 1971.

———. *Rafael Serra y Montalvo, obrero incansable de nuestra independencia*. Havana: Unión de Escritores y Artistas de Cuba, 1975.

Díaz Soler, Luis M. *Historia de la esclavitud negra en Puerto Rico*. San Juan: Editorial de la Universidad de Puerto Rico, 1981. First published 1953.

Duany, Jorge. *The Puerto Rican Nation on the Move: Identities on the Island and in the United States*. Chapel Hill: University of North Carolina Press, 2002.

———. "Reconstructing Racial Identity: Ethnicity, Color, and Class among Dominicans in the United States and Puerto Rico." *Latin American Perspectives* 25, no. 3 (1998): 147–72.

Dye, Nancy Schrom. "Modern Obstetrics and Working-Class Women: The New York Midwifery Dispensary, 1890–1920." *Journal of Social History* 20, no. 3 (Spring 1987): 549–64.

Dzidzienyo, Anani, and Suzanne Oboler, eds. *Neither Enemies nor Friends: Latinos, Blacks, Afro-Latinos*. New York: Palgrave Macmillan, 2005.

Erman, Sam. "Meanings of Citizenship in the U.S. Empire: Puerto Rico, Isabel Gonzalez, and the Supreme Court, 1898 to 1905." *Journal of American Ethnic History* 27, no. 4 (2008): 5–33.

Escalona, Martha Silvia. *Los cabildos de africanos y sus descendientes en Matanzas*. Matanzas: Ediciones Matanzas, 2008.

Estrade, Paul. *Martí en su siglo y en el nuestro*. Havana: Centro de Estudios Martianos, 2008.

Fernández, José B., and Jerrell Shofner. "Martyrs All: The Hero of Key West and the Inocentes." *Tequesta* (1973): 31–39.

Fernández Robaina, Tomás. *El negro en Cuba, 1902–1958: apuntes para la historia de la lucha contra la discriminación racial*. Havana: Editorial de Ciencias Sociales, 1994.

Ferrer, Ada. *Freedom's Mirror: Cuba and Haiti in the Age of Revolutions*. Cambridge: Cambridge University Press, 2014.

———. *Insurgent Cuba: Race, Nation, and Revolution, 1868–1898*. Chapel Hill: University of North Carolina Press, 1999.

Ferrer Cuevas, Manuel. *José Maceo y Grajales (el León de Oriente)*. Havana: Editorial "Ros," 1943.

Field, Phyllis F. *The Politics of Race in New York: The Struggle for Black Suffrage in the Civil War Era*. Ithaca, NY: Cornell University Press, 1982.

Figueroa, Luis A. *Sugar, Slavery, and Freedom in Nineteenth-Century Puerto Rico*. Chapel Hill: University of North Carolina Press, 2005.

Finch, Aisha K. *Rethinking Slave Rebellion in Cuba: La Escalera and the Insurgencies of 1841–1844*. Chapel Hill: University of North Carolina Press, 2015.

Flores, Juan. "'Que Assimilated, Brother, Yo Soy Asimilao': The Structuring of Puerto Rican Identity in the U.S." *Journal of Ethnic Studies* 13, no. 3 (January 1, 1985): 1–16.

Foner, Philip S. *Antonio Maceo: The "Bronze Titan" of Cuba's Struggle for Independence*. New York: NYU Press, 1977.

Forment, Carlos E. *Crónicas de Santiago de Cuba*. Santiago de Cuba: Editorial Arroyo, 1953.

Fradera, Josep Maria. *Colonias para después de un imperio*. Barcelona: Edicions Bella-terra, 2005.

Franco, José Luciano. *Antonio Maceo: apuntes para una historia de su vida*. Havana: Edito-rial de Ciencias Sociales, 1989.

Fraser, Gertrude Jacinta. *African American Midwifery in the South: Dialogues of Birth, Race, and Memory*. Cambridge, MA: Harvard University Press, 1998.

Fraunhar, Alison. "Marquillas Cigarreras Cubanas: Nation and Desire in the Nine-teenth Century." *Hispanic Research Journal* 9, no. 5 (December 1, 2008): 458–78.

Friss, Evan. "Blacks, Jews, and Civil Rights Law in New York, 1895–1913." *Journal of American Ethnic History* 24, no. 4 (Summer 2005): 70–99.

Fusté, José I. "Translating Negroes into Negros: Rafael Serra's Transamerican En-tanglements between Black Cuban Racial and Imperial Subalternity, 1895–1909." In *Afro-Latin@s in Movement: Critical Approaches to Blackness and Transnationalism in the Americas*, edited by Petra R. Rivera-Rideau, Jennifer A. Jones, and Tianna S. Paschel, 221–45. New York: Palgrave Macmillan, 2016.

Gaines, Kevin K. *Uplifting the Race: Black Leadership, Politics, and Culture in the Twentieth Century*. Chapel Hill: University of North Carolina Press, 2012.

García Muñoz, Montserrat. "La documentación electoral y el fichero histórico de diputados." *Revista General de Información y Documentación* 12, no. 1 (2002): 93–137.

Gardner, Martha. *The Qualities of a Citizen: Women, Immigration, and Citizenship, 1870–1965*. Princeton, NJ: Princeton University Press, 2009.

Gatewood, Willard B. *Aristocrats of Color: The Black Elite, 1880–1920*. Fayetteville: University of Arkansas Press, 2000.

———. "Black Americans and the Quest for Empire, 1898–1903." *Journal of Southern History* 38, no. 4 (1972): 545–66.

———. *Smoked Yankees: Letters from Negro Soldiers*. Fayetteville: University of Arkan-sas Press, 1987. First published 1971.

Gerstle, Gary. *American Crucible: Race and Nation in the Twentieth Century*. Princeton, NJ: Princeton University Press, 2017.

Gilbert, David. *The Product of Our Souls: Ragtime, Race, and the Birth of the Manhattan Musical Marketplace*. Chapel Hill: University of North Carolina Press, 2015.

Glasser, Ruth. *My Music Is My Flag: Puerto Rican Musicians and Their New York Com-munities, 1917–1940*. Berkeley: University of California Press, 1997.

Glymph, Thavolia. "Rose's War and the Gendered Politics of a Slave Insurgency in the Civil War." *Journal of the Civil War Era* 3, no. 4 (2013): 501–32.

Godreau, Isar P. "Slippery Semantics: Race Talk and Everyday Uses of Racial Termi-nology in Puerto Rico." *Centro Journal* 20, no. 2 (2008): 5–33.

González Veranes, Pedro N. *La personalidad de Rafael Serra y sus relaciones con Martí*. Havana: La Verónica, 1943.

González-Ripoll Navarro, María Dolores. "La emigración cubana de Cayo Hueso (1855–1896): independencia, tabaco y revolución." *Revista de Indias* 58, no. 212 (1998): 237–54.

Goodman, James E. "For the Love of Stories." *Reviews in American History* 26, no. 1 (1998): 255–74.

Grandío Moráguez, Oscar. "The African Origins of Slaves Arriving in Cuba." In *Ex-tending the Frontiers: Essays on the New Transatlantic Slave Trade Database*, edited by David Eltis and David Richardson, 176–200. New Haven, CT: Yale University Press, 2008.

Gravlee, Clarence C. "Ethnic Classification in Southeastern Puerto Rico: The Cultural Model of 'Color.'" *Social Forces* 83, no. 3 (March 2005): 949–70.

Greenbaum, Susan. "Afro-Cubans in Tampa." In *Afro-Latin@s in the United States: A Reader*, edited by Miriam Jiménez Román and Juan Flores, 51–61. Durham, NC: Duke University Press, 2010.

Grimké, Francis J. "The Second Marriage of Frederick Douglass." *Journal of Negro History* 19, no. 3 (1934): 324–29.

Guerra, Lillian. *The Myth of José Martí: Conflicting Nationalisms in Early Twentieth-Century Cuba*. Chapel Hill: University of North Carolina Press, 2005.

Guridy, Frank Andre. *Forging Diaspora: Afro-Cubans and African Americans in a World of Empire and Jim Crow*. Chapel Hill: University of North Carolina Press, 2010.

Hall, Gwendolyn Midlo. *Slavery and African Ethnicities in the Americas: Restoring the Links*. Chapel Hill: University of North Carolina Press, 2005.

Harris, Marvin. "Referential Ambiguity in the Calculus of Brazilian Racial Identity." *Southwestern Journal of Anthropology* 26, no. 1 (April 1, 1970): 1–14.

Helg, Aline. "Black Men, Racial Stereotyping, and Violence in the U.S. South and Cuba at the Turn of the Century." *Comparative Studies in Society and History* 42, no. 3 (July 1, 2000): 576–604.

———. *Our Rightful Share: The Afro-Cuban Struggle for Equality, 1886–1912*. Chapel Hill: University of North Carolina Press, 1995.

Hellwig, David J. "The African-American Press and United States Involvement in Cuba, 1902–1912." In *Between Race and Empire*, edited by Lisa Brock and Digna Castañeda Fuertes, 70–84. Philadelphia: Temple University Press, 1998.

Hernández Sainz, Mariela, and Moraima Martel Martínez. "La práctica social de las comadronas en Nuevitas antes del Triunfo de la Revolución." *Humanidades Médicas* 6, no. 1 (April 2006). http://scieloprueba.sld.cu/scielo.php?script=sci_arttext&pid=S1727-81202006000100006&lng=es&nrm=iso.

Hevia Lanier, Oilda. *El directorio central de las sociedades negras de Cuba (1886–1894)*. Havana: Editorial de Ciencias Sociales, 1996.

Hidalgo Paz, Ibrahim. *Cuba, 1895–1898: contradicciones y disoluciones*. Havana: Centro de Estudios Martianos—Centro Juan Marinello, 1999.

Hobbs, Allyson Vanessa. *A Chosen Exile: A History of Racial Passing in American Life*. Cambridge, MA: Harvard University Press, 2014.

Hochschild, Jennifer, and Brenna Powell. "Racial Reorganization and the United States Census 1850–1930: Mulattoes, Half-Breeds, Mixed Parentage, Hindoos, and the Mexican Race." *Studies in American Political Development* 22, no. 1 (2008): 59–96.

Hodes, Martha. *White Women, Black Men: Illicit Sex in the Nineteenth-Century South*. New Haven, CT: Yale University Press, 1999.

Hoffnung-Garskof, Jesse. "To Abolish the Law of Castes: Merit, Manhood, and the Problem of Colour in the Puerto Rican Liberal Movement, 1873–92." *Social History* 36, no. 3 (August 1, 2011): 312–42.

———. "The Migrations of Arturo Schomburg: On Being Antillano, Negro, and Puerto Rican in New York, 1891–1917." *Journal of American Ethnic History* 21, no. 1 (2001): 3–49.

————. *A Tale of Two Cities: Santo Domingo and New York after 1950*. Princeton, NJ: Princeton University Press, 2008.

————. "Telling a Transnational History of Race." Under review.

————. "The World of Arturo Schomburg: Afro-Latinos, African Americans, and the Antillean Independence Movement, 1879–1914." In *Afro-Latin@s in the United States: A Reader*, edited by Miriam Jiménez Román and Juan Flores, 70–91. Durham, NC: Duke University Press, 2010.

Holt, Thomas C. *Children of Fire: A History of African Americans*. New York: Hill and Wang, 2011.

Horrego Estuch, Leopoldo. *Juan Gualberto Gómez: un gran inconforme*. Edited by Oilda Hevia Lanier. Havana: Editorial de Ciencias Sociales, 2004. First published 1948.

Hostos, Adolfo de. *Ciudad murada, ensayo acerca del proceso de la civilización en la ciudad española de San Juan Bautista de Puerto Rico, 1521–1898*. Havana: Editorial Lex, 1948.

Ibarra, Jorge. *Cuba, 1898–1921: partidos políticos y clases sociales*. Havana: Editorial de Ciencias Sociales, 1992.

————. "Martí and Socialism." In *José Martí, Revolutionary Democrat*, edited by Christopher Abel and Nissa Torrents, 83–107. London: Athlone Press, 1986.

Iglesias Utset, Marial. "José Martí: mito, legitimación y símbolo. La génesis del mito martiano y la emergencia del nacionalismo republicano en Cuba (1895–1920)." In *Diez nuevas miradas de historia de Cuba*, edited by José A. Piqueras Arenas, 201–26. Castelló de la Plana: Universitat Jaume I, 1998.

————. *Las metáforas del cambio en la vida cotidiana: Cuba 1898–1902*. Havana: Union Ediciones, 2003.

Itzigsohn, José, Silvia Giorguli, and Obed Vázquez. "Immigrant Incorporation and Racial Identity: Racial Self-Identification among Dominican Immigrants." *Ethnic and Racial Studies* 28, no. 1 (2005): 50–78.

Jacoby, Karl. *The Strange Career of William Ellis: The Texas Slave Who Became a Mexican Millionaire*. New York: W. W. Norton and Company, 2016.

James, Winston. *Holding Aloft the Banner of Ethiopia: Caribbean Radicalism in Early Twentieth-Century America*. London: Verso, 1998.

Jiménez de Wagenheim, Olga. *El grito de Lares: sus causas y sus hombres*. Río Piedras: Ediciones Huracán, 2004.

Jiménez Román, Miriam, and Juan Flores, eds. *Afro-Latin@s in the United States: A Reader*. Durham, NC: Duke University Press, 2010.

Johnson, James Weldon. *Along This Way: The Autobiography of James Weldon Johnson*. Boston: Da Capo Press, 2000. First published 1933.

————. *The Autobiography of an Ex-Colored Man*. Boston: Sherman, French, and Co., 1912.

————. *Black Manhattan*. New York: A. A. Knopf, 1930.

Jones, Jennifer A. "Afro-Latinos: Speaking through Silences and Rethinking the Geographies of Blackness." In *Afro-Latin American Studies: An Introduction*, edited by Alejandro de la Fuente and George Reid Andrews, 569–605. Cambridge: Cambridge University Press, 2018.

Kanellos, Nicolás. *En otra voz: antología de la literatura hispana de los Estados Unidos*. Houston: Arte Publico Press, 2002.

―――. "Hispanic American Intellectuals Publishing in the Nineteenth-Century United States." *Hispania* 88, no. 4 (2005): 687–92.

Kinsbruner, Jay. *Not of Pure Blood: The Free People of Color and Racial Prejudice in Nineteenth-Century Puerto Rico.* Durham, NC: Duke University Press, 1996.

Kinzer, Stephen. *The True Flag: Theodore Roosevelt, Mark Twain, and the Birth of American Empire.* New York: Macmillan, 2017.

Kramer, Paul A. "Empires, Exceptions, and Anglo-Saxons: Race and Rule between the British and United States Empires, 1880–1910." *Journal of American History* 88, no. 4 (2002): 1315–53.

Lane, Jill. *Blackface Cuba, 1840–1895.* Philadelphia: University of Pennsylvania Press, 2005.

Laurent Perrault, Evelyn. "Invoking Arturo Schomburg's Legacy in Philadelphia." In *Afro-Latin@s in the United States: A Reader,* edited by Miriam Jiménez Román and Juan Flores, 92–98. Durham, NC: Duke University Press, 2010.

Law, Robin. "Ethnicity and the Slave Trade: 'Lucumi' and 'Nago' as Ethnonyms in West Africa." *History in Africa* 24 (1997): 205–19.

Leal, Rine. *La selva oscura: de los bufos a la neocolonia (historia del teatro cubano de 1868 a 1902).* Havana: Editorial Arte y Literatura, 1982.

Leavitt, Judith. *Brought to Bed: Childbearing in America, 1750–1950.* Oxford: Oxford University Press, 1986.

Lee, Erika. "Immigrants and Immigration Law: A State of the Field Assessment." *Journal of American Ethnic History* 18, no. 4 (1999): 85–114.

Lee, Sonia Song-Ha. *Building a Latino Civil Rights Movement: Puerto Ricans, African Americans, and the Pursuit of Racial Justice in New York City.* Chapel Hill: University of North Carolina Press, 2014.

Lindsey, Treva B. "Black No More: Skin Bleaching and the Emergence of New Negro Womanhood Beauty Culture." *Journal of Pan African Studies* 4, no. 4 (2011): 97–116.

Llaverías y Martínez, Joaquín. *Los periódicos de Martí.* Havana: Imprenta Pérez, Sierra y Co., 1929.

Logan, Enid Lynette. "Each Sheep with Its Mate: Marking Race and Legitimacy in Cuban Catholic Parish Archives, 1890–1940." *New West Indian Guide / Nieuwe West-Indische Gids* 84, no. 1–2 (January 1, 2010): 5–39.

Logan, John R., Weiwei Zhang, and Miao David Chunyu. "Emergent Ghettos: Black Neighborhoods in New York and Chicago, 1880–1940." *American Journal of Sociology* 120, no. 4 (January 2015): 1055–94.

Logan, Rayford. *The Betrayal of the Negro, from Rutherford B. Hayes to Woodrow Wilson.* Boston: Da Capo Press, 1997. First published 1954.

Lomas, Laura. "'El negro es tan capaz como el blanco': José Martí, 'Pachín' Marín, Lucy Parsons, and the Politics of Late-Nineteenth-Century Latinidad." In *The Latino Nineteenth Century,* edited by Rodrigo Lazo and Jesse Alemán, 301–22. New York: NYU Press, 2016.

―――. *Translating Empire: José Martí, Migrant Latino Subjects, and American Modernities.* Durham, NC: Duke University Press, 2008.

López, Alfred J. *José Martí: A Revolutionary Life.* Austin: University of Texas Press, 2014.

López Mesa, Enrique. *La comunidad cubana de New York: siglo XIX.* Havana: Centro de Estudios Martianos, 2002.

López Valdés, Rafael L., and Ricardo E. Alegría. *Pardos y morenos esclavos y libres en Cuba y sus instituciones en el caribe hispano.* San Juan: Centro de Estudios Avanzados de Puerto Rico y el Caribe, 2007.

Love, Eric. *Race over Empire: Racism and U.S. Imperialism, 1865–1900.* Chapel Hill: University of North Carolina Press, 2005.

Lovejoy, Henry B. "Old Oyo Influences on the Transformation of Lucumí Identity in Colonial Cuba." PhD diss., University of California at Los Angeles, 2012.

Lucena Salmoral, Manuel. "El derecho de coartación del esclavo en la América española." *Revista de Indias* 59, no. 216 (May 1, 1999): 357.

Mañach, Jorge. *Martí, el apóstol.* Havana: Las Americas Publishing Company, 1963.

Martínez, María Elena, David Nirenberg, and Max-Sebastián Hering Torres, eds. *Race and Blood in the Iberian World.* Berlin: Lit Verlag, 2012.

Martínez Alier, Verena. *Marriage, Class, and Colour in Nineteenth Century Cuba.* Cambridge: Cambridge University Press, 1974.

Martínez Heredia, Fernando, Rebecca J. Scott, and Orlando García Martínez, eds. *Espacios, silencios y los sentidos de la libertad: Cuba entre 1878 y 1912.* Havana: Ediciones Unión, 2001.

Martínez Vergne, Teresita. *Shaping the Discourse on Space: Charity and Its Wards in Nineteenth-Century San Juan, Puerto Rico.* Austin: University of Texas Press, 1999.

Martínez-Fernández, Luis. *Protestantism and Political Conflict in the Nineteenth-Century Hispanic Caribbean.* New Brunswick, NJ: Rutgers University Press, 2002.

Mata, Iacy Maia. *Conspirações da raça de cor: escravidão, liberdade e tensões raciais em Santiago de Cuba (1864–1881).* Campinas: Editora UNICAMP, 2015.

Matos Rodríguez, Félix. "Spatial and Demographic Change in Nineteenth-Century San Juan, Puerto Rico, 1800–1868." *Journal of Urban History* 25, no. 4 (May 1, 1999): 477–513.

McFarland, Gerald. *Inside Greenwich Village: A New York City Neighborhood, 1898–1918.* Amherst: University of Massachusetts Press, 2001.

Mercadal, Carles. "¿Ciudadanos o súbditos de 'La siempre fiel'? Derechos políticos, derechos civiles y elecciones en Cuba (1878–1895)." *Illes i imperis,* no. 5 (2001): 81–107.

Meriño Fuentes, María de los Ángeles. *Gobierno municipal y partidos políticos en Santiago de Cuba (1898–1912).* Santiago de Cuba: Ediciones Santiago, 2001.

Merleaux, April. *Sugar and Civilization: American Empire and the Cultural Politics of Sweetness.* Chapel Hill: University of North Carolina Press, 2015.

Miles, Tiya. *Ties That Bind: The Story of an Afro-Cherokee Family in Slavery and Freedom.* Berkeley: University of California Press, 2005.

Miller, Ivor. *Voice of the Leopard: African Secret Societies and Cuba.* Jackson: University Press of Mississippi, 2010.

Mills, Quincy. *Cutting along the Color Line: Black Barbers and Barber Shops in America.* Philadelphia: University of Pennsylvania Press, 2013.

Minnesota Population Center. *National Historical Geographic Information System: Version 2.0.* Minneapolis: University of Minnesota, 2011.

Mirabal, Nancy Raquel. *Suspect Freedoms: The Racial and Sexual Politics of Cubanidad in New York, 1823–1957.* New York: NYU Press, 2016.

Mitchell, Michele. *Righteous Propagation: African Americans and the Politics of Racial Destiny after Reconstruction.* Chapel Hill: University of North Carolina Press, 2004.

Moliner Castañeda, Israel. *Los cabildos afrocubanos en Matanzas.* Matanzas: Ediciones Matanzas, 2002.

Montejo Arrechea, Cármen. "Minerva: A Magazine for Women (and Men) of Color." In *Between Race and Empire*, edited by Lisa Brock and Digna Castañeda Fuertes, 33–48. Philadelphia: Temple University Press, 1998.

Moses, Wilson Jeremiah. *Alexander Crummell: A Study of Civilization and Discontent.* New York: Oxford University Press, 1989.

Muller, Dalia Antonia. *Cuban Émigrés and Independence in the Nineteenth Century Gulf World.* Chapel Hill: University of North Carolina Press, 2017.

Muraskin, William. *Middle-Class Blacks in a White Society: Prince Hall Freemasonry in America.* Berkeley: University of California Press, 1975.

Navarro, Miguel Ángel Esteban. "De la esperanza a la frustración: 1868–1873." In *El republicanismo en España (1830–1977)*, edited by Nigel Townson and Alicia Alted Vigil, 87–112. Madrid: Alianza Editorial, 1994.

Negron Portillo, Mariano. *Las turbas republicanas, 1900–1904.* Río Piedras: Ediciones Huracán, 1990.

Nelson, Wolfred. *Five Years at Panama: The Trans-Isthmian Canal.* New York: Belford Company Publishers, 1889.

Neumann Gandía, Eduardo. *Verdadera y auténtica historia de la ciudad de Ponce.* San Juan: Instituto de Cultura Puertorriqueña, 1987.

Novoa, Adriana. "José Martí and Evolution: An Analysis on Nation and Race." In *Interdisciplinary Essays on Darwinism in Hispanic Literature and Film*, edited by Jerry Hoeg and Kevin S. Larsen, 169–204. Lewiston: Edwin Mellen Press, 2009.

Offner, John L. *An Unwanted War: The Diplomacy of the United States and Spain Over Cuba, 1895–1898.* UNC Press Books, 1992.

Ojeda Reyes, Félix. *Peregrinos de la libertad, documentos y fotos de exilados puertorriqueños del siglo XIX localizados en los archivos y bibliotecas de Cuba.* Río Piedras: Editorial de la Universidad de Puerto Rico, 1992.

O'Neill, Luis Pumarada. "National Register of Historic Places, Bridges of Puerto Rico, Land Transportation in Puerto Rico." Washington, DC: US Department of the Interior, March 1992.

Ortiz, Paul. *Emancipation Betrayed: The Hidden History of Black Organizing and White Violence in Florida from Reconstruction to the Bloody Election of 1920.* Berkeley: University of California Press, 2006.

Orum, Thomas T. "The Politics of Color: The Racial Dimension of Cuban Politics during the Early Republican Years, 1900–1912." PhD diss., New York University, 1975.

Osofsky, Gilbert. "Race Riot, 1900: A Study of Ethnic Violence." *Journal of Negro Education* 32, no. 1 (1963): 16–24.

Padrón Valdés, Abelardo. *El general Flor Crombet: el francesito criollo.* Havana: Editorial de Ciencias Sociales, 2012.

Painter, Nell Irvin. *Standing at Armageddon: The United States, 1877–1919.* New York: W. W. Norton and Company, 1989.

Palmer, Colin A. "Defining and Studying the Modern African Diaspora." *Journal of Negro History* 85, no. 1–2 (January 1, 2000): 27–32.

Pappademos, Melina. *Black Political Activism and the Cuban Republic.* Chapel Hill: University of North Carolina Press, 2011.

Paquette, Robert L. *Sugar Is Made with Blood: The Conspiracy of La Escalera and the Conflict between Empires over Slavery in Cuba.* Middletown, CT: Wesleyan University Press, 1990.

Pascoe, Peggy. *What Comes Naturally: Miscegenation Law and the Making of Race in America.* Oxford: Oxford University Press, 2009.

Patterson, Tiffany Ruby, and Robin D. G. Kelley. "Unfinished Migrations: Reflections on the African Diaspora and the Making of the Modern World." *African Studies Review* 43, no. 1 (April 2000): 11–45.

Paz, Ibrahím Hidalgo. *Martí en España, España en Martí: 1871–1874.* Havana: Centro de Estudios Martianos, 2007.

Pedreira, Antonio Salvador. *El periodismo en Puerto Rico.* Havana: Imprenta Ucar, García y Cía., 1941.

Perera Díaz, Aisnara, and María de los Ángeles Meriño Fuentes. *Para librarse de lazos, antes buena familia que buenos brazos: apuntes sobre la manumisión en Cuba (1800–1881).* Santiago de Cuba: Editorial Oriente, 2009.

Pérez, Francisco, and Rodolfo Sarracino. *La Guerra Chiquita, una experiencia necesaria.* Havana: Editorial Letras Cubanas, 1982.

Pérez, Lisandro. *Sugar, Cigars, and Revolution: The Making of Cuban New York.* New York: NYU Press, 2018.

Pérez, Louis A. *On Becoming Cuban: Identity, Nationality, and Culture.* Chapel Hill: University of North Carolina Press, 1999.

———. *Cuba and the United States: Ties of Singular Intimacy.* Athens: University of Georgia Press, 2003. First published 1988.

———. *Cuba between Empires, 1878–1902.* Pittsburgh: University of Pittsburgh Press, 1983.

———. *Cuba: Between Reform and Revolution.* Oxford: Oxford University Press, 2006.

———. *Cuba in the American Imagination: Metaphor and the Imperial Ethos.* Chapel Hill: University of North Carolina Press, 2008.

———. *To Die in Cuba: Suicide and Society.* Chapel Hill: University of North Carolina Press, 2005.

———. "Politics, Peasants, and People of Color: The 1912 'Race War' in Cuba Reconsidered." *Hispanic American Historical Review* 66, no. 3 (1986): 509–39.

Pérez de la Riva, Juan. *El barracón: esclavitud y capitalismo en Cuba.* Barcelona: Crítica, 1978.

Pérez-Stable, Marifeli. "Estrada Palma's Civic March: From Oriente to Havana, April 20–May 11, 1902." *Cuban Studies* 30 (January 1, 2000): 113–21.

Peterson, Carla L. *Black Gotham: A Family History of African Americans in Nineteenth-Century New York City.* New Haven, CT: Yale University Press, 2011.

Picó, Fernando. *Al filo del poder: subalternos y dominantes en Puerto Rico, 1739–1910.* Río Piedras: Editorial de la Universidad de Puerto Rico, 1993.

———. *Educación y sociedad en el Puerto Rico del siglo 19: consideraciones en torno a la escolarización primaria y sus limitaciones.* San Juan: Centro de Estudios de la Realidad Puertorriqueña, 1983.

———. *1898 la guerra después de la guerra.* Río Piedras: Ediciones Huracán, 2004. First published 1987.

Pletch, Andrés. "Isle of Exceptions: Race, Law, and Governance in Cuba, 1825–1856." PhD diss., University of Michigan, 2017.

Plochet, Alberto, and David A. Plochet Lardoeyt. *El capitán Plochet recuerda a José Martí.* Santiago de Cuba: Ediciones Santiago, 2003.

Porter, Edwin S. *Panorama Water Front and Brooklyn Bridge from East River.* New York: Thomas A. Edison Inc., 1903. https://www.loc.gov/item/00694364/.

Portuondo Zúñiga, Olga. "El padre de Antonio Maceo, ¿venezolano?" *Del Caribe,* no. 19 (1993): 93–97.

Poyo, Gerald E. "Cuban Revolutionaries and Monroe County Reconstruction Politics, 1868–1876." *Florida Historical Quarterly* 55, no. 4 (April 1, 1977): 407–22.

———. *With All, and for the Good of All: The Emergence of Popular Nationalism in the Cuban Communities of the United States, 1848–1898.* Durham, NC: Duke University Press, 1989.

Putnam, Lara. *Radical Moves: Caribbean Migrants and the Politics of Race in the Jazz Age.* Chapel Hill: University of North Carolina Press, 2013.

Quesada y Miranda, Gonzalo de. *Así fue Martí.* Havana: Editorial Gente Nueva, 1977.

Quigley, David. *Second Founding: New York City, Reconstruction, and the Making of American Democracy.* New York: Hill and Wang, 2003.

Quintana, Jorge. "La expulsión de Venezuela de Francisco Gonzalo Marín." *Revista del Instituto de Cultura Puertorriqueña* 37 (October 1967): 27–32.

Quintero Rivera, Angel G. *Patricios y plebeyos: burgueses, hacendados, artesanos, obreros.* Río Piedras: Ediciones Huracán, 1988.

———. "The Somatology of Manners: Class, Race, and Gender in the History of Dance Etiquette in the Hispanic Caribbean." In *Ethnicity in the Caribbean,* edited by Gert Oostindie, 152–81. London: Macmillan Education Ltd., 1996.

———. *Workers' Struggle in Puerto Rico: A Documentary History.* New York: Monthly Review Press, 1976.

Ramírez, C. Rafael. "El vínculo de Martí con el Plan Gómez-Maceo de 1884." *Eureka* 2, no. 3 (June 2011): 2–10.

Ramos-Perea, Roberto. *Literatura puertorriqueña negra del siglo XIX escrita por negros.* San Juan: Ateneo Puertorriqueño—Editorial LEA—Archivo Nacional de Teatro y Cine, 2009.

Ramos-Zayas, Ana Yolanda. *Street Therapists: Race, Affect, and Neoliberal Personhood in Latino Newark.* Chicago: University of Chicago Press, 2012.

Reid-Vazquez, Michele. "Tensions of Race, Gender, and Midwifery in Colonial Cuba." In *Africans to Spanish America: Expanding the Diaspora,* edited by Sherwin K. Bryant and Rachel Sarah O'Toole, 186–205. Champaign: University of Illinois Press, 2012.

———. *The Year of the Lash: Free People of Color in Cuba and the Nineteenth-Century Atlantic World.* Athens: University of Georgia Press, 2011.

Ripoll, Carlos. "The Falsification of José Martí in Cuba." *Cuban Studies* 24 (1994): 3–38.

Rivera-Rideau, Petra R., Jennifer A. Jones, and Tianna S. Paschel, eds. *Afro-Latin@s in Movement: Critical Approaches to Blackness and Transnationalism in the Americas.* New York: Palgrave Macmillan, 2016.

Rivero, Yeidy M. *Tuning out Blackness: Race and Nation in the History of Puerto Rican Television.* Durham, NC: Duke University Press, 2005.

Rivero Muñiz, José. "La lectura en las tabaquerías, monografía histórica." *Separata de la Revista de la Biblioteca Nacional* 2, no. 4 (December 1951): 190–258.

———. "Los cubanos en Tampa." January 1958. Arte Público Hispanic Historical Collection, EBSCO.

Rivers, L. E., and C. Brown Jr. "African Americans in South Florida: A Home and a Haven for Reconstruction-Era Leaders." *Tequesta* 56 (1996): 5–23.

Roberts, John Storm. *The Latin Tinge: The Impact of Latin American Music on the United States.* Oxford: Oxford University Press, 1998.

Roca, Alfredo Jácome. "La Emulsión de Scott en la cultura hispanoamericana." *Revista Medicina* 27, no. 2 (2005): 122–27.

Rodríguez-Silva, Ileana M. *Silencing Race: Disentangling Blackness, Colonialism, and National Identities in Puerto Rico.* New York: Palgrave Macmillan, 2012.

Rogler, Charles. "The Morality of Race Mixing in Puerto Rico." *Social Forces* 25, no. 1 (October 1, 1946): 77–81.

Roig de Leuchsenring, Emilio. *Martí en España.* Havana: Cultural, S.A., 1938.

Rojas, Rafael, and Licia Fiol-Matta. "The Moral Frontier: Cuba, 1898. Discourses at War." *Social Text*, no. 59 (1999): 145–60.

Roldán de Montaud, Inés. *La Restauración en Cuba: el fracaso de un proceso reformista.* Madrid: Editorial CSIC, 2001.

Ronning, C. Neale. *José Martí and the Emigré Colony in Key West: Leadership and State Formation.* New York: Praeger, 1990.

Rooks, Noliwe M. *Hair Raising: Beauty, Culture, and African American Women.* New Brunswick, NJ: Rutgers University Press, 1996.

Ruggles, Steven, Katie Genadek, Ronald Goeken, Josiah Grover, and Matthew Sobek. *Integrated Public Use Microdata Series: Version 6.0* [database]. Minneapolis: University of Minnesota, 2015.

Sánchez González, Lisa. *Boricua Literature: A Literary History of the Puerto Rican Diaspora.* New York: NYU Press, 2001.

Sánchez Korrol, Virginia. *From Colonia to Community: The History of Puerto Ricans in New York City.* Berkeley: University of California Press, 1994.

Sartorius, David A. *Ever Faithful: Race, Loyalty, and the Ends of Empire in Spanish Cuba.* Durham, NC: Duke University Press, 2013.

———. "My Vassals: Free-Colored Militias in Cuba and the Ends of Spanish Empire." *Journal of Colonialism and Colonial History* 5, no. 2 (September 23, 2004).

Scarano, Francisco Antonio. *Sugar and Slavery in Puerto Rico: The Plantation Economy of Ponce, 1800–1850.* Madison: University of Wisconsin Press, 1984.

Schmidt-Nowara, Christopher. *Empire and Antislavery: Spain, Cuba, and Puerto Rico, 1833–1874.* Pittsburgh: University of Pittsburgh Press, 1999.

———. "From Slaves to Spaniards: The Failure of Revolutionary Emancipationism in Spain and Cuba, 1868–1895." *Illes i Imperis*, no. 2 (1999): 177–90.

Schneider, Dorothee. "The New York Cigarmakers Strike of 1877." *Labor History* 26, no. 3 (Summer 1985): 325–52.

Scott, Rebecca J. *Degrees of Freedom: Louisiana and Cuba after Slavery.* Cambridge, MA: Harvard University Press, 2005.

———. "Microhistory Set in Motion: A Nineteenth-Century Atlantic Creole Itinerary." In *Empirical Futures: Anthropologists and Historians Engage the Work of Sidney W. Mintz*, edited by George Baca, Aisha Khan, and Stephan Palmié, 84–111. Chapel Hill: University of North Carolina Press, 2009.

———. "Public Rights, Social Equality, and the Conceptual Roots of the Plessy Challenge." *Michigan Law Review* 106, no. 5 (2008): 777–804.

———. *Slave Emancipation in Cuba: The Transition to Free Labor, 1860–1899.* Princeton, NJ: Princeton University Press, 1985.

Scott, Rebecca J., and Jean M. Hébrard. *Freedom Papers: An Atlantic Odyssey in the Age of Emancipation.* Cambridge, MA: Harvard University Press, 2012.

Seigel, Micol. *Uneven Encounters: Making Race and Nation in Brazil and the United States.* Durham, NC: Duke University Press, 2009.

Senior, Olive. *Dying to Better Themselves: West Indians and the Building of the Panama Canal.* Kingston: University of the West Indies Press, 2014.

Serrano García, Rafael, ed. *España, 1868–1874: nuevos enfoques sobre el sexenio democrático.* Valladolid: Junta de Castilla y León, Consejería de Educación y Cultura, 2002.

Shofner, Jerrell. "Cuban Revolutionaries and the 1876 Election Dispute." *American Chronicle* 1 (1972): 21–25.

Simmons, LaKisha Michelle. *Crescent City Girls: The Lives of Young Black Women in Segregated New Orleans.* Chapel Hill: University of North Carolina Press, 2015.

Sinnette, Elinor Des Verney. *Arthur Alfonso Schomburg, Black Bibliophile and Collector: A Biography.* Detroit: Wayne State University Press, 1989.

Sippial, Tiffany A. *Prostitution, Modernity, and the Making of the Cuban Republic, 1840–1920.* Chapel Hill: University of North Carolina Press, 2013.

Smallwood, Stephanie E. *Saltwater Slavery: A Middle Passage from Africa to American Diaspora.* Cambridge: Harvard University Press, 2008.

Smith, Matthew J. *Liberty, Fraternity, Exile: Haiti and Jamaica after Emancipation.* Chapel Hill: University of North Carolina Press, 2014.

Stepan, Nancy. *The Hour of Eugenics: Race, Gender, and Nation in Latin America.* Ithaca, NY: Cornell University Press, 1991.

Stubbs, Jean. "Social and Political Motherhood of Cuba." In *Engendering History: Caribbean Women in Historical Perspective*, edited by Verene Shepherd, Bridget Brereton, and Barbara Bailey, 296–317. New York: Palgrave Macmillan, 1995.

———. *Tobacco on the Periphery: A Case Study in Cuban Labour History, 1860–1958.* Cambridge: Cambridge University Press, 1985.

Suárez Findlay, Eileen. *Imposing Decency: The Politics of Sexuality and Race in Puerto Rico, 1870–1920.* Durham, NC: Duke University Press, 1999.

Summers, Martin Anthony. *Manliness and Its Discontents: The Black Middle Class and the Transformation of Masculinity, 1900–1930.* Chapel Hill: University of North Carolina Press, 2004.

Tarragó, Rafael E. "La lucha en las Cortes de España por el sufragio universal en Cuba." *Colonial Latin American Review* 18, no. 3 (December 1, 2009): 383–406.

Thomas, Lorrin. *Puerto Rican Citizen: History and Political Identity in Twentieth-Century New York City.* Chicago: University of Chicago Press, 2010.

———. "Resisting the Racial Binary? Puerto Ricans' Encounter with Race in Depression-Era New York City." *Centro Journal* 21, no. 1 (2009): 5–35.

Thornbrough, Emma Lou. "The National Afro-American League, 1887–1908." *Journal of Southern History* 27, no. 4 (November 1961): 494–512.

Tinajero, Araceli. *El Lector: A History of the Cigar Factory Reader.* Translated by Judith E. Grasberg. Austin: University of Texas Press, 2010.

———. "El Siglo, La Aurora y la lectura en voz alta en Cuba, 1865–1868." *Revista iberoamericana* 72, no. 214–16 (2006): 171–83.

Tirado García, Modesto. "Los que conocieron a Martí." *Revolución y Cultura*, no. 33 (May 1975): 26–28.

Todd, Roberto H. *Julio José Henna, 1848–1924.* San Juan: Cantero, Fernández and Co., 1930.

Toledo, Josefina. *Sotero Figueroa, editor de Patria: apuntes para una biografía.* Havana: Editorial Letras Cubanas, 1985.

Torres-Saillant, Silvio. "One and Divisible: Meditations on Global Blackness." *Small Axe* 13, no. 2 (2009): 4–25.

———. "The Tribulations of Blackness: Stages in Dominican Racial Identity." *Callaloo* 23, no. 3 (2000): 1086–111.

Trelles, Carlos M. "Bibliografía de autores de la raza de color de Cuba." *Cuba Contemporánea* 42, no. 19 (January 1927): 30–78.

Twinam, Ann. "The Etiology of Racial Passing: Constructions of Informal and Official 'Whiteness' in Colonial Spanish America." In *New World Orders, Violence, Sanction, and Authority in the Early Modern Americas*, edited by John Smolenski and Thomas J. Humphrey, 249–72. Philadelphia: University of Pennsylvania Press, 2005.

———. *Public Lives, Private Secrets: Gender, Honor, Sexuality, and Illegitimacy in Colonial Spanish America.* Stanford, CA: Stanford University Press, 1999.

———. *Purchasing Whiteness: Pardos, Mulattos, and the Quest for Social Mobility in the Spanish Indies.* Stanford, CA: Stanford University Press, 2015.

Urban Transition Historical GIS Project. Providence: Brown University, 2015.

Valdés, Vanessa Kimberly. *Diasporic Blackness: The Life and Times of Arturo Alfonso Schomburg.* Albany: SUNY Press, 2017.

Van Norman, William C. "The Process of Cultural Change among Cuban Bozales during the Nineteenth Century." *The Americas* 62, no. 2 (2005): 177–207.

Wade, Peter. "Images of Latin American Mestizaje and the Politics of Comparison." *Bulletin of Latin American Research* 23, no. 3 (2004): 355–66.

Wallace, Aurora. "A Height Deemed Appalling: Nineteenth-Century New York Newspaper Buildings." *Journalism History* 31, no. 4 (Winter 2006): 178–89.

Warren, Louis S. *Buffalo Bill's America: William Cody and the Wild West Show.* New York: Vintage Books, 2005.

Washburne, Christopher. "The Clave of Jazz: A Caribbean Contribution to the Rhythmic Foundation of an African-American Music." *Black Music Research Journal* 17, no. 1 (1997): 59–80.

Waugh, Joan. "'Give This Man Work!': Josephine Shaw Lowell, the Charity Organization Society of the City of New York, and the Depression of 1893." *Social Science History* 25, no. 2 (May 1, 2001): 217–46.

Xi, Wang. *The Trial of Democracy: Black Suffrage and Northern Republicans, 1860–1910.* Athens: University of Georgia Press, 1997.

Zacaïr, Philippe. "Haiti on His Mind: Antonio Maceo and Caribbeanness." *Caribbean Studies* 33, no. 1 (2005): 47–78.

Zeuske, Michael. "Clientelas regionales, alianzas interraciales y poder nacional en torno a la 'Guerrita de Agosto.'" *Illes i imperis* (January 1, 1999): 127–56.

———. "Hidden Markers, Open Secrets: On Naming, Race-Marking, and Race-Making in Cuba." *New West Indian Guide* 76, no. 3–4 (July 1, 2002): 211–41.

INDEX

Note: Page numbers in italic type indicate photographs and maps.